THE NEW WEST VIRGINIA ONE-DAY TRIP BOOK

For My Parents

THE NEW WEST VIRGINIA ONE-DAY TRIP BOOK

COLLEEN ANDERSON

More Than
200 Affordable
Adventures
in the
Mountain State

To wonderful
West Virginia
adventures!
Colleen Anderson

EPM Publications, Inc.
McLean, Virginia

Library of Congress Cataloging-in-Publication Data

Anderson, Colleen, 1950–
The new West Virginia one-day trip book : more than 200 affordable adventures in the Mountain State / Colleen Anderson.
p. cm.
ISBN 1-889324-13-2
1. West Virginia—Tours. I. Title.
F239.3.A63 1998
917.5404 ' 43—dc21 98-22753
CIP

EPM Publications, Inc., 1003 Turkey Run Road
McLean, VA 22101
Printed in Canada

Cover design by Tom Huestis
Book design by Scott Edie, E Graphics
Cover Photographs:
Front Cover: View of the New River Gorge from Grandview. Stephen J. Shaluta, Jr., WV Division of Tourism and Parks.
Back Cover: Handmade quilt. Michael Keller, WV Division of Culture and History.
Whitewater rafting. Courtesy of Class VI River Runners, Inc.

Contents

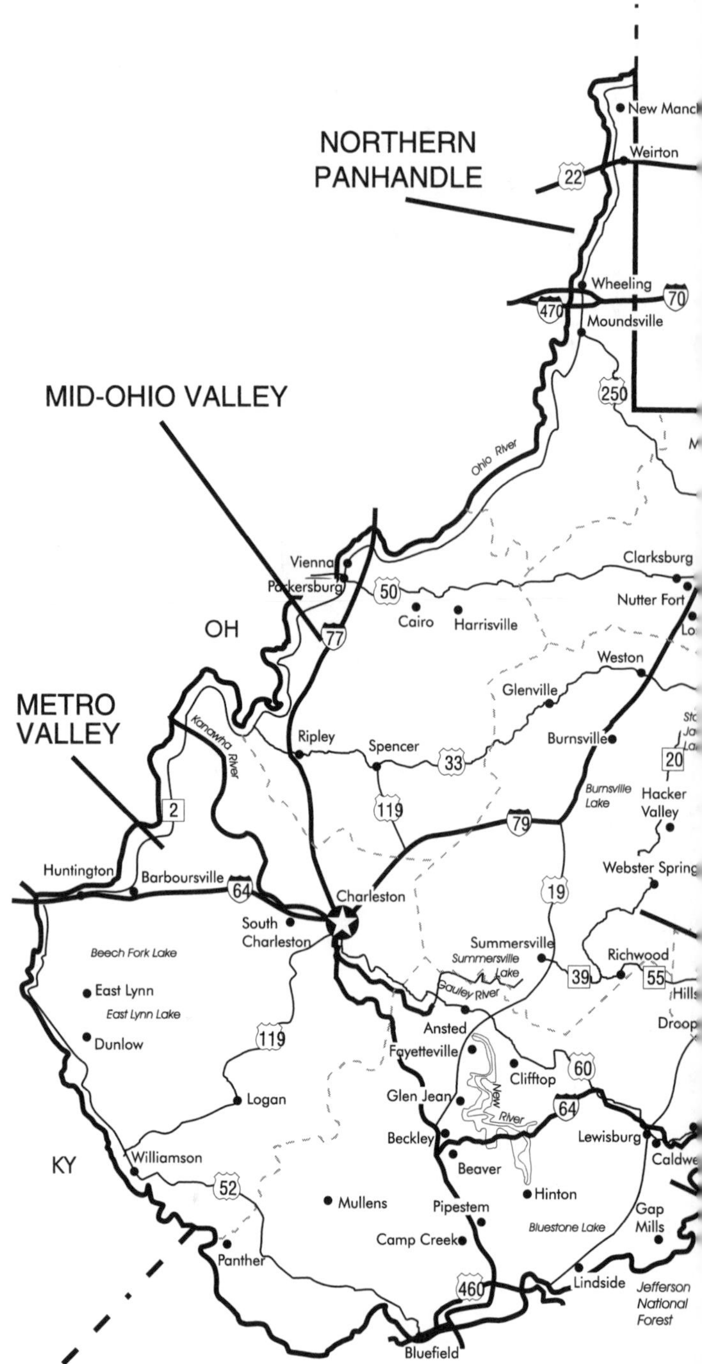
NORTHERN PANHANDLE
MID-OHIO VALLEY
METRO VALLEY
OH
KY
Weirton
Wheeling
Moundsville
Ohio River
Vienna
Parkersburg
Cairo
Harrisville
Clarksburg
Nutter Fort
Weston
Glenville
Burnsville
Burnsville Lake
Hacker Valley
Ripley
Spencer
Kanawha River
Huntington
Barboursville
Charleston
South Charleston
Webster Springs
Summersville
Summersville Lake
Gauley River
Richwood
Beech Fork Lake
East Lynn
East Lynn Lake
Dunlow
Ansted
Fayetteville
Clifftop
Logan
Glen Jean
New River
Beckley
Lewisburg
Beaver
Williamson
Hinton
Mullens
Pipestem
Gap Mills
Bluestone Lake
Camp Creek
Panther
Lindside
Jefferson National Forest
Bluefield
22
470
70
250
50
77
33
119
79
2
64
19
39
55
60
52
460
20

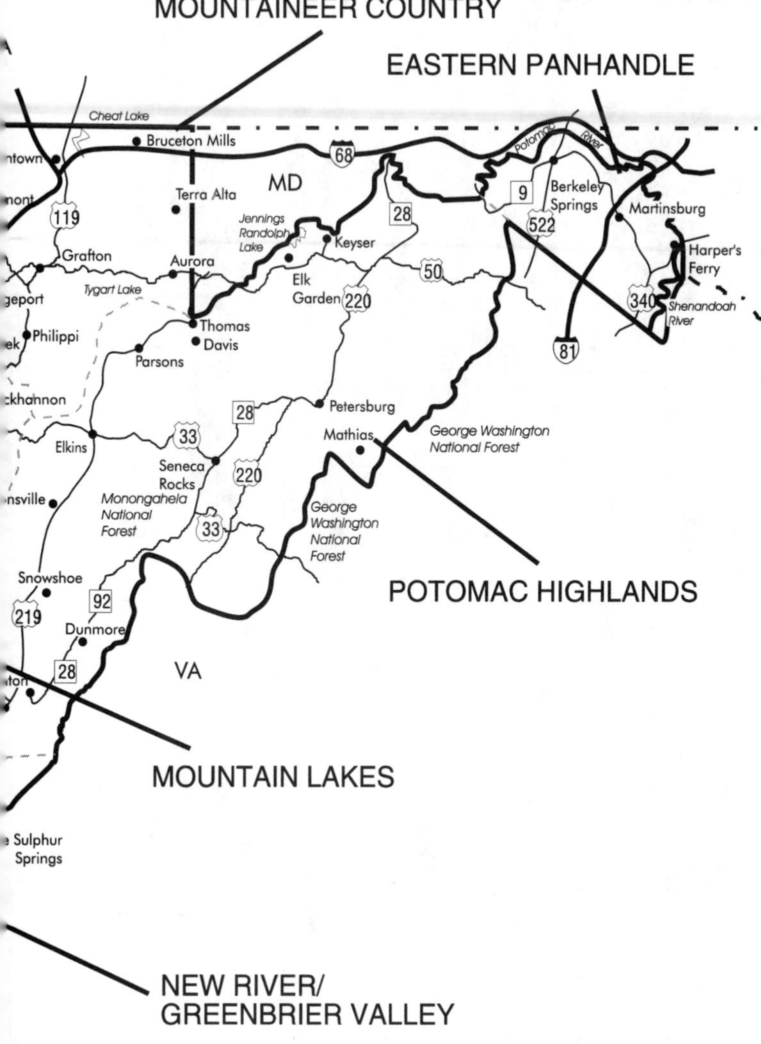

Courtesy of the West Virginia Division of Tourism

Some of the 50 miles of hiking trails in Otter Creek Wilderness double in winter for cross-country skiing. STEPHEN J. SHALUTA, JR.

Welcome to West Virginia

West Virginians love their state fiercely. I cannot think of another place on earth that has inspired so many songs and poems, let go of her children so reluctantly or called them home again with such an intensity of longing. A visit to the Mountain State—even for one day—will show you why.

Wild natural beauty, from the hawk-high promontories of Dolly Sods to the deep gorge of the ancient New River. Fascinating history and lore, from a tragic island love story to a steel-drivin' legend to a flamboyant lady spy. Recreational adventures of all kinds—on ridgetops and rivers, on trains and trams, in balloons above the land or caverns underneath it. Heirloom-quality handcrafts. Festivals that celebrate strawberries, buckwheat, fiddling, dandelions, octogenarians, ramps, potatoes, pumpkins, gospel music, glass and bass, just to mention a few. Combine all these with a sense of fun and friendliness that will tempt you to stay a little while longer. That's West Virginia.

This guide, the ninth in EPM's series of One-Day Trip Books, brings you more than 200 short, affordable excursions in the Mountain State, many of which can be combined for a diverse one-day outing. It is organized into eight travel regions, following the format used by the West Virginia Division of Tourism. Each entry includes the details you'll need to plan ahead: directions, telephone numbers and addresses, hours of operation, prices and helpful tips. If you haven't visited West Virginia before, you may be surprised to learn that some of the state's most appealing attractions are absolutely free, and many others very modestly priced.

Because the suggestions in this book are primarily for day trips, my research did not include restaurants or lodgings. However, I have included a few—in some cases, it was clear that a particular restaurant or inn also deserved mention for its historical significance, and in some cases they were just too good to leave out.

At the back of the book you'll find several appendices, including a chart that can help you plan a visit to one of West Virginia's excellent state parks; lists of whitewater rafting outfitters, ski resorts, hunting and fishing guides and biking organizations; a guide to the state's covered bridges and even a list of wineries. Finally, there's a calendar of events chock-full of festivals in every month of the year.

Each section of this guide opens with a map showing the locations of travel destinations within the region. Detailed highway maps are available at no charge from the Division of Tourism; you can also pick up free maps at West Virginia welcome centers and rest stops on interstate highways, as well as at many of the locations listed in this book.

The pen-and-ink drawings that appear in various places throughout this edition were made by artist William D. Goebel, and are from a large collection of West Virginia artwork. For more information about the artist and his work, please contact William D. Goebel, PO Box 75036, Charleston, WV 25375. You may also contact him by e-mail (artking@citynet.net) or phone him at (304)344-0009.

Our rugged mountains can make for severe weather and hazardous driving conditions in winter; some attractions are open only in summer or may close early due to unpredictable weather. When the weather is uncertain, be sure to call ahead to check hours and road conditions. In snowy weather, a four-wheel drive vehicle is advisable on some mountain roads. In all seasons, drive with care in West Virginia. Although roads are well maintained and quickly cleared after snowfalls, rural routes can be narrow and sharply curved. Watch for and obey the signs that indicate safe speeds on curves, warnings of rock falls or road work, animal crossings and school safety zones. Be especially watchful for deer on West Virginia's roads.

The choice of destinations for this book came from a variety of sources, beginning with valuable guidance from the Division of Tourism and the patient help of a great many local and regional Convention and Visitors Bureaus, for which I am deeply grateful. At the beginning of each section are listed the addresses, phone numbers and (when available) web sites of organizations and agencies that will help you make the most of your trip. The West Virginia Division of Tourism's toll-free number can put you in touch with hundreds of destinations, including most of the state's parks and forests. Call them at (800)CALL-WVA or visit their web site: www.state.wv.us/tourism.

This guide was also shaped by nearly thirty years of personal exploration in the state that has accepted me as an adopted daughter—years of listening to stories at the knees of quilters, watching sunsets from mountaintops, square dancing to lively fiddle tunes, inhaling the aroma of steaming apple butter at fairs and festivals, splashing in creeks and rivers, visiting small and large museums, getting lost on back roads, falling asleep in state park cabins and historic mansions, laughing and learning and getting to know the good people I call my neighbors. I love this place. I hope you will, too.

C.A.

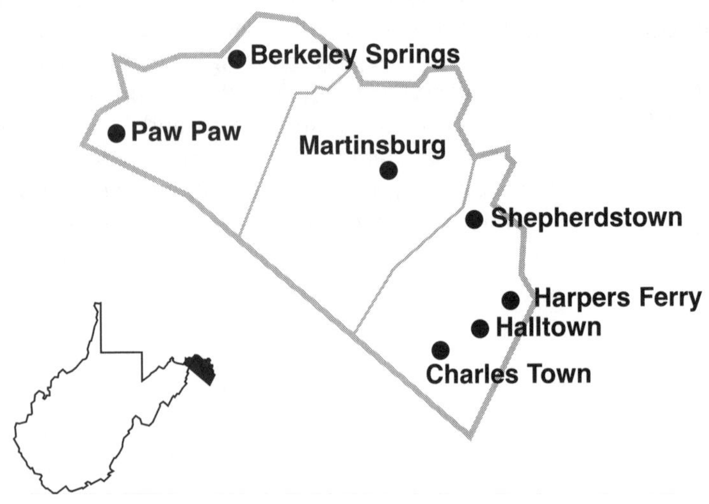

BERKELEY SPRINGS
- Berkeley Springs State Park & Downtown
- Cacapon State Park
- Coolfont Resort and Conference Center

CHARLES TOWN
- Historic Charles Town and Walking Tour

HALLTOWN
- Halltown Memorial Chapel

HARPERS FERRY
- Harpers Ferry National Historical Park

MARTINSBURG
- Blue Ridge Outlet Center
- Historic Martinsburg Walking Tour

PAW PAW
- Paw Paw Tunnel

SHEPHERDSTOWN
- Historic Shepherdstown Walking Tour
- James Rumsey Monument
- O'Hurley's General Store

Eastern Panhandle

Sandwiched between Maryland and Pennsylvania, closer to the nation's capital than the capital of its own state, the Eastern Panhandle's very shape raises questions about why it is part of West Virginia. The answers explain a measure of the region's popularity: the land that comprises Morgan, Berkeley and Jefferson counties was the source and site of fierce struggle during the Civil War—the war that gave birth to the Mountain State. In Harpers Ferry, where abolitionist John Brown made his stand against slavery, thousands come each year to relive and learn from history. In Martinsburg, travelers still board trains at the depot where the vital railroad link between east and west was severed and restored nine times between 1861 and 1864.

The history that beckons visitors goes back even further. George Washington and many of his relatives considered Charles Town and Berkeley Springs delightful places to live and relax; Shepherdstown traces its beginnings back to the early 18th century, and counts steamboat pioneer James Rumsey among its favorite sons as well.

The past has never come alive in such splendid surroundings. Victorian mansions-turned-inns, shaded streets and boulevards, excellent restaurants and a thriving arts community all await you in the Eastern Panhandle. You can browse in small, charming antique shops or hunt for bargains at the big Blue Ridge Outlet Center; sit and sip ale in an 18th-century pub or stand and cheer for your favorite horse at the Charles Town Races; park your car on the promontory rated one of America's outstanding scenic spots or walk through an arched, half-mile-long tunnel deep into the heart of a mountain.

If outdoors is where you want to be, the Panhandle's rolling hills, rivers and rich farmland make for some of the most scenic views anywhere—not to mention some of the best golfing, hiking, biking, rafting and fishing. Whatever your interests, the Eastern Panhandle is the gateway to a great getaway, and the perfect place to make your own memorable history.

For more information on visiting the Eastern Panhandle contact:

Charles Town Visitors Bureau, PO Box 815, Charles Town, WV 25414.

Jefferson County Chamber of Commerce, Inc., PO Box 426, Charles Town, WV 25414-0426. Phone (800)624-0577 or (304)725-2055. Contact them by e-mail (chamber@jefferson-county.com) or visit their web site (www.jeffersoncounty.com/chamber).

Jefferson County Convention and Visitors Bureau, PO Box A, Harpers Ferry, WV 25425. Call (800)848-TOUR or (304)535-2627. Contact them by e-mail (visitors@intrepid.net) or visit their web site (www.jefferson.county.com/cvb).

Martinsburg/Berkeley County Convention and Visitors Bureau, 208 South Queen Street, Martinsburg, WV 25401. Call (800)498-2386 or (304)264-8801, visit their web site (www.travelwv.com) or contact them by e-mail (info@travelwv.com).

Shepherdstown Visitor Information Center, 102 East German Street, Shepherdstown, WV 25443. Call (304)876-2786.

Travel Berkeley Springs, Inc., 304 Fairfax Street, Berkeley Springs, WV 25411. Call (800)447-8797 or (304)258-9147 or visit their web site (www.berkeleysprings.com).

West Virginia Welcome Center (Route 340 at Harpers Ferry): (304)535-2482.

Berkeley Springs

In 1776, George Washington and some of his friends soaked in the warm mineral springs of a place they named Bath, after the well-known town in southwestern England. Washington's satisfaction with the spa treatment for his rheumatic fever is recorded on a plaque: "I myself benefited by the water and am not without hope of making a cure of me...." The sparkling mineral water—good for drinking as well as soaking—still flows at a rate of 2,000 gallons per minute and maintains a constant temperature of 74.3 degrees. And more than two centuries later, the town known as **Berkeley Springs** remains a mecca for seekers of health and well-being.

The best way to see downtown Berkeley Springs is on foot. Be sure to stop by Travel Berkeley Springs (304 Fairfax Street) to pick up helpful brochures, maps and news about current goings-on. (There is *always* something fun going on in Berkeley Springs.) The office is open between 9:00 a.m. and 5:00 p.m. Monday through Saturday. Call (800)447-8797 or (304)258-9147.

Berkeley Springs State Park and Downtown

Bustling **Berkeley Springs State Park**, which also serves as the town square, is proof that good things come in small packages. One of the tiniest of the state parks, it may also be the most unique. Its **Old Roman Bath**, open year-round and in continuous use since 1784, is not only picturesque but functional; nine separate private bathing rooms, each with a 750-gallon ceramic tile bath that holds four adults comfortably, are available for half-hour or one-hour rentals. On the second floor of the Old Roman Bath is a museum. Nearby, a public swimming pool is open during the summer months. Also on the park grounds are Lord Fairfax's public tap, where you're likely to see someone filling gallon jugs with the famous water, and a stone bathtub where George Washington is said to have bathed. (If he did, he must have been cramped; the tub is quite small and narrow.)

At the south corner of the square is the **Main Bath House**. Here you can enjoy a relaxing soak in spring water heated to 102 degrees, a session in a steam cabinet and a full-body massage. The atmosphere in the bath house, built in the 1930's, is serenely spartan; and, at $35, the 50-minute spa treatment is a very affordable luxury. Open from 10:00 a.m. to 6:00 p.m. every day of the year except for major holidays, the baths are extremely popular, especially on weekends and holidays, so make reservations at least a month in advance: Call (800)CALL-WVA and ask for Berkeley Springs State Park, or call the park directly at (304)258-2711.

Tip: If you can't get an appointment at the Main Bath House, ask about other spa options in Berkeley Springs. Visitors can now choose a dazzling variety of spa services from no fewer than three other facilities and several independent massage and bodywork therapists.

But there is more to Berkeley Springs than baths and backrubs. Along with the rest of West Virginia's Eastern Panhandle, Berkeley Springs and surrounding Morgan County are history-rich. Pick up a handy guide to historic treasures from Travel Berkeley Springs, or simply stroll and read the plaques identifying the original owners in the 1776 town. If you want to shop, you can browse two antique malls and a pretty row of specialty shops with inviting awnings. When you get hungry, good food abounds; some favorite gathering places are **Tari's Cafe and Gourmet Market, The Country Inn**, **LaFonte Italian Cafe** and **Maria's Garden and Inn**. Take in a film at **The Star Theatre**, a vintage movie house featuring current films, and be sure to check out the arts kiosk in front of the movie house to see what's happening at **The Ice House**, the town's art and community center.

Whatever the weather, this town loves to celebrate! From January through March, you can join the fun at the Winter Festival of the Waters, which includes the **Toast To The Tap**, a nationally renowned water competition; and the **Spa Feast**, a luxurious sampler of spa services. In April, there's **Uniquely West Virginia**, a taster's heaven of homegrown foods and wines; in August, a tour of area art and craft studios; in October, the **Apple Butter Festival**; and, all year long, free concerts in Berkeley Springs State Park and other locations.

The mysterious fortress that towers above the town is **Berkeley Castle**. Built of local sandstone in 1885, this faithful replica of an English Norman castle was given as a wedding gift by Colonel Samuel Taylor Suit to his young bride. Current owner Walter Bird, who salvaged and restored the castle after many years of neglect, claims his is the "only truly royal castle in America." At no cost, you are welcome to admire the grand entrance hall, which is paneled in wood, draped in brocade and dominated by a huge fireplace. For a fee, guided tours of the rest of the house are conducted. Call the owner at (304)258-4000.

Three miles west of Berkeley Springs on Route 9 is the Panorama Outlook just beneath **Prospect Peak**. Pull off the road and take a look; in good weather, you can see mountains in four states—West Virginia, Maryland, Pennsylvania and Virginia—as well as the Potomac and Cacapon rivers. A marker at the outlook says: "National Geographic rates this scene among America's outstanding beauty spots." If you turn around and look toward the mountain, instead of toward the view, you'll see **Fluted Rocks**, along the road, which are actually the base of Prospect Peak.

Directions: From I-70, take Route 522 south six miles to Berkeley Springs State Park or, from I-81, take Route 522 north at Winchester, VA and travel about 34 miles. The park is at 121 South Washington Street, a block down Fairfax Street from Travel Berkeley Springs.

Cacapon Resort State Park

The long ridge of Cacapon Mountain dominates the view from almost anywhere in **Cacapon Resort State Park**, and offers not only breathtaking views at the summit but nearly 30 forested miles of hiking and horse trails. One of four state resort parks, Cacapon is equally well suited for a day trek or an overnight stay. The 6,000-acre park is close enough to Berkeley Springs to serve as a home base for exploring that town and the area, but far enough away to feel like an escape.

Golfers like the challenge of Cacapon's 18-hole championship

German stonemasons were paid eight cents an hour to build the walls of Berkeley Castle three feet thick. DAVID FATTALEH

course designed by Robert Trent Jones. A full-time pro is on hand for lessons. Considered one of the country's finest golf courses, it doubles as a playground for cross-country skiers in the winter. Nearby, Cacapon Lake is great for fishing, swimming and rowing; and there are tennis courts, stables, an arts and crafts center and plenty of picnic areas. Guided horse rides are an especially popular activity. A year-round recreation program assures that there will always be something to do and learn; weekend activities range from dances to craft demonstrations to nature hikes.

If you want to stay overnight, there are many lodging options, all reasonably priced: 30 fully-equipped cabins; the 11-room Old Inn with its own private dining room (ideal for groups up to 25); or the Lodge, a cozy and comforting 50-room facility, complete with restaurant and gift shop. Rooms are clean and simple, and the restaurant overlooks the fairway. For more information call (800)CALL-WVA or (304)258-1022, or write Cacapon Resort State Park, Berkeley Springs, WV 25411.

Directions: Take Route 522 south from Berkeley Springs for about ten miles. Follow the signs.

Coolfont Resort and Conference Center

Just minutes from Berkeley Springs is **Coolfont Resort**, a relaxing place to spend a day—or a week. Ensconced in a spacious valley between Warm Springs Ridge and Cacapon Mountain, Coolfont offers spa services, swimming, fishing, boating, horseback riding, tennis, volleyball and miles of hiking trails on 1,350 wooded acres. Lodging at Coolfont ranges from deluxe chalets to campsites. Day travelers can enjoy a healthful meal at **The Treetop House Restaurant**; aptly named, it overlooks 14-acre Lake Siri, and bird feeders at nearly every window put you, literally, within inches of finches and chickadees enjoying their meal as you enjoy yours.

The resort was born of a whim nearly four decades ago, when Sam Ashelman got snowed in at Berkeley Springs during an early spring camping trip. An advertisement for a "Beautiful Estate" caught his attention; he looked at the property, loved it instantly, and soon found himself the owner of, yes, a beautiful estate—complete with a historic manor house. Some years later, fate delivered another gift: his wife Martha, who first visited Coolfont as a guest. For 20 years the two have worked collaboratively to build their dream—a place for "refreshing, renewing, and restoring your mind and senses in a natural environment."

Coolfont's **Spectrum Spa** offers a full range of services, from full-body massage to a black mud and aloe body treatment. A popular package is their "Spa for a Day." This $120 package includes an exercise class, a delicious low-fat lunch, a choice of two among several one-hour spa services and access to the resort's solar-heated pool, hot tubs, exercise studios and sauna. One of the most comprehensive fitness centers in the Mid-Atlantic, Coolfont offers short-term or week-long packages for those who want to slim down, tone up, manage stress, stop smoking or learn to cook healthy meals. There's even a massage workshop for couples—a class that has revitalized marriages as well as muscles, according to Martha.

The focal point of Coolfont is the **Manor House**, where Coolfont's owners reside. (Some rooms are available for overnight guests, too.) Built early in the century by philosopher and author Herbert Quick, the architecturally original manor house is on the National Register of Historic Places. With its two-story portico, maple floors, lovingly built-in cabinetry, curved cherry staircase and music room, the Manor House makes a lovely setting for a regular series of free classical music concerts. For reservations or information, call Coolfont at (304) 258-4500 or toll-free at (800)888-8768, or write to Coolfont, Berkeley Springs, WV 25411.

Directions: From the intersection of Route 9 and Route 522 in Berkeley Springs, follow Route 9 west for one mile. Turn left on Cold Run Valley Road, and follow it for 3½ miles. Coolfont's Treetop House is on the left.

Charles Town

Historic Charles Town and Walking Tour

A teenaged George Washington surveyed this area in 1748 and liked it so much that he encouraged his half-brother Lawrence Washington to buy land here, and later invested his own surveyor's earnings in 550 acres nearby. When Lawrence died, George's youngest brother Charles inherited the land upon which he founded, in 1786, the town that bears his name. Happy Retreat, Charles's home, still stands here and is listed on the National Register of Historic Places. Other Washington family homes located in the immediate vicinity of **Charles Town** include Beall-Air, Claymont Court, Harewood, Blakeley, Cedar Lawn and Richwood Hall. Although these homes are privately owned and not open to the public, some of them are at times included on the annual House and Garden Tour of historic Charles Town, usually held the last weekend in April. For information write: Tour Director, PO Box 1166, Shepherdstown, WV 25443.

If you approach Charles Town from the east on Route 340, you'll find the Chamber of Commerce before you actually reach downtown, at 201 Frontage Road. Stop here to get copies of a county map and an attractive brochure that will lead you on a self-guided walking tour. Call them at (304)725-2055 or (800)624-0577. You can also pick up area information from the **Charles Town Visitors Bureau** located in The Antique Center at 200 West Washington Street.

The walking tour starts you out at the **Jefferson County Courthouse**, famous as the site of two of only three treason trials held in the U.S. prior to World War II. Here in 1859, abolitionist John Brown, wounded and lying on a cot during the proceedings, was convicted and condemned to death. In 1922, the same courthouse was the first of three venues for the trial of William Blizzard, charged with treason and murder for his part in the "March on Logan" during the Mine Wars, labor struggles that raged in the state during the early 1900s. That trial ended in a jury deadlock, and Blizzard was never retried. Guided tours of the courthouse are conducted at 1:00 and 3:00 p.m. on Saturdays and Sundays from April through November. For information about private tours and December candlelight tours, call tour guide Nan Furioso at (304)728-7713.

Another fascinating stop on the tour is the **Jefferson County Museum** at 200 East Washington Street, where you'll learn more about John Brown's trial and see, among other artifacts, his revolver, the handcuffs that bound him and the wagon that carried him with his black walnut coffin to the gallows in a field now occupied by the Victorian brick **Gibson-Todd House**. The museum is open April through December from 10:00 a.m. to 4:00 p.m. Monday through Saturday. Call (304)725-8628.

After extensive renovations, the 1912 **Old Opera House** (corner of George and Liberty streets), with its gracious curved balcony, can accommodate nearly 300 theatergoers for live comedies, drama and musicals year-round. For season schedule and ticket information, including group rates, call (888)900-SHOW or (304)725-4420.

If you want to watch something that moves a little more quickly, make your way to the **Charles Town Races**. Live horse races are run on Wednesday, Friday, Saturday and Sunday during summer months, with additional races Mondays several times a year; races from other tracks are simulcast seven days a week. Video lottery terminals are also open seven days a week. Admission and parking are free, so if you're lucky you may come out ahead. For an up-to-date race schedule, write Charles Town Races, PO Box 551, Charles Town, WV 25414 or call (800)795-7001. And, for turbo-driven speed thrills, try watching (or participating in) motorcycle or car racing at **Summit Point Raceway**, eight miles west of Charles Town on Route 13. Races run from March through November at this 28-

year-old track. Call (304)725-8444 or write Summit Point Raceway, PO Box 190, Summit Point, WV 25446.

Directions: From I-70 or I-270, travel about six miles west of Harpers Ferry on Route 340 to reach Charles Town.

Halltown

Halltown Memorial Chapel

If you are driving on Route 340 between Harpers Ferry and Charles Town, you will pass a tiny jewel of a church by the roadside. With Gothic windows and small attached buttresses, it looks as if it might have been transported from the English countryside hundreds of years ago, but **Halltown Memorial Chapel** was built of native limestone in 1901 to serve as a center for the Halltown African-American community. The Halltown Union Colored Sunday School, as it was known then (although some white children attended classes), was built entirely by volunteers. Its elegantly simple design is not the work of any known architect, but more likely a reflection of Shenandoah Valley black laborers' experience with limestone construction since slave times. In the 1980s, when the small chapel was in serious disrepair, Halltown residents once again came together, this time to restore it. It is on the National Register of Historic Places.

Directions: Beside Route 340 in Halltown, about 1½ miles west of Harpers Ferry.

Harpers Ferry

Harpers Ferry National Historical Park

Two rivers (Shenandoah and Potomac) and three states (Maryland, Virginia and West Virginia) converge at Harpers Ferry. And, each year, about half a million people visit this village in the Blue Ridge foothills. It is a spectacularly beautiful setting, but most people come here with history in mind—and the history of **Harpers Ferry** is dramatic and multi-layered. The town has witnessed landmark events in industrial and transportation history, the struggle to end slavery, the Civil War and the education of former slaves. In fact, the whole town of Harpers Ferry is an historic district, much of which is part of the National Historical Park.

Early settlers ran a ferry service in the mid 1700s, among them Robert Harper, for whom the town is named. In the last decade of the 18th century, the United States Armory and Arsenal was built here at President George Washington's urging. It subsequently produced more than 600,000 muskets, rifles and pistols and employed, at times, more than 400 workers. In the 1830s, the convergence of two railroad lines and the Chesapeake and Ohio Canal spurred economic growth; by the 1850s, the town had some 3,000 inhabitants, about ten times its present population.

The town's name, however, is most closely associated with abolitionist John Brown, who in 1859 chose Harpers Ferry as the starting point for his planned uprising against slavery. Hoping to use the arsenal's weapons, he and 21 others (among them three of his own sons and five free African-Americans) seized the armory and several other locations. Thirty-six hours later, with most of his band killed or wounded by Federal troops, Brown was captured in the armory fire enginehouse, now known as "John Brown's Fort." His trial and hanging in nearby Charles Town riveted the nation's attention on the moral issue of slavery and prefigured civil war.

Although ravaged by floods during the latter part of the 19th century, much of the town has been restored and is part of the **Harpers Ferry National Historical Park**.

The Information Center on Shenandoah Street is a good place to begin your visit. To help visitors make sense of the town's layered past, the Park Service has identified six themes that weave through the town's history: Natural History, Industry, Transportation, John Brown's Raid, the Civil War and African-American History. Pick up an orientation map and ask which walking tours will be conducted that day by park rangers (daily in summer, weekends in fall and spring). Walk northeast on Shenandoah Street to find the **John Brown Museum**, where you can see a display on the abolitionist and the turbulent times in which he lived. Follow the map to John Brown's Fort, and stroll a bit further to take in the convergence of the Shenandoah and the Potomac rivers at "The Point." Retrace your steps along Shenandoah Street to the other restored 19th-century buildings like the Provost Marshal's Office and the Dry Goods Store. The exhibit at the replicated Philip Frankel & Co. clothing store explains the evolution of clothing production from hand sewn to machine made and its impact on daily life. You may be told that Victorian men wore up to eight layers of clothing (women, more) and that a pair of man's handmade shoes in the 1800s cost $1.00.

Not part of the national park but an interesting stop is **John Brown's Wax Museum** on High Street, where the abolitionist's

A young visitor gets a hands-on history lesson at Harpers Ferry's annual event, "Election Day—1860."

COURTESY HARPERS FERRY NATIONAL HISTORICAL PARK

career, youth to gallows, is recreated in life-sized tableaux. The museum operates daily, 9:00 a.m. to 5:00 p.m., from mid-March through mid-December, weekends only during the winter months. For information about rates and group discounts, write Wax Museum, Harpers Ferry, WV 25425 or call (304)535-2792.

You'll also find the National Park Service's Black History and

Civil War museums along High Street. At the former, take time to pick up one of the telephone handsets in the "Black Voices from Harpers Ferry" exhibit, and hear the stories of John Douglas, Isaac Gilbert and other African-Americans who helped shape history.

For a truly inspiring view of the rivers and surrounding mountains, follow the stone steps up the hill from High Street. You'll pass the small stone Harper House, oldest surviving structure in the park (1775-1782), and St. Peter's Catholic Church, built in the 1830s. Continue to **Jefferson Rock** and enjoy a view that belies the fact that Harpers Ferry is only 275 feet above sea level. Jefferson claimed this sight was worth "a voyage across the Atlantic." The path goes on to Harper Cemetery, where you can easily locate Robert Harper's gravestone in a special walled section. At the top of the hill is the former campus of **Storer College**. Now used as a training center by the Park Service, it was one of the first black colleges in the nation. Harpers Ferry was a refuge for runaway slaves during the Civil War; and in 1867, six years to the month after John Brown's raid, classes for freed slaves began here. The college and town also served as the meeting place for the second conference, in 1906, of the Niagara Movement, which led to the formation of the NAACP.

You can easily spend a full morning exploring the National Park exhibits, browsing the **Harpers Ferry Historical Association Bookstore** on Shenandoah Street and peeking into quaint shops along side streets. **Harpers Ferry Walking Tours** (not associated with the National Park) offers a leisurely 45-minute guided tour of the town; stop by 490 Washington Street or call them at (304)535-6836. Another option is the short walk to **Virginus Island,** a now-abandoned island that held a thriving 19th-century industrial town. Although there are no intact buildings, interpretive signs will tell you about businesses and life on the island.

If you crave more strenuous exercise, the news is good: just as earlier transportation routes converged to make Harpers Ferry an industrial center, newer recreational routes make it a mecca for hikers and bikers. The **Appalachian Trail** passes through a section of the park and town, and the Appalachian Trail Conference national headquarters are here in Harpers Ferry. Pick up maps at 799 Washington Street, call (304)535-6331 or write Appalachian Trail Conference, PO Box 807, Harpers Ferry, WV 25425. Walking or biking the towpath along the old **C&O Canal** is one of the most beautiful ways see the countryside. Cross the Potomac footbridge to the Maryland side and pick up the path paralleling the Potomac; a favorite bike trip is the 11-mile stretch upriver to Shepherdstown. Also, the National Park Service offers maps for several loop hikes; walkers rate the

Maryland Heights Trail most popular for its view of Harpers Ferry from the cliffs on the Maryland side of the Potomac.

A few special events are worth noting. One is **Old Tyme Christmas**, two weekends in early December, sponsored by the Harpers Ferry Merchant Association. The National Park Service sponsors a celebration that coincides with the first weekend. Call (800)848-TOUR for more information about this weekend of candlelight, garlanded streets, caroling and other traditional holiday fun. Another is **Election Day 1860**, sponsored by the National Park Service, a living-history event that includes political debates, speeches and rallies. Call (304)535-6298 for information about this and other park activities, or write Harpers Ferry National Historical Park, Box 65, Harpers Ferry, WV 25425. On Friday, Saturday and Sunday nights from May through the first week in November, **Harpers Ferry Ghost Tours** will take you on an evening stroll through Harpers Ferry, complete with stories about what happened in various historic buildings. The tour takes about an hour, costs $2.00 per person and begins at 8:00 p.m. in front of the **Hot Dog Haven** at 173 Potomac Street, across from the railroad station. During April, ghost tours are conducted on Saturdays only. In October and November, reservations are a must. Call (304)725-8019 for more information or to make reservations.

National Park facilities are open year-round 8:00 a.m. to 5:00 p.m., and to 6:00 p.m. from Memorial Day to Labor Day. For information on walking tours call (304)535-6298. Closed Christmas Day. Because parking is extremely limited in the town, the Park Service requests that visitors park at the **Cavalier Heights Visitors Center** and take the shuttle into town. Admission to the park is $5.00 per car. This fee allows admission for seven consecutive days. The fee for cyclists and walk-ins is $3.00 per person.

Directions: The park is located approximately 20 miles southwest of Frederick, MD, via US 340. Signs along Route 340 will also direct you to the town's visitors center.

Martinsburg

Founded in 1778 by General Adam Stephen and named for a nephew of Lord Fairfax, **Martinsburg** was a thriving center of culture and commerce before the Civil War and a bitterly contested place during the war; the town changed hands as many as 60 times. With seven historic districts and a wealth of individual sites on the National Historic Register, Martinsburg has a fond awareness of its past and a healthy appreciation of the present, including a lively arts scene and a jam-packed calendar of events.

Blue Ridge Outlet Center

With all that history, why do most folks come to Martinsburg? To shop! Over a million people a year flock to discount outlets housed in four beautifully converted turn-of-the-century woolen mills located on the site of a Civil War skirmish. Whether they know it or not, shoppers tread the halls of history while they hunt for bargains. The buildings are within easy walking distance of each other, and handy maps will help you find your way to more than 50 name-brand retailers featuring savings up to 70 percent off regular retail prices. You'll appreciate the bright, airy atmosphere of the rehabilitated structures almost as much as the great prices.

The outlet center is open 10:00 a.m. to 6:00 p.m. Monday through Wednesday, 10:00 a.m. to 9:00 p.m. Thursday through Saturday, and 11:00 a.m. to 6:00 p.m. Sunday, except for major holidays. Call (800)445-3993 or (304)263-SHOP. You can also contact the **Blue Ridge Outlet Center** by e-mail (trice@intrepid.net) or visit their web site (www.outletcenter.com).

Directions: From I-81, take the King Street Exit to Queen Street in Martinsburg. Turn right on Queen Street and proceed two blocks to Stephen Street, then right to the outlet center at 315 West Stephen Street.

Tip: Weekend traffic is heavy, so come early to find nearby parking.

Historic Martinsburg Walking Tour

A good place to begin an exploration of Martinsburg is the stately **Boarman House** at 208 South Queen Street, one of oldest brick buildings in town. In the foyer you'll see portraits of Rear Admiral Charles Boarman, for whom the house is named; his naval career (1811–1879) spanned 68 years and three wars. You'll find the very helpful **Martinsburg/Berkeley County Convention and Visitors Bureau** on the ground floor. The visitors center is open 9:00 A.M to 5:00 p.m. Monday through Friday, and 11:00 a.m. to 3:00 p.m. Saturday and Sunday. Pick up a walking tour brochure (an excellent driving tour is also available), but don't leave without going upstairs to find out what's on exhibit at the **Boarman House Arts Center**. With a special emphasis on West Virginia artists, the center sponsors changing shows of art and craft ranging from traditional to contemporary. Boarman House Arts Center also maintains the **Art-**

Space Open Studio, an artist-in-residence program: artists are granted temporary studio space at the center, conduct workshops and are often on hand to talk with visitors. You'll find some lovely jewelry, paintings, textiles, ceramics and other treasures in the arts center's gift shop. Their annual Christmas Show & Sale, from mid-November through Christmas, features work by almost 100 artisans. Gallery hours are 10:00 a.m. to 5:00 p.m. Monday through Friday, 10:00 a.m. to 2:00 p.m. on Saturday. Call (304)263-0224.

Your walking tour of Martinsburg will take you through five of the town's seven historic districts and past dozens of the many National Register sites here.

Some, like the **Belle Boyd House**, are fairly bursting with lively stories worth learning. Considered the best example of Greek Revival architecture in Martinsburg, the house/museum at 126 East Race Street was the childhood home of West Virginia's most famous Civil War spy. An actress and author as well, the flamboyant Belle Boyd was a tireless self-promoter, as this excerpt from an 1860 letter to her cousin Willie illustrates: "I weigh 106-1/2 pounds. My form is beautiful. My eyes are of a darker blue and so expressive. My hair of a rich brown and think I tie it up nicely....Indeed I am decidedly the most beautiful of all your cousins." A year later, 18-year-old Belle shot a Union soldier and began her career as a Confederate courier. Her further exploits included a stint in jail, a London acting career, three husbands and five children. Her autobiography, *Belle Boyd in Camp and Prison*, has been republished and is available at the Ben Boyd Book Store in the house, which also contains the Berkeley County Historical Society and a very well-maintained genealogy library that serves Berkeley, Jefferson and Morgan counties. It's open to the public 10:00 a.m. to 4:00 p.m. Monday through Saturday. Behind the house and also open to visitors is one of the prettiest gardens you are likely to find anywhere—historian Don Wood, who maintains the house and grounds, has filled it with over 100 varieties of roses, Belle Boyd's favorite flower. Call (304)267-4713 for more information.

The first rails of the Baltimore and Ohio Railroad reached Martinsburg in 1842, and the **B&O Roundhouse**, shops and other facilities were finished in 1849, establishing the town as a commercial hub. When the Civil War broke out, both North and South struggled to control the vital railroad link. In 1861, Stonewall Jackson led troops that destroyed much of the complex. Rebuilt by the Union, it was destroyed and rebuilt eight more times between 1861 and 1864! The roundhouse, which dates from 1866, is still an impressive structure, and the restored ticket house still serves as a depot for Amtrak travelers. Walk around to the back of the historical marker at 229 E. Martin Street (to the side that rail passengers see), and you'll learn that this railyard was the site of another, later struggle: in 1877, B&O workers went on strike here to protest a cut in wages, sparking a huge nationwide strike. Federal troops were called in for the first time in a labor dispute, and more than 50 railroad workers lost their lives before the strike was crushed.

Built in 1902, the **Apollo Theater**, at 128 E. Martin Street, was designed by Reginald Geare, architect for the well-known Knickerbocker Theater in Washington, D.C. Over the years it has been the home of vaudeville shows, concerts and movies; it currently serves as Martinsburg's center for live community theater. Call (304)263-6766 for a performance schedule.

If you see nothing else in Martinsburg, do visit the founder's home. Perched on a hill above Tuscarora Creek at 309 East John Street, the native limestone **Adam Stephen House** occupies Lot 104 of the 255 acres upon which General Adam Stephen platted Martinsburg. An acquaintance of George Washington and a distinguished surgeon and soldier in the American Revolution, the Scottish-born doctor also operated a nearby mill, a distillery and an armory, and served as the first sheriff of Berkeley County. The furnishings of the house reflect the period of 1750-1830; of special interest are the 1785 pianoforte and Chippendale mirror. The first Saturday in June is designated General Adam Stephen Day in Martinsburg; at the Adam Stephen House, expect an all-day gala with arts, crafts, music and dancing.

Next-door, the **Triple Brick Museum**, so called because it was once divided into three separate dwellings to house workers on the B&O Railroad, contains an eclectic gathering of local historical artifacts. You'll see button and spoon collections, old glassware, flax- and wool-spinning wheels, early surveying equipment, quilts and some intriguing hands-on exhibits children will love. Both the museum and the Adam Stephen House are open to the public May through October, 2:00-5:00 p.m. on Saturday and Sunday only. To arrange a tour at other times call (304)267-4434.

From July through Halloween, Martinsburg's own bona fide ghost hunter and captivating storyteller Susan Crites conducts **Graveyard Tours** on Friday nights and tours of **Haunted Historic Martinsburg** on Saturday evenings. Tours last about an hour and cost $8.00 for adults, $6.00 for elementary students. Call the "Ghostline" at (304)267-0540 for reservations or more information.

If your touring style is driving instead of walking, make sure you pick up the excellent driving tour guide at the Convention and Vis-

General Adam Stephen built his house on a hill in Martinsburg, the town he laid out nearly 200 years ago.

COURTESY GENERAL ADAM STEPHEN HOUSE

itors Bureau. Of special significance, and only about two miles from downtown Martinsburg, is the **Vanmetre Ford Bridge**, a lovely three-arch stone bridge across Opequon Creek. Built in 1832, it is the oldest intact bridge in the state.

And, if you find the Martinsburg area too interesting for a single day, your night's lodging can also be a National Historic Register site. You might try **Boydville** (circa 1812), a grand old mansion that survived the Civil War by direct intervention of President Lincoln. Belle Boyd, Henry Clay and Stonewall Jackson all visited here; the inn has welcomed presidents, generals, ambassadors and senators. Call (304)263-1448 for rates and reservations, or write to La Rue Frye, Boydville, The Inn at Martinsburg, 601 South Queen Street, Martinsburg, WV 25401. Another excellent inn with a fascinating past is **Aspen Hall Inn**, located under a canopy of large locust trees next to the babbling Tuscarora Creek. Quakers built it of limestone over 200 years ago, and proprietors Gordon and LouAnne Claucherty have restored it magnificently. If you stay, ask them to show you the secret room and the wall where they uncovered the date 1788 and the builders' signatures. Call (304)263-4385 for rates and reservations, or write Aspen Hall Inn, 405 Boyd Avenue, Martinsburg, WV 25401.

Directions: Martinsburg is just off I-81, about 12 miles south of I-70.

Tip: About 12½ miles west of Martinsburg on Route 9 and Mountain Lake Road, **The Woods Resort** has direct access to over 70 miles of hiking trails, 27 holes of golf, indoor and outdoor swimming, tennis, massage, luxury accommodations with fireplaces and whirlpool tubs, fine dining and more. Reserve tee times at least five days in advance by calling (304)754-7222 or call (800)248-2222 for a brochure.

Paw Paw

Paw Paw Tunnel

Fourteen years (1836-1850) in the building, the **Paw Paw Tunnel** is considered one of the engineering feats of the 19th century. German and Irish workers used only hand tools to fashion the 25-foot-high Roman arch that extends slightly over half a mile through Sorrell Ridge near Paw Paw. (Both town and tunnel are named for the pawpaw tree, *Asimina triloba,* which bears North America's largest native edible fruit and grows abundantly throughout West Virginia.) Part of the C&O Canal, long ago drained of water, the tunnel is now open to hikers and bikers only. If you walk through, you may want a flashlight. Please don't disturb the bats you may find, but *do* try singing—the reverberation lends voices a haunting quality.

Directions: Paw Paw is at the western edge of Morgan County. From Berkeley Springs take Route 9 west to Route 29. Follow Route 29 north to Paw Paw. Drive through town and across the bridge into Maryland. Immediately after crossing the bridge, you'll be on Maryland Route 51. The parking lot for the tunnel is one-fourth mile further on the right.

Shepherdstown

Shepherdstown was settled in the early 1730s and incorporated in 1762, and claims to be West Virginia's oldest incorporated town. The earliest European arrivals were Germans who called it Mecklenberg. In 1798, the town was renamed Shepherd's Town in honor of its founder, Thomas Shepherd, and in 1867, when it was granted a charter by the new state of West Virginia, it became Shepherdstown. By any name, it is the favorite town of many a visitor.

Revolutionary war buffs know Shepherdstown as the jumping-off point for the legendary Bee Line march, in which the first large contingent of southern volunteers hiked overland in record time to reinforce George Washington's fledgling Continental Army near Boston.

On December 3, 1787, two decades before Fulton's *Claremont* first steamed up the Hudson River, James Rumsey made a successful trial of his steam-powered boat here on the Potomac before a large crowd of onlookers. The boat was the first to operate on the principle of water jet propulsion, and Shepherdstown still considers itself the birthplace of the steamboat.

During the Civil War, General Lee's troops retreated across the Potomac at Pack Horse Ford after the battle at nearby Antietam on September 17, 1862, leaving this town's homes, churches and other buildings filled with the wounded and dying. Shepherdstown changed hands many times during the Civil War but, unlike nearby Harpers Ferry, it was spared burning, and many old homes survived the war intact. Both towns suffered devastating floods, and neither ever fully regained the commercial prominence of its antebellum years.

Shepherd College, which occupies about a third of the town and continues to grow, has been here since 1871 and lends Shepherdstown a friendly college atmosphere. The campus is home to the up-and-coming **Contemporary American Theatre Festival**. For several weeks each July, the professional resident theater presents four new American plays in rotating repertory. Puppetry, music, dance and visual arts round out the festival. For more information about plays and prices, call (800)999-CATF.

Historic Shepherdstown Walking Tour

Shepherdstown's main street, German Street, is lined with shade trees, charming shops, restaurants and taverns. You'll also find good books, herbs and natural foods, fine handmade jewelry, ceramics and other crafts in quaint, historic settings. Stop by the cheery **Visitor Information Center** at 102 E. German Street, open 10:00 a.m. to 4:00 p.m. seven days a week, or call (304)876-2786. Ask for your free copy of a recently updated and very comprehensive walking tour guide; it will lead you past almost fifty historic sites without wearing out your shoe leather. Here are a few highlights:

The tour begins at the **Entler Hotel**, on the northwest corner of Princess and German streets. Open 11:00 a.m. to 5:00 p.m. Saturday and 1:00 to 4:00 p.m. Sunday, May through October, the hotel was built in three successive stages beginning in 1790, with the final construction finished in 1815. After nearly a century of success as an inn, the building was acquired in 1921 by Shepherd College and used over the years as student housing, faculty apartments and a storage warehouse. When the college made plans to demolish the old building, the community rallied to save it. Now on the National Register of Historic Places, it serves as a community museum and headquarters for the Historic Shepherdstown Commission.

A fan-shaped glass window divides the first floor into formal reception parlors. Stop to admire the beautifully crafted desks made by German artisans in the early 1800s.

Walking upstairs, you may notice the ruddy color of the banister. It was stained with a mixture of blood and milk, a not-uncommon treatment for wood in the early 1800s (look for this in Belle Boyd's Martinsburg homeplace, too) that is remarkably resistant to removal efforts.

Upstairs are a furnished hotel bedroom, a Victorian sitting room, and five rooms containing local historical and American Indian artifacts. Admission to the museum is free, but donations are encouraged. Call (304)876-0910 for more information.

To the rear of the Entler Hotel, on the same property, is the **Rumsey Steamboat Museum**, which houses a half-size working replica of the first Rumsey steamboat and a display about the inventor. You may ask to see the boat anytime during museum hours. Adjacent to the hotel on Princess Street is the **Little House**, a charming, two-story house in miniature, ten feet high and less than ten feet wide, which has fueled the dollhouse fantasies of little girls in Shepherdstown since 1928. It's open during the Christmas holidays; otherwise, peek through the windows.

Walk west along German Street for two blocks to find the **Opera House**, advertising "the finest in films since 1909." One of first theaters to make the transition from silent movies to "talkies," it has been lovingly restored by owners Pam and Rusty Berry and features week-long runs of contemporary and art films. Stop by 131 West German Street to pick up a thoughtful guide to the current month's film offerings, or call (304)876-3704.

Shepherdstown founder Thomas Shepherd was also a miller, a position of importance in his time, and the mill he built around 1739 is worth a stroll past the corner of High and Mill streets, even though the property is privately owned and not generally open to the public. Powered by the Town Run, the **Thomas Shepherd Gristmill** wheel is one of the largest overshot water wheels in the world at 40 feet in diameter. A recent restoration has put it in working order.

Directions: Shepherdstown is about seven miles east of Martinsburg on Route 45 and nine miles north of Harpers Ferry on Routes 340 and

Waiters have replaced tellers and the old bank vault is now a wine cellar at Shepherdstown's Yellow Brick Bank Restaurant.

COLLEEN ANDERSON

230. From Hagerstown, take Route 65 south to Sharpsburg, then Route 34 west across the Potomac River and into Shepherdstown. From Frederick, take Route 340 west to Route 230, just past Harpers Ferry, and follow Route 230 north to Shepherdstown.

Tip: Some of Shepherdstown's most interesting structures also house its best eateries. Highly recommended is the **Yellow Brick Bank**, a modified Beaux Arts-style brick building that curves elegantly around the northeast corner of Princess and German streets. It is notable for its unusual wine cellar (in the former bank's vault) and first-rate cuisine. And a meal at the **Old Pharmacy Cafe** (138 East German Street) is just what the doctor ordered: good food in the authentic surroundings of a former pharmacy with its original 1911 marble soda fountain, tin ceiling and oak cases filled with old pharmaceutical jars. Check out the chalkboard in the window of the **Mecklenburg Inn** (locals call it "The Meck") for featured entertainers or, if it's Tuesday night, join in the open-mic session yourself.

James Rumsey Monument

Looming incongruously over the Potomac River from its perch on a hillside a few blocks from downtown, the **James Rumsey Monument** commemorates the inventor's first demonstration of his steamboat on December 3, 1787. Sleek and modern in appearance, as befits a man ahead of his time, the monument is a tall Ionic column supporting a globe.

The son of a Maryland blacksmith and farmer who learned most of his engineering skills from his father, Rumsey moved to Bath (now Berkeley Springs) to start an inn. Neighbor George Washington noticed his competence and later made him manager of construction for the new Potowmack Navigation Company. He moved his workshop to Shepherdstown and there refined his revolutionary propulsion system for boats, a steam-activated piston engine that pumped water from an intake under the boat through the keel to produce jet action. In December 1787, he proved his mechanical know-how by operating his prototype craft, the *Rumseian Experiment,* against the Potomac's current—at an amazing three knots per hour!

Today, Rumsey's memory is kept alive by an active Rumseian Society dedicated to publicizing the inventor's accomplishments. The group planned and financed the construction of a half-scale replica of the *Rumseian Experiment,* which was successfully launched during Rumsey's bicentennial in 1987. This boat is the one you'll see behind the Entler Hotel; if you want to see it afloat, call the Rumseian Society for a demonstration schedule: (304)876-6907.

Directions: Follow Mill Street north until it dead-ends near the river.

O'Hurley's General Store

If you want to meet the builder of the *Rumseian Experiment* replica, Jay Hurley, you'll find him at 205 East Washington Street in Shepherdstown. Jay is also the genial proprietor of a recreated turn-of-the-century store. At **O'Hurley's General Store**, clerks in period dress ring up such merchandise as fruit presses, pocket watches, cast iron and enamel pots, wooden toys, harness bells, rush chairs, brass hardware and other authentic items that might have been sold in the early 1900s. Should you need it, you can even buy an anvil, a steam engine or a coffin! In this jam-packed store, with Celtic music as a background, you'll also find clothing, crafts and a col-

Jay Hurley and friend, Kate, greet visitors to O'Hurley's General Store and its time-tested treasures. HARRIET WISE

lection of homesteading tools you'll have fun trying to identify.

For nearly 20 years, Jay and whoever cares to join him have been making music at Thursday night jam sessions; these days musicians and spectators gather in a brand new room, the Great Hall. Reminiscent of the late 1700s, with an open-timber frame and wooden-pegged structure, the room is warmed by candlelight and an open-hearth cooking fireplace with a bread oven.

And if Jay's name is Hurley, who are the O'Hurleys? Ask, and you'll hear the colorful tale of Colonial-era stonemason Eliphalet O'Hurley and his true love Jenny, the parents of Grandad Seamus. Jay claims it is the early history of the O'Hurley clan—or at least a good story.

Out back, visit and watch blacksmith Daniel Tokar, who can craft almost anything—a needle or a garden gate, an anchor or a baby's spoon—in pewter, iron, copper, brass or silver.

O'Hurley's General Store is open 10:00 a.m. to 7:00 p.m. Tuesday through Saturday, noon to 6:00 p.m. Sunday. Closed Mondays. Call (304)876-6907.

Directions: 205 East Washington Street, at the east edge of Shepherdstown near the railroad tracks on Route 230.

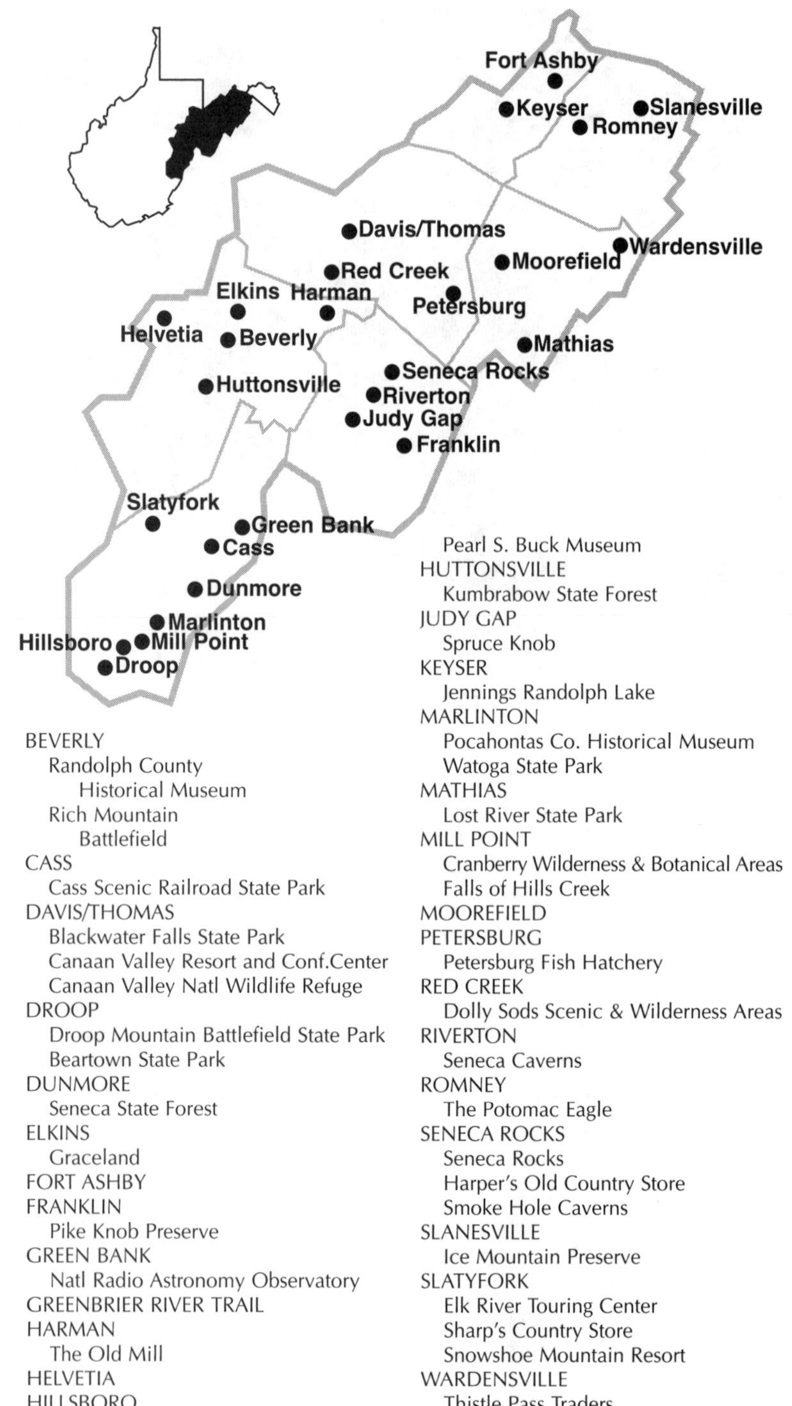

BEVERLY
- Randolph County Historical Museum
- Rich Mountain Battlefield

CASS
- Cass Scenic Railroad State Park

DAVIS/THOMAS
- Blackwater Falls State Park
- Canaan Valley Resort and Conf.Center
- Canaan Valley Natl Wildlife Refuge

DROOP
- Droop Mountain Battlefield State Park
- Beartown State Park

DUNMORE
- Seneca State Forest

ELKINS
- Graceland

FORT ASHBY

FRANKLIN
- Pike Knob Preserve

GREEN BANK
- Natl Radio Astronomy Observatory

GREENBRIER RIVER TRAIL

HARMAN
- The Old Mill

HELVETIA

HILLSBORO
- Pearl S. Buck Museum

HUTTONSVILLE
- Kumbrabow State Forest

JUDY GAP
- Spruce Knob

KEYSER
- Jennings Randolph Lake

MARLINTON
- Pocahontas Co. Historical Museum
- Watoga State Park

MATHIAS
- Lost River State Park

MILL POINT
- Cranberry Wilderness & Botanical Areas
- Falls of Hills Creek

MOOREFIELD

PETERSBURG
- Petersburg Fish Hatchery

RED CREEK
- Dolly Sods Scenic & Wilderness Areas

RIVERTON
- Seneca Caverns

ROMNEY
- The Potomac Eagle

SENECA ROCKS
- Seneca Rocks
- Harper's Old Country Store
- Smoke Hole Caverns

SLANESVILLE
- Ice Mountain Preserve

SLATYFORK
- Elk River Touring Center
- Sharp's Country Store
- Snowshoe Mountain Resort

WARDENSVILLE
- Thistle Pass Traders

Potomac Highlands

With ridges rising to 4,000 feet, the Appalachians make West Virginia "the tallest state in the East," and most of the state's lofty peaks are in the Potomac Highlands, where the Allegheny Front runs like a spine down its length. Much of the region lies within the Monongahela National Forest. Large populations of deer, songbirds and other wildlife thrive here, and unspoiled wilderness areas and nationally significant wetlands support a rich botanical diversity.

In spring, trout-stocked rivers beckon fly-casting fishermen. In summer, the same waterways are just right for canoes, kayaks, rafts and inner tubes to glide through groves of rhododenron, past beautiful farmland and small towns. In fall, hunters head home weighed down with quail, turkey and venison from the huge forest. And in winter the woodland trails attract cross-country skiers, while the steep mountains boast several major downhill ski resorts.

Climb a mountain to a silent, haunting Civil War battle site and come down to hear a champion fiddler perform. Trek through wild backcountry during the day and sit down to a gourmet meal in the evening. Learn about black holes and exploding stars at a world-famous observatory, then watch our own moon rise between the awesome peaks of Seneca Rocks. The Potomac Highlands are lands of plenty for travelers, and most of the wonders are natural—miles of mountain vistas, deep forests, sparkling rivers, vast and splendid caverns.

You'll find history here, if you look, along with arts and music and plenty of festive events—but you'll find it all against backdrop of natural grandeur. Best of all, it doesn't cost much to enjoy the fresh mountain air, deep-green forest and clean water; a day trip to the Potomac Highlands confirms that the best things in life are free or nearly so. Pack a lunch. Put on your hiking boots. Bring the camera.

For more information on visiting the Potomac Highlands contact:

Grant County Chamber of Commerce, PO Box 1366, Petersburg, WV 26847. Call (304)257-2722.

Hampshire County Chamber of Commerce, HC 63, Box 3550, Romney, WV 26757. Call (304)822-7221.

Mineral County Chamber of Commerce, 75 South Mineral Street, Keyser, WV 26726. Call (304)788-2513.

Pendleton County Visitors Commission, PO Box 610, Franklin, WV 26807. Call (304)358-7573.

Pocahontas County Tourism Commission, PO Box 275, Marlinton, WV 24954. Call (800)336-7009, contact them by e-mail (ptct@neumedia.net) or visit their web site (www.pocahontas.org).

Potomac Highlands Travel Council, 1200 Harrison Avenue, Elkins, WV 26241. Call (304)363-8400 or visit the web site (wvweb.com/potomac_highlands).

Randolph County Convention and Visitors Bureau, 200 Executive Plaza, Elkins, WV 26241, phone (800)422-3304 or (304)636-2717. Visit their web site (www.randolphcountywv.com) or contact them by e-mail (bpritt@neumedia.net).

Tucker County Convention and Visitors Bureau, PO Box 565, Davis, WV 26260. Call (800)782-2775 or (304)259-5315 or visit their web site (wvweb.com/www/CANAAN_VALLEY.html).

Beverly

Randolph County Historical Society Museum

Six miles south of Elkins, the small town of Beverly was the homeplace of Lemuel Chenoweth, widely known and respected as a builder of covered bridges. Prior to the Civil War, the bustling town boasted a hat factory, two boot and shoe shops, two tailor shops, three saddlery shops and even a toy factory. Learn about the town's lively antebellum history and the devastation that accompanied the Civil War at the **Randolph County Historical Society Museum** in the **Blackman-Bosworth Store** building. Built as a mercantile store about 1828 by David Blackman and operated by him until the Civil War, it was occupied by both Union and Confederate armies and used for a time as a commissary. Along with Civil War artifacts and displays, you'll find inscriptions written by soldiers on some upstairs walls. After the war, the building was again used as a store, and has also served as a post office and a print shop. The Historical Society purchased and restored it in 1973, and it is listed on the National Register of Historic Places. If genealogy is your interest, the same building houses the **Allegheny Regional Family History Society Library**, where friendly archivist Madeline Crickard helps researchers trace their roots. Volunteers at both the museum and library will be glad to give you information about walking tours of historic Beverly.

Directions: Beverly is six miles south of Elkins on Routes 219 and 250. You'll find the museum and library at the northwest corner of Court and Main streets. (The turn-of-the-century **Beverly Bank** is at the same intersection.) The museum is open on Saturdays from 1:00 to 5:00 p.m. and on Sundays from 1:00 to 4:00 p.m. Admission is free, but donations are welcome. For more information, call the curator at (304)636-1958. The number for the genealogy library is (304)636-1959.

Rich Mountain Battlefield

On July 11, 1861, in one of the earliest engagements of the Civil War, Union troops under the command of General McClellan routed Confederates holding the pass over Rich Mountain near Beverly. The victory was the decisive battle of McClellan's 1861 campaign and led to a withdrawal of Confederate forces from the northwestern counties of Virginia.

The historic battlefield is now a quiet place, but wander and look; you'll find moving reminders of the struggle and bloodshed, such as the sandstone boulder into which is crudely engraved, by a soldier, the words

Clay Jackson
shot and killed
here 1861

Hidden in the woods and worn indistinct by lichens and rain for more than a century, the boulder still speaks eloquently, reminding visitors that someone cared enough about Clay Jackson to scrape grooves into hard stone and leave a declaration of a life lived and lost.

For more information about the battlefield and camp, call (304)637-RICH or write to Rich Mountain Battlefield Foundation, Inc., PO Box 227, Beverly, WV 26253.

Directions: From Route 250 in Beverly, drive west on Rich Mountain Road. The battlefield is about five miles up the mountain. About a mile and a half further, at the mountain's western base, are the remains of Camp Garnett, a Confederate base. Look for signs of extensive entrenchments on the north side of the road.

Cass

Cass Scenic Railroad State Park

The Shay logging locomotive was invented to do the impossible—climb the steepest grades, swing around hairpin curves and negotiate frail temporary tracks, all the while hauling incredibly heavy loads from forest to mill. Back in 1911, West Virginia led the nation with over 3,000 miles of logging railroad line. It is all gone now, except for the 11 miles you'll travel on the **Cass Scenic Railroad**. Instead of timber, the huge locomotives haul passengers in old logging flatcars that have been refurbished in cheery green and red.

The ride is exciting not for its speed—about five miles per hour—but for the sheer power of the restored steam locomotives. One of the Cass locomotives is the last Shay ever built and, at a hefty 162 tons, the largest still in existence. Listen as the great pistons start pulsing, the gears begin turning, the wheels find traction, and the train pulls away from the once-booming lumber town of Cass. With thick, black smoke belching from its stack and the incomparable sound of the steam whistle at crossings, the train takes you past an old water tower (where the locomotive's tanks are filled), a repair shop and a graveyard of antique rail equipment, through forest and up switchbacks to **Whittaker Station**. Here you can picnic and return within 1½ hours, or continue onward for the 4½ hour trip to **Bald Knob**, the second-highest point in West Virginia at 4,842 feet, where you may see eagles and, on a clear day, the state of Virginia.

Cars are fitted with speakers for the guide's narrative, and brakemen in each car will gladly answer questions. Soot, smoke and cinders may occasionally blow backwards from the engine; consider wind direction before you choose your seat, and be prepared to turn your head.

From Memorial Day through September 1, trains to Whittaker Station run three times a day (10:50 a.m., 1:00 p.m. and 3:00 p.m.) and trains to Bald Knob leave once a day, at noon. During September and October the same schedule applies to weekends only. There are special fall foliage runs during October, and some dinner train and holiday trips, including the Halloween Train.

If you don't have time to ride, bring your camera and watch the train chug out of the station—the sound of that steam whistle is just as good when you're a spectator! Also, you can visit the restored buildings near the station, where you'll learn about the town's lively history: the Cass Country Store, full of railroad memorabilia; the Wildlife Museum; and the Historical Museum and Cass Showcase, a miniature of the town in earlier days with model trains demonstrating how timber was transported and processed.

If you want to stay over, the Shay Inn and several refurbished cottages are available. Please note that pets are not allowed in cabins or on trains. Fares are as follows: to Whittaker Station, $10.00-$12.00 for adults (higher prices are for weekend trips), $6.00-$8.00 for ages 5-12. To Bald Knob, $14.00-$16.00 for adults, $8.00-$10.00 for ages 5-12. Children under five ride free. Fall color trips are slightly more expensive. Dinner trains are $25.00 adult, $15.00 children. Fares include admission to the Wildlife Museum, Historical Museum and Cass Showcase. For more information or reservations, call (800)CALL-WVA or (304)456-4300, visit the web site (wvweb.com/www/CASS_RAILROAD.html) or write Cass Scenic Railroad, Box 107, Cass, WV 24927.

Directions: Cass is located on Route 66 between Route 28/92 and Route 219. From Route 28/92, turn four miles north of Dunmore. From Route 219, the turn to Cass is at Slatyfork.

Davis/Thomas

A century ago, the West Virginia Central and Pittsburgh Railway Company characterized the town of **Davis** this way: "Davis stands more than 3,000 feet above the level of the sea and is one of the loftiest cities in the State. It is already becoming a favorite resort for tourists and only needs to be advertised to make it the great mecca for sea coast resorters in summer." They had it right—except for the season. Both Davis and nearby **Thomas** (two miles north on Route 32) are indeed wonderful in the summer, but nowadays the seasons during which they become "the great mecca" are fall foliage time and winter ski season.

Thanks to those skiers and leaf-peepers, Davis and Thomas have become places to enjoy a tasty meal, take in a play or find the perfect gift. **My Grandpa's Attic** is located in the former Davis Supply Store, built at the turn of the century by the Babcock Lumber and Boom Company. Its 8,000 square feet are now filled with antiques and collectibles. Call (304)259-2270. For fine West Virginia arts and crafts, visit **The Art Company** in Davis. Open seven days a week, this cooperative features artfully displayed paintings, toys, quilts, jewelry, fiber arts and much more. Call (304)259-4218. Both stores are right in the center of town on Route 32. In Thomas, the place to meet is **Sweet's Body & Soul Cafe**, where you'll find a little bit of everything, from live music and excellent coffee in the atmosphere of an old English pub to homemade breads and soups, books, crafts, clothing and plenty of good conversation. The cafe opens at 9:00 a.m. every day and stays open until 7:00 p.m. Sunday through Thursday, until 9:00 p.m. on Friday and until 10:00 p.m. on Saturday (live music night). Call (304)463-4427 to find out when the next poetry reading or storytelling session is scheduled. For a schedule of festivals and performances in the area, many of them at the **Cottrill Annex** on Front Street in Thomas (next-door to the 1902 Cottrill's Opera House, currently under renovation), call the box office at (304)463-4522. For more information about either town, call the Tucker County Convention and Visitors Bureau at (800)782-2775 or (304)259-5315.

Blackwater Falls State Park

You'll hear **Blackwater Falls** before you see it. Follow your ears—and other visitors—to the easily accessible boardwalk and a view that provides the backdrop for treasured snapshots in photo albums all over the world. Tourists love Blackwater Falls in every season, and no wonder—plunging from a height of five stories, the famous falls qualify as one of West Virginia's most dramatic natural wonders. Beyond them, the Blackwater River tumbles along through a wooded eight-mile gorge lined with rhododenron and hemlock. In fact, it is the acids from decaying hemlocks and red spruce needles that give the water its "blackness."

This is ski country, and the park's second-biggest attraction is snow. Blackwater is full of beautiful trails, many of which become excellent cross-country ski routes in the winter, and the park's Nordic Ski Center can outfit you completely.

In any season, Blackwater's trails are among the most pleasing you'll find, winding through spruce, maple, beech, and hemlock groves, over rocky outcroppings and to smaller falls. One trail connects with the Monongahela National Forest trail system; another popular hike is to Canaan Valley State Park, about 8½ miles away. The easiest and most traveled is the paved **Gentle Trail** from the road near the lodge to a wheelchair-accessible observation deck.

Like many of West Virginia's state parks, Blackwater Falls maintains a busy schedule of activities: the Septemberfest Senior Fling, the astronomy weekend for beginning and advanced star gazers, wildflower observation hikes and and plenty of other special events. If you have time, you may want to visit nearby **Fairfax Stone Monument**; ask at the park lodge or nature center for directions to this stone marker that was significant in determining the final boundary between West Virginia and Maryland.

The recently refurbished lodge at Blackwater Falls perches on the rim of the Blackwater Canyon (diners in the lodge restaurant have a particularly good view) and the park has 25 cabins scattered throughout the woods. Lodge and cabins are used year-round. From the last Saturday in April through October 31, there are also 65 camping sites. Office hours are 8:00 a.m. to 4:00 p.m. seven days a week. The park is open 6:00 a.m. to dark. Call (800)CALL-WVA or (304)259-5216, visit the web site (wvweb.com/www/BLACKWATER_FALLS.html) or write Blackwater Falls State Park, Drawer 490, Davis, WV 26260.

Directions: Coming from the south, take Route 33 from Elkins to Harman, then Route 32 north to the park. From the north, take Route 219 to Thomas, then Route 32 south to the park.

Tip: This is a popular destination. For peak seasons, make cabin or lodge reservations as much as a year in advance.

Canaan Valley Resort and Conference Center

Legend has it that this valley's name originated with a pioneer in the 1750s who, upon seeing the place for the first time, cried, "Behold, the Land of Canaan." The comparison with the Promised Land isn't much of a stretch. With its craggy mountains and deep forests, rushing streams and fragile wetlands, botanical diversity and abundant wildlife, the Canaan Valley might be the most nearly celestial bit of Almost Heaven, West Virginia.

Maybe that's why two of the most popular state parks are here, less than ten miles apart. Nestled in this bowl of land over 3,200 feet above sea level, **Canaan Valley Resort and Conference Center** is in the perfect place to take advantage of the region's extended snow season. This is the state park system's major winter sports complex, catering to downhill skiers with chairlifts, snow-making equipment and a ski school. Canaan visitors can enjoy the snow on tubes, snowshoes and cross-country skis as well. There's also a well-stocked ski shop.

In spring, cross-country ski trails turn into wildflower walks. The 18 miles of trails include terrain that ranges from wetland to forest to scenic outlook. One easy trail follows a boardwalk from the park headquarters/nature center to the lodge, past a beaver pond, over marsh and meadow. The park has an especially active and varied schedule of nature programs—lectures, walks and slide shows, star gazing, bird and butterfly watches, fishing expeditions and more.

Lodging options include the 250-room lodge, 23 fully-equipped vacation cottages and 34 deluxe campsites. When the snow's not flying, visitors enjoy the resort's 18-hole championship golf course and outdoor Olympic-sized pool. Any season is right for indoor swimming or a relaxing soak in the hot tub at the indoor spa and health club.

The park is open for day visitors 6:00 a.m. to 10:00 p.m. year-round. The lodge is open 24 hours a day. To make overnight reservations, call (800)622-4121 or (304)866-4121; you can also visit their web site (wvweb.com/www/cvresort.html) or write Canaan Valley Resort and Conference Center, HC 70, Box 330, Davis, WV 26260.

Directions: The park is about ten miles north of Harman on Route 32. (From the east, take Route 55 to Harman and follow Route 32 north. From the west, follow Route 33 to Harman, then take Route 32 north.) Traveling north on Route 32, you'll find the park office and nature center on the right. Stop here for brochures, or continue to the resort's lodge.

Canaan Valley National Wildlife Refuge

America's 500th National Wildlife Refuge and the only one wholly within West Virginia's boundaries is the **Canaan Valley National Wildlife Refuge**. Its establishment in 1994 recognized the Canaan Valley as a rare treasure with nationally significant wetlands.

Some say that Canaan Valley is "a little bit of Canada gone astray." The high altitude and cool, moist climate here have created a unique natural protectorate for 40 different wetland and upland plant communities supporting 580 different species of plants. It is the largest freshwater wetland area in the central and southern Appalachians, and the many northern species found in the valley make it a virtual living museum of the Ice Age in West Virginia.

The valley supports equally diverse wildlife populations, with 290 species of mammals, birds, reptiles, amphibians and fishes known or expected to occur there. Canaan is the breeding and fall migration concentration area for the nation's largest breeding unit of American woodcock, and you may see many other migratory species, including raptors, waterfowl, wading birds, shorebirds and songbirds.

For more information about the refuge, call (304)637-7312 or write Canaan Valley National Wildlife Refuge, PO Box 1278, Elkins, WV 26241.

Directions: There are mowed nature trails on the Freeland Road tract across from the White Grass Ski Touring Center on Freeland Road off Route 32. Hiking is also permitted on the roads and trails of the Beall tract. It is located on Old Timberline Road, off Cortland

Road just north of Beechy Lumber Company. Feel free to enter even if the gate is locked. Call or write the above address for a map of these and other tracts.

Droop

Droop Mountain Battlefield State Park

This is the oldest state park in West Virginia. At 287 acres, it is small by comparison to some, but the view is big indeed—the park stands on a mountain plateau overlooking the beautiful Greenbrier Valley. Consider combining a picnic in this park with a visit to Beartown, Watoga and Cranberry Glades Botanical Area—the parks are very different from one another, and the foursome make a good sampler of the variety of landscapes in West Virginia.

It's hard to believe that this serene hilltop was the scene of one of West Virginia's largest Civil War engagements. On November 6, 1863, nearly 7,000 men fought and there were more than 400 casualties, some of whom may still be buried on park grounds. Part of the battlefield has been restored and is marked for visitors.

At the small park museum you'll find exhibits of bayonets, shells, revolvers and other artifacts, many of them found on the grounds—even a wedding band left by a fleeing Confederate soldier. Read about the battle in a displayed *New York Times* account dated November 21, 1863. If the ranger is on hand, ask him to tell you about the cannon outside and the adjacent graveyard.

You can hike on 3½ miles of trails that vary from steep to nearly level. Some lead to war trenches and mountain springs, others to scenic overlooks or caves. Horse Heaven Trail ends at a cliff from which dead horses were thrown after the bloody battle.

The park is open 6:00 a.m. to 10:00 p.m. year-round. Camping is not allowed. For more information, call (304)653-4254, visit their web site (wvweb.com/www/DROOP_MOUNTAIN.html) or write Droop Mountain State Park, HC 64, Box 189, Hillsboro, WV 24946.

Directions: On Route 219, 15 miles south of Marlinton and 27 miles north of Lewisburg.

Beartown State Park

There are holy places in West Virginia, and **Beartown State Park** is one of them. This jumble of huge sandstone boulders, formed millions of years ago by receding and returning ancient oceans, then slowly eroded by wind and rain, has an aura of sanctuary and mystery, of deep joy and wild sorrow. Ferns and mosses soften the rocks. Lichens create colorful abstract paintings. Hemlocks spring from crevices and form a lacy ceiling through which sunlight falls in filtered spangles. Especially on a misty day, it is easy to imagine wood sprites and nymphs meeting here, and not at all hard to see why local legend claims that bears once lived in the house-sized stone formations.

A half-mile boardwalk, skillfully constructed to lead you deep into the maze-like wonderland, is marked with interpretive signs. You will pass a remarkable hemlock that has survived two lightning strikes and a chestnut and oak grown together like Siamese twins. As tempting as it might be to leave the boardwalk and explore, don't. The ecology here is extremely fragile, and this natural gem cannot be replaced. Camping is strictly prohibited, and park rules ask you not to bring food and beverages on the boardwalk.

The gate to the parking area is closed during winter (November to March), but you are welcome to walk in. The only thing more magical than Beartown in summer morning mist is Beartown in snow. Superintendent Mike Smith, who also oversees Droop Mountain Battlefield State Park, will open the gate on request. Call (304)653-4254 or visit their web site (wvweb.com/www/BEARTOWN.html). The park is open 8:00 a.m. to dusk, April 1 through October 31.

Directions: On Route 219 about seven miles south of Hillsboro or 26 miles north of Lewisburg. For further information write Beartown State Park, HC 64, Box 189, Hillsboro, WV 24946.

Dunmore

Seneca State Forest

The Seneca tribe hunted and fished in the mountains of West Virginia long ago, and their name is honored in West Virginia's oldest state forest. This one is ideal for sportsmen or those who want a real escape from the urban. Nearly 12,000 acres of woodlands and the pristine, trout-stocked Seneca Lake make it a favorite hunting and fishing spot. Serious hikers enjoy the 23 miles of challenging trails. For mountain bikers, there are a total of 38 miles, and the Greenbrier River Trail is easily accessible nearby.

Seven rental cabins are available, two beside the river and five around the lake. The rental price includes the use of a rowboat.

A boardwalk leads through Beartown's fascinating forest of rock formations, caves, ferns, and hemlocks. LARRY BELCHER

(Cabin #4, if you're lucky enough to get it, is tucked into its own private cove. There's a dock for the rowboat; forest rules prohibit swimming.) These cabins are rustic: stone fireplaces, fully-equipped kitchens with refrigerator and wood-burning stove, gas lights, bed linens and towels. There is no running water, but hand pumps are conveniently available, and the forest office has coin-operated, hot showers for camping and cabin guests.

Day-trippers are welcome, too, and you'll find picnic facilities and playground equipment for children. Admission to the park is free. Weekly cabin rentals range from $224.00 for a three-person cabin to $402.00 for an eight-person cabin, and are also available on a weekend or nightly basis. Camping costs $7.00 a night. The camping/cabin season runs from the last week in April to the first week in December. For a complete price list and reservations call (800)CALL-WVA or (304)799-6213 or write Seneca State Forest, Route 1, Box 140, Dunmore, WV 24934.

Hours for access to the forest and lake are 6:00 a.m. to 10:00 p.m. year-round. Office hours are 8:30 a.m. to 4:30 p.m. weekdays and 10:00 a.m. to 2:00 p.m. on weekends in season. During winter, the office is closed on weekends.

Directions: Take Route 28 south from Dunmore for about four miles to the forest entrance. From Marlinton, take Route 39 east to Route 28. Go north about 11 miles.

Elkins

In the last years of the 19th century and the first years of the 20th, Henry Gassaway Davis and his son-in-law Stephen Benton Elkins were two of the most influential businessmen in West Virginia—with vast holdings in coal mining, railroads, logging, banking and other commercial ventures. Although both maintained principal homes in other states, they preferred to spend their summers in the cool mountain climate of the town they named for the latter. Here they established **Davis and Elkins College**, built palatial summer homes, entertained presidents and managed their financial and political careers.

The turn-of-the-century boom town is booming in a different way these days. The town of **Elkins** was recently ranked #28 in both *America's Hundred Best Small Art Towns and The 100 Best Small Towns.* That enviable position owes much to the same climate and natural beauty that attracted Davis and Elkins a century ago, but also to a new generation of residents whose interests have made Elkins a mecca for traditional arts and music.

You'll find the Randolph County Convention and Visitors Bureau on the southeast corner of the intersection of Routes 33, 250 and 219, across the street from McDonald's restaurant. Stop in and pick up a walking tour guide to historic buildings in downtown Elkins.

Their hours are 8:30 a.m. to 5:00 p.m. Monday through Friday and 9:00 a.m. to 5:00 p.m. on weekends. Call (800)422-3304 or (304)636-2717 or write Randolph County Convention and Visitors Bureau, 200 Executive Plaza, Elkins, WV 26241.

You'll begin your tour at what was originally called the **Western Maryland Railroad Station** at the corner of Railroad and Third avenues. Built in 1908, it's a good example of turn-of-the-century architecture. Continue on the self-guided tour to 25 other locations, all within a few blocks of one another.

When you reach the **Starr Hotel** building at 224 Davis Avenue (#3 on the walking tour), you may want to stop at the friendly **Augusta Bookstore and Starr Cafe**. You can find a good selection of area hiking and river guidebooks here, or enjoy a fresh cup of coffee and the cafe's most popular original entree, a tender and tangy mix of acorn squash, sesame chicken and vegetables. Hours are 9:00 a.m. to 9:00 p.m. Monday through Friday and 10:00 a.m. to 9:00 p.m. Saturday. Call (304)636-7273.

Lovers of fine art and crafts will probably be tempted across the street to **Artists at Work**, a juried cooperative gallery at 329 Davis Avenue, so named because the artists often work on their wares while minding the shop. You'll find baskets, paintings, jewelry, woodworks, photographs, textiles, prints, pottery, furniture and wearables by some 20 talented regional artists. It's open 10:00 a.m. to 5:00 p.m. Monday through Saturday, 1:00 to 4:30 p.m. Sunday. Call (304)637-6309.

Considering its prominent position, it would be hard to leave Elkins without seeing the **"Iron Horse,"** a statue of Henry Gassaway Davis. It is on Randolph Avenue, across Sycamore Street from the **Davis Memorial Presbyterian Church**, a pretty chapel erected by Henry and Thomas Davis in memory of their parents. Sycamore Street leads to Davis and Elkins College.

Each year in July and August, the hilly, wooded college campus is dedicated to the passing along of folkways. Thousands of students of all ages, from all over the world, flock here to learn from master craftsmen, musicians and dancers. The **Augusta Heritage Center** and its summer schedule of workshops has grown from a few classes to five weeks of workshops ending in a three-day public festival in mid-August. For more information about the summer workshops or other activities at Augusta Heritage Center, call (304)637-1209, contact them by e-mail (augusta@euclid.DnE.wvnet.edu) or write Augusta Heritage Center, Davis and Elkins College, 100 Campus Drive, Elkins, WV 26241.

Directions: Elkins is at the junction of Routes 33 and 219.

Graceland

What Henry Gassaway Davis considered a summer home, most of us would call a castle. In 1893, he completed the mansion he first called Mingo Moor, then Mingo Hall and finally **Graceland** in honor of his youngest daughter Grace. It is said that when Grace married Arthur Lee in 1898, the lavish reception at Graceland was followed by a honeymoon trip to Tokyo, where Grace attended a party given by the emperor, picked up an acorn, brought it home with her and planted an oak tree that still stands beside the home.

From this modified Queen Anne-style mansion, West Virginia's Senator Davis could oversee his railroad yards or look east toward his son-in-law's equally huge estate, **Halliehurst** (named for Hallie, Davis's daughter and Elkins's wife). The estates had orchards, gardens, livestock, a dairy, an ice house and a greenhouse. For recreation? A nine-hole golf course, two tennis courts and a bowling alley.

Built of locally-quarried sandstone and abundantly topped with gables, dormers and turrets (including a four-story octagonal tower that rises to an open-air belvedere), Graceland is roofed in Vermont red slate ornamented with broad bands of fish-scale shingles. Impressive as it is outside, stepping inside will give you a better idea of the sheer scale: within the enormous, two-story great hall are a massive fireplace and a grand stairway leading to an open balcony. Huge stained and leaded-glass windows filter the north light entering the room. Above the fireplace is a 15-foot mural of Blackwater Falls. In the parlor and the library, to the right, you'll see fine examples of the mansion's interior paneling in a variety of native hardwoods, including oak, bird's-eye maple, cherry and walnut. All in all, there were originally 35 rooms for family use, with additional rooms for servants and storage.

Both Graceland and nearby Halliehurst have been brilliantly restored within the past few years, and the two mansions, along with the ice house and estate gate house, form a National Historic District. Halliehurst serves as administrative offices for Davis and Elkins College and is not open for public tours—but Graceland is operated as an inn and restaurant, and you are unlikely to find a more sumptuous stay anywhere in the region. If you want to experience the opulence, call (800)624-3157, visit their web site (wvweb.com/GRACELAND) or write Graceland Inn, Davis and Elkins College, Elkins, WV 26241.

Fort Ashby

The large, hand-hewn log structure sitting very near Route 46 in **Fort Ashby** looks peaceful enough, but its origin recalls a time of violent change. In the middle of the 18th century, this area was considered the extreme edge of the frontier and was vulnerable to Indian attack at any time. In 1755, when Colonel George Washington directed that a chain of 69 forts be built so that settlers in the new territory could seek safe refuge, Fort Ashby was among the first to be constructed. Today, it is the only one still standing. It took its name from Captain John Ashby, who took shelter here after escaping from Indians and later commanded the fort.

Now a museum, the building encloses a massive chimney 14 feet wide and four feet thick; the large doors on the sides of the building were designed to accommodate horses dragging in huge logs to be rolled into the fireplace. Much of the interior woodwork and wrought iron is original, although most articles on display are from the 19th century. Fort Ashby, which has also served as a school and residence, was purchased by the Daughters of the American Revolution in 1927 and has been open to the public since 1939. Admission is free, but donations are appreciated, and you must call in advance to arrange a visit: (304)298-3319, -3926, -3318 or -3722. For more information, write Fort Ashby, Box 233, Fort Ashby, WV 26719.

Directions: Fort Ashby is at the intersection of Route 46 and Route 28, 12 miles east of Keyser, WV.

Tip: Lovers of fine West Virginia crafts, folk art, glassware and antiques—even if they are not avid shoppers—will want to follow Route 28 six miles southeast from Fort Ashby (or eight miles north from Romney) to nearby Springfield to visit **Three Sisters**, a showcase of the state's finest. In addition to seeing handcrafted bird houses, pottery, furniture, wearables, toys and much more, you'll hear West Virginia music and taste West Virginia foods—and the Christmas room is a great place to pick up a handmade ornament at any time of the year. The shop, on Route 28 in tiny Springfield, is open 10:00 a.m. to 6:00 p.m. Monday through Saturday and 11:00 a.m. to 6:00 p.m. Sunday, spring to fall. Winter hours are less predictable, so call (304)822-8880 or write Three Sisters, PO Box 482, Springfield, WV 26763. If you do end up spending money, you can feel good about it—Three Sisters is an enterprise of the Hampshire County Committee on Aging.

Fort Ashby is the only remaining fort of 69 such structures George Washington ordered to protect the frontier in 1755.

COURTESY FORT ASHBY CHAPTER, DAR

Franklin

Pike Knob Preserve

High and lonely, **Pike Knob Preserve** offers some of the most impressive views in the state. The Nature Conservancy owns this 750-acre preserve in Pendleton County, which features a virgin red pine stand next to **Nelson Sods**, large open meadows near the crest of Pike Knob at an elevation of over 4,000 feet. The preserve is also known for its Appalachian grass balds, natural clearings with rare plant species. You'll see panoramic views of Spruce Mountain and surrounding valleys.

The preserve is scenic in all seasons. Autumn foliage can be spectacular from this vantage point, and the preserve is excellent for fall hawk-watching. In winter, expect peace and solitude, and be prepared for bone-chilling winds.

Directions: From Franklin, travel 4.4 miles west on Route 33. Turn left on an unmarked gravel road. After 100 yards, take the right branch of a fork. Continue on the main gravel road up the mountain, bearing right at several forks. Eventually the road becomes impassable for vehicles; park and follow the trail uphill to a gap. At the crest, follow the trail to the right. It climbs to the summit of Pike Knob. From the gap to the top of the mountain is less than a mile; the trail is only moderately difficult, but it's a steady uphill climb. From Judy Gap (the intersection of Routes 33 and 28), travel east on Route 33 for 8.7 miles, past Reeds Creek Road, and make a sharp right onto the gravel road. Continue with above directions.

Green Bank

National Radio Astronomy Observatory

The drive along Route 92 through the Tygart Valley beside the long Cheat Mountain ridge is arguably one of the most beautiful stretches of highway in West Virginia. If you find yourself pondering the mysteries of the universe while traveling it, you're not alone. Out here in the middle of the Monongahela National Forest, scientists at the **National Radio Astronomy Observatory** (NRAO) are searching the heavens for answers to some very fundamental questions: How big is space? When were the galaxies created? Who or what else is out there?

The observatory is one of the world's major sites for receiving and analyzing radio waves from space. Scientists from all over the globe come here to study pulsars, black holes, galaxies, exploding stars, globular clusters and other objects billions of light years away. Seven telescopes are currently in operation, including the world's largest equatorially mounted telescope, which rotates in all directions to measure both long and short radio waves.

The real "star" of this stargazer's paradise, though, is the huge new telescope currently under construction and scheduled to be in operation by 1999. Standing taller than the Statue of Liberty, it will be the world's largest fully steerable radio scope with a reflecting surface larger than two football fields. Its enormous receiving capacity will assure Green Bank's position as the premier radio astronomy observatory in the 21st century.

The observatory occupies 2,600 acres in Deer Creek Valley, protected by surrounding mountains from unwanted man-made radio interference. To assure that purity, the NRAO mandates what radio waves are allowed to enter the "quiet zone" of 13,000 square miles. It is the world's only region where public and private radio transmissions are restricted.

To begin your tour, a staff member will point out displays and introduce a 12-minute slide show giving an overview of the observatory and its operations. You will learn astounding facts: that the sun's radio waves reach earth in eight minutes; the nearest star's in 4.3 years; the farthest galaxy's in billions of years. You'll find out why scientists prefer pulsars as the most accurate measure of time. Staffers will answer your questions about space, time and the possibility of extraterrestrial life, then lead a bus tour around the facility, pointing out specific scopes and explaining their special features. Afterwards, visit the gift shop in the tour center or enjoy a picnic lunch outside, among songbirds and grazing deer.

Hours: Tours begin every hour on the hour, from 9:00 a.m. to 4:00 p.m. every day, mid-June though Labor Day. From Memorial Day to mid-June and during the months of September and October, tours are on weekends only. There is no fee, and cameras are welcome. Call (304)456-2011 or write NRAO, PO Box 2, Green Bank, WV 24944.

Directions: On Route 92 about 25 miles northeast of Marlinton and 53 miles southeast of Elkins.

Greenbrier River Trail

This rail-to-trail conversion has been rated one of the top hiking trails in the United States, and almost any section of its 75 miles will show you why. It parallels the Greenbrier River from Caldwell to Cass, traversing 35 bridges and two tunnels. Easily accessible from a number of entry points, the trail passes beside or near a number of state parks and forests (Watoga, Droop Mountain Battlefield, Beartown, Cass, Greenbrier, Calvin Price and Seneca).

While thrill-seeking mountain bikers may choose other routes, the **Greenbrier River Trail's** nearly-level grade (less than 1 percent) and packed gravel surface make it ideal for children and novice bikers. It's also fine for jogging and, in winter, cross-country skiing. **Marlinton** (mile post 56) is the largest town on the trail and best for food supplies, medical aid and tourist information. Stop at the Marlinton Railroad Depot, now restored as an information center, for maps and brochures.

One of the most beautiful sections of the trail—a favorite of the naturalist at Watoga State Park—is the stretch between Renick (24.5) and Horrock (29.6). To get to it, take Route 219 to County Route 11. At the bottom of the hill, before crossing the bridge, look for a parking lot and trail access. These five miles of trail are particularly entrancing in spring, when the redbud, trillium and Dutchman's-breeches are blooming. Head north and look for Canada geese, wood ducks and other migratory fowl where the river splits to form islands. Bird watchers have recorded 21 different types of warblers here in two days. Around mile post 27, wild turkeys roost in a swampy area. Beech, tulip poplar and river birch line the riverbanks.

North of mile post 65 and on the north side of 511-foot **Sharp's Tunnel and Bridge**, you may see people putting canoes or inner tubes into the water. When the water is high enough, they'll enjoy a leisurely 45-minute float that will take them around the mountain and right back to the south side of the same tunnel. A favorite sight for hikers and bikers is the graceful gothic arch at the north end of this tunnel, which was built in 1900.

Tips: For biking the trail, north to south is the easier direction. Fat tires are recommended. Bring drinking water; although the Greenbrier is one of the cleanest rivers in the state, the water is not potable. For a map and trail guide write Superintendent, Watoga State Park, Marlinton, WV 24954 or call (304)799-4087. You can also get information from the Greenbrier River Trail Association, HC 69, Box 7, Slatyfork, WV 26291.

Harman

The Old Mill

The three-story, white frame gristmill straddling the Dry Fork River looks almost too picturesque to be real. But it is real and it still works, the water-powered turbine turning the half-ton millstones that grind grain into flour. Ask for a tour!

The Old Mill is better known as a museum and retail artisan shop. Listed on the National Register of Historic Places, the 1877 building is filled with antique engines, spinning wheels and other period artifacts, along with homemade preserves, handmade rugs, iron and woodwork, glassware and pottery by West Virginia crafters. Upstairs are two large looms where someone is usually weaving.

There are plenty of hands-on activities. Grind your own flour with a hand grinder, or stick your arm into the "feely box" and guess which of four grains you are examining. Watch live bees working in a glass-encased hive, or try your hand at weaving on the small loom.

The Old Mill is open 10:00 a.m. to 5:00 p.m. Monday through Saturday, from Memorial Day to Labor Day weekends. Admission is free, though donations are welcome. Call (304)227-4466 for more information, or write The Old Mill, Harman, WV 26270.

Directions: One mile north of Harman on Route 32.

This beekeeper's hut, also an inn where guests sip coffee around a pot-bellied stove, is one of ten restored buildings in the Swiss village of Helvetia.

Helvetia

If there is such a thing as a West Virginia Brigadoon, it is the tiny hamlet of **Helvetia** (population: 25) tucked into a remote niche of the Potomac Highlands. Settled in 1869 by a group of Swiss immigrants who really ended up here by accident, it grew to a substantial farming community of 500 people in its prime. For many years, children in Helvetia spoke Swiss German until they started school. That has changed, but the town's pride in its Swiss heritage has not.

Called Helvetia after the original Latin name for Switzerland, the entire town of Helvetia is on the National Register of Historic Places. The industrious descendants of the original settlers have preserved ten historic buildings. One, a settler's cabin, is now a museum filled with artifacts, including the original Swiss flag the pioneers brought with them over a century ago. Others include a church, library, beekeeper's hut (now a cozy inn featuring breakfast around a pot-bellied stove in the kitchen) and one-room schoolhouse. If guests are not staying at the inn, ask to see the innkeeper's collection of early farm implements, clothing, books and musical instruments. Entrance to all buildings is free. The church is open all day, and the museum is open noon to 4:00 p.m. Sundays from May to October.

Most of the time, Helvetia promises peace and quiet in beautiful surroundings. Park at the wood-heated Hutte restaurant, cross the bubbling stream to the common, inhale the fresh air, peek in the store and post office. Twice a year, though, this little village bursts into song and dance. One festival, **Fasnacht** (the Saturday before Ash Wednesday) celebrates the end of winter and includes masks, costumes and the burning of Old Man Winter in effigy. On the second weekend in September, Helvetians and plenty of helpers gather for the **Helvetia Fair**, an annual harvest celebration with a farm animal parade and cheese making.

Whether you come from Elkins or Buckhannon, getting to Helvetia involves a long, curvy drive through forested mountains. That's part of its appeal. Drive carefully, and don't be surprised to see deer, owls or even West Virginia's state mammal, the black bear.

For information about the town, inn or restaurant, call (304)924-6435 or write Eleanor Mailloux, Swiss Village of Helvetia, Helvetia, WV 26224.

Directions: From Buckhannon, take Route 20 to French Creek, then Route 46 to Helvetia. From Elkins, take Route 250 south and turn onto Route 46 at Mill Creek. Follow Route 46 to Helvetia.

Tip: When in Helvetia, put your picnic plans on hold and head for the **Hutte Restaurant** instead. Homemade specialties include sausage, cheese, sauerbraten, sauerkraut and a substantial Stout Soup. On Sundays, the "Bernerplatte" brunch is a real treat. Bring a healthy appetite—the Swiss pride themselves on hearty meals. Just beyond the restaurant is a stable with goats. Human kids are welcome to feed the animals.

Hillsboro

Pearl S. Buck Museum

Pocahontas County seems to grow literary women. Longtime West Virginia poet laureate Louise McNeill's roots were in this area, and Pearl Buck, the first American woman to receive both the Nobel Prize for Literature and the Pulitzer Prize (for *The Good Earth*), was born in Hillsboro.

Her missionary parents, having lost earlier children to sickness, returned to the United States for Pearl's birth in 1892 and stayed until she was a few months old before resuming their vocation in Asia. Pearl Buck herself spent 40 years of her life in China.

The handsome two-story brick and wood manor that serves as the **Pearl Buck Museum** was built between 1860 and 1880 by the Stultings, Buck's maternal grandparents—a replica of the house they left behind in Holland. The interior is furnished with period pieces and shows off her grandparents' carpentry skills as well as the relative affluence of the family. Walnut cabinets in two rooms flanking the entrance hold memorabilia reflecting the rich blend of East and West that shaped the author's long and productive writing life. Copies of her hundreds of novels and short stories, many of which have been translated into over 60 languages, line the bookshelves. A costumed guide will answer questions and show you original furniture such as an eight-day clock, rope bed and dresser handmade by Buck's grandfather. You'll learn the origin of the expressions "sleep tight" and "pop goes the weasel." Ask about the secret hiding place in the attic steps.

Guided tours are available from May 1 to October 31, 9:00 a.m. to 5:00 p.m. Monday through Saturday and 1:00 to 5:00 p.m. on Sunday. Admission is $4.00 for adults and $1.00 for children. Phone (304)653-4430 or write Pearl S. Buck Museum, PO Box 126, Hillsboro, WV 24946.

Directions: On Route 219 one-fourth mile north of Hillsboro and about ten miles south of Marlinton.

Tip: If you're in the mood for aged cheddar, homemade peanut butter or hand-dipped ice cream, stop at the **Hillsboro General Store**. Along with antiques, West Virginia-made foods, buckwheat flour, horse plows, handcrafted gifts, mountain bike supplies, fly-fishing gear and Shaker-style furniture, you'll find deli specialties and a full line of groceries. They're open 9:00 a.m. to 5:00 p.m. Monday through Saturday and noon to 5:00 p.m. on Sunday, weekends only in winter. Phone (304)653-4414. If mountain music makes you happy, you'll want to visit Dwight and Elaine Diller's shop, **Morning Star Folk Arts**. Dwight is a well-known traditional musician; in addition to a collection of traditional West Virginia music, the couple sells dolls, original pastels of West Virginia wildflowers, pottery, glass and other West Virginia-made items. They're open 11:00 a.m. to 6:00 p.m. Monday through Saturday from Memorial Day until the leaves are gone, weekends until Christmas. Phone (304)653-4397. Both stores are on Route 219 in Hillsboro.

Huttonsville

Kumbrabow State Forest

If you want to experience life without electricity for a night or a week—cook over a wood stove, read by gaslight, and haul water from a well—consider a rustic cabin at **Kumbrabow State Forest**. West Virginia's highest state forest, with elevations ranging from 3,000 to 3,855 feet above sea level, it is also one of the most remote and rugged. The name Kumbrabow may sound like an Indian word, but it was derived by combining parts of the names of three families who were instrumental in the forest's early development: KUMp, BRAdy and BOWers.

Built by the Civilian Conservation Corps in the 1930s, Kumbrabow's five rustic cabins are furnished with stone fireplaces, wood-burning stoves, and gas lights and refrigerators. They have no running water, but pit toilets are available and water may be drawn from nearby wells. All cabins are equipped with cooking utensils, dishes, flatware, bed linens and towels, and are open from late April through early December. Thirteen rustic campsites are available during the same season.

Kumbrabow's trails are open for day hikers, too, and you'll find ample picnic areas with fireplaces, drinking water and restroom facilities. You are likely to see deer, turkey and ruffed grouse along the trails; bears and bobcats have also been spotted. A state license is required for hunting, which is allowed in season. With the appropriate license, you can also enjoy fishing in Mill Creek, a stream whose swift, cold waters provide an excellent environment for native brook trout.

For more information, call (800)CALL-WVA or (304)335-2219 or write Kumbrabow State Forest, PO Box 65, Huttonsville, WV 26273.

Directions: Off Route 219, 24 miles south of Elkins and seven miles south of Huttonsville. Turn onto a rock base road at Elkwater and follow it to the forest. If you are traveling north on Route 219, the turn is eight miles from Valley Head. Another access to the forest is from Route 15, turning onto a rock-base road at Monterville.

Tip: Then again, you could simply go hiking at Kumbrabow and stay overnight at the **Hutton House**. The antique-filled Queen Anne Victorian home is on the National Register of Historic Places, and the view of the Laurel Mountains from the wraparound porch may keep you lingering over your gourmet breakfast. It's on Route 219/250 in Huttonsville. Call (800)234-6701 or (304)335-6701 or write Hutton House, PO Box 88, Huttonsville, WV 26273.

Judy Gap

Spruce Knob

At 4,861 feet, **Spruce Knob** is the highest point in West Virginia. It's worth the drive, if only to watch the vegetation change from beech, birch, oak and other hardwoods to mountain ash, scrub spruce and other other alpine flora that can withstand wind and severe cold. If you have plenty of time, you can turn the trip into an all-day excursion; or stay longer and take advantage of the plentiful campsites and over 60 miles of hiking trails in the area.

A scenic but indirect route is to approach Spruce Knob from Route 33 (20 miles west of Harman) by way of Rich Mountain Road along lovely Gandy Creek. Stop to fish, picnic or simply admire the red spruce, hemlocks and cascading falls. Along the way is 25-acre **Spruce Knob Lake**, with a wheelchair-accessible pier and one-mile trail around the lakeshore. The serene lake is also fine for canoes and rowboats, but swimming is not allowed.

When you reach Spruce Knob, park your car and walk through the whispering one-sided spruces, shaped by prevailing westerly winds, to the observation tower. To the west, you'll be gazing out over the Monongahela National Forest and Middle Mountain Range. To the north are the Alleghenies and to the east, miles and miles in the distance, the Shenandoahs. Walk the half-mile Whispering Spruce Trail from the parking area, where June brings lady slippers and July pink mountain laurel and rhododenron. Later, huckleberries and blueberries may tempt you. Feel free to pick and eat berries, but keep an eye out for bears, copperheads and rattlers.

For more information call the Seneca Rocks Visitors Center at (304)567-2827 or the Potomac Ranger Station at (304)257-4488, or write HC 59, Box 240, Petersburg, WV 26847.

Directions: There are quicker routes to Spruce Knob, if you're in a rush to reach the top. From the east, take Briery Gap Road (County Road 33/4 at Gateway General Store) two miles south of Riverton off Route 33, for 2½ miles to Forest Road 112 and follow the signs to Spruce Knob. From the south, turn left off Route 28 south of Cherry Grove onto 28/10 and follow it for 11 miles to the lake, then follow signs to the summit. From the north, take Whitmer Road (County Road 29) south from Route 33 to Whitmer (8.3 miles). Continue south on the same road for 10.3 miles and turn left on Forest Road 1 for 2½ miles to the lake.

Tip: Weather conditions here are unpredictable. Bring a sweater even in summer. Watch for patches of fog in damp weather. Winter travel is discouraged.

Keyser

Mineral County is one of West Virginia's well-kept secrets—quiet and rural, full of wildlife, water, pretty country drives and unexpected pleasures. Its county seat, **Keyser**, is a friendly home base from which to explore the area, including nearby Fort Ashby [see entry]. You'll find the **Mineral County Chamber of Commerce** at the back of the parking lot next to the Candlewyck Inn on Keyser's main thoroughfare, Mineral Street. Hours may vary, but someone is usually there on weekday mornings. Call (304)788-2513 or write Mineral County Chamber of Commerce, 75 South Mineral Street, Keyser, WV 26726.

A favorite local gathering place is the restored 1902 **Candlewyck Inn** at 65 South Mineral Street, where you can enjoy a good meal in an atmosphere of lacy curtains, hanging brass lamps and other Victorian finery. Just inside the door, be sure to peek at the framed front page from the September 23, 1869 edition of the *Mineral County Gazette*. (The story headlined "A Perfidious Wretch" is worth the trip to Keyser.) The inn is also a lodging. Call (800)446-5863 or (304)788-6594 for rates and reservations. If you crave a burrito or a gourmet burger, visit the nearby **Stray Cat Cafe**. Call (304)788-0505.

Although it is privately owned and not available to tour, you can drive or walk past a Keyser landmark, the **Old Stone House**, on Armstrong Street Extended. The oldest building in Keyser, the handsome stone house was built in 1815 by Edward McCarty and his sons. It served as both a prison and hospital during the Civil War.

Keyser is home to **Potomac State College**, very much a part of the community. Highland Arts Unlimited sponsors a lively season of performing arts events at the college's Church-McKee Auditorium on campus. For a schedule of upcoming performances call (304)788-0111 or write Highland Arts Unlimited, Inc., PO Box 63, Keyser, WV 26726.

In nearby Claysville, at the intersection of Routes 50 and 93 about eight miles south of Keyser, history lovers will want to look at the **Claysville Church**, a pretty clapboard structure built in 1860. It was used for services by both Union and Confederate soldiers during the Civil War. Church and grounds are now owned by the Mineral County Historical Society. One-fourth mile south of the church on Route 93 is a 200-year-old log house that originally served as a way station for mail carriers to change horses between Keyser and Petersburg. Now restored, the two-story **Antique Log House of Claysville** has begun a new life as an antique and gift shop. Owners Frank and

Linda Roleff have a particular liking for toys and oak furniture. It's open 10:00 a.m. to 5:00 p.m. Saturdays and 1:00 to 5:00 p.m. Sundays, other times by chance or appointment. Call (304)788-5129 for more information about either the church or log house, or write Antique Log House, HC 72, Box 136, New Creek, WV 26743.

Directions: Keyser is at the junction of Routes 220 and 46, about 20 miles southwest of Cumberland, MD.

Jennings Randolph Lake

West and south of Keyser, near the small town of Elk Garden, the U.S. Army Corps of Engineers maintains **Jennings Randolph Lake**. Originally called Bloomington Lake, this flood-control, water quality and recreation project was renamed in 1987 to honor longtime U.S. Senator Jennings Randolph. The dam across the North Branch of the Potomac River, one of the largest rolled earth and rockfill dams east of the Mississippi, took ten years to complete and controls a drainage area of 263 square miles. During summer, it stores some 31 billion gallons of water.

Because the North Branch of the Potomac forms the state boundary, the lake shares shoreline with Maryland. On the West Virginia side are a scenic overlook, visitors center, picnic area, boat launch and campground, all accessible from Route 46. An interesting feature at the West Virginia Overlook is the "Waffle Rock," a unique, 300-million-year-old geological formation with an orderly geometric pattern that looks as though it's waiting for warm maple syrup. There are 87 campsites at the Robert W. Craig Memorial Campground. You can borrow horseshoe, basketball and other sports equipment or take a walk along a three-fourths-mile interpretive trail.

With all that water held back, fishing is a favorite pastime at Jennings Randolph Lake (there is a fishing pier reserved for persons with disabilities), but the dam may be most well known for the water it lets out, in four carefully controlled springtime releases that make for four weekends of high-excitement whitewater rafting on the North Branch of the Potomac. Release dates for each year are available after January 1 by calling (304)355-2346 or writing Reservoir Manager, Jennings Randolph Lake, PO Box 247, Elk Garden, WV 26717.

Scenic overlooks are open year-round, dawn to dusk. Boat launch and picnic areas are open from April 1 to October 30, and the campground opens May 1 for a camping season that runs through mid-October.

Directions: Off Route 46 between Keyser and Elk Garden. Look for signs leading to the campground, boat launch, and West Virginia access road leading to the picnic area and overlook.

Marlinton

Pocahontas County Historical Museum

If you drive through **Marlinton** in the summer months, you'll find the **Pocahontas County Historical Museum** worth a look. The two-story frame house facing the Greenbrier River was built by banker Frank Hunter for his bride in 1904. It was placed on the National Register of Historic Places in 1976 and is maintained by the Pocahontas County Historical Society.

When you walk in, you'll see displays of Indian artifacts and historical photographs. Other first-floor rooms feature Civil War, logging and railroad history. There's a stuffed black bear and a Bible printed in 1690, thought to be the first in Pocahontas County. On the sun porch is a "cooling board" used to prepare corpses for burial. If you are a fan of Pearl Buck's writing, this museum's collection of the author's signed novels will whet your appetite for the Pearl S. Buck Museum in nearby Hillsboro [see entry].

Upstairs is the Society's collection of farm implements, tools and medical instruments, as well as early machines for weaving, spinning and washing clothes.

The museum property extends to the river, and the picnic tables are there for visitors. Explore the grounds to find an authentic log cabin, dating from about 1840, and a cemetery, the resting place of Confederate soldier Woodsie Price. Some say his ghost wanders through the museum at night.

The museum is open 11:00 a.m. to 5:00 p.m. on weekdays, 1:00 to 5:00 p.m. on Sundays, June 13 through Labor Day, and the admission fees are modest: $1.00 for adults and $0.50 for ages 12-18. Children under 12, free.

Directions: About one-fourth mile south of Marlinton on Route 219.

Tip: Driving through Marlinton on Route 219, look at the old Chesapeake and Ohio Railroad Station and imagine back to 1900, when the timber industry brought the railroad here. Its arrival was celebrated with a huge town rally on October 26, 1900, and the **Marlinton Railroad Depot** was completed in February of the following year. The depot, on the National Register of Historic Places, was restored for the second time after a devastating flood in 1985.

Watoga State Park

The largest of West Virginia state parks, **Watoga** encompasses 10,100 acres of mountainous Pocahontas County. It takes its name from the Cherokee—"Watauga" or "river of islands"—for the wide, shallow Greenbrier River, which forms several miles of the park's boundary. Watoga is one of the most popular state parks, with a comforting, old-fashioned feel that brings visitors back year after year to rent cabins or campsites.

With all that space, it's natural that naturalists would gravitate to Watoga. Summer nature activities may include bird hikes around 11-acre **Watoga Lake**, stream stomps to the river to collect aquatic insects and fish, wildflower walks and hiking on dozens of trails. Bear sightings at Watoga have been reported, and you should be surprised if you *don't* see whitetail deer on your way up to the **T.M. Cheek** picnic area on one of the park's high ridges. If you're an amateur naturalist, the park's **Brooks Memorial Arboretum** is a good place to get acquainted with regional plants and wildlife. Join in a fishing contest and, just before sunset, head for the beaver dam for the park's "backyard beaver watch." Keep in mind that feeding animals in the park is prohibited.

Fishing is a favorite pastime at Watoga. You can rent a paddleboat or rowboat to fish in the lake. Warm-water fishermen like the nearby Greenbrier River, while trout fishermen head for Laurel Run, six miles from the administration building.

Visit the game court and recreation building near the swimming pool for tennis, shuffleboard, croquet, badminton, volleyball, horseshoes and Ping-Pong. Playground equipment and picnic tables are nearby. You can rent horses at the park's stables. Recreational facilities are open from Memorial Day through Labor Day, and some are open until the end of October.

Watoga's 33 cabins and 88 campsites are much in demand. Make cabin reservations well ahead of time. From the first week in April through the end of October, weekly cabin rentals for deluxe cabins range from $504 to $720 for four- and eight-person cabins. Standard cabins rent for less. Nine deluxe cabins are available year-round for weekly or weekend rentals, and campsites are also rented year-round. Pets are not allowed in or near the cabins. The park is open for day travelers from dawn to dark, year-round. Park office is open 8:00 a.m. to 8:00 p.m. Memorial Day to Labor Day, 8:30 a.m. to 4:30 p.m. weekdays and 9:00 a.m. to 5:00 p.m. weekends the rest of the year. Call (800)CALL-WVA or (304)799-4087, visit the park's web site (wvweb.com/www/WATOGA.htma) or write

Watoga State Park, Star Route 1, Box 252, Marlinton, WV 24954.

Directions: Look for signs on Route 219 just north of Hillsboro. Follow the road to miles to the west park entrance. A second option is to turn south from Route 39 at Huntersville and go nine miles to the north entrance of the park.

Tip: If you prefer primitive camping and unmarked hiking paths, you may want to know that Watoga is adjacent to **Calvin Price State Forest**, a large tract of 9,482 acres, mostly undeveloped. Fishing is great here, as is hunting in season. Contact Watoga State Park for more information about the forest.

Mathias

Lost River State Park

The river doesn't really get lost, it merely disappears underground for a couple of miles, to reappear as the Cacapon River. What gets lost at **Lost River State Park** is the stress and strain of everyday life. One of the oldest of West Virginia's state parks, it is also one of the most serene and relaxing.

Miles of horse and hiking trails wind through the 3,712 acres of park woods. For one spectacular view, climb to the **Cranny Crow Overlook** at 3,200 feet above sea level. Or pack a lunch and hike the park's longest trail to **Miller's Rock**, where craggy spruce trees cling to lichen-covered outcroppings overlooking mile upon mile of mountains. A walk around the immediate park grounds will inevitably lead you to the **Lee Museum**, a simple white cabin "Light Horse Harry" Lee built in 1800 on this land he received as a grant in return for his military leadership during the Revolutionary War.

Recreation is not limited to walking. You'll find tennis, badminton, horseshoes, croquet, basketball, archery and volleyball at the park's recreation center near the pool, and playground equipment scattered throughout the park. Summer months are filled with special activities: history and wildflower walks, scavenger hunts, slide programs, movies and children's activities. Lost River's trails are especially good for horseback riding. The stables are generally open 9:00 a.m. to 7:00 p.m. daily (reduced hours in the fall), and riding fees are $15.00 for the first hour and $10.00 for each additional hour.

The park's 24 cabins (nine deluxe, 15 standard) are tucked into private spaces among the trees and provided with fully-equipped kitchens, cooking utensils, tableware, towels, blankets, linens, baths with showers and—especially comforting in fall and winter—

huge stone fireplaces with an endless supply of firewood. Because it's such a family-friendly place and so close to Washington (about 2½ hours), these cabins are heavily booked. Plan eight months or more in advance, but don't hesitate to inquire at the last minute about possible cancellations. Weekly rentals range from about $300.00 to $600.00 depending upon the cabin and the number of guests. Nightly and weekend rentals are available from Labor Day to the second weekend in June. Deluxe cabins are heated and open year-round. Standard cabins open the last weekend in April and close the fourth Monday in October.

There is a restaurant at Lost River State Park, open seasonally. Hours may vary, so check with park personnel before you make dinner plans. The park is open year-round, 6:00 a.m. to 10:00 p.m. Office hours are 8:00 a.m. to 4:00 p.m. Monday through Friday and 10:00 a.m. to 3:00 p.m. on weekends. Call (800)CALL-WVA or (304)897-5372, visit their web site (wvweb.com/www/LOST_RIVER.html) or write Lost River State Park, HC 67, Box 24, Mathias, WV 26812.

Directions: From the town of Mathias, turn west off Route 259 and follow the secondary road four miles to the park entrance.

Tip: When you go sightseeing, note the **John Mathias Homestead**, the log structure at the junction of Lost River State Park Road and Route 259. It dates from 1797 and is a good example of early architecture in the state. You'll find a very nice crafts cooperative, **Lost River Craft Cooperative**, seven miles south of Baker on Route 259. A 150-year-old barn is now home to a tasteful selection of juried crafts, homemade foods and wines. At the same location is the **Lost River Museum**, a treasure trove of old tools, wagons, utensils and photographs. Open 10:00 a.m. to 5:00 p.m. daily except Wednesday and Thursday, Memorial Day through Veterans Day, and weekends only through mid-December. For more information call (304)897-6169 or -5847. A short walk up the road is **Uncommon Things**, owned by former Peace Corps volunteers whose inventory reflects their interest in American history as well as folk art from other countries. You'll find everything from American country furniture to embroidery done by Laotian hill-tribe women to copperware and textiles from Turkey. And, in the pasture nearby, three uncommon animals—friendly miniature donkeys named Rocky, Rosie and Buckwheat. Open April through December, 11:00 a.m. to 5:00 p.m. Friday through Monday. Phone (304)897-6788.

Mill Point

Cranberry Wilderness and Botanical Areas

The **Cranberry Wilderness Area**, under the care of the U.S.D.A. Forest Service, is a 36,000-acre area being allowed to grow without any logging or other land-disturbing activities. Together with the 750-acre **Cranberry Glades Botanical Area**, it is considered to be among the most significant biological environments in Allegheny Mountains.

Undisturbed, the bogs (locally called "glades") are being taken over by maple, hemlock, yellow birch and red spruce. One venerable yellow birch is 300 years old. The wilderness is home to many songbirds, deer and small mammals.

Some plants in the bogs (acidic wetlands) originated from plant life left after the ice age 10,000 years ago. These plants are now more commonly found in Canada. Four of the most accessible and representative bogs are found in **Cranberry Glades**, a natural, 3,400-foot-high "bowl" of tundra-like environment, kept unusually cool by surrounding mountains. Park in the parking lot and follow the half-mile boardwalk through the glades. Along the way you may see snake-mouth orchids, Indian pipe, cinnamon fern, monkshood, jack-in-the-pulpit, skunk cabbage, trillium, trout lily, jewelweed, mountain laurel and elderberry. Harmless snakes, frogs, mice, warblers, finches, woodpeckers, thrushes and owls are also at home here.

The wheelchair-accessible boardwalk is open 24 hours a day; early morning is best for observing birds and wildlife. Removal of plants or animals is strictly prohibited in the glades. Bicycles and pack animals are not permitted on the glades boardwalk, and dogs must be leashed.

Forest Service staff conduct tours at 2:00 p.m. on Saturdays and Sundays from Memorial Day to Labor Day. The **Cranberry Mountain Nature Center**, located at the junction of Route 150 and Route 39/55, presents a variety of nature-related programs including a video on the Cranberry Glades. The center is open Memorial Day to Labor Day and on weekends the rest of the year (except for December) from 9:00 a.m. to 5:00 p.m. Phone (304)653-4826 or 653-8564.

Backpacking is permitted in the wilderness area for parties of ten or fewer. Motorized vehicles and mechanical transportation are prohibited, and horse use is discouraged. If you go into the wilderness area, be sure to register at the nature center.

Directions: Take Route 219 south from Marlinton about eight miles to Mill Point. Take Route 39/55 about six miles to the Nature Center. The entrance to the boardwalk is .6 miles beyond the center on Route 39/55. If you are coming south on Route 219 from Slatyfork, consider taking Route 150, part of the **Highland Scenic Highway**. (Be advised: it is not maintained in winter months, and travel there is not recommended.)

Falls of Hills Creek

This roadside gem begins with a walkway that leads to a view of the second-highest waterfall in West Virginia. A three-fourths-mile trail leads down a steep gorge to a series of three falls that cascade 25, then 45 and finally a dramatic 65 feet. The walkway to the first falls is wheelchair-accessible. If you walk all the way to the bottom of the gorge, bear in mind that the hike back up is strenuous.

Directions: The **Falls of Hills Creek** is located along Route 39/55, 5½ miles west of the Cranberry Mountain Nature Center.

Moorefield

Although not as often as nearby Romney, **Moorefield** changed hands several times during the Civil War. In August 1864, Confederate General McCausland slept here while Union soldiers slipped into the area and attacked at dawn, routing his troops. And it was here, a few months later, that local heroes McNeill's Rangers, a Confederate partisan unit, surprised General Benjamin Kelley's forces and chased them all the way to Keyser (then known as New Creek).

McCausland spent his fateful night at **McMechen House**, a three-story Greek Revival home built in 1853 by Samuel McMechen. You can sleep there, too, in the lovingly restored home-turned-inn, among McMechen family furniture, photographs and other memorabilia—and it's a safe bet you'll enjoy your breakfast more than General McCausland did. Owners Bob and Linda Curtis also operate an antique store, and serve weekend dinners from early May through the end of October. In warm weather, guests and diners enjoy the hemlock-shaded deck. Call (304)538-7173, or write McMechen House Inn, 109 N. Main Street, Moorefield, WV 26836.

Next-door, the **McCoy-McMechen Theater**, a 1927 movie palace once called McCoy's Grand, has been converted to a community theater and museum. This and the nearby **Dr. Bowen House**, formerly a pharmacy and now a museum and headquarters for the **Hardy County Historical Society**, are open during Hardy County

Heritage Weekend (the last full weekend in September) and by appointment. Write the Historical Society, c/o 111 N. Main Street, Moorefield, WV 26836.

Among other interesting structures on Moorefield's Main Street are the 1788 **Old Stone Tavern** at 117 S. Main, now a private home (said to be haunted by its owner, who reportedly insisted upon being buried in the basement); the **Gamble-Maslin House** at 131 S. Main, where Justice Thomas Maslin hid Confederate sympathizers in a secret cellar; and the **Dr. H.M. Gamble Home** at 202 S. Main, built in the 1850's with brick fired on the site. Dr. Gamble was a soldier, physician and surgeon. Fluent in several languages, he founded the West Virginia Medical Society and was also an avid botanist, whose personal collection of plants formed the basis of the West Virginia University Herbarium.

Stroll down Winchester Avenue to the east, just past Rosemary Lane, for a look at a particularly lovely Victorian Gothic restoration, the **Downing Cottage**. If you continue on Winchester Avenue for less than half a mile, you'll come to the **Olivet Cemetery**, where you'll be rewarded with a panoramic view of Moorefield and mountains.

Directions: Moorefield is at the junction of Route 55 and Route 220/28.

Tip: Just three miles south of Moorefield, on Route 220 and 55 adjacent to the Valley View Golf Course, you'll find **West-Whitehill Winery**. Stop in Saturday or Sunday between 1:00 and 5:00 p.m. for a taste of proprietor Steve West's award-winning wines, or call (304)538-2605 or (304)538-7990.

Petersburg

Petersburg Fish Hatchery

The state fish hatchery at Petersburg, one of the oldest in the West Virginia, was built by the Civilian Conservation Corps in the 1930s. It was here, in the 1950s, that a particular, bright golden strain of rainbow trout first emerged. Isolated and bred, the fish has earned Petersburg the title "home of the golden trout."

Outside are four rock-walled ponds used for brood fish and production. If you are lucky enough to be traveling through the area between mid-September and late October, you'll see golden trout in all stages of growth—tiny hatchlings, week-old, year-old and two-year-old fish. A bit earlier, between August 1 and mid-September, you can watch fish spawning on Tuesday mornings.

The hatchery is open year-round, seven days a week, from 7:30 a.m. to 3:30 p.m. Although there are no picnic tables, you're welcome to spread a blanket between the ponds and picnic among the flashing golden fins. Feeding the fish is not allowed. For more information call (304)257-4014.

Directions: From Petersburg, follow Route 220 south. At the edge of town, turn onto Fish Hatchery Road/Airport Road. Pass the airport and industrial park. The hatchery is at the end of the paved road, about two miles from Petersburg.

Tip: If seeing all that trout makes you hungry, order a meal of rainbow trout at **Brooke's Landing Restaurant** on Route 220 in Petersburg. It won't be from the local hatchery (their fish all go into streams), but it will be fresh from another West Virginia hatchery. The Sunday buffet, from 11:00 a.m. to 3:00 p.m., is an all-you-can-eat bargain at $6.95. Call (304)257-2355. The restaurant is part of a complex that also includes the historic **Hermitage Inn**, listed on the National Register of Historic Places, which has been headquarters for Union officers during the Civil War, circuit court judges, sequestered juries and many honeymooners. Stay the night or just stop to browse in the inn's pleasant craft and book shop, where you'll find a selection of regional books and handcrafts. Call (304)257-1711 or, for reservations only, (800)437-6482.

Red Creek

Dolly Sods Scenic and Wilderness Areas

The high, windswept plains of Dolly Sods, a tract of more than 10,000 acres within the Monongahela National Forest, form an "island" of wild country in West Virginia where the climate and plant life resemble northern Canada. The plateau is a place of boundaries, natural and man-made. It comprises parts of four counties (Grant, Randolph, Pendleton and Tucker) and is a secondary continental divide—southern portions are drained by Red Creek, which eventually feeds the Mississippi, while water from northern parts of the plateau makes its way via Stoney Creek to tributaries of the Potomac and the Chesapeake Bay. This land was once covered by a red spruce and hemlock forest that was burned in the 1880s. Its name comes from German settlers probably named Dahle (the spelling is open to dispute) who grazed livestock on the densely matted bluegrass ("sods") that thrived in a place otherwise uncharitable to agriculture.

The **Dolly Sods Scenic Area** was created in 1970 to protect the scenic qualities of an area north of Forest Road 19, which traverses the southern boundary of the Wilderness Area. Accessible by narrow mountain roads, this is the most visited part of Dolly Sods—and, as its name implies, an area of dramatic views. It encompasses about 2,000 acres along Forest Road 75 and includes **Red Creek Campground**, short hiking trails, picnic areas and rocky outlooks with panoramic views, among them the popular Bear Rocks overlook. Large limestone boulders are scattered throughout the area.

From late spring until October, Dolly Sods puts on a changing botanical show. If you come here in early May, you may see the frothy white bloom of service trees ("sarvis" is the more popular name here) along Forest Road 75, along with clumps of wild bleeding-heart, the clustered white blossoms of alder-leaved viburnum and gently fragrant trailing arbutus. The rosy azaleas of early June give way or sometimes overlap with the pink mountain laurel of late June, which in turn yields to rosebay rhododendron, West Virginia's state flower.

Late summer is blueberry time at Dolly Sods. Actually, both blueberries and huckleberries grow here, the former in greater abundance. You can tell the difference by eating them: blueberries have many tiny seeds, almost too small to notice; the larger seeds of huckleberries tend to get caught in teeth. Feel free to pick and eat both. Bears love the blueberry thickets, too, so look up from your harvesting from time to time, and watch for snakes as well. On the Northland Loop Trail, just south of the campground, you may see the tiny, carnivorous sundew plant along the boardwalk through the bog. Look for the bright blue of gentian in open meadows and swamps during September. By late September or early October you may find native cranberries, a delicacy.

As the goldenrods and asters fade, autumn brings to Dolly Sods what some consider its finest display of color. Thousands of acres of blueberries, huckleberries and chokeberries form a blazing sea of red, throwing the dark spruces and pines into contrast. The mountain ash, or rowan, fruits in brilliant orange sprays of color, and three species of deciduous holly cling to their bright red fruits.

Fall is also prime time for bird lovers. For many years, the Allegheny Front at Dolly Sods has served as an important station for the scientific study of bird migration and dispersal. Volunteers from the Brooks Bird Club use fine-gauge nylon nets to carefully trap, examine, band and release thousands of migratory birds—mostly thrushes, warblers, vireos, sparrows, flycatchers and finches, but also elusive owls and even hawks. Because these bird banders work under federal and state permits, only a few individuals are permitted to participate, but you may be lucky enough to watch them if you are in the area on a morning between mid-August and mid-October.

The birds that bring greater numbers of autumn visitors to Dolly Sods are hawks. Dolly Sods is on one of the major flight channels from north to south. From mid-September until early October, chances are you will see the unforgettable sight of a flock of migrating broad-winged hawks; or, at the very least, enjoy awe-inspiring scenery in the company of other humans who have gathered in hopes of spotting the noble birds.

Within the past 150 years, Dolly Sods has been logged, burned, grazed and even used as a military training ground during World War II. In the 1930s and 1940s, however, the Forest Service and Civilian Conservation Corps began efforts to reforest the area with red pine and spruce. **Dolly Sods Wilderness Area** was designated in 1975, specifically to allow nature to take its course. Protected from further disturbances, this area may eventually return to its primitive state.

These 10,215 acres of wilderness are prized by backcountry lovers. The refuge of some rare or elusive species—the Cheat Mountain salamander and the bobcat, the northern flying squirrel and the snowshoe hare—it also supports weasel, mole, shrew, mice, raccoon, skunk, woodchuck, fox, deer and bear populations. Trail maps are available, but you should know that the nine trails here are not marked for inexperienced hikers, and the wilderness area is an easy place to get lost. The Forest Service stresses that topographic maps and compasses, plenty of previous hiking experience and good map-reading skills are essential. There are no shelters and no bridges over creeks. Motorized vehicles, bicycles and other wheeled vehicles are prohibited in the wilderness area.

Although it is not part of the Dolly Sods Wilderness Area, the **Flatrock and Roaring Plains Backcountry** south of Forest Road 19 is another beautiful part of the Allegheny Plateau, with plenty of bogs, berries and windswept plains. The trails in this area are marked with blue blazes and signs at all junctions. However, the trails are rugged and wet, and hikers here should take the same precautions they would take in the wilderness area: carry maps and compasses, be prepared for changeable weather, bring drinking water and wear high-visibility clothing during hunting seasons.

For more information, or to purchase maps or hiking guides, contact the Potomac Ranger Station, Route 3, Box 240, Petersburg, WV 26847, phone (304)257-4488 (weekdays); or the Seneca Rocks Visitors Center, PO Box 13, Seneca Rocks, WV 26884, phone (304)567-2827 (open daily, except winter).

Directions: From Petersburg, follow Route 28/55 south to Jordan Run Road. Turn right and go one mile up Jordan Run Road to Forest Road 19. Turn left and follow Forest Road 19 six miles to Dolly Sods Scenic Area. From Canaan Valley, follow Route 32 south to the Laneville Road. Turn left and follow the Laneville Road ten miles to the Dolly Sods Scenic Area.

Tips: Be aware that traveling to Dolly Sods involves driving on narrow, rough gravel roads. Heavy traffic makes for dusty conditions on some weekends. Forest service roads are not plowed; travel during winter is not recommended.

Riverton

Seneca Caverns

Within 12 miles of Seneca Rocks, in opposite directions, are two commercial caverns, Seneca and Smoke Hole [see entry], where you can take a guided tour through a separate world beneath the mountains. Each has its own awe-inspiring ambience and variety of limestone formations.

Seneca Caverns, the largest of West Virginia's commercial underground caves and the only one with a gemstone mining operation, is three-fourths mile long and, at its deepest point, 165 feet below the earth's surface. Although you'll want to bring a sweater, the cave's constant temperature of 54 degrees Fahrenheit makes it a good shelter in extreme weather, and explains why arrowheads and other artifacts have been found here. Europeans discovered the cavern in 1790.

Underground rivers carved these caverns millions of years ago, and they were thrust above water level during the ice age, perhaps by an earthquake. Drop by drop, seepage through limestone formed the stalagmites, stalactites, columns and flowstone visitors see today, formations you can still hear growing as you walk through the caves.

You'll see a number of rooms, including the Grand Ballroom, which could easily accommodate several hundred people, and Mirror Lake, where the limestone formations are reflected in an underground pool. These and other magical scenes are heightened by skillful lighting. However, the passageways can be slippery, so wear shoes with good traction, keep children close at hand and—

no matter what the tour guide tells you—leave your pets behind. The cavern's staff will make arrangements to accommodate persons in wheelchairs (please call ahead), but backpack or front baby carriers are recommended instead of strollers for youngsters. The guided tour takes 45 to 55 minutes.

Getting to Seneca Caverns involves a scenic bonus—the drive through German Valley, a wide and fertile area of farmland between the mountains. The caverns, less commercialized than most such operations, are in a rustic setting with a minimum of obtrusive signage. There's plenty of free picnicking space as well as a new restaurant. Tours are given year-round, weather permitting, at the following rates: $7.50 for adults, $6.75 for seniors, $3.75 for children 6-11, under age 6 free. For group rates, call (304)567-2691, visit their web site (www.senecacaverns.com) or write Seneca Caverns, Route 9, Box 61, Riverton, WV 26814.

Directions: From Seneca Rocks, take Route 33 south through Riverton and follow the signs to the entrance.

Tip: If it's a weekend, you may want to stop at the **Riverton Cash Store** on your way to Seneca Caverns. Built in 1900 by Charles Grant Teter, the old post office and store is now a museum and shop with crafts, locally-made jams and jellies, antiques and a collection of Fenton glassware. It's a nice place to sit around an old-timey pot-bellied stove and trade yarns with owner Charles Teter, a fifth-generation Teter who has worked in the store since he was "able to count." To find him, go to Riverton, make the turn toward Seneca Caverns, go one block, turn right, go approximately 100 yards and look for the store on the right.

Romney

Romney residents claim that their town shares with Shepherdstown the distinction of being West Virginia's oldest (both were incorporated in 1762). During the Civil War, Romney changed hands as many as 56 times—three times in one day! Thomas "Stonewall" Jackson headquartered here for a time during the war. Reportedly, he was so angered by an order to abandon Romney to the Yankees that he threatened to resign his commission.

Today, Romney's peaceful aspect belies its Civil War troubles. A day or afternoon here will yield pleasures to satisfy a surprising variety of interests. Be sure to visit **The Bottling Works**, Mike Smith's personal museum of Coca-Cola memorabilia—everything from vintage bottles to bottling equipment, uniforms and oodles of promotional items—housed in the former Coca-Cola bottling plant at 426 Main Street. Built in 1939, the plant was managed by Mike's grandfather; his father was a bottler, and Mike himself drove a route truck. Ask to see his pet restoration project, a 1947 delivery truck. Open Friday through Sunday, May through September, 10:00 a.m. to 6:00 p.m., daily during October, and Saturday 10:00 a.m. to 5:00 p.m. in November and December. Call (304)822-4783 for more information.

If soft drinks are not your cup of tea, how about a taste of West Virginia wine? **Schneider's Winery** in Romney is one of four wineries clustered in a relatively small area of Hampshire and Hardy counties [see appendix]. You'll find it on a beautiful hilltop: Go about 2½ miles east of town on Route 50 and turn left on Jersey Mountain Road (immediately before the Mountain Top Truck Stop). Go exactly two miles to the winery, a blue building on the left. Hours are noon to 6:00 p.m. Wednesday through Saturday and 1:00 to 6:00 p.m. on Sunday. Call (304)822-7434.

Antique lovers will insist upon spending at least an hour exploring 10,000 square feet of antique furniture and collectibles at **The Brass Frog Antiques**, on Route 50 at the eastern edge of town. Hours are 10:00 a.m. to 5:00 p.m. weekdays, except for Tuesday, and 10:00 a.m. to 6:00 p.m. weekends. Call (304)822-5542 or (304)298-4800.

On a nice day, you might take a leisurely canoe float through "The Trough," the famous scenic stretch of the South Branch of the Potomac River, accessible only by river or rail. **Trough General Store**, about 9½ miles south of Romney on River Road, can outfit you with canoes, shuttle service, food and other supplies. Store hours vary, but you can make advance reservations for trips by calling (304)822-7601.

Chances are you'll find Romney and the rest of the South Branch Valley worth more than a day. If so, historic **Hampshire House 1884**, at 165 North Grafton Street, is a good place to spend the night. At this completely restored period inn, you can relax in front of an alcohol-burning fireplace or outside in the Minnie Peters garden. Full country breakfasts and personal attention are hallmarks. Call (304)822-7171 for rates and reservations.

Directions: Romney is at the junction of Route 28 and Route 50.

The Potomac Eagle

If you don't want to paddle a canoe, do take advantage of the other way to see "The Trough," by riding **The Potomac Eagle**. The train's name is no coincidence: you are very likely to spot an American

The Potomac Eagle travels through the Trough, a narrow gorge that is one of West Virginia's few nesting areas for bald eagles.

COURTESY THE POTOMAC EAGLE

bald eagle as you make the three-hour excursion through the tranquil valley of the South Branch of the Potomac. The narrow gorge is one of West Virginia's few nesting areas for the once-endangered bird, and they are sighted on nine excursions out of ten. The train moves slowly enough for you to enjoy a profusion of wildflowers, evergreens, mixed hardwoods and wildlife: hawks, deer, beaver and even fish beneath the crystal-clear waters.

The trip from Romney follows the river to Sycamore Bridge near Moorefield before returning. It is especially popular during fall foliage season. The station opens one hour before the train departs, with boarding about 30 minutes in advance. If you arrive early, **Mountain Traditions Arts & Crafts Guild**, located at the train station, is a nice place to browse.

For coach cars, the fares are $20 for adults, $18 for seniors over 59, and $12 for children 3-12 (under three, free); for the first class club car, where lunch is served, the fare is $44. From May 16 to June 27, the train runs Saturday at 1:00 p.m. From July 4 to early September, the schedule expands to Saturdays and Sundays at 1:00

p.m. From mid-September to the end of the month, trains run Sunday at 1:00 p.m. and twice on Saturday, at 10:00 a.m. and 2:00 p.m. And in October, it's seven days a week: Monday through Friday departures vary through the month, and on Saturdays and Sundays the train leaves at 10:00 a.m. and 2:00 p.m. Throughout the season, there are special all-day round trips between Romney and Petersburg. Call (800)22-EAGLE for more information, or write The Potomac Eagle, 2306 35th Street, Parkersburg, WV 26104. You can also visit their web site (wvweb.com/www/potomac_eagle/).

Directions: On Route 28, 1½ miles north of Romney.

Tip: Reservations are recommended, especially for groups of 20 or more and during fall foliage season. No alcoholic beverages, smoking or pets are allowed on the train. And remember that eagles are protected by law; there are stiff fines for anyone caught near nesting areas.

Seneca Rocks

Seneca Rocks

Driving east along Routes 33 and 55 from Harman, a few miles past the small town of Onego (say "one" and "go"), you will come upon an unforgettable sight—huge Tuscarora sandstone rocks lunging straight out of the earth to a height of 900 feet. **Seneca Rocks** is one of the most visually thrilling (and most photographed) landmarks in West Virginia. The towering giants were formed over 200 million years ago at the end of the Paleozoic geologic era, when the ancestral continents of Africa and North America collided, bending and buckling rock layers deep within the earth's crust. Indian folklore celebrated them, and they have been shown on maps since the first European settlers arrived.

Surely Native Americans climbed these peaks before someone, probably a surveyor, carved "D.B. Sept. 16, 1908" into the sandstone cliffs. During the 1940s, U.S. Army troops were trained here in preparation for climbing European mountains. Seneca Rocks is still considered by many to be the most challenging climb in the East.

Although the face of Seneca Rocks is a challenge for skilled or supervised climbers with proper equipment, the trail to the top of the rocks is a safe, albeit steep, 1.3-mile walk to an observation platform 40 feet below the top of the ridge line—and the view of the gentle farmland below is worth the hike.

Sadly, the **Seneca Rocks Visitors Center** lost everything, including its collection of historical photographs, when it burned in 1992. However, old postcards show an unusual 30-foot, 20-ton pinnacle, called the Gendarme, that rested between the large humps at the top of the cliffs until it tumbled down in October 1987.

The visitors center is open daily, Easter through Thanksgiving, from 9:00 a.m. to 5:30 p.m. and weekends only, 9:00 a.m. to 4:30 p.m, the rest of the year. The center offers displays and an 11-minute video of Spruce Knob-Seneca Rocks National Recreation Area. Books and maps are for sale here, as well.

Directions: Located near the junction of Route 33 and Route 28/55 in Pendleton County. Another spectacular peak, **Champe Rock**, is six miles north on Route 28/55.

Tip: If you can, plan your visit to coincide with late afternoon: the rocks are particularly dramatic when viewed from the west in the glow of the setting sun. And if gazing up at Seneca Rocks gives you the urge to climb them, you'll find two climbing schools operating from April through October at the junction of Routes 33 and 28. **Seneca Rocks Climbing School**, next to Harper's Store, has been teaching climbers for almost a quarter of a century and was the first guide service in the eastern United States to be accredited by the American Mountain Guides Association. Services include basic and intermediate classes, private guiding and safety courses. Call (800)548-0108 or (304)567-2600 or write Seneca Rocks Climbing School, Box 53, Seneca Rocks, WV 26884 for prices and reservations, or visit their web site (www.gendarme.com). Another highly respected and accredited climbing school and guide service, **Seneca Rocks Mountain Guides**, is across the road from the general store. Call them at (800)451-5108 or (304)567-2115, reach them by e-mail (SenecaTrad@aol.com) or write Seneca Rocks Mountain Guides, Box 223, Seneca Rocks, WV 26884. If you've never climbed and want an inexpensive, safe introduction to the sport, try the **Seneca Rocks Gym** next-door—for $10, they'll outfit you with helmet, harness and shoes and show you how to scale a man-made cliff beside the road. Phone (800)451-5108.

Harper's Old Country Store

It really is old, it really is Joe Harper's, and its country store atmosphere is the genuine item. Since 1902 members of the Harper family have operated this store—the current proprietor is the great-great-grandson of the founder—and they haven't changed it much. The original oiled hardwood floors, antique metal ceiling, shelving and counters are all in place, along with a vintage cash register and a mind-boggling mix of bait, sheepskins, sassafras roots, Indian headdresses and Daniel Boone-style raccoon caps. You can buy gas, beer and soft drinks downstairs—but you'll probably want to head upstairs to the **Front Porch Restaurant** for a slice of fresh-dough pizza, an American lamb sandwich or a meal-in-itself hot apple dumpling. Prices are very reasonable and the view from the porch is priceless—you'll be looking up at Seneca Rocks and the surrounding Alleghenies.

The store is open year-round from 7:00 a.m. to 8:30 p.m. weekdays and Saturday, 7:30 a.m. to 8:00 p.m. Sunday. The restaurant is also open seven days a week, from 11:00 a.m. to 9:00 p.m. Saturday and Sunday and 11:00 a.m. to 10:00 p.m. Monday through Friday. Call (304)567-2586 to reach the store; the restaurant's phone is (304)567-2555.

Directions: At the junction of Route 33 and Route 28/55, across from Seneca Rocks.

Smoke Hole Caverns

The "World's Longest Ribbon Stalactite," a huge limestone formation weighing 2½ tons and measuring 13 by 16 feet, thought to be between five and six million years old, is found at **Smoke Hole Caverns**. Kids will also love what is touted as the state's largest souvenir store. This complex of caverns, restaurant, store and lodgings on Route 28/55 is more commercialized then nearby Seneca Caverns. The walk through the caverns is somewhat easier, but usually more crowded.

A legend claims that the name "Smoke Hole" originated from the smoke venting from the cavern ceiling when Indians used the caves for curing meat during frigid weather. Civil War soldiers hid ammunition here, and moonshiners set up stills during Prohibition. The caves were opened to the public in 1942.

Guided tours lead through the Room of a Million Stalactites and turn around in the Queen's Room. You'll see a multi-tiered flowstone formation called the Alaskan Glacier—the backdrop for a colorful, man-made "northern light show"—as well as the Perfect Column, a formation with the graceful curves of sculptured drapery, and a room where the formations appear to defy gravity by growing sideways. Passageways are wet but well lighted. Wear comfortable shoes and bring a sweater, because the temperature will not deviate from 56 degrees Fahrenheit. Admission is $7.50 for adults, $5.00 for ages 5-12, and free for children under five. The caverns are open year-round. Hours are 9:00 a.m. to 7:00 p.m. Memorial

The world's longest ribbon stalactite, over five million years old, grows one cubic inch every 125 years in Smoke Hole Caverns.

Courtesy Smoke Hole Caverns

Day through Labor Day and 9:00 a.m. to 5:00 p.m. the rest of the year. For more information about the caverns or lodging, call (800)828-8478 or (304)257-4442 or write Smoke Hole Caverns, HC 59, Box 39, Seneca Rocks, WV 26884.

Directions: On Route 28/55 about 13 miles north of Seneca Rocks and eight miles south of Petersburg.

Slanesville

Ice Mountain Preserve

If you are an experienced hiker with a botanical bent, you will not want to miss **Ice Mountain Preserve**. The Nature Conservancy owns the 150-acre preserve on which a steep rock slope releases cold air all year long. As a result, several rare plants such as bristly rose and twinflower are found here and nowhere else in West Virginia. The preserve also has a high, rocky overlook, **Raven Rocks**, from which you can see much of western Hampshire County on a clear day. Guided hikes are free on the third Thursday and second Saturday of each month, but be advised that Ice Mountain is open by reservation only to groups of fewer than 15 people.

Directions: Slanesville is about 15 miles south and west of Paw Paw on Route 29. For specific meeting point and reservations, you must call at least two weeks in advance (304)345-4350 or write The Nature Conservancy of West Virginia, PO Box 3754, Charleston, WV 25337.

Tip: The trails are steep. Wear good hiking shoes and be prepared for climbing. You'll want to bring your own lunch and drinks and, if you own them, binoculars.

Slatyfork

Elk River Touring Center

In the past few years, West Virginia has come into its own as a mountain-biking destination. The **Elk River Touring Center**, established in 1982, was the first mountain biking center in the state and remains a standard-setter. It's also the home of the **West Virginia Fat Tire Festival** [see calendar of events], the premier bike festival in the region.

You can consult Elk River Touring Center for self-guided tours on the area's many trail systems, hire a guide for a tailor-made half-day or full-day trip or, best of all, get in on one of the center's guided trips or clinics. Some, like the singletrack weekend for families, are designed with kids in mind, with fairly level riding and plenty of free time for splashing in swimming holes and storytelling around the campfire. Others, like the Twin Peaks adventure, are seriously demanding treks full of tight, tricky, steep and twisted trails that will thwart all but the most accomplished bikers. The center offers equipment rentals, sales and full repair service.

Elk River Touring Center also offers cabins, bed-and-breakfast rooms and a good restaurant, open to anyone. For information or reservations, call (304)572-3771, visit their web site (www.ertc.com) or write Elk River Touring Center, HC 69, Box 7, Slatyfork, WV 26291.

Directions: On Route 219 in Slatyfork, 47 miles south of Elkins and 15 miles north of Marlinton.

Tip: Whether you're just off the trail or just driving through, the fresh rainbow trout at The Inn and Restaurant at Elk River is the best eating around.

Sharp's Country Store

Eleanor Roosevelt, several governors and thousands of others have walked the squeaky oak floors and peered into the antique wood and glass display cases at **Sharp's Country Store**. The large display windows no longer feature fashions of the day, as they did in the 1927; instead, you'll see tools and artifacts such as shoes from 1880, a 1930 foot measure and a collection of native American chestnuts from trees that were lost to disease in the 1920s.

Inside is much, much more—rows of dark shelves filled with everything from maple syrup to T-shirts, exhibits including a stuffed golden eagle shot in 1909, Indian weapons and Civil War relics, flea market treasures and fresh bait. Founder L.D. Sharp started his business in 1884 at the age of 12; the current owner, his granddaughter Linda, aims to preserve both the history and the homey ambience of this Slatyfork landmark. It remains a favorite gathering place for local old-timers as well as a welcoming haven for weary travelers. Stop by for gas, hand-dipped ice cream and stories. Hours are 6:30 a.m. to 8:00 p.m. Monday through Friday, 10:00 a.m. to 6:00 p.m. Saturday and 11:00 a.m. to 6:00 p.m. Sunday.

Directions: Located on Route 219, four miles south of Snowshoe Mountain Resort.

Snowshoe Mountain Resort

Not far from Slatyfork is the community of Snowshoe, which has grown up along with the resort of the same name. Twenty years ago, **Snowshoe** was known only as a ski resort. With 54 slopes and trails and 11 lifts at two large winter areas, the Snowshoe/Silver Creek complex remains one of the major winter destinations in the East. But nowadays, the spring thaw doesn't send people home—it brings them back again, for a smorgasbord of outdoor adventures in all seasons. From golf at the Hawthorne Valley course, rated by *Golf Magazine* as one of the "best new courses in the United States," to 150 miles of mountain biking trails that range from leisurely level rides to heart-thumping uphills and knuckle-whitening downhills, Snowshoe offers more than just skiing. Add tennis, horseback riding, hiking on 11,000 acres, and a busy calendar of special events like the **Snowshoe Symphony Festival** (with the West Virginia Symphony Orchestra under the baton of Maestro Thomas Conlin), **Appalachian Echoes** music/poetry celebration, a red-hot chili cook-off and the **Wild Hare Mountain Biking Festival**, and you begin to get the idea: once you get here, it's hard to leave.

The resort's four lodges, five restaurants and shops make Snowshoe a good home base for exploring many other places in Pocahontas County. For more information call (304)572-1000, visit their web site (www.snowshoemtn.com) or write Snowshoe Mountain Resort, PO Box 10, Snowshoe, WV 26209.

Directions: From Slatyfork, follow Route 219 north and east to Route 66. Turn right and follow Route 66 east to the turn-off for Snowshoe. From Cass, take Route 66 west.

Wardensville

Thistle Pass Traders

West Virginia's scenic highways and byways don't get any better than Route 55, which winds its way through much of the Potomac Highlands. Simply driving this road, exploring as you go, would make a good theme for an expedition in the Mountain State. If you do that, you'll discover a wonderful craft shop near the Virginia border in Wardensville.

Look for a log cabin nestled at the edge of a wooded area. Handmade by local laborers to the specifications of shop owners Margaret Janes and Linda Scott (who grew up in a log cabin herself), **Thistle Pass Traders** offers a fine collection of crafts, books and music by West Virginians. From handwoven baskets and candles to ghost stories and children's songs, the inventory represents the owners' continuing search for the highest quality in West Virginia-made wares.

Visitors are sometimes surprised by what they find. "Sometimes they come in with one idea and by the time they leave we certainly hope they have a better understanding of Appalachia—that it's more than just coal mines," says Scott. The shop is open all year, but hours change seasonally and weather is a "big factor." For more information call (304)897-6048 or write Thistle Pass, HC 67, Box 27AA, Mathias, WV 26812.

Directions: On Route 55, 5½ miles east of Wardensville.

BUCKHANNON
Little Hungary Farm Winery

BURNSVILLE
Bulltown Historic District and Burnsville Lake

FRENCH CREEK
WV State Wildlife Center

GLENVILLE
Cedar Creek State Park

JANE LEW
Masterpiece Crystal & The Glass Swan

RICHWOOD

SUMMERSVILLE
Carnifex Ferry Battlefield State Park
Summersville Dam and Lake

WESTON
Jackson's Mill Historic Area
Stonewall Jackson Lake State Park and Dam

Mountain Lakes

Sparkling, shining, still as glass or tumbling over falls and through rocky creekbeds, water is the main attraction of the Mountain Lakes. It brings boaters, anglers, water skiers, scuba divers and swimmers in warm weather—and in fall, when water from Summersville Lake is unleashed into the Gauley River, it sends whitewater rafters downriver on the ride of a lifetime. One of West Virginia's largest lakes, the new Stonewall Jackson Lake is chock-full of bass, crappie, bluegill, walleye and catfish—and the skies above entertain eagles, hawks and osprey. The muskie wait in winding Cedar Creek. On summer mornings at Burnsville Lake, fishermen intent on outwitting the wily bass rise early at the lake-side campground. And those who want to watch, not catch, the wildlife, love to see the otters frolic at the West Virginia State Wildlife Center in French Creek.

The water flows in a region rich with history, a great deal of it easily accessible to visitors. From the thunderous Civil War reenactments at Carnifex Ferry Battlefield State Park to the frontier and colonial living-history presentations at Bulltown Historic District to the working gristmill and museum at Jackson's Mill, the past is not exactly a thing of the past here.

Stroll through the Victorian architecture of Weston. Dig into delectable ramps, those savory wild leeks, in Richwood or Clay. Tap your feet to fiddle music at a bluegrass or old-time festival. Sip honey wine made from an Old World recipe in Buckhannon. Scout for antiques and crafts in small town shops. Relax with a cup of homegrown tea on an organic herb farm. Rediscover the pleasures of peace and quiet in West Virginia's Mountain Lakes.

For more information on visiting the Mountain Lakes contact:

Buckhannon/Upshur Chamber of Commerce, PO Box 442, Buckhannon, WV 26201. Call (304)472-1722.

Lewis County Convention and Visitors Bureau, PO Box 379, Weston, WV 26452. Call (304)269-7328.

Richwood Area Chamber of Commerce, PO Box 267, Richwood, WV 26261. Call (304)846-6790.

Summersville Convention & Visitors Bureau, PO Box 231, Summersville, WV 26651. Call (304)872-3722.

Buckhannon

Little Hungary Farm Winery

He treats his grapevines and his bees like beloved children—and both have rewarded Ferenc Androczi's tender care with Melomel, the signature wine from his **Little Hungary Farm Winery**. Speaking in a heavy Hungarian accent, the former library sciences professor eagerly shows off his product, a mixture of honey, grapes, apples and pears. The award-winning concoction is made according to the traditional recipe Androczi learned from his own father and grandfather, aged in oak barrels and served up to appreciative tasters. Each year's wine, he explains, is a bit different, for each year the grapes and honey are unique. Drink a cup of Melomel a day, according to Androczi, and you'll live to be 150; a spry octogenarian, Androczi is a good advertisement.

Free tours and tastings are available whenever Androczi is in. "I don't give tours after midnight," he jokes. If you visit, allow yourself time to enjoy the winemaker's stories as well as his mead-like beverage. To arrange a tour call (304)472-6634 or write Little Hungary Farm Winery, Route 6, Box 323, Buckhannon, WV 26201.

Directions: From I-79, take Exit 99 and follow Route 33 east to Buckhannon. Take the first Buckhannon exit, turn right at the light, and go just over a mile on South Kanawha Street (Route 20) to the winery. It is opposite the Kroger supermarket.

Tip: Buckhannon is the home of **West Virginia Wesleyan College**, and the tree-shaded campus in the middle of town is a pleasant place for a stroll. While you're there, check out the Sleeth Art Gallery in McCuskey Hall. Call (304)473-8432 for information about upcoming exhibitions.

Burnsville

Bulltown Historical Area and Burnsville Lake

When the U.S. Army Corps of Engineers dammed the Little Kanawha River to create **Burnsville Lake**, they carefully disassembled, moved and reconstructed the historic log structures that now form **Bulltown Historical Area**. The picturesque complex, located at the front gate of the **Bulltown Campground**, represents different kinds of dwellings and lifestyles in central West Virginia from 1815 to 1870. Living-history demonstrations reenact 19th-century daily occupations such as quilting, washing, apple-butter- and soap-making, gardening and weaving. Bulltown is also notable as the site of a 12-hour Civil War skirmish on October 13, 1863.

Begin your visit at the interpretive center and watch the six-minute slide show on Burnsville and its facilities. Here you'll also find historical exhibits and artifacts, including a huge salt box used for curing meat. Civil War and turn-of-the-century memorabilia are also included. At 2:00 p.m. each day, you can join a guided tour of the houses, church and battlefield; at other times, follow the one-mile interpretive trail on your own.

The **Cunningham Farmhouse** was built about 1815. You can see a bullet hole in one wall, made when the house was seized by Union forces during the war. The nearby granary is the oldest outbuilding on the farm. The Cunningham House is an example of a log home that was subsequently covered with boards and painted white.

Continuing your walk, you'll come to the **Johnson House**, with its cat-and-clay chimney (made of mud and boards instead of stone), built around 1883 by a freedman. The trail then takes you along the old **Weston and Gauley Bridge Turnpike**, used by both Union and Confederate forces to transport troops and supplies. Up on the hill, elegant in its austere simplicity, is **St. Michael's**, one of the earliest Catholic churches in the Mountain Lakes region, where men and women sat separately during Sunday services. At 11:00 a.m. each Sunday in season, a special tour focuses on the development of religion in Appalachia, with an explanation of bell tolling and the significance of the service (or sarvis) berry and tree. At the site of the Union fortifications, a reenactment of the Battle of Bulltown takes place bianually in October. Children who miss school during summer can try out an unusual "subscription school" program, offering a 19th-century Appalachian education with lessons, games and homework from authentic period textbooks. Most of the children who attend are from the adjacent Bulltown Campground on Burnsville Lake.

The 986-acre lake and surrounding area are popular for swimming, water skiing, fishing, boating and hiking. Anglers catch largemouth bass, walleye, crappie and catfish. The muskellunge fishing is reportedly as good as it gets in the state.

The interpretive center is open 10:00 a.m. to 6:00 p.m. May 1 to September 1. From September 1 to October 15, the hours are 10:00

a.m. to 4:00 p.m. The center is closed October 15 to May 1. Large groups should prearrange tours by calling (304)452-8170. The Bulltown Campground is operated by the U.S. Army Corps of Engineers, which maintains 270 campsites available from the first week of April to December 1. For reservations and information call (304)452-8006 or (304)853-2371 or -2398 (fishing), or write: Ryan Davis, Burnsville Lake, HC 10, Box 24, Burnsville, WV 26335.

Directions: Traveling from the north on I-79, take Route 19 south to the Bulltown entrance, about 15 miles south of Ireland. From the south, take the Flatwoods exit off I-79 and follow Route 19 north for approximately ten miles.

Tip: If you're in the mood for local theater or live music, you may find it on weekends at the **Landmark Studio for the Arts**. It's at 405 Main Street in nearby Sutton, a few miles south of the Flatwoods exit on I-79. The acoustically excellent performance space, a converted 1896 Victorian church in Sutton's Historic District, is home to the West Virginia Landmark Players and the Braxton County High School's Eagle Theatre. For more information call (304)765-3766 or write Olga Gioulis, 268 N. Hill Street, Sutton, WV 26601.

French Creek

West Virginia State Wildlife Center

As you stroll through the wooded, 1.25-mile trail through the new, state-of-the-art **West Virginia Wildlife Center**, you'll find no reason to pity the animals: instead of being cooped up in small cages, they have 300 acres of woods, open meadow and rocks in which to roam. The animals are so at home in their surroundings that it's easy for them—and visitors—to forget they are captives.

This modern zoological park actually has a long history. In the early part of the 20th century, uncontrolled exploitation of natural resources in West Virginia led to a sharp decline in the state's wildlife, and conservationists vigorously promoted game refuges as a means of protecting diminishing species. The French Creek Game Farm, opened in 1923, proved not to be a good way of restocking wildlife—pen-raised animals do not develop the skills to live in the wild—but it was enormously popular with the public. The new Wildlife Center, opened in 1986, is dedicated to presenting a realistic and factual understanding of West Virginia's wildlife by displaying the animals in their natural habitat.

During the season, you'll see elk and bison, a mountain lion, a timber wolf, a coyote, white-tailed deer, wild boar, black bear and many common and not-so-common small animals. A new exhibit allows visitors to watch playful river otters, one of the species nearly driven to extinction in the early 1900s, from above and below water level, revealing the full power and grace of these aquatic mammals. Owls, eagles, waterfowl and other birds are also displayed in natural settings.

Interpretive signs along the paved trail help visitors learn about each animal's history, biology and relationship with humans. Guided tours for groups are also available. The small entrance fee is a bargain—and you'll have the satisfaction of knowing you are helping to finance planned expansions, including a nocturnal animal exhibit, reptile display, aquarium and auditorium.

Admission to the Wildlife Center is $2.00 for adults and $1.00 for children aged 3-15. Groups of 12 or more get a real deal: $1.00 for each adult and ten cents per child. These prices are in effect from April 1 to October 31. From November 1 to March 31, you are welcome to walk the trail at no charge—many people come here regularly for exercise—but in cold weather the animals make up their own minds about if and when to emerge from their warm den areas.

Directions: The center is located 12 miles south of Buckhannon on Route 20. If you are driving south on I-79, take Exit 99 and follow Route 33 east to Route 20. If you are driving north on I-79, take Exit 67 and follow Routes 19 and 4 about 33 miles to Rock Cave and Route 20. For more information call (304)924-6211 or write West Virginia Wildlife Center, Box 38, French Creek, WV 26218.

Tip: Not far from the Wildlife Center is 8,292-acre **Holly River State Park**, a fine place for a picnic, hike or overnight stay. The park's features include nine standard cabins, 88 campsites, a restaurant, playground, game courts, swimming pool, one-room schoolhouse museum and seasonal recreation and nature programs. Call (304)493-6353 or (800)CALL-WVA or write Holly River State Park, PO Box 70, Hacker Valley, WV 26222. The park is located 32 miles south of Buckhannon on Route 20. From the Wildlife Center, continue south on Route 20.

Glenville

Cedar Creek State Park

The verdant, rolling hills and wide valleys of Gilmer County make a perfect setting for a park, and **Cedar Creek State Park** is a gem of a recreation area, especially for those who crave serenity, pastoral scenery and good fishing.

Two historic structures distinguish this park. One is the campground check-in station, a restored log cabin that served first as a home and, from 1928 to 1982, the last log gas station in West Virginia. The other is a reconstructed one-room schoolhouse complete with old desks, inkwells and a potbellied stove. Guided tours are offered on Saturdays in summer.

Cedar Creek itself is a meandering brook that offers good muskie fishing in the summer, but the park also has a series of popular, seasonally stocked fishing ponds with trout, bass and catfish. For a leisurely ride around the largest pond, you can rent a paddleboat. If you like hiking, you'll find 14 miles miles of trails lacing the oak and poplar forests of this 2,483-acre park, though you'll have to share them with abundant wildlife—deer, turkey, geese, squirrel, rabbit and groundhog.

For a nominal fee, the park offers miniature golf, tennis, basketball, volleyball, croquet, softball and swimming. (The pool is open 11:00 a.m. to 6:45 p.m. daily from Memorial Day weekend through Labor Day.) Look for a weekly schedule of nature and recreation programs at the campground check-in station.

There are 45 generously spaced campsites (35 with electric hookups and parking pads), each with its own grill and picnic table. Hot showers and laundry facilities include one handicapped-accessible facility. A 10-site group camp is also available by reservation, and the park store offers grocery items, souvenirs and supplies.

Park hours for day visitors are 6:00 a.m. to 10:00 p.m. For more information or to reserve campsites call (304)462-7158 or (800)CALL-WVA or write Cedar Creek State Park, Rt. 1, Box 9, Glenville, WV 26351.

Directions: From I-79, take the Burnsville/Glenville exit and follow Route 5 west to Glenville. The park is located south of Glenville and four miles east of U.S. routes 33/119.

Tip: Each June, tiny Glenville rings with mountain music during the **West Virginia State Folk Festival** [see calendar of events]. So if you plan to stay at Cedar Creek State Park in mid-June, be sure to make reservations well in advance.

Jane Lew

Masterpiece Crystal and The Glass Swan

At one time almost a hundred glass factories operated in West Virginia. Although most of them no longer exist, there are still many opportunities to watch and learn about glassmaking in the Mountain State. One is **Masterpiece Crystal** in Jane Lew. The factory's specialties include handblown items with delectable names: Apples, Strawberries, Crystal Kisses, Ice Cubes, Rain Drops and Bluebirds, among others. The outlet store also features handmade stemware, barware, decanters, bells, candle holders, votives and decorative marbles. You'll also find some West Virginia-made crafts in the shop, including handcrafted candles to go with your new crystal candle holders.

Tours are conducted from 9:00 a.m. to 3:00 p.m. Monday through Friday. The outlet is open 9:00 a.m. to 5:00 p.m. seven days a week. Call (304)884-7841 or (800)624-3114 or write Masterpiece Crystal, PO Box 848, Jane Lew, WV 26378.

Directions: From I-79, take Exit 105. Go west on Route 7 for three-fourths mile, then north on Route 19 for one-fourth mile. Turn left on Trolley Street and go 75 yards to the outlet.

Although tours are not offered at **The Glass Swan**, the owners of this outlet, George and Carol Williams, are a talented couple known for their handmade marbles, paperweights and cobalt blue dinnerware, all available at the store. An extra bonus: Carol is an expert hand-cutter who can personalize your crystal selections with flowing designs or monograms. Small jobs may be completed while you wait—or you can choose to have The Glass Swan carefully pack and ship your hand-decorated treasures. Outlet hours are Monday through Saturday 9:00 a.m. to 5:00 p.m. Call (304)884-8014 or write The Glass Swan, Box 736, Weston, WV 26452.

Directions: From I-79, take Exit 105 to Route 19. At the intersection, go left directly into parking lot.

Richwood

Nestled on the banks of the Cherry River, **Richwood** is a good place to stock up on supplies for outdoor activities, being the southern gateway to the Monongahela National Forest and the Cranberry Wilderness Area [see entry] and the southwestern terminus for the **Highland Scenic Highway**, which winds through the national forest past the Cranberry Mountain Nature Center, Cranberry Glades and the Falls of Hills Creek [see entries], as well as campgrounds, hiking trails and scenic overlooks.

In 1901, the town was established as a mill site for the Cherry River Boom and Lumber Company. It has also been home to many other industries, most of them dependent on wood: a clothes pin factory, a paper mill, a tannery, and wagon-hub and shovel-handle factories. These days, small and friendly Richwood is the beginning (or the end, depending upon which way you walk it) of the brand-new **Cranberry Tri-River Rail Trail**, a 14½-mile trail that includes a depot, a trestle and a haunted tunnel. From Richwood, the trail makes its way north and west—down the Cherry River, up the Gauley and across the Cranberry, ending just beyond Sarah's Tunnel. Legend has it that the tunnel's ghost haunts the scene of an unsolved, long-ago homicide.

The trail passes through the towns of Fenwick, Holcomb, Curtin and Woodbine, all historic lumber towns. A cooperative project of trail clubs, Scouts, local governments and the Georgia Pacific Corporation, the new rail trail was officially dedicated in the spring of 1997. It's a bit bumpy in places, but it goes through some beautiful country. For more information write the West Virginia Rails-to-Trails Council, PO Box 8889, South Charleston, WV 25303.

Come spring, the traffic on trails and roads is likely to be heading *toward* Richwood for one of the state's oldest and biggest ramp feeds. Home of the National Ramp Association and self-described as the Ramp Capital of the World, Richwood has hosted the **Feast of the Ramson** [see calendar of events] since 1937. The ritual springtime meal celebrates an aromatic wild leek, *Allium tricoccum*. Its broad leaves are among the first greens of the season—but it's the bulbous root ramp lovers hunt, scrambling up mountainsides and digging in shady hollows. For the Richwood festival, townspeople gather and clean thousands of pounds of the savory plant.

Ramps taste rather like green onions—but not quite. Truth to tell, they *taste* delicious. Most folks like ramps fried up with potatoes or eggs or ham. Adventurous and whimsical cooks have also prepared them pickled, boiled, stuffed and stewed—in soups, souffles, salads, omelets and and hors d'oeuvres. Some connoisseurs eat them raw. If you eat them, however, be forewarned: cooked or raw, ramps leave a lingering odor. You can expect to have "ramp breath," and your traveling companions (unless they, too, have partaken) will be able to detect a distinctive, ramp-like odor about you for up to three days. For real ramp fans, the stinky aftereffect is part of the fun. (The late Jim Comstock, a Richwood native and admitted prankster, once mixed ramp juice with the printing ink for his newspaper, the *West Virginia Hillbilly,* and suffered the consequences: a reprimand from the Postmaster General and a stern warning to cease and desist.)

If ramps are, as some say, a healthful spring tonic, perhaps that's why Richwood is also the site for the **Past 80 Party** each June, free for anyone old enough to attend.

For more information about the trail, the scenic highway or Richwood events, call (304)846-6790 or write the Richwood Area Chamber of Commerce, PO Box 267, Richwood, WV 26261.

Directions: Richwood is between Summersville and Marlinton on Routes 39 and 55.

Summersville

Carnifex Ferry Battlefield State Park

This 156-acre state park commemorates a Civil War battle that had a great impact on West Virginia history. Beginning on September 10, 1861, General William S. Rosecrans led an attack that forced Confederate General John B. Floyd to abandon his position and retreat, under cover of nightfall, into the Gauley River gorge and across the river. The removal of the Confederate presence from the northwestern counties of then-Virginia cleared the way for the political process that eventually resulted in the creation of West Virginia.

Each year in September, a reenactment with about 300 participants revives the smoke and thunder of the Battle of Carnifex Ferry. The reenactors' clothing, weapons and campsite are authentic reproductions, except that they use no real bullets or bayonets. But you can learn how muskets are loaded—a complicated, awkward process of biting off the end of a paper cartridge, pouring gunpowder down the barrel, setting the bullet on the top of the powder with a ramrod and priming the piece with a cap before firing. An experienced soldier could perform this ritual and fire his weapon three times a minute.

If you miss the reenactment, there is plenty of other action at **Carnifex Ferry Battlefield State Park** in autumn, when whitewater rafting on the Gauley River is at its exciting best. The park overlooks provide a first-rate place from which to watch furiously paddling rafters guide their boats down the river.

A small museum, **Patterson House**, displays battle artifacts during the summer. Museum hours are 10:00 a.m. to 5:00 p.m. on

Hundreds of participants take part in the annual reenactment at Carnifex Ferry Battlefield State Park. Claude Levet

weekends and holidays, Memorial Day to Labor Day. The park also offers picnic facilities, hiking trails, game areas and playground equipment. Some facilities are operated on a seasonal basis. For more information call (304)872-0825 or (800)CALL-WVA or write Carnifex Ferry Battlefield State Park, Route 2, Box 435, Summersville, WV 26651.

Directions: Located on the Gauley River via Route 129. From Route 19 south of Summersville take Route 129 west to Carnifex Ferry Road.

Summersville Dam and Lake

The U.S. Army Corps of Engineers built the **Summersville Dam** to control flooding on the Kanawha and Gauley Rivers. The project's byproduct is an aquatic playground for fishermen, scuba divers, water skiers, boaters, rafters and kayakers. The 2,790-acre lake works its fingers into 60 miles of shoreline in the hills. Much of this shoreline contains sandstone cliffs, making it a favorite rock-climbing destination.

In summer, the huge dam—one of the largest earth-filled dams east of the Mississippi—keeps **Summersville Lake** 1,652 feet above sea level. Stocked with trout, bass, walleye, bluegill and catfish, it's a popular fishing lake. Between Labor Day and Columbus Day, however, controlled releases send the water downriver at the rate of 2,600 cubic feet per second, creating some of the most thrilling whitewater conditions in the world.

Picnic, boat launch, camping facilities and a wildlife management area with nature trails accommodate both day trippers and overnighters. Stop at the visitors center, open 7:15 a.m. to 4:00 p.m. Monday through Friday, to get maps and brochures and to see a water safety video. Group tours are available, too. Call (304)872-3412 or write Resource Manager, Summersville Lake, U.S. Army Corps of Engineers, RR #2, Box 470, Summersville, WV 26651.

Tip: Good food and wine are both to be found in Summersville! If your idea of a day trip includes a relaxing, delicious meal at the end, make a reservation at the **Country Road Inn** just outside of Summersville. Hailed by *Southern Living,* the *Mobil Travel Guide* and many others, the farmhouse restaurant features a sumptuous Italian banquet cooked by the Jarroll family under the watchful eye of matriarch Mama Jarroll. Prices range from $14.95 to $23.95 and include everything from hors d'oeuvres to Mama's Chocolate Tortoni. Reservations are requested. Call (304)872-1620 or (888)439-8852. You'll find the restaurant eight miles west of Summersville on Route 39.

You may also wish to tour **Kirkwood Winery**, home of the September **Grape Stomping Festival** [see calendar of events] and the **Cork Poppin' Chili Fest**, held Memorial Day weekend. Offering year-round tours and tastings of over three dozen French hybrids, American varietals and other fruit wines, Kirkwood is located three miles north of Summersville. To get there from Summersville, drive three miles north on Route 19 and turn right on Phillips Run Road. Go 1.3 miles to the winery. Call (304)872-7332.

Weston

A small town with attractions to suit many and varied interests, **Weston** is also the county seat of Lewis County. On your way into town on Route 33/119, look for the Farmer's Market on the right, where a good selection of local produce is available in season.

Begin your visit by picking up maps and brochures at the **Lewis County Convention and Visitors Bureau** at 345 Center Avenue. It is located in an old red brick, one-room schoolhouse, just 24 feet wide and 40 feet long, known until the early 1950s as the Weston Colored School. The Convention and Visitors Bureau carries on the tradition of education by featuring changing historical exhibits about the county. The hours are 10:00 a.m. to 4:30 p.m. Monday through Friday. Call (304)269-7328 or write Lewis County Convention and Visitors Bureau, P.O. Box 379, Weston, WV 26452.

If you like turn-of-the-century architecture, you'll enjoy walking in Weston's neighborhoods of gingerbread-trimmed houses and Victorian mansions. Be sure to notice the **Jonathan-Louis Bennett House** at 148 Court Avenue, now serving as Lewis County's public library. Built in 1875 in the High Victorian Italianate style, it was deeded to the town on the condition that its exterior never be changed. The original bracketed cornices, latticework and roof tower make it an eye-catching sight. Inside, most rooms are closed to the public, but you can still look at a few of the original furnishings, including a rolltop desk and an impressive chandelier. The library is open 10:00 a.m. to 6:00 p.m. Monday through Friday and 10:00 a.m. to 2:00 p.m. Saturday. Due to limited staff, tours are self-guided. For more information, write Louis Bennett Library, Box 740, Weston, WV 26452.

Also worth seeing, and just a few blocks from the library, is the **Citizen Bank** at 201 Main Street. The bank, considered by some to be the finest example of Art Deco architecture in the state, is noteworthy not only for the ornamental detail in the original structure, but also for the ingenious blending of the old building with a 1980 addition. Inside, the 45-foot-high ceiling bears the state seal in 24-karat gold leaf. Also note the carving around the lobby entrance door and the American walnut paneling. On the upper level, directors meet around a conference table of walnut, tiger wood and bird's-eye maple. Bank personnel are justifiably proud of the building and welcome visitors. Open 8:30 a.m. to 3:00 p.m. Monday through Thursday and until 5:30 p.m. on Fridays.

Look across the West Fork River from Weston to see an enormous hand-cut stone edifice, formerly **Weston State Hospital**, the state's oldest institution (1864).

Of special interest to genealogy students, the **West Virginia Genealogical and Historical Library and Museum**, dedicated to the study of genealogical history in the central West Virginia area, is located in the historic **Horner School** on Route 33 east of Weston. Hours are 10:00 a.m. to 8:00 p.m. Monday and Thursday; 10:00 a.m. to 3:00 p.m. Tuesday, Wednesday and Friday; and 10:00 a.m. to 2:00 p.m. Saturday. Call (304)269-7091. To get there from I-79, take Exit 99 and go 2 1/2 miles east on Route 33 to the Horner/Georgetown

Road. Turn left. The school is at the intersection.

Lovers of natural foods and herbs will find at least two sources of organically grown herbs near Weston. **La Paix Farm**, a small organic herb and produce farm near Weston, offers tours, workshops and a retail shop. The farm's original house was a log cabin reputedly used as a safe house by the Underground Railroad. Owner Myra Bonhage-Hale asks visitors to make a $5.00 purchase in return for tours of nine display gardens, well-marked woodland walks and a relaxing cup of herbal tea. In addition to dried herbs and books, fresh herbs and plants are available in season. Tours are by appointment only. To schedule a tour, get directions or find out about workshops in growing and harvesting herbs, mushrooms and greens, call (304)269-7681 or write La Paix Farm, HC 64, Box 17, Alum Bridge, WV 26321.

Another farm offering a wide variety of medicinal and culinary herbs, **Smoke Camp Crafts** also features 50 varieties of old-fashioned jams and jellies made with wild and organically cultivated fruits, not to mention a delightful variety of soothing, homegrown herb teas. "If we are home, we are open," say owners Dot and Bob Montgillion, but you must call to arrange tours and nature walks. You can also request a mail-order list. Call (304)269-6416 or write Smoke Camp Crafts, Route 1, Box 263-SS, Weston, WV 26452.

Directions: Weston is just off I-79 at Exit 96.

Jackson's Mill Historic Area

Thomas J. "Stonewall" Jackson, considered by many to be the greatest commander of the Civil War, spent much of his childhood on his grandparents' farm after being orphaned at a young age. The sawmill where Jackson worked (until he left for West Point at 18) produced the milled timber for a large gristmill built in 1841, which still stands on the banks of the West Fork River. Now on the National Register of Historic Places after years of careful restoration, it is the only remaining structure of the original Jackson family homestead and the keystone of the growing **Jackson's Mill Historic Area**. With a fresh coat of white paint, the 40-foot-square building is now a museum with 2½ stories of antique tools and artifacts, including a huge storage bin hand-hewn from the trunk of a gum tree in 1895, a 75-gallon apple-butter kettle, a straw flattener (for making straw hats), a Sabo varmint trap, a cheese press and a selection of old wooden washing machines.

Also part of the complex is the working **Blaker Mill**, originally built in 1794. Disassembled stone by stone, the mill was moved from its original location in the southern part of the state and and rebuilt here by dedicated volunteers. Even when it's not operating, it will amaze you to take a look at the huge gears that move the mill; at 11:00 a.m. and 2:00 p.m. on most Saturdays, the wheels actually turn. You can buy a bag of freshly ground flour at the nearby gift shop.

The McWhorter Cabin, built over 200 years ago, has served as a post office, church and meeting house as well as home to the Henry McWhorter family, who lived for 37 years in this cabin that measures 18 feet by 24 feet. It has been part of the Jackson's Mill Historic Area since 1927. Another log structure, **Mary Conrad's Cabin**, was originally located in Roanoke, West Virginia and now serves as a visitors center and gift shop for the historic complex. The newest addition to the complex is a modern log building with a deck from which you are invited to feed the ducks and fish in the placid mill pond.

The historic complex is part of the 500-acre **Jackson's Mill State 4-H Conference Center**. Its gracious lodge, cabins and dining hall create a favorite place for gatherings and festivals, including the **Stonewall Jackson Heritage Arts and Crafts Jubilee** [see calendar of events], which draws approximately 60,000 people each Labor Day weekend for mountain music, food, crafts and reenactments. Other festivals and events are ongoing.

There is a modest admission fee for the Historic Area. Hours are 10:00 a.m. to 5:00 p.m. every day except Monday from Memorial Day to Labor Day. Open weekends only in early May and early October. For more information call (304)269-5100 or write Jackson's Mill Historic Area, Route 1, Box 210-WVU, Weston, WV 26452.

Directions: If you are traveling from the north, take Exit 105 from I-79. Follow Route 19 south approximately seven miles to Jackson's Mill Road. From the south, take Exit 99 and follow Route 33/119 approximately two miles to Jackson's Mill Road. Follow Jackson's Mill road for 2½ miles and enter through the second gate after the one-lane bridge.

Stonewall Jackson Lake State Park and Dam

A few miles south of Weston is one of the newest parks in the state system. The 1,833-acre **Stonewall Jackson Lake State Park** is very popular for boating and fishing, especially for bass, crappie, bluegill, walleye and catfish. The damming of the West Fork River resulted in one of West Virginia's largest lakes, with 2,650 surface acres of water and over 82 miles of shoreline. Unlike some dammed lakes, **Stonewall Jackson Lake** is accessible for boating year-round. A modern marina provides docking for boaters and slips for 374 boats. Also docked here is a sternwheeler that takes visitors out for excursions and dinner cruises. Plans are underway for the park to become one the state's resort parks, with a 150-room lodge, golf course, pool and spa. Currently there are 34 camping sites near the lake.

Begin your visit at the **U.S. Army Corps of Engineers Visitors Center** in the administration building near the dam, where you can pick up a map of the lake and safety information. In season, tours of the dam are conducted. There is a state park visitors center as well, near the marina, where the ranger will give you information on fishing, hunting and wildlife. On the nature trails and on the water, birders are likely to see songbirds of various kinds as well as hawks, eagles and osprey attracted by the lake's abundant supply of fish.

Admission to the park is $1.00 per vehicle, April 1 to mid-September. The Corps visitors center is open year-round, every day, from 8:00 a.m. to 4:00 p.m. Tours are given Sunday from 1:00 to 4:00 p.m., Memorial Day to Labor Day, and group tours are available on request or by appointment. Call (304)269-4588. The state park visitors center is open year-round, 8:00 a.m. to 4:30 p.m. Monday through Friday. Park hours are 6:00 a.m. to 10:00 p.m. For more information, call (304)269-0523 or (800)CALL-WVA or write Stonewall Jackson Lake State Park, Route 1, Box 0, Roanoke, WV 26423.

Directions: From I-79 take Exit 91 (Roanoke) and follow Route 19 south for 3½ miles to the park entrance. For dam site, take Exit 96, turn left and go one-half mile to visitors center.

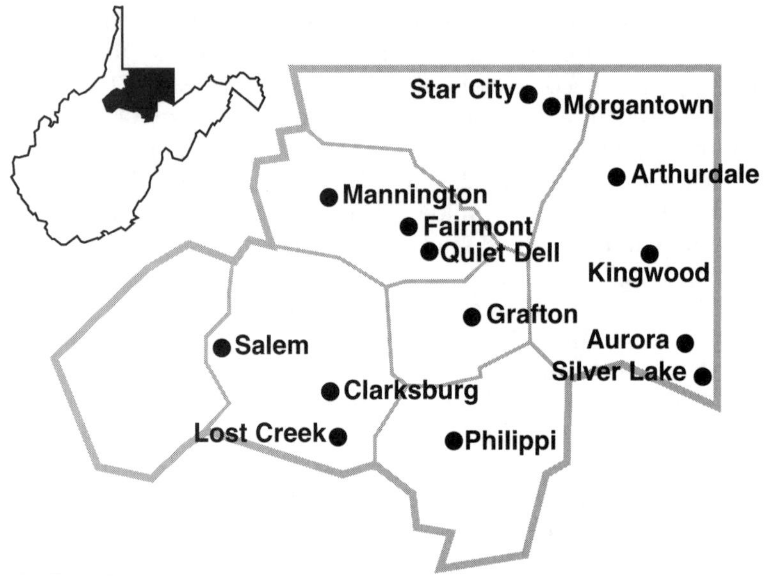

ARTHURDALE

AURORA
- Cathedral State Park

CLARKSBURG

FAIRMONT
- High Gate
- Marion Cty. Historical Soc. Museum
- Pricketts Fort State Park
- Valley Falls State Park

GRAFTON
- International Mother's Day Shrine
- Tygart Lake State Park and Dam

KINGWOOD
- West Virginia Northern Railroad

LOST CREEK
- Watters Smith Memorial State Park

MANNINGTON
- Mannington Round Barn and West Augusta Historical Society Museum

MORGANTOWN
- West Virginia University
  - University Tour
  - Core Arboretum
  - Personal Rapid Transit (PRT)
- Chestnut Ridge Park
- Coopers Rock State Forest
- Easton Roller Mill
- Forks of Cheat Winery
- The Old Stone House

PHILIPPI
- Barbour County Historical Museum
- Philippi Covered Bridge

QUIET DELL
- West Virginia Mountain Products Co-op

SALEM
- Fort New Salem

SILVER LAKE
- Our Lady of the Pines

STAR CITY
- Gentile Glass Company

Mountaineer Country

Mountaineer Country is a study in contrasts: a vibrant blend of exciting history and breathtaking natural beauty, and a pleasing mix of urban amenities and down-home comforts.

The region borrows its name from West Virginia University's beloved football team—the cheers of loyal fans literally ring off the hillsides on fall Saturdays—and their home of Morgantown offers visitors a colorful variety of entertainments: theater, music, dining, shopping, a beautiful walk among wildflowers or a smooth ride on a space-age transit system. Nearby is a spectacular overlook at Coopers Rock State Park.

The region is rich in gorgeous waterways. Both the Cheat and Tygart rivers offer all manner of aquatic recreation, from whitewater rafting and canoeing in some sections to large dammed lakes where fishing, swimming, boating and water skiing are the preferred activities.

Two reconstructed forts bring pioneer times into the present with living-history programs, and museums and historical sites throughout the region commemorate famous and not-so-famous West Virginians—from the founder of Mother's Day in Grafton to two anonymous mummies in Philippi.

Spend a spiritual hour among the virgin hemlocks at Cathedral State Park. Drive across a covered bridge built a decade before the Civil War. Sink your teeth into a plate of incomparable pasta in Clarksburg, a town that celebrates its Italian heritage. Tour a Tudor mansion in Fairmont. Ride the rails in Kingwood. Whatever you choose, you'll probably choose to come again.

For more information on visiting Mountaineer Country contact:

Belington Convention and Visitors Bureau, Crim Avenue, Belington, WV 26250. Call (304)457-1225.

Bridgeport-Clarksburg Convention and Visitors Bureau, 109 Platinum Drive, Suite B, Eastpointe, Bridgeport, WV 26330. Call (800)368-4324 or (304)842-7272 or visit their web site (www.bridgeport-clarksburg.com).

Grafton-Taylor Convention and Visitors Bureau, 214 West Main Street, Room 207, Grafton, WV 26354. Call (304)265-3938.

Greater Morgantown Convention and Visitors Bureau, 709 Beechurst Avenue, Morgantown, WV 26505. Call (800)458-7373 or (304)292-5081 or visit their web site (www.MGTN.com).

Marion County Convention and Visitors Bureau, 110 Adams Street, Fairmont, WV 26554. Call (800)834-7365 or (304)368-1123, or visit their web site (www.westvirginia.com/marion).

Philippi Convention and Visitors Bureau, 124 N. Main Street, Philippi, WV 26416. Call (304)457-1225.

Preston County Convention and Visitors Bureau, PO Box 860, Arthurdale, WV 26520. Call (800)571-0912 or (304)864-4601.

Arthurdale

In August 1933, a tall woman stepped out of a car to visit the homes of destitute, unemployed mining families in Scotts Run, West Virginia. Her heartfelt response to their plight was to initiate one of the most ambitious and far-reaching social experiments ever attempted by the United States government.

The woman was Eleanor Roosevelt, and the dream she made happen was called **Arthurdale**—the first of some 100 homestead resettlement communities throughout the country. With the unemployed miners providing labor, 165 homesteads were erected on the site of a large farm. Each had a house, a cellar, a small barn and two to five acres of land. Community property included a community building, forge, store, barber shop, weaving room, furniture display room, administration building, crafts rooms, a filling station, school buildings, factories, an inn, a health center and a gristmill.

Like most resettlement communities, Arthurdale lost its federal funding in the 1940s, and some critics said the New Deal experiment had been a failure. Arthurdale residents—and there are still some original homesteaders here, along with all 165 original homes—disagree with that assessment. Stop at the visitors center in the Administration Building and pick up a self-guided driving tour of the town, all of which is on the National Register of Historic Places. Take time to visit the restored forge, too. You'll learn a great deal about the Depression era, and you will meet some people who have kept Eleanor's dream alive in their hearts as well as their homes.

The visitors center is open noon to 5:00 p.m. Saturdays and 2:00 to 5:00 p.m. Sundays during summer. Tours are available by appointment year-round. For more information, call (304)864-3959 or write Arthurdale Heritage, Inc., PO Box 850, Arthurdale, WV 26520.

Directions: Arthurdale is on Route 92, about 16 miles southeast of Morgantown. From Morgantown, take Route 7 to Route 92, then Route 92 south to Arthurdale. The Administration Building will be on your right.

Aurora

Cathedral State Park

The light filtering through lacy patterns of hemlock needles recalls stained-glass windows. At your feet, ferns and mossy fallen trees tell of an endless cycle of death and rebirth. This 133-acre park is a small, fragile gem. It is appropriately named, for you cannot stand underneath the massive hemlocks here without feeling the kind of reverent awe a great cathedral inspires. And the sense of awe is inevitably mixed with sorrow: **Cathedral State Park** protects the last remnant of mixed virgin timber in West Virginia, the only suggestion of what this land must have looked like before Europeans set foot here.

The woods include yellow birch, red oak, black cherry, maple, chestnut, beech and other hardwoods. But the most commanding presences here are hemlocks, many of which are centuries old. One, the **Centennial**, is considered the largest hemlock east of the Mississippi, with a circumference of 21 feet, a height of 121 feet, and a spread of 68 feet. Some experts believe this tree is over 500 years old.

Even though you will always be within earshot of traffic on Route 50, this is a lovely, reflective atmosphere for a gentle, leisurely walk. Seven miles of trails wind through the park, crossing small brooks and streams. The massive trees lead your eye upward. Wildflowers, mosses, ferns and fungi soften the way underfoot, but the canopy above is so dense that there is not much understory vegetation. The small forest is home to many birds.

During the years when the rest of the state was logged, these woods were saved because they were on private property, the centerpiece of the Brookside Inn and Resort. Later, the property was sold to the state under the condition that it "never be touched with axe or saw." In 1966 the park entered the National Registry for Natural History Landmarks as an "area that possesses exceptional value in illustrating the natural history of the United States."

You'll find trail maps in the parking area. The park hours are 6:00 a.m. to 10:00 p.m. every day of the year. Absolutely no camping, hunting or fishing is allowed. Restrooms are closed from the first frost until April 1. The resident caretaker gives a tour every Wednesday at 1:00 p.m. Memorial Day to Labor Day. To arrange special tours at other times, call (304)735-3771 or write Caretaker, Cathedral State Park, Route 1, Box 370, Aurora, WV 26705.

Directions: From Grafton take Route 50 east about 25 miles to Aurora. The park is about a mile east of Aurora, within a few miles of the Maryland state line.

Tip: Summertime is beautiful, but there is nothing quite like Cathedral State Park in the hush of snow.

Clarksburg

Clarksburg was the birthplace of Thomas J. "Stonewall" Jackson in 1824. A deeply religious man whose personal life was marked by continuing loss and tragedy, he was a brilliant military strategist. Jackson earned his nickname when he led a brigade at the first battle of Bull Run, and General Barnard Elliott Bee proclaimed, "See, there stands Jackson like a stone wall." When he was wounded and lost his left arm at Chancellorsville, Robert E. Lee lamented, "He has lost his left arm, but I have lost my right arm." Jackson died from his wounds on May 10, 1863. Look for a statue of the great leader in front of the Harrison County Courthouse at West Main and Third streets in downtown Clarksburg.

Another statue on the courthouse square, by West Virginia sculptor Bill Hopen, honors the area's immigrants. During the late 1800s and early 1900s, coal mining brought a booming economy—and a huge influx of immigrants, especially from Ireland, Greece and Italy—to the Clarksburg/Bridgeport area. Among them were the skilled stonemasons who gave this city its variety of architecture. A walk through the Clarksburg Downtown Historic District is a visual feast for anyone who loves Late Victorian architecture. Stand on almost any downtown corner, with Italianate and Renaissance-style buildings surrounding you, and it's not hard to imagine the bustle of the "Boom Years" of coal mining. Especially worthy of mention are the **Waldo Hotel**, at the corner of 4th and West Pike streets, a seven-story Moorish design dating from 1904, and the old **Clarksburg Municipal Building** at 227 West Pike Street, circa 1888, with its multi-gabled roof and stone parapets.

One of the loveliest and most significant structures in Clarksburg, however, predates the building boom of the late 1800s. **The Waldomore**, a graceful Greek Revival mansion next-door to the Public Library on Pike Street, was built in 1839 by Waldo Potter Goff. It was the birthplace of Nathan Goff, a federal judge and U.S. Senator, and is now on the National Register of Historic Places. Used as the community library from 1931 to 1974, the Waldomore currently houses the West Virginia History and Genealogical Collection, the Guy W. Tetrick collection of family histories and other historical and genealogical material. The great hall downstairs is used for community functions and houses a grand piano that is occasionally rolled down the street for performances at the **Robinson Grand Theater**. Hours are 9:00 a.m. to noon and 1:00 to 5:00 p.m. on Monday, Tuesday, Wednesday and Friday. Thursday hours are 9:00 a.m. to noon, 1:00 to 4:00 p.m. and 5:00 to 8:00 p.m., and Saturday hours are 9:00 a.m. to noon. Call the Public Library at (304)624-6512 for more information, or write the Harrison County Genealogical Society, PO Box 387, Clarksburg, WV 26302.

Walk down Main Street between Monticello Avenue and Goff Plaza to see some of the town's most beautiful older homes. One of them, a lovingly restored Victorian "painted lady" at 151 Main Street, is also a delightfully comfortable bed-and-breakfast inn. Call the **Main Street B&B** at (304)623-1440.

Once a year, Clarksburg's Italian heritage takes over the town. Rated as one of the top 100 ethnic events in North America, the **West Virginia Italian Heritage Festival** is truly an outpouring of Italian love, pride, music, dance and wonderful food for all to enjoy. The festival takes place every year over Labor Day Weekend, but you don't have to wait for a festival to find good Italian food in the Clarksburg/Bridgeport area—excellent pasta meals are almost as common as Italianate architecture!

Stop by the **Bridgeport-Clarksburg Convention and Visitors Bureau** to pick up maps, brochures and dining recommendations, or call (800)368-4324 or (304)842-7272. You can also visit their web site (www.bridgeport-clarksburg.com) or write 109 Platinum Drive, Suite B, Bridgeport, WV 26330.

Directions: The Convention and Visitors Bureau is just off I-79. Take Exit 119 (Route 50), and go east towards Bridgeport. Follow the signs to Eastpointe shopping center at Emily Drive. Turn right into the shopping center at Emily Drive, then immediately left. Go to the end of the street, 109 Platinum Drive. To reach Clarksburg from I-79, go west on Route 50 and take one of several Clarksburg exits.

Fairmont

High Gate

Fairmont visitors driving or walking on Fairmont Avenue between 8th and 9th streets cannot help but notice **High Gate**, a magnificent Tudor Revival mansion that occupies the entire block. Named for the tall iron gates and fence surrounding the mansion and carriage house, High Gate was built in 1910 by coal magnate James Edwin Watson. It has been designated a National Historic Landmark.

Watson's choice of architect Horace Trumbauer—a famed "rich man's architect" who designed for clients such as George Jay Gould and Cornelius Vanderbilt III—was a good one. The immense, multi-gabled, half-timbered structure exemplifies Edwardian opulence. Seven huge, almost sculptural chimneys rise from the red roof.

The main house at High Gate is privately owned and occupied, but the High Gate Carriage House and Gardens are now owned by the Friends of High Gate, a non-profit preservation group, and are available for tours and rentals. High Gate is a popular place for readings, lectures and receptions. If you tour, take time to look at the old photographs. To make advance arrangements for a tour, call (304)366-5779. For rental information call (304)367-9494 or write Friends of High Gate, PO Box 957, Fairmont, WV 26555-0957.

Directions: From I-79, take Exit 137 (Downtown). Follow Route 310 north to Route 250, and go south on Route 250 (Fairmont Avenue) for four blocks. High Gate is on the right.

Marion County Historical Society Museum

This 1911 sandstone house, which is on the National Register of Historic Places, was originally built as the sheriff's home. That explains its strategic location between the courthouse and the jail: by walking through the causeway from the second floor to the jail, the sheriff could check on prisoners without going outside. On lease to the Marion County Historical Society, the house is now a three-story museum of donated memorabilia and antiques.

If you prefer to see the rooms in their chronological order, start on the third level with the Marion County Room. Here you'll see items such as cradles, paintings and quilts. In the Artifacts room you can look over an old doctor's kit and many reminders of early schools in Marion County. Children also love the working model railroad.

On the second floor, the Children's Room is filled with period toys and dolls. In rooms that span the years 1820-1890, you'll find artifacts from Marion County's Civil War history and representations of a fertile period of mechanical invention that spawned the telephone, telegraph, electric lights, the reaper and the sewing machine.

The Twenties Room will give you a sense of the wealth and exhilaration of the early years of the 20th century, and the first level dining room is set for a time of prosperity. (As a result of the coal boom and and other industries, Fairmont in 1920 was home to more millionaires per capita than any other town in the country.)

As you come downstairs to the first level, notice the wrought iron bannister. And, before you leave the museum, be sure to read the framed headline from the *New York Herald*, April 15, 1865, announcing the death of President Lincoln and the search for John Wilkes Booth.

The museum is free, but donations are appreciated. The hours are 10:00 a.m. to 2:00 p.m. Monday through Friday, year-round; from Memorial Day to Labor Day, the museum is also open 10:00 a.m. to 2:00 p.m. on Saturday.

Directions: From I-79 take Exit 37 (Downtown). Bear left at McDonald's onto Route 310. Go through three lights and turn right over the old bridge, then left onto Adams Street. The courthouse sits on the corner and the museum is beside it.

Pricketts Fort State Park

"Living in old times was hard. Women and children cried a great deal and the men and boys cussed a lot. And everybody prayed enough, in church, in the fields, in the woods, wherever and whenever they had the feeling for it.... We put up with a lot of trouble but we stayed brave, and God was by us every minute...." —Kesiah Batten Shearer (1776-1872)

Displayed in an exhibit in the **Pricketts Fort Visitors Center**, this excerpt sets the scene for a vivid living-history lesson. In this reconstructed frontier fort from the late 1700s, professional costumed interpreters share the history of frontier families while they demonstrate frontier living and crafts.

Park at the visitors center and buy your tickets to the fort, reconstructed in 1976, and the Job Prickett House. It's also a good idea to stop in the exhibit area to watch the introductory video, review maps and artifacts and get an overview of early settlement days.

Jacob Prickett, Sr., his wife and ten children were among the earliest settlers to this part of western Virginia, a land of rich soil, huge hardwood trees and abundant wildlife. Initially tolerant of the European settlers, Native Americans were increasingly angered by their

Living history interpreters at Pricketts Fort State Park demonstrate weaving, gunmaking and other 18th-century skills.

COURTESY PRICKETTS FORT STATE PARK

destruction of forests and wildlife. In 1774 the Indians declared war. For protection, the settlers built a refuge to which they could retreat when their homes were under siege. For 20 of the 25 years it stood (1774-99), the fort was in active use, a safe place for the lucky settlers who had time to grab children and whatever essentials they could before their homes were destroyed. Between 80 and 100 families (about 1,000 people in all) waited out the sieges, which could last from a few hours to as long as seven weeks.

Prickett's land was chosen for the fort because of its high vantage point and proximity to water and a major travel route, the nearby Monongahela River. Originally, a 150-yard stockade discouraged attacks on the fort itself.

From early spring through late fall, Indians attacked homes and individuals at any time with no warning. Jacob Prickett's 16-year-old son, Isaiah, was murdered and scalped within sight of the fort; his companion, Susan Oxx, was abducted and never found. You'll learn from interpreters that scalping was not a practice originating with Native Americans, but a bounty ritual learned from French trappers, and that the mutilation did not necessarily result in death—luckier victims might heal within two years, although they would never grow hair again.

In the **Meeting House**, you can watch the preparation of simple meals at the large fireplace, or try your hand at carding wool, which an interpreter may spin into yarn as you watch. Weavers demonstrate their craft on old looms and explain how flax, the common man's cotton, was grown and turned into clothing—a labor-intensive process in which a simple petticoat could represent two years of processing, spinning and weaving. You can examine a gun under construction in the gun shop, help pump the bellows in the blacksmith shop and watch one craftsman make containers and drinking cups out of cows' horns.

In contrast to the spartan fort is the relative luxury of the **Job Prickett House** a few yards (but quite a few years) away. The handsome two-story brick home was built by Jacob's great-grandson in 1860, 60 years after the fort was dismantled. Furnished in "late farmhouse Victorian" and period antiques, many originals from the Prickett family, its glass windows, high ceilings and well-equipped kitchen show how quickly this region changed from frontier to prosperous farmland during the early 19th century. The 18 Pricketts who were raised in this house lived in an affluence their ancestors could hardly have imagined.

Pricketts Fort hosts several special events during the year. Springtime brings traditional Appalachian fiddling, dulcimer playing and banjo picking during a music weekend. Summer encampments demonstrate lifestyles of eastern settlers between 1700 and 1799. The smell of apples (in cider and butter forms) sweetens the **Fall Festival**, and in late November and December **Christmas at Pricketts Fort** presents crafts and gifts by candlelight [see calendar of events].

Since 1983, volunteers have performed a full-length outdoor drama during selected evenings in July. Visitors find *Pricketts Fort: An American Frontier Musical* a wonderful way to learn the fort's history. Reservations are recommended. Call ahead for specific dates and times.

Pricketts Fort is open from mid-April to the end of October, 10:00 a.m. to 5:00 p.m. Monday through Saturday and noon to 5:00 p.m. Sunday, with extra hours till 8:00 p.m. on performance nights. Special tours can be arranged in advance. Admission is $5.00 for adults, $4.50 for seniors and $2.50 for ages 6-12. Children under 6 visit free. (Theater tickets, sold separately, are $9.00, $8.00 and $4.50 for adults, seniors and children, respectively.) Last admission ticket sold at 4:30 p.m. For more information, call (800)CALL-WVA or (304)363-3030, visit their web site (www.dmssoft.com/pfort) or write Pricketts Fort Memorial Foundation, Route 3, Box 407, Fairmont, WV 26554.

Directions: From I-79 take Exit 139, north of Fairmont. Then follow signs to fort, about two miles. Watch out for the narrow bridge that accommodates only one car at a time.

Tip: Allow a minimum of two hours here. The setting beside the water is a lovely picnic spot. The Museum Shop at the visitors center has a variety of high-quality handmade toys, recordings, candles, cards, crafts, books and other gift items.

Valley Falls State Park

The rapid fall of the Tygart River known as Valley Falls is the centerpiece of this 1,145-acre day park. Large slabs and room-sized boulders of sandstone proliferate along the narrow canyon floor, inviting sunbathers and many picnickers. The controlled water flow from the Tygart Dam also makes this a good place for bass to feed and breed.

More than 12 miles of interlocking hiking and mountain biking trails wind through the park, including the relatively level, 3.2-mile **Rhododendron Trail** and the **Wild Turkey Trail** (1.2 miles), which takes you up a steep incline to follow a ridgetop trail.

There's a family feel to Valley Falls. Children find plenty of playground equipment, and families enjoy the volleyball and horseshoe pitching areas. The park has a large number of picnic tables and a shelter. You'll also find the remains of a sawmill and gristmill once powered by these falls, built by W.W. Fetterman in the mid-19th century.

Park hours are 7:00 a.m to dusk seven days a week, year-round. The road can be icy and hazardous during the winter, so you may want to call ahead in cold weather. For more information, call (304)367-2719 or write Valley Falls State Park, Route 6, Box 244, Fairmont, WV 26554.

Directions: From I-79, take Exit 137 (Downtown) and follow Route 310 south for seven miles. Turn right at the Valley Falls State Park sign and go two miles to the park entrance.

Grafton

International Mother's Day Shrine

It seems right that Mother's Day should have been initiated in West Virginia, where family and home are all-important. The idea began with Anna Jarvis, a Grafton schoolteacher and one of 12 children of Anna Reeves Jarvis. The elder Anna was a community activist who organized women's groups to improve sanitation and health conditions and to care for injured soldiers, both Union and Confederate, during the Civil War. After the war, she played a large role in reuniting the divided community.

On the second anniversary of her mother's death, the second Sunday in May, 1907, Anna Jarvis organized a small, private service to honor her mother, and announced her intentions to promote a national holiday. The following year, on May 10, 1908, a congregation of 407 attended the first official Mother's Day service, held in the same church where Anna Reeves Jarvis had taught Sunday School for 20 years. Miss Jarvis sent 500 white carnations, to be given to each son, daughter and mother in attendance.

With Anna Jarvis spearheading efforts at the state and national level, the idea of a holiday for mothers was quickly accepted. In 1910 Governor William Glasscock issued the first Mother's Day's proclamation. In 1914 President Woodrow Wilson approved a congressional resolution proclaiming the second Sunday in May (the anniversary of Anna Reeves Jarvis's death) as Mother's Day. Within a short time it was adopted internationally.

Historic Andrews Church became the **International Mother's Day Shrine** when it was incorporated on May 15, 1962. Built in 1873, the church is a handsome two-story brick building. If you visit, take note of the original wooden pews and stained-glass windows. On the entrance level are photographs of the mother and daughter whose loving bond created an international holiday.

Hours are 9:30 a.m. to 3:30 p.m. Monday through Friday, April 15 to October 31. A special Mother's Day service is held on the holiday every year at 2:30 p.m. Guided tours are available, but you should make prior arrangements for groups by calling (304)265-1589 or -1177 or writing International Mother's Day Shrine, PO Box 457, Grafton, WV 26354. Admission is free but donations are appreciated.

Directions: 11 E. Main Street in Grafton, one mile south of the junction of Routes 50 and 119.

Tip: Parking on Main Street is limited, but there is plenty of space in back of the church.

Four miles south of Grafton on Route 119/250 you pass through the town of Webster. Here the 1854 home of Granville and Anna Jarvis (the elder), the **Anna Jarvis Birthplace**, has been restored by the Thunder on the Tygart Foundation. Across the road is **Ocean Pearl Felton Historic Park**, used as an encampment by General

George B. McClellan during the Civil War. The museum/gift shop is open 10:00 a.m. to 6:00 p.m. Tuesday through Sunday, and there's a **Mother's Day Festival** the second weekend of each May. Guided tours are $4.00 for adults, $3.00 for seniors and $2.00 for students, with no charge for children under six. Call (304)265-5549 to arrange for tours.

Tygart Lake State Park and Dam

The centerpiece of this popular state park is an 11-mile-long lake that spreads its fingers into the wooded valleys south of Grafton. Created by the U.S. Army Corps of Engineers in the 1930s for flood control, the lake is a favorite for scuba divers, fishermen, swimmers, boaters and water skiers. You should expect a lot of company here on any warm summer day, but you'll find that the lake's size and many inlets allow for many people to enjoy it without feeling crowded.

Tygart Lake's water quality is so high that stocking is not necessary to maintain healthy populations of bass, muskie, crappie, perch and walleye. The **Tygart Lake Marina** offers complete boat servicing and launching facilities as well as boat rentals. Swimmers are welcome and lifeguards are on duty at the beach area. Hikers and naturalists enjoy trails around the shoreline and through the 2,134-acre park, and the park naturalist schedules slide programs, bird walks, guided hikes and other nature programs during the summer season.

If you have time to stay overnight, you'll find that one of the best things about Tygart Lake is the lodging. The 20-room wood-paneled lodge is on a promontory above the lake, with a panoramic view of the waterfront from the restaurant. Or you can choose one of ten deluxe vacation cottages, completely furnished for housekeeping with cooking utensils, dishes, linens, towels and blankets. Lodge and cabins are available from April 1 through December 31. If you want to camp, a 40-unit camping area is open from late April to October 31.

From April 1 to December 31, the park is open seven days a week, 8:30 a.m. to 10:00 p.m. Winter hours are 8:30 a.m. to 4:30 p.m. Monday through Friday. All facilities are closed January to early April, but the park is open daily from dawn to dusk. For more information, call (800)CALL-WVA or (304)265-3383. For lodge reservations, call (304)265-2320. You may also visit the park's web site (wvweb.com/www/TYGART_LAKE.html) or write Tygart Lake State Park, Route 1, Box 260, Grafton, WV 26354.

After you've had enough sun, an interesting way to round out a day at Tygart Lake is to stop at the U.S. Army Corps of Engineers visitors center and learn how the **Tygart Dam** created this lake. Completed in 1938, Tygart is one of the oldest and largest concrete dams east of the Mississippi. A ten-minute video explains the history and construction of the dam. If you can arrange to be here on a Wednesday during summer, you'll get a complete tour of the dam—inside and underneath—by the Corps park ranger. But you can stroll out onto the walkway anytime during park hours to get a feeling of the enormous power here.

The visitors center is open 7:30 a.m. to 3:45 p.m. every day of the year; tours of the dam are given every Wednesday at 12:45 p.m. during June, July and August; during September and early October, tours are Saturday at 12:45 p.m. Call (304)265-1760 for more information, or write Area Resource Manager, Tygart Lake, Route 1, Box 257, Grafton, WV 26354.

Directions: From Grafton, take Route 50 to South Grafton and follow signs to the park and dam.

Kingwood

West Virginia Northern Railroad

You'll want to be waiting at the depot in Kingwood when Conductor Bob calls, "All Aboard!" Since 1882, trains have rolled past homes, farms and especially coal mines in Preston County. The **West Virginia Northern Railroad** travels the same tracks that, during the heyday of coal mining, bore the weight of up to 21,000 coal cars a year. You'll see both present-day coal mining operations and remnants of mines long closed—along with wildflowers in spring, lush greenery in summer and brilliant foliage in autumn. Keep your eyes open for whitetail deer and wild turkey.

In addition to regular passenger cars, open-air touring cars are popular in good weather. Including the layover at the restored historic Tunnelton B&O Depot, the trip takes three hours. Groups as small as two persons can charter one of the railroad's tiny four-wheel track inspection cars.

Fares for the ride are $12.00 for adults and $6.00 for ages 3-12. Group rates are available. Rain or shine, the train runs at 11:00 a.m. and 3:00 p.m. on Saturdays, Sundays and holidays from Mid-May through October, with special weekday fall foliage runs at noon during October. The schedule is expanded during the **Preston County Buckwheat Festival** in late September [see calendar of events]. For reservations and information about special events like the **Northern Nightmare Express**, call (304)329-3333 or write Kingwood Northern, Inc., PO Box 424, Kingwood, WV 26537.

Directions: On Route 7 (Sisler Street) at the east end of Kingwood. Follow the signs that say "Excursion Train."

Lost Creek

Watters Smith Memorial State Park

This 532-acre park's swimming pool and playground, trails and picnic areas alone would make it an inviting place, but its real attraction is for history lovers. **Watters Smith Memorial State Park** is also an historic farmstead with a number of original structures made from hand-hewn logs. It is dedicated to the memory of Watters Smith and his descendants, who worked the surrounding land for four generations, from 1796 to the early 1900s.

The best way to appreciate the historic area of the park is to begin at the visitors center, which also houses a fascinating museum of pioneer implements and artifacts, including a "shaving horse" on which shingles like the ones on the old buildings were cut. There you'll receive a nicely detailed brochure with a self-guided tour of other structures: the horse and cattle barn, mill room, corn crib, hog pen, cellar, woodworking shop, blacksmith shop and barn. On the site of Watters Smith's original cabin is a hand-hewn log cabin once located in Beech Fork State Park. If you're lucky, you'll be here when a demonstration of soap-making, quilting or hearthstone cooking is in progress. Another completely refurbished Smith residence on the grounds, a typical example of sturdy farmhouses built by hand in the 19th century, includes many original furnishings as well as other antiques.

Guided tours of the **Smith House Museum** and the visitors center are conducted daily, 11:00 a.m. to 7:00 p.m., Memorial Day to Labor Day. Travelers are welcome to walk in year-round, from 8:00 a.m. to dusk, but restrooms and park gates are closed between October 15 and April 15. Call (304)745-3081 or write Watters Smith Memorial State Park, PO Box 296, Lost Creek, WV 26385.

Directions: From I-79, take Exit 110 (Lost Creek) and follow the signs for seven miles to the park. Visitors traveling Route 19 should turn off at West Milford and follow signs three miles to the park.

The 1912 Round Barn in Mannington now houses antique farm equipment and artifacts instead of cows.

STEPHEN J. SHALUTA, JR.

Mannington

Mannington Round Barn and West Augusta Historical Society Museum

Although they are not uncommon in Pennsylvania-Dutch country, round barns in West Virginia are rare. The only restored round barn in the state, is now owned, along with the nearby school museum, by the West Augusta Historical Society. A cupola, built to ventilate stored hay, adds a touch of grace to the structure—and affords a lovely view of the surrounding hills.

The shape, although a challenge to build, was popular because it allowed farmers to store their hay in the spacious loft of the barn, eliminating the need to haul silage from another storage place. Farmer Amos C. Hamilton built this one as a dairy barn in 1912, making an ingenious addition to the design: he built the barn into the side of the hill, which allowed him to drive a wagon directly into the loft.

Besides sheltering cows and storing feed, the barn served as the farmer's home and the center of a 400-acre farm. Your tour is likely to start in the apartment, where you'll see photos of the Hamilton family, including Amos's stern, snuff-dipping grandmother.

The barn's floor, roof and rib-like rafters are nearly all original. On three levels, you'll see a wealth of artifacts and farm equipment, including harness, buckets, a surrey, a bee smoker, fruit dryers, butter churns, milk coolers, lard presses, corn shellers, and an enormous, horse-drawn potato picker. You'll learn about the spring-fed watering system, designed so cows could turn it on and off themselves, and natural gas deposits on the property that provided heat for the barn. Children will like the homemade wooden bobsled capable of carrying a dozen riders.

Nor will they mind a trip to the former Wilson School in downtown Mannington, which now houses the **West Augusta Historical Society Museum**. Also built in 1912, and practically whispering with nostalgic memories, the old school's bright, spacious classrooms now hold an eclectic and fascinating jumble of donated historical treasures: brass ox-horn covers, an 1886 music box, a portable pantry that was carried on wagon trains, an elegant hand pumper (a forerunner of the vacuum cleaner), early paper currency and a surrey that converts into a sleigh.

Take note of the 1912 school board's rules for teachers' conduct: "You will not marry during the school term; you will not wear a dress shorter than two inches above the ankle; you must wear at least two petticoats; you may not loiter downtown in the ice cream store...or keep company with men; you may not smoke cigarettes...or dress in bright colors."

Outside in the schoolyard, a colorful 1912 caboose holds a miniature railroad museum. A small log cabin, built in 1870 by George Washington Price on Dead Fall Road in Wetzel County, has been moved here, restored and furnished with items authentic to its era.

The museum and barn, which request separate $2.00 donations for adults ($0.50 for children), are open Sundays from 1:30 to 4:00 p.m. May through September, or by appointment at any time. Call (304)986-2636, (304)986-1089 or (304)825-6650; or write West Augusta Historical Society, PO Box 414, Mannington, WV 26582.

Directions: To the barn, take Route 250 north from Fairmont about 12 miles. Just after passing a shopping mall, turn left on Flaggy Meadow Road and follow signs. To the museum, continue into Mannington on Route 250; the brick school is on your right.

Morgantown

Morgantown is a fast-growing, sprawling community. Groups of backpack-toting young people everywhere (roughly a third of the population) let you know at once that it's a college town, but Morgantown has plenty to offer any visitor. To make the most of it, make your first stop the **Greater Morgantown Convention and Visitors Bureau** at 709 Beechurst Avenue. You'll enjoy seeing the building that houses the visitors center in any case: the **Seneca Center** is a handsome and very creative renovation of a turn-of-the-century glass factory. Now it is full of upscale shops and a restaurant, but the red water tower and 100-foot glass furnace chimney reflect the original purpose of the 1898 structure. Pause on the entrance level to see a gallery-like display of glass, tools, photos and explanatory murals.

Town founder Zackquill Morgan, who settled here in 1768, was the son of Morgan Morgan, the state's first recorded permanent settler; and Morgantown was among the first dozen incorporated towns in the state. A quiet residential community on the Monongahela river, it changed with the coming of the railroad in 1886 to a bustling industrial center.

Stop at the visitors center for a brochure with a self-guided walking tour of the downtown area. Many of Morgantown's older buildings date from the turn of the century—and many of these were designed by the same man, the prolific Elmer Jacobs, whom the Morgantown *New Dominion* once credited with "almost all of the architectural beauty" of the town. Also of interest is the 1891 Romanesque Revival **Monongalia County Courthouse**. In the center of the historic district at 243 High Street, its square comes alive with free noontime concerts every Tuesday, Wednesday and Thursday from July to October.

The visitors center is open 8:30 a.m. to 5:00 p.m. Monday through Friday. Call (800)458-7373 or (304)292-5081, visit their web site (www.MGTN.com) or write Greater Morgantown Convention and Visitors Bureau, 709 Beechurst Avenue, Morgantown, WV 26505.

Directions: From I-79, take Exit 155 (Star City) and go 2½ miles south on Route 19 (turns into Beechurst Avenue) to Seneca Center. From I-68, take Exit 1 (South University Avenue) and go four miles north on Route 119.

West Virginia University

If Morgantown can be called the heart of Mountaineer Country, **West Virginia University** is the heartbeat. Established in 1867 as a land grant institution, the state's largest university is home-away-from-home to more than 22,000 students from all 55 counties, all 50 states and 85 countries around the world. On two growing campuses, students attend 14 separate colleges offering 165 degree programs—and also enjoy a lively extra-curricular atmosphere, which you can share. From theater performances to concerts, art exhibits to sports events, museums to munchies, a nature walk or a ride on one of the most efficient public transportation systems in operation, you can find it somewhere on the WVU campus.

If you want to come for a football game, you'd better plan ahead. The WVU Mountaineers, the school's Big East football team, surely can boast the most loyal and spirited student (and former student) body anywhere. Fans pack the 63,500-seat **Mountaineer Field** to cheer on the team and the "Pride of West Virginia" marching band, recently honored as the number one marching band in the country. In the parking lot, some bumper stickers read, "I bleed blue and gold."

University Tour

Although it has a friendly, small-college atmosphere, WVU is a comprehensive university; the best way to get a good overview of the school is to take the bus/walking tour offered by the **University Visitors Center**. The tour of both campuses—Downtown and Evansdale/Health Sciences—lasts about two hours, beginning at the center with a short film and information session. Then you'll board the bus with an enthusiastic student tour guide who will point out important buildings on the Evansdale/Health Sciences campus. In addition to Mountaineer Field, highlights include:

The **Coliseum**, which seats up to 14,000 for basketball and other sports events as well as concerts.

The **Creative Arts Center,** featuring rotating art exhibits and the West Virginia Public Theater, which stages dozens of off-Broadway performances each year. In addition to student and faculty performances, visiting artists and companies share their music, theater and dance talents. For an in-depth tour, call (304)293-4841 to make arrangements.

Ruby Memorial Hospital, WVU's teaching hospital, part of the Robert C. Byrd Health Sciences Center complex.

The **Mineral and Energy Museum**, with a huge collection of artifacts from the state's mining history, in the Mineral and Energy Resources Building. Call (304)293-4211 to arrange for a separate tour.

The **Cook-Hayman Pharmacy Museum** in the Health Sciences Center, a fascinating look at apothecary history. Call (304)293-5101 for a tour.

The bus then takes you to the downtown campus. WVU's campus has been rated by *USA Today* as one of the safest in the nation—and you'll see for yourself that it's one of the prettiest. The bus will take you briefly through downtown Morgantown. (On your own, you can explore the more than 100 specialty shops and 40 restaurants and taverns.) The hub of WVU's downtown campus is the **Mountainlair**, ranked among the top student unions in the country. With its theater, food court, computer labs, convenience store, deli, post office, bakery, pleasant study rooms and many meeting rooms, it is the liveliest place on campus, especially during events like **FallFest**, **Mountaineer Week** (a celebration of West Virginia heritage) and the annual lecture series, **Festival of Ideas**.

Across the street from the Mountainlair is the historical heart of WVU. **Woodburn Circle's** three handsome brick and stone buildings, all on the National Register of Historic Places, formed the core of the original school. **Martin Hall**, the oldest building on campus, was completed in 1870, and is home to the journalism school.

Hours: The visitors center is open from 9:00 a.m. to 6:00 p.m. Monday through Friday, 9:00 a.m. to 4:00 p.m. Saturday and noon to 4:00 p.m. Sunday. Guided tours are conducted at 11:00 a.m. and 2:30 p.m. Monday through Friday and 10:00 a.m. and 12:30 p.m. on Saturday—except on home football game days! A self-guided tour on cassette tape is also available. Call ahead to make arrangements or to check out a video or CD-ROM: (800)344-WVU1 (ext. 2). You may also visit their web site (www.wvu.edu) or write WVU Visitors Center, PO Box 6009, Morgantown, WV 26506. Tours are free, but you must make reservations.

Directions: From I-79 take Exit 155 (Star City) and follow campus signs, going about one mile (past Holiday Inn). Stay in the left lane and turn left on Patteson Drive. The visitors center is about 200 yards on the right, in a one-story brick building at 120 Patteson.

Core Arboretum

As you board the bus to leave the Evansdale/Health Sciences campus and head for the downtown campus of WVU, your tour guide will point out the **Core Arboretum**. If you want to take a beautiful

The award-winning Personal Rapid Transit system carries 16,000 riders a day to classes on West Virginia University's two campuses. Visible behind the PRT car is part of WVU's historic Woodburn Circle.

walk, come back here. Especially in spring, this 70-acre park holds botanical treasures to delight you, whether or not you know your wildflowers and trees.

Founded in 1948, the arboretum is named in honor of Dr. Earl L. Core, a distinguished and beloved West Virginia botanist, educator and author. An elevation drop of about 200 feet from the entrance on Beechurst Avenue to the Monongahela River makes for a variety of natural habitats in which hundreds of species of native West Virginia trees, shrubs and flowers thrive. Many of the woody plants are labeled.

There are three miles of trails, including a short circular trail as well as some rather steep and challenging ones. All are well-marked, and maps throughout the park will keep you from getting lost. In April, you can see hillsides of Virginia bluebells and much more—join the guided wildflower walk at 2:00 p.m. on the last three Sundays of the month, or simply explore on your own. In early May, look for a profusion of purple dwarf larkspur. The Core Arboretum is open dawn till dusk, for foot travelers only, year-round. For more information, call (304)293-5201, visit their web site (www.as.wvu.edu/biology/bioar.html) or write Core Arboretum, WVU Department of Biology, PO Box 6057, Morgantown, WV 26506.

Directions: On Beechurst Avenue just south of Patteson Drive, next-door to the Coliseum. (You must be traveling south on Beechurst to enter the arboretum parking lot. You may also park in the Coliseum lot.)

Tip: Want a more level walk? The WVU campus borders the 51-mile **Caperton Trail**, a rails-to-trails project that extends from nearby Fairmont through Morgantown to the Pennsylvania border.

Personal Rapid Transit (PRT)

On your bus tour around town, you'll probably notice little white cars traveling on their own elevated tracks. These are part of the most modern transit system in the world, one that connects the university campuses safely, comfortably, quickly and, for students, free of charge. The cars hold up to 20 people and travel at a top speed of 30 miles per hour—and, when classes are in session, they transport 16,000 riders a day. The longest ride on the five-stop trip is only 11½ minutes, and the system is designed so that any passenger can take a car to the desired destination without stopping at any intervening station—that's the "personal" part of the transit system. The system operates on a flexible schedule, with computer coordination of all 73 cars.

Powered by electricity without polluting the air, the environmentally friendly system has also proven extremely safe: since its inception in 1975, more than 46 million people have traveled over 17 million miles in the system's 73 cars without a single accident. Although the individual cars require no operators, stations are monitored by camera; new riders quickly learn from a chastising voice, broadcast through nearly invisible speakers, what constitutes inappropriate behavior.

A joint project of the U.S. Department of Transportation and the university, the system cost about $120 million and, as a demonstration project, has served as a model for large cities with major transportation problems. The PRT has recently been rated Best of Class (surpassing the Disney monorail!) by *New Electric Railway Journal.*

For non-students, the ride costs $0.50, and you must have exact change in quarters. Hours are Monday through Friday from 6:30 a.m. to 10:15 p.m. and Saturday from 9:30 a.m. to 5:00 p.m. Closed Sundays, holidays and university vacation days. For more information call (304)293-5011 or write Personal Rapid Transit, WVU, PO Box 6565, Morgantown, WV 26506.

Directions: Board at one of the five stops—Walnut Street, Beechurst Avenue, Engineering (near Patteson Drive and Monongahela Boulevard), Towers (near Towers Drive and University Boulevard), and Medical Center (at WVU hospital).

Chestnut Ridge Park

Just east of Morgantown is **Chestnut Ridge Park**, a Monongalia County recreation area with rustic and modern cabins, tent and trailer camping, trails, picnic tables and shelters, a nature center and two lakes for swimming and fishing. Full hook-up and pull-through RV sites are available at the Sand Springs Camping Area. This area also features a swimming pool, miniature golf and game room, as well as lodge rental rooms. Chestnut Ridge is a popular center for many activities and festivals, including nature walks, workshops, cross-country ski lessons, a **Haunted Woods Festival** and the **West Virginia Wine and Jazz Festival** in September [see calendar of events]. For more information call (304)594-1773 or write Chestnut Ridge Park, Route 1, Box 267, Bruceton Mills, WV 26525.

Directions: From I-68, take Exit 15 (Coopers Rock). If traveling west off exit ramp, turn right; if traveling east, turn left. When you come to a stop sign turn right on Old Route 73 and continue for about one-fourth mile, then turn left onto Sand Springs Road. Follow it for about 1½ miles until the road forks. Bear left and follow it for about one mile to the park office.

Coopers Rock State Forest

The view of Cheat Lake and River 1,200 feet below draws more than 400,000 people a year to the overlook at **Coopers Rock State Forest**. And no wonder: the sandstone overhang, balanced above cliffs and massive boulders, offers a truly breathtaking outlook. For

West Virginians and others who value the view, it looks even better these days: the state's recent purchase of more than 2,000 acres directly across from the overlook assures that the spectacular view will be there for future generations to enjoy.

Hikers and cross-country skiers love Coopers Rock. The largest of the state forests at nearly 13,000 acres, it is laced with miles and miles of trails. Three of the most popular are the Virgin Hemlock Trail (2.4 miles round trip) to a hemlock grove over 300 years old; Raven Rock Trail (4 miles round trip), which ends at an overlook with a view of the river; and Rock City Trail (2 miles round trip), an easy, level walk that leads to a wonderland of huge boulders with many crevices to explore.

Several trails pass by the **Henry Clay Iron Furnace**, which in the early 1800s supported a community of more than 1,000—an era during which nearby Morgantown's population was only about 400. Because of the combination of resources (iron ore, limestone and timber) and the river transportation route, this area along the Cheat was one of the country's major iron centers during the first half of the 19th century. Later, loggers claimed the forest; by the time the state purchased the land in 1936, most of the woods had been logged and burned. The Civilian Conservation Corps built many rustic structures here during the 1930s, some of which still stand and are on the National Register of Historic Places. One of them is the large stone-and-wood picnic shelter near the overlook.

There is a concession stand on the park grounds. Trails are open during daylight hours all year. The campgrounds and road (except for cross-country skiing) are closed from the first Sunday in December to April 1. No rock climbing is allowed on the scenic vistas, including the overlook. Also, be aware that hunting is allowed. During hunting seasons (October through February), wear bright-colored clothing, preferably orange.

Directions: From Morgantown take I-68 east about ten miles to Exit 15. For more information call (304)594-1561 or write Coopers Rock State Forest, Route 1, Box 270, Bruceton Mills, WV 26525.

Tip: Near Coopers Rock State Forest is the northern terminus of the **Allegheny Trail**, West Virginia's first long distance hiking trail, stretching 330 miles from the Mason-Dixon Line on the West Virginia/Pennsylvania border to the Appalachian Trail atop Peters Mountain in Monroe County. Marked throughout its length with yellow blazes, the trail is intended for human foot travel and not recommended for mountain bicycles, other wheeled vehicles or horses. (Some segments, however, are excellent for cross-country skiing when the snow falls.) It passes through four state parks, two state forests and three national forests.

It skirts the Otter Creek National Wilderness Area and is only a few miles from both the Dolly Sods and Cranberry Wilderness Areas. For more information call (304)296-5158 or write Allegheny Trail, c/o 633 West Virginia Avenue, Morgantown, WV 26505. A postpaid copy of the *Hiking Guide to the Allegheny Trail* is available for $8.00 by writing the same address.

Easton Roller Mill

In the 1800s the mill was the economic and social center of many communities. The **Easton Roller Mill**, near the Morgantown airport, is one of the few remaining steam-driven mills in the Mid-Atlantic. Although it has not operated since 1930, it remains in excellent condition and is lovingly cared for by the Monongalia Historical Society.

Built between 1864 and 1867 of hand-hewn oak timbers, the mill initially operated as a gristmill. At 3½ stories, the mill boasts an impressive brick chimney and many fine decorative details, testimony to the skill and pride of the craftsmen who built it.

Inside, if you take a tour, you'll see equipment for two milling techniques: part of the old millstone system and the newer roller mills. The mills were driven by a steam engine originally powered by coal. The corn sheller and crusher show that the mill was also important for processing animal feed. On the second floor are large storage bins and sieves. Here grain was purified and dressed to become flour, the whiter and finer the better. (Dark flour was not recognized as healthful during the 19th century.) On the top floor, notice the elevator heads that controlled the transportation of of grain through the mill.

The Easton Roller Mill is open the first and third Sundays from May 1 to October 30, 12:30 to 4:30 p.m. Tours by appointment any time of the year. Admission is free but donations are appreciated. To make tour arrangements, call (304)599-0833 or write Monongalia Historical Society, PO Box 127, Morgantown, WV 26505.

Directions: From I-68 take Exit 7 towards town. Go one mile, turn left onto Route 119 South and turn left onto the first blacktop road. The mill stands about one-fourth mile on the right.

Forks of Cheat Winery

For a lovely drive and a taste of excellent West Virginia wine, make your way to the **Forks of Cheat Winery** six miles north of Morgantown. The drive to this small, family-run winery will take you through picture-pretty farmland and put you in the mood for a sip of Susan and Jerry Deal's award-winning wines.

In operation since 1990, Forks of Cheat has grown steadily from a production of 500 to 6,000 gallons a year. They cultivate 12 acres with French hybrid and American grapes. Their four white wines range from a fruity Niagara to a dry, crisp Villard Blanc. The Delaware Blush is light and dry. White wine devotees will especially want to try the Seyval. Most of the reds are from French hybrids: Foch, Leon Millot and Dechaunac.

When you tour, you'll be amazed to learn that two people run the production end of this wine-making operation. All the grapes here are hand-picked, pressed, crushed and left to ferment, with sugar added, in large, air-tight containers. Before bottling it, they filter the wine six times. With the proper equipment, two people can bottle and cork about 22 cases of wine an hour.

Your tour will cover the entire process from vine to wine. Leave time for tasting afterwards in the sampling area. Tours and tasting Monday through Saturday from 10:00 a.m. to 5:00 p.m. and Sundays (except for January through March) from 1:00 to 5:00 p.m. Call (304)598-2019 or (304)599-8660 or write Forks of Cheat Winery, Route 4, Box 224E, Morgantown, WV 26505.

Directions: From I-68, take Exit 7 (Pierpont Road) to Route 119 and go north about 3 1/2 miles before turning right onto Stewartstown Road (second paved road on right). Continue 1.9 miles to the winery on your left.

Tip: Forks of Cheat Winery was instrumental in starting the popular annual **West Virginia Wine and Jazz Festival** at nearby Chestnut Ridge Park in September [see calendar of events]. If you enjoy tasting, plan to attend and sample the fruits of eight or more West Virginia wineries, along with gourmet food and live music.

The Old Stone House

Pressed between commercial buildings, this tiny and charming house—it resembles the setting for a child's favorite story—looks as pretty as it must have when it was built in 1795 by Jacob Nuze. The oldest stone dwelling in Monongalia County, it has been on the National Register of Historic Places since 1972.

Following a colorful history as a tavern, pottery, tannery, tailor shop, church and residence, the two-story cottage is now a craft and gift shop owned and operated by the non-profit Service League of Morgantown. West Virginia artisans are the stars here, and many of the ceramics, glassware, woodworks, paintings and other items are made by local artists. A small second-hand resale operation supplements craft and art sales to support community projects like school libraries and children's theater. Hours are 10:00 a.m. to 2:00 p.m. Monday through Saturday.

Directions: At 313 Chestnut Street, the house is easily accessible by PRT (one-half block from the Walnut Street stop). For more information call (304)296-7825.

Philippi

Barbour County Historical Museum

After you cross the **Philippi Covered Bridge** [see entry], you'll probably want to know more about this antebellum engineering feat. Stop by the **Barbour County Historical Museum**, which occupies the restored 1911 Baltimore & Ohio depot at the east end of the bridge.

In addition to historical information about the bridge and plenty of Civil War memorabilia, including cannonballs and a drum played at Appomattox, the museum is home to two most unusual ladies: the Philippi mummies, two 19th-century asylum patients whose bodies were mummified in 1888 by Graham Hamrick, a part-time undertaker. Confined to the West Virginia Hospital for the Insane (later called Weston State Hospital) during life, the mummies traveled all over the world with the Barnum & Bailey Circus after their deaths. Back home in West Virginia now and over a century old, they rest in glass-topped wooden caskets in one room of the museum. Though covered in mud, they "survived" the catastrophic flood of 1985 and are still holding a job, in a way: the $1.00 fee for viewing the mummies funds a scholarship.

General admission to the museum is free, but donations are welcome. Museum hours are 11:00 a.m. to 4:00 p.m. Monday through Saturday and 1:00 to 4:00 p.m. Sunday, Memorial Day through September, and by appointment at other times. To schedule a tour, call (304)457-4846 during museum hours or (304)457-3349 at other times, or write Jim Ramsey, Curator, Barbour County Historical Museum, 225 Garnett Street, Philippi, WV 26416.

Directions: On Route 250 in Philippi, at the east end of the Philippi Covered Bridge.

Philippi Covered Bridge

West Virginia boasts many covered bridges [see appendix for a complete list], but if you see only one, make it the large one that crosses the Tygart River in Philippi. This is one of the most celebrated covered bridges in the United States. Built in 1852 and designed by Lemuel Chenoweth, the 285-foot "double barrel" bridge was larger and longer than most bridges of its time and was an important link on the old Staunton-Parkersburg turnpike. Today, it is the nation's only two-lane covered bridge serving a federal highway (Route 250).

On June 2, 1861, the bridge was the site of the first land battle of the Civil War. Bloodless but decisive, the battle went to Union General B.F. Kelley; General George A. Porterfield's hasty retreat to nearby Beverly was called the "Philippi races."

The bridge at Philippi has endured floods, fires and structural modifications. Renovations in 1938 replaced the wooden deck with concrete. In 1989, the bridge was severely damaged by fire; the subsequent restoration, using hand tools and original construction techniques, returned the bridge to its pre-Civil War appearance.

Philippi is the northernmost point of a self-guided **Civil War Auto Tour** which follows Routes 219 and 250 south through portions of the Monongahela National Forest. For scenery lovers and/or Civil War buffs, this tour is highly recommended. It includes 16 sites of interest, among them Cheat Summit Fort, Droop Mountain Battlefield and Rich Mountain Battlefield [see entries for the latter two in Potomac Highlands section]. For more information about the self-guided tour, call (304)636-1800 or write U.S.D.A. Forest Service, Monongahela National Forest, 200 Sycamore Street, Elkins, WV 26242.

Directions: From Elkins, follow Route 92/250 northwest. The covered bridge is on Route 250 at Philippi.

Tip: For another self-guided tour, this one of Civil War sites in the Tygart Valley, stop by the Philippi Convention and Visitors Bureau at 124 Main Street or call (304)457-1225.

Quiet Dell

West Virginia Mountain Products Co-op

There's hardly ever a dull moment at this craft co-op. No matter when you arrive, you'll probably find someone demonstrating spinning, weaving, singing, quilting, tole painting or one of the many other arts and crafts practiced by the approximately 75 members. There are no paid employees; each member volunteers time and effort toward the operation of the lively shop. Even the caged bunny at the entrance makes a contribution, donating his Angora fur for scarves.

When 75 craftspeople collect their wares, imagine the array! Stained glass, wooden wares, clothing, jewelry, hand-braided rugs, dolls, toys, quilts, pillows, metalware, West Virginia music and mountain foods—the list could go on and on. The group has also produced a cookbook of Appalachian recipes.

Their activities are directed as much toward public education as to the support of artists. In addition to demonstrating and selling their crafts, they sponsor several seasonal events: the **Spring Fling**, **Mountain Merriment**, **Fall Frolic** and **Christmas Open House**. The co-op is open 10:00 a.m. to 5:00 p.m. Monday through Saturday and 1:00 to 5:00 p.m. Sunday, year-round. for more information call (304)622-3304 or write West Virginia Mountain Products, Inc., Route 1, Box 215-B, Mt. Clare, WV 26408.

Directions: Located in Quiet Dell. From I-79 take Exit 115 to Route 20. Turn south on Route 20 and go 0.2 mile. Look for the shop on a hill on your right (in back of a gas station).

Salem

Fort New Salem

When you enter the inner courtyard of **Fort New Salem**, a collection of log buildings representing a frontier settlement of the 19th century, you will feel that you have indeed stepped back at least a century. The original settlers, a group of Seventh Day Baptists from New Jersey, came here in 1792. Their history and that of diverse groups who settled north-central West Virginia come alive in a multitude of demonstrations and hands-on activities that reflect the years from 1792 to 1901.

Under the auspices of Salem-Teikyo University, the fort serves as an educational center as well as a busy museum. Here, college students can pursue a Master of Arts degree in education with an emphasis on Appalachian folklife while they share the region's rich cultural heritage with some of the thousands of school children and tourists who visit Fort New Salem every year. Less than a mile from the main campus, where public workshops augment its programs, the replicated settlement serves as a living classroom for the passing on of traditional crafts and folkways.

Depending upon when you visit, you are likely to see—and try your hand at—weaving, printing, blacksmithing, paper marbling, tinsmithing, carpentry, needlework, quilting, hearth cooking, can-

Log structures at Fort New Salem represent the history of West Virginia's mountain people from 1792-1901.

COURTESY FORT NEW SALEM, SALEM-TEIKYO UNIVERSITY

dle-dipping, basketry and storytelling. The costumed interpreters are warm, friendly and especially patient with children.

Begin at **The Sign of the Three Barrels**, the visitors center at the fort's entrance. If you are lucky, Fort New Salem's director Carol Schweiker will be on hand to tell you about some of the many ways in which she is sharing West Virginia frontier culture with students and families: celebrations of spring, harvest time and holidays; educational programs that combine learning about folk ways with modern-day math, science and social studies; and "sampler camps" in which students spend a whole day immersed in herbal lore, Appalachian music, crafts and more.

Work your way clockwise around the settlement, through the **Blockhouse** and **Meeting House**, the spiritual center of a frontier community (also used for trials and schooling). Visit the **Tin Shop** and the **Old Kitchen**, where you'll marvel that a family of 12 to 15 people might have shared this small space. The old loom and cupboards are authentic.

At the **Apothecary**, bundled herbs are drying overhead, and you'll learn that the pioneers gathered them for many purposes—to heal, dye textiles, repel insects, and sweeten the air. At the **Basket Shop**, 80-something Charlie Randolph, Fort New Salem's resident basketmaker, will show you his techniques. Nearby, a "settler" in period costume will tell you a West Virginia ghost story while she fashions a rag doll before your eyes. Dip your own candles in a large vat of hot beeswax. Before you leave, relax at the **Green Tree Tavern** with a mug of steaming apple cider.

Fort New Salem opens its formal season in late April. It is open 10:00 a.m. to 5:00 p.m. weekdays only through May. From Memorial Day through October, hours are 10:00 a.m. to 5:00 p.m. Wednesday through Sunday. There are special seasonal events, including a **Dulcimer Festival**, throughout summer and fall. December features the **Spirit of Christmas in the Mountains** celebration. Admission is $4.00 for adults, $1.50 for children ages 6-12. Special rates may be in effect during celebrations, and group and senior rates are available. For more information about special events or group reservations call (304)782-5245 or write Fort New Salem, Salem, WV 26426.

Directions: From Clarksburg, take Route 50 west about 12 miles to the exit at Route 23 and follow signs to Fort New Salem.

Tip: Allow at least an hour here, maybe more. This is a mini-scale Williamsburg without the congestion, and the many hands-on activities are so inviting that you may find it hard to leave.

Silver Lake

Our Lady of the Pines

Hidden from the road by tall pine trees, this tiny chapel in the village of Silver Lake is said to be the smallest church in 48 states. The miniature stone church measures 24 feet by 12 feet outside and just 16 feet by 11 feet inside—a snug fit for a maximum of 12 worshipers in six pews.

The altar crosses and linens, Stations of the Cross, tabernacle and candle holders were all handmade to fit the small proportions. Colored light pours into the chapel through six stained-glass windows. A painting on wood of the Last Supper hangs from the altar.

Mr. and Mrs. P.L. Milkint built the tiny church in 1957-58 in memory of their parents, and thousands of people visit every year. The grounds are carefully tended, and the chapel is open to the public during the day from spring to fall. There is no admission charge, although you may wish to drop a penny into the wishing well on the grounds.

If you'd like to send a postcard in addition to offering up a prayer and a penny, look for the miniature post office—claiming to be "the smallest mailing office"—right next-door to the church.

Directions: On Route 219 in Silver Lake, about eight miles north of Thomas.

Star City

Gentile Glass Company

Since the early part of this century, four generations of the Gentile family have carried on the tradition of making glass paperweights. West Virginia's first paperweight factory, **Gentile Glass Company** also opened the area's first outlet store in 1947. The family continues to produce fine cut crystal and paperweights that are sold throughout the country at affordable prices. Mr. Gentile, the founder, and his wife Gertrude (also known as the First Lady of Glass Paperweights) are usually to be found in the company's outlet store, and will gladly tell visitors about their family's history and art.

Be sure to go downstairs and watch for yourself as skilled glass artists use the ancient "off hand" process to create beautiful paperweights. You are also welcome to visit the factory's cutting department, where Gentile's master craftsmen, still mostly family, produce and individually hand cut their crystal ware. In addition to the famous Morgantown Rose pattern, which they cut for many glass factories locally and throughout the country, the company specializes in custom hand-cut patterns and individually monogrammed glassware. Gentile Glass also distributes glassware for other West Virginia manufacturers; you are sure to find a treasure of your own in their large showroom.

Plant tours are given Monday through Friday, 8:00 to 11:00 a.m. and 12:30 to 2:30 p.m. Outlet hours are 8:00 a.m. to 4:00 p.m. Monday through Friday and 8:00 a.m. to noon on Saturday. For more information, call (304)599-2750.

Directions: In Star City, about three miles north of Morgantown. From I-79, take Exit 155 to Route 7 East to Route 19 South, over the bridge. Turn left at the first light, go one block to University Avenue, then go left down the hill one block and turn right on Industrial Avenue. Gentile Glass is just half a block further, at 425 Industrial Avenue.

BETHANY

CHESTER
- Mountaineer Race Track & Gaming Resort

MOUNDSVILLE
- Grave Creek Mound Historic Site
- Old West Virginia Penitentiary

NEWELL
- Homer Laughlin China Company

NEW MARTINSVILLE
- Dalzell-Viking Glass

NEW VRINDABAN
- Prabhupada's Palace of Gold

SISTERSVILLE

WELLSBURG
- Brooke Glass Company

WHEELING
- Capitol Music Hall
- Centre Market
- Challenger Learning Center
- Oglebay Park Resort & Conference Center
  - Mansion Museum
  - Waddington Gardens & Oglebay Shops
  - Good Zoo
  - Festival of Lights
- Stifel Fine Arts Center
- Victorian Wheeling Landmark Tours
- West Virginia Independence Hall
- Wheeling Artisan Center
- Wheeling Suspension Bridge

Northern Panhandle

The state's long, slender Northern Panhandle, bounded by the Ohio River on the west and Pennsylvania on the east, is one of the most captivating, diverse, fun regions of West Virginia. The Ohio River, historically a vital artery for the region's industry, transportation and recreation, remains a strong and beautiful presence in the life of the region.

The city that was once called the Gateway to the West, Wheeling, is now the entry point for a multitude of travelers' joys, ranging from a delightful walk through Victorian history to concerts in an historic music hall to a great big wonderland of a park to an amazingly realistic simulated voyage on a space vehicle. And the gateway to the West is still there: for over 150 years, the Wheeling Suspension Bridge has spanned the Ohio, and you can still drive or walk its historic length. From November to February, the glitter of Wheeling's Festival of Lights brings more than a million visitors to town.

In nearby Moundsville, the glitter comes from gold—more gold than most people have seen in one place, at the fabulous Palace of Gold. For a real change of scenery, take in the palace and tour the Old Moundsville Penitentiary on the same day. Steep yourself in ancient history at Grave Creek Mound State Park. Pick up a place setting at the world's largest dinnerware factory in Newell. Walk in the footsteps of a visionary philosopher in Bethany. Ride the only remaining ferry across the Ohio in pretty Sistersville. Tour glass factories in New Martinsville and Wellsburg. And don't forget to take in West Virginia's natural splendor along the way.

For more information on visiting the Northern Panhandle contact:

Historic Bethany, Bethany College, Bethany, WV 26032. Visit their web site (www.bethanywv.edu), contact the information center by e-mail (historic@mail.bethanywv.edu) or call (304)829-7285.

New Martinsville Chamber of Commerce, 200 Main Street, PO Box 271, New Martinsville, WV 26155. Call (304)455-3825.

Sistersville City Hall, 200 Diamond Street, Sistersville, WV 26175. Call (304)652-6361.

Wellsburg Chamber of Commerce, 600 Colony Center, Wellsburg, WV 26070. Call (304)737-2787.

Wheeling Convention and Visitors Bureau, 14th and Main streets, Wheeling, WV 26003. Visit their web site (www.wheelingcvb.com), contact them by e-mail (whcvbwv@access.mountain.net) or call (800)828-3097 or (304)233-7709.

Bethany

About half an hour's drive north from Wheeling is **Bethany**, a place as pretty as its name. This town of tree-shaded streets, a small general store and enough historic buildings to qualify the whole village for the National Register of Historic Places is also the home of one of the best liberal arts colleges in the country, according to *U.S. News and World Report*.

Bethany College may be small in size (about 800 students), but its founder's philosophy was not. Alexander Campbell, who established the school as the state's first degree-granting college in 1840, was a debater, educator, businessman, statesman, editor, philosopher and a leading influence in one of America's indigenous religious movements, the Disciples of Christ. A passionate believer in education and an eloquent proponent of its role in freedom, his words of 150 years ago seem not in the least outdated: "Intelligence and freedom are but two words for the same thing. An intelligent community will always be free; an ignorant one, never. As we advance in education, as we promote universal intelligence, we promote universal freedom."

Campbell lived and worked for half a century here in a "gentleman farmer's house" and donated the land for the first church in Bethany, where he often preached. Surviving his first wife and their eight children, he reared another family of six and lived to to be almost 80. His distinguished career and visionary writings mark Bethany's character today.

The **Historic Bethany Information Center** (Delta Tau Delta Founder's House), located a block from the Bethany campus, is housed in the first restored building in Bethany, which was built in the 1850s with bricks fired in one of the the town's early kilns. Here you can arrange a guided tour of Campbell's home and church or get information for a self-guided walking/driving tour of historic Campbell sites. Group tours must be arranged in advance. The center is open 9:00 a.m. to 5:00 p.m. Tuesday through Friday. Brochures are also available at the Alexander Campbell Mansion

Old Main at Bethany College, one of the best examples of Collegiate Gothic architecture in the country.

COURTESY BETHANY COLLEGE

and the College Information Center on the main campus (near entrance), open 9:00 a.m. to 4:00 p.m.

The architectural highlight of the Bethany campus is the **Old Main** building. Begun before the Civil War, it suffered fire, alterations and long delays before it achieved its present appearance in 1911. During the 1980s, the college embarked on a $4-million restoration of the structure. Considered among the earliest and best examples of early collegiate Gothic architecture in the United States, it is often compared to similar buildings at the University of Virginia. Its 400-foot-long facade is broken by five arched entrances and topped by a stately clock tower rising more than 140 feet. Old Main's Gothic exterior conceals a renovated interior that accommodates present-day classroom requirements such as computer facilities. The Academic Parlor on the second level (which can be seen by appointment only) contains five handsome Edward Troye oil paintings.

From the campus, walk east on Route 67 to the edge of the village and the **Old Bethany Meeting House**. Built in 1850, this church sits on the original site and retains some of the stonework from the first Bethany church (1835). During services, men and women sat separately in straight-backed pews, and entrances on either side of the pulpit discouraged latecomers. The meeting house is open for tours by appointment only.

Walk or drive east on Route 67 for about a mile to the **Alexander Campbell Mansion**. The house dates from the 1790s when Campbell's father-in-law, a cabinet maker, built the three-story structure of hand-hewn oak timbers. Its height and real glass windows defined it as a "mansion" in its time. Notice the hand-tooled molding in the walnut-paneled parlor, where Campbell married Margaret Brown in 1811. (He bought the house from her father not long afterward.) As his family and fame increased, Campbell added a school room, dormitory, dining room, porch and the elegant "Strangers Hall," with its hand-painted French wallpaper, where he entertained James A. Garfield, Henry Clay and Jefferson Davis, among others.

Owned by the college, the mansion was reopened to the public in 1990 after extensive restoration. The rooms contain mostly original Campbell family furnishings. The fieldstone basement held the original kitchen and fireplace. Partly to escape domestic distractions, Campbell built himself a small separate study, hexagonal in shape, with a cupola. Here, a few yards from the main house, he wrote his sermons, studied for his debates, composed many of his 59 volumes and directed his printing, farming and sheep raising endeavors. Glass-enclosed bookcases still line the walls. A spring house and one-room schoolhouse also survive on the grounds.

Down the road a few steps, on a hillside, is "God's Acre," the **Campbell Cemetery**, where Campbell rests with 13 of his 14 children, many of his descendants, other leaders of his religious movement and former presidents of Bethany College. A monument of Italian marble marks the college founder's gravesite.

Admission to the Campbell Mansion is $4.00 for adults and $2.00 for students. It is open April through October, 10:00 a.m. to noon and 1:00 to 4:00 p.m. Tuesday through Saturday and 1:00 to 4:00 p.m. on Sunday. The last tour begins at 3:00 p.m. From November through March, the mansion is open by appointment only. For more information call (304)829-7285, visit their web site (www.bethanywv.edu), contact the information center by e-mail (historic@mail.bethanywv.edu) or write Historic Bethany, Bethany College, Bethany, WV 26032.

Directions: From Wheeling take Route 88 north to Route 67 east (right turn) to Bethany, less than a mile from the junction.

Chester

Mountaineer Race Track & Gaming Resort

If the thrill of live thoroughbred racing makes your blood race, you'll find it at the **Mountaineer Race Track & Gaming Resort** in Chester. This is a gaming paradise—live thoroughbred racing on mile dirt and turf tracks; simulcast racing from race tracks across the country such as Santa Anita Park, Churchill Downs and Hollywood Park; and the added fun of video gaming in the resort's Speakeasy and Hollywood Knights gaming saloons, where 1,000 machines challenge you to try your luck at video slots, blackjack, poker and keno.

After the excitement, the best bet for relaxing is in one of the resort's two outdoor pools, on the golf or tennis courses, or in the Resort Lounge (where you can indulge in more video slots, if you please). The resort's 100-room hotel and restaurants feature dining and lodging packages. For more information, call (800)804-0468 or (304)387-2400, visit their web site (www.mtrgaming.com) or write Mountaineer Race Track & Gaming Resort, PO Box 358, Chester, WV 26034.

Directions: On Route 2 just south of Chester, look for signs to the resort.

Moundsville

Grave Creek Mound Historic Site

Traders, hunters and fishers in a widespread area along the Ohio Valley from about 1,000 B.C. to 200 A.D., the Adena were the first of the "mound builders," an important group of prehistoric people from the Woodland Period. They buried their dead under large, conical mounds ranging from 20 to 300 feet in diameter. The mound at **Grave Creek Mound Historic Site**, one of two National Historic Landmark archeological sites in West Virginia, is the largest such mound in the world. Its construction required the moving of 60,000 tons of dirt—carried in baskets, without the use of wheel or horse! Originally encircled by a moat 40 feet wide and five feet deep, the mound measures 69 feet high and 295 feet in diameter at the base. It probably took 100 years (250-150 B.C.) to complete.

In 1838, excavators penetrated two chambers and found skeletons, shells, ornaments and a flat sandstone tablet inscribed with markings whose significance they still debate. Later drilling yielded stone tools and flints. Some authorities believe that people of rank were buried here; cremation was the standard burial. Today the burial site and the adjacent **Delf Norona Museum** are the nucleus of the seven-acre historic site. Plans for the future include an archaeological research and curation facility.

The walk to the top of the landscaped mound is an easy, five-minute climb, and the museum—contemporary, bright and particularly fascinating for a curious child—houses a collection of Adena tools, pipes, pottery and ornaments. Displays show how an Adena community lived and built their mounds.

The site, including a gift shop, is open year-round, Monday through Saturday, 10:00 a.m. to 4:30 p.m. and 1:00 to 5:00 p.m. on Sunday. It is closed on holidays. Access to the mound closes at 4:00 p.m. Admission is $3.00 for adults and $2.00 for children aged 6-16. Phone (304)843-4128, or write Grave Creek Mound Historic Site, Box 527, Moundsville, WV 26041.

Directions: From Wheeling, take Route 2 south to Moundsville. The address is 801 Jefferson Avenue, one block east of Route 2, between 8th and 10th streets.

Tip: If mound builders and archeology are your special interests, call ahead to make arrangements for a lecture.

Old West Virginia Penitentiary

A few years ago, "going up to Moundsville" was a phrase that could strike terror into the heart of even a hardened criminal. The **Old West Virginia Penitentiary** in Moundsville, a forbidding, neo-Gothic stone structure built in 1866, was "not a nice place to be," in the understated words of one former prison guard who now guides visitors through the damp, musty interior of the old prison. As many as 2,357 inmates lived here at one time, sometimes two or three in each five-by-seven-foot cell. The penitentiary was closed in 1995 after it was declared uninhabitable by the state's Supreme Court.

You'll begin your tour of Moundsville at the main gate, and have your "mug shot" taken before entering the prison by way of a footbridge. Inside the main hall are several exhibits, including a collection of shanks—deadly weapons crafted by inmates out of innocuous articles such as bed springs, eating utensils, combs and scissors. There's also a letter from Charles Manson, who pleaded with the warden for a transfer to Moundsville because he was homesick for the hills.

You'll see cells—some decorated with pin-up calendars and painted with psychedelic patterns—where inmates spent their lives, and "Old Sparky," the electric chair where the lives of nine inmates ended (85 others died by hanging) before West Virginia barred capital punishment in 1965. From the exercise yard, a small square surrounded by walls topped with razor wire, look up at the four gun towers, once manned by guards with high-powered rifles and the authority to shoot at their discretion.

Upon leaving, you'll probably feel a sense of lightness and relief. Knowing you don't have to spend the night in the penitentiary is worth the admission fee!

Tours are conducted on the half-hour Tuesday through Sunday, 10:00 a.m. to 5:00 p.m., and last approximately 90 minutes. Admission is $8.00 for adults, $5.00 for children under 11 and free for those under four. Discounts are available for groups of 20 or more. Call (304)845-6200 or write West Virginia State Penitentiary Tours, 818 Jefferson Avenue, Moundsville, WV 26041.

Directions: The penitentiary is across the street from Grave Creek Mound Historic Site, just off Route 2 in Moundsville. From Route 2, take either 10th or 11th Street and travel east to Jefferson Avenue.

Newell

Homer Laughlin China Company

Newell is on the Ohio River almost at the tip of West Virginia's narrow Northern Panhandle, between Ohio and Pennsylvania. Thirty-seven acres of this small town are occupied by a company that has touched the lives of most Americans, whether they know it or not; the **Homer Laughlin China Company** has produced more dinnerware than any other pottery in the United States.

Founded in 1871 by two brothers, Homer and Shakespeare Laughlin, the company prospered after winning an 1876 competition for producing chinaware that rivaled the whiteness of European potteries. More than a century later, Homer Laughlin's most collected pattern is not white, but brilliantly multi-colored. Fiesta, the richly-hued Art Deco line developed by Frederick Hurten Rhead in 1935, was produced by the company for 37 years and reintroduced, in softer pastel shades, as a regular line in 1986. Its popularity among collectors has steadily increased over the years. Collectors are always on the lookout, in flea markets and attics and Grandma's old cabinets, for an original Fiesta teacup, dinner plate or pitcher—and collectors' prices far exceed the original cost of the once-common, "everyday" dinnerware.

The company's reputation for quality and innovation remains unrivaled. It produces a myriad of patterns in more than a dozen basic shapes, and creates custom designs for more than 1,500 restaurants and hotels internationally. The Homer Laughlin China Company employs more than 1,100 people and is one of the only completely lead-free potteries in the world.

Although you won't find an overlooked, original Fiesta cup or saucer on your visit here, do look for bargains in the retail store, where many of the company's patterns are discounted. The retail outlet is open 9:30 a.m. to 5:00 p.m. Monday through Saturday and noon to 5:00 p.m. Sunday. Factory tours are conducted at 10:30 a.m. and 1:00 p.m, Monday through Friday. Groups of 10 or more should call for reservations. Be prepared to walk the half-mile tour route. For more information, call (800)452-4462, visit the company's web site (www.hlchina.com) or write Homer Laughlin China Company, Newell, WV 26050.

Directions: On Route 2 in Newell. From Ohio, take Route 11 or 7 to East Liverpool, cross the Ohio River into West Virginia on the Newell Bridge and go one mile south on Route 2. From Pennsylvania, take Route 30 west to Route 2 by way of Chester, West Virginia.

New Martinsville

Dalzell-Viking Glass

One of West Virginia's oldest and most respected glass companies, in operation since 1902, **Dalzell-Viking** specializes in hand-pressed tableware. Their wide range of dinnerware includes formal, simple patterns in rich, intense colors like ruby red and cobalt blue; dramatic gold accent pieces; frilly collectors' favorites including berry bowls and covered butter dishes; stemware in a rainbow of colors; and much more. If you love to mix and match to create elegant table settings, you'll have lots of fun in Dalzell-Viking's outlet store. And you'll find discontinued items and good quality seconds at great bargain prices.

Free factory tours are offered Monday through Friday from 9:15 a.m. to 4:00 p.m. Groups are requested to call ahead for arrangements. All tours begin at the outlet center, which is open 9:00 a.m. to 5:00 p.m. seven days a week. For more information, or to make group reservations, call (304)455-2900 or write Dalzell-Viking, PO Box 459, New Martinsville, WV 26155.

Directions: Dalzell-Viking is on Route 2 in New Martinsville. From Wheeling, take Route 2 south to New Martinsville and turn right onto Parkway at the first traffic light south of the New Martinsville bridge to Ohio. There is good signage.

Tip: How about something sweet to put on your Dalzell-Viking dinnerware? Just eight miles east of New Martinsville is **ThistleDew Farm**, one of the state's oldest commercial honey producers. Tours are available, and the gift shop has a variety of nut and honey toppings, a good-enough-to-eat-by-the-spoonful raspberry honey mustard, hand-dipped candles, beeswax skin cream and lip balm, and—of course—pure honey. After 23 years, owners Steve and Ellie Conlon are still crazy about honey, and some folks think Steve is just plain crazy—a few times a year, at fairs and festivals like the **West Virginia Honey Festival** in September [see calendar of events], he dons a buzzing beard of live bees. For more information call (304)455-1728 or (800)85-HONEY or write ThistleDew Farm, RD 1, Box 122, Proctor, WV 26055.

Directions: From Route 2 north of New Martinsville, take Route 89 (Proctor Creek Road) east eight miles to the old Grandview Schoolhouse, now ThistleDew Farm.

New Vrindaban

Prabhupada's Palace of Gold

In 1965, a 69-year-old man arrived in New York with seven dollars in his pocket and a fervent call to spread the message of the Krishna Consciousness movement in the West. Within ten years, Srila Prabhupada's movement had become a worldwide sensation, with tens of thousands of converts who built 120 temples on six continents. One of those temples waits for visitors who follow the signs from Route 250 east of Moundsville up three miles of steep farmland, past cows and mobile homes, to **Prabhupada's Palace of Gold**.

The dazzle of gold and the shapes of domes and turrets appear suddenly, as you round a curve. If you gasp in disbelief, you won't be the first to do so. Chanting voices accompany you through the gate, fountains bubble and the fragrance of a thousand roses wafts through the air.

Prabhupada's Palace was begun in 1973 by devotees at the New Vrindaban Hare Krishna community. The faithful followers of Prabhupada's teachings, many without training in construction arts, worked for six years to create this spectacular palace. Once the largest Hare Krishna community in the nation, New Vrindaban now has about 200 residents.

Tours are conducted every half hour, beginning in the palace named for the beloved guru, who died in 1977. Although he did not live to see the completion of the palace, he visited here twice and expressed his approval. As well he might: with its gold-leafed surfaces, Austrian crystal chandeliers, hand-carved Indian teak, handcrafted stained glass and 254 tons of hand-cut Italian marble and Iranian onyx, it would be a nearly incredible feat by anyone's standards.

Your tour will probably start in the west gallery. Here, light shimmers from the chandeliers (designed and made entirely by hand by a devotee with no formal training), pours through peacock-motif stained-glass windows, bounces from the mirrored ceiling and glints off polished marble floors. Each of the four radiantly blue peacock windows—the motif, associated with Lord Krishna, is repeated throughout the palace—contains 1,500 pieces of hand-shaped glass.

The tour proceeds to the gilded study, where a likeness of Prabhupada appears to be hard at work translating sacred texts from Sanskrit to English. The statue leans over a marble-topped desk near an ornately hand-carved teak altar. Walls and floor are elaborately decorated with inlaid marble, and the ceiling gleams with solid

Rising from the mountains like a mirage, the gilt turrets of Prabhupada's Palace of Gold shimmer and shine. DAVID FATTALEH

gold. As in the other rooms, large bouquets of fresh flowers stand in tall brass vases.

The apartment, with Prabhupada's bedroom, bathroom and dressing room, is similarly aglow with gold, crystal, gleaming marble and warm teak. Nearly a thousand flowers are hand-painted onto the ceiling. (One wonders how anyone could fall asleep!) The bathroom fixtures are 22-karat gold plate, and the marble sink weighs 300 pounds.

Devotees gather three times daily for kirtan chanting ceremonies in the temple. Like the famous palaces of India, Prabhupada's Palace is lavishly decorated with inlaid marble—50 varieties of marble, imported from France, Italy, Canada and the Middle East. The temple's 25-foot-high dome features 18 murals with scenes of Lord Krishna's life and a rare antique French chandelier. The centerpieces of the room are the altar and golden, jewel-studded throne upon which sits another likeness of Prabhupada—this one arrayed in richly embroidered raiments and wearing necklaces of fresh flowers, although the guru himself lived the life of an ascetic.

By the time visitors emerge from the temple, they are usually ready for a visual rest after the onslaught of glittering gold, shimmering crystal and gleaming marble. It's a good time to visit the gift shop, which features many imported items from India, or to adjourn to the **Palace Restaurant**. You can order papadam or pizza from the all-vegetarian menu, and the food is quite good.

When you're ready, explore the palace gardens and terraces. Two levels of terraces surround the palace; from them, you can see West Virginia, Ohio and Pennsylvania. Waterways hold lotuses and water lilies. In the **Garden of Time**, to the east of the palace, geraniums, marigolds, zinnias, blue salvias, dahlias and a prize-winning collection of roses reign.

A short drive leads past a swan lake to a conference center and the **Interfaith Temple of Understanding**, with its huge stained-glass ceiling, where religious ceremonies are conducted several times a day. Also nearby are a guest lodge, health food store and snack bar.

Escorted tours of Prabhupada's Palace are available April through August, 10:00 a.m. to 8:00 p.m. From September to March, hours are 10:00 a.m. to 5:00 p.m. The restaurant is open May through August, 11:00 a.m. to 9:00 p.m. daily. In September and October, the restaurant is open weekends only, though catering is available year-round. Suggested donation for the tour is $5.00 for adults, $3.00 for ages 6-18 and free for children under six. For group tour reservations call (304)843-1812 or (304)845-1207, e-mail (palaceofgold@juno.com) or write Palace of Gold, RD 1, Box 319, Moundsville, WV 26041.

Directions: From I-70, take I-470 to Bethlehem (Exit 2). Take Route 88 south eight miles to Route 250. Turn left and follow Route 250 south to Limestone (about two miles), then look for the large sign on the left. Turn left and drive four miles to the palace.

Sistersville

Midway between Wheeling and Parkersburg on Route 2 is a little town that seems to float quietly in the backwaters of the Ohio River. But **Sistersville** at the turn of the century was a rowdy boomtown of more than 13,000 with saloons, gambling casinos, hotels, an opera house and theaters that hosted vaudeville artists and New York shows.

All of that came after 1889, when oil was discovered here. Derricks sprouted up along streets, in backyards and on hillsides; meanwhile, newly rich men built an eclectic collection of homes and businesses. The oil boom ended by 1915, and Sistersville returned to its former life as a small, quiet place. What remains is a Victorian jewel of a town, a large portion of which is a National Historic District.

Stop in at the **Sistersville City Hall,** an American Colonial Revival structure built in 1897 on the diamond-shaped square that marks the center of town, and pick up a self-guided walking tour of Victorian Sistersville. (City Hall is at 200 Diamond Street, or call (304)652-6361.) You can also find the guide at several other locations in town, including the historic hotel that begins the tour.

The Wells Inn was established in 1894 and formally opened in 1895 with pomp and publicity; the *Sistersville Daily Review* called its opening banquet and ball "one of the notable events of the city" and went on to extol the hotel for its "most fashionable shades" of upholstery and carpets into which "the foot sinks." Of the salesmen's sample room, the newspaper boasted, "It is in keeping with the pale of the truth to state no handsomer room was ever furnished for the 'knights of the grip' to spread their wares before customers." With recent, million-dollar renovations, the Wells Inn is once again the grand old gal of the boomtown era; today's visitors enjoy not only the Victorian atmosphere but a 32-room, full-service hotel and conference center with a good restaurant, indoor pool, pub and bakery. Special weekend "romance packages" make the Wells Inn a popular destination for honeymoons and anniversaries. Call (304)652-1312 or write the Wells Inn, 316 Charles Street, Sistersville, WV 26175.

Many beautifully maintained turn-of-the-century homes can be found along Main Street. Special highlights include cast iron fences, turrets and lots of stained and beveled glass. Other notable stops on the walking tour include the **Little Sister Oil Well**, a monument to the the hundreds of oil wells drilled during the boom days, that comes to life during the annual **Oil and Gas Festival** [see calendar of events]; the **Townhouse Gallery**, an art center and gallery with changing exhibits in the beautifully restored Queen Anne-style home at 718 Main Street; and **Bankers' Corner**, with an anonymous human face carved into the panel above the old Union National Bank building at 629 Wells Street. The **General Store**, a friendly emporium in the old **Farmers and Producers Bank Building**, at 628 Well Street, features stained-glass windows, original tin ceilings and two full floors of West Virginia-made arts, crafts and foods.

A dollar and 15 minutes of your time will get you a round-trip ride on the only remaining ferry on the Ohio River. The **Sistersville Ferry** docks at the landing at the end of Catherine Street and operates from 7:00 a.m. to 5:00 p.m. Monday through Friday, 8:00 a.m. to 5:00 p.m. Saturday and 9:00 a.m. to 5:00 p.m. Sunday. Human passengers ride for $0.50 and the charge for a car (maximum four cars per trip) is $2.00. There's no regular schedule; the ferry operator keeps an eye out for passengers on the landing. Even if you have no burning desire to cross the Ohio to Fry, the five-minute trip in the small, cheery, red-trimmed paddleboat is worth the price.

Directions: On Route 2 about midway between Parkersburg and Wheeling. Sistersville is also accessible from Ohio Route 7 by crossing the bridge to Route 2 at New Martinsville, or in Fry, Ohio by way of the Sistersville Ferry.

Wellsburg

Brooke Glass Company

No fewer than five glass companies operated in Wellsburg during its heyday, the first dating from 1814. **Brooke Glass Company**, the only remaining one, occupies a site that has been a glass manufacturing plant since 1879. Three generations of the Rithner family have owned the company.

This small, hand-operated factory does not produce one-of-a-kind art pieces or crystal stemware, but specializes in lamp and lighting fixture parts, hand-painted lamps and giftware. The company is also a source for tailor-made orders, such as matching antique pieces, and is known for its colored glass in over 20 different shades.

The educational tour explains the composition of glass (70 percent sand, 20 percent soda ash and the rest chemicals that determine color) as well as how the molten material is press-blown, cooled, shaped into cast-iron molds and decorated, etched or painted. Each piece is inspected for flaws after it cools. For the frosted look we see on some light shades, pieces are dipped by hand into an acid bath. In another room, you'll watch skilled artists paint designs on the glass by hand.

Twice-daily tours begin at the gift shop, where many of the company's wares are offered for sale, and are conducted at 10:00 a.m. and 2:00 p.m. Monday through Friday, except for major holidays and the plant's two-week vacation period beginning July 1. (However, you may take a video tour during those weeks.) Gift shop hours are 9:30 a.m. to 5:00 p.m. Monday through Saturday. Visitors under the age of 15 are not allowed on the tour unless accompanied by an adult. Groups of school-age children are not permitted.

Directions: Located at 6th and Yankee streets. From Wheeling, take Route 2 north about 16 miles to downtown Wellsburg and follow Route 2 to 6th Street. Brooke Glass Company is across the street from a gas station.

Wheeling

Wheeling is a town with something for everyone, and you'll probably find that one day isn't nearly enough time to get the "Wheeling feeling," a heady blend of history, science, arts, outdoor recreation, great music, great food and great shopping. Don't waste a moment—begin at the **Wheeling Convention and Visitors Bureau** at the corner of 14th and Main streets, just across the street from the Wheeling Artisan Center and next to the Civic Center, to pick up maps and information about the city, or call (800)828-3097 or (304)233-7709.

Capitol Music Hall

Country music fans know Wheeling as the home of ***Jamboree USA***, the second-oldest country music radio program (next to the *Grand Old Opry*) and one of America's oldest live radio broadcasts. You can be part of the live show at **Capitol Music Hall**. West Virginia's oldest and largest theater, it was built in 1928 and is a classic example of the opulence and grandeur of early theaters. With its rich brocade and red velvet decor, it's reminiscent of the Paris Opera House. Stars such as Tanya Tucker, Willie Nelson, Alan Jackson and Lorrie Morgan perform here on Saturday nights, in a tradition dating back to 1933. On other nights, the theater is the venue for Broadway touring musicals—*Cats* and *Phantom of the Opera* are a couple of the most recent—as well as comedy and beloved entertainers like Bobby Vinton and Englebert Humperdinck.

Capitol Music Hall is also home to the **Wheeling Symphony** and several other music and dance groups. Recently, the theater has made extensive upgrades to lighting and stereo equipment and added two 10-foot projection screens for larger-than-life viewing. Fans and stars alike love its warmth, beauty and fine acoustics.

Box office hours are 9:00 a.m. to 5:00 p.m. Monday through Friday and 9:00 a.m. to 9:00 p.m. Saturday. For information about upcoming concerts and events, call (800)624-5456 or (304)234-0050, visit their web site (www.jamboreeusa.com) or write Capitol Music Hall, 1015 Main Street, Wheeling, WV 26003.

Directions: From I-70, take Exit 1A to downtown Wheeling. Go through two lights, and you'll see the music hall on your right.

Centre Market

In the late 19th century, every major city had a market house, the bustling center of commerce and community. Wheeling was no exception—and in Wheeling, the old-time market is still vibrant and active. **Centre Market** really includes two historic market houses, the 1853 Upper Market House and the Lower Market House, built in Wheeling's Victorian prime in 1890.

The **Upper Market** is the only cast-iron columned market—hollow Roman Doric columns cast in Wheeling—in the country, with every other column innovatively designed to do double-duty as a downspout for the roof. This market house, originally open but enclosed in 1886, has been in continuous operation since the 19th century.

The **Lower Market House**, a Romanesque brick structure, has central brick arches adorned with four carved stone medallions depicting different animal heads—bull, ram, stallion and boar. Flanking the two market houses are historic commercial buildings, many of which, along with the Market itself, are listed on the National Register of Historic Places.

Centre Market is a fun place to browse. You'll find antiques and collectibles, handmade jewelry and crafts. When you get hungry, stop in the old-fashioned ice cream parlor, order the fish market's world-famous fish sandwich or choose from ethnic foods that reflect Wheeling's melting-pot culture.

Hours are 10:00 a.m. to 6:00 p.m. Monday through Thursday, 10:00 a.m. to 7:00 p.m. Friday and 10:00 a.m. to 6:00 p.m. Saturday, with extended holiday hours. There's plenty of convenient parking at Centre Market Parking Garage. For more information call (304)234-3878 or write Centre Market Commission, PO Box 6888, Wheeling, WV 26003.

Directions: On Market Street between 20th and 22nd Street. From I-70 eastbound, take Exit 1A, go south on Main Street to 22nd Street. Turn left and look for the market one block ahead, on right. (Parking is on left.) From I-70 westbound, merge into right lane before the Wheeling Tunnel and take Exit 1A immediately after the tunnel. Turn left on Main Street. Follow above directions from Main Street.

Challenger Learning Center

On the campus of **Wheeling Jesuit University** is a space-age learning facility that can take you for a ride you won't forget. One of a growing national network of centers established in memory of the Challenger Space Shuttle, the **Challenger Learning Center** is an exciting, hands-on way for children and adults to sharpen their math, science and teamwork skills. Part of the university's **NASA Classroom of the Future**, the Challenger Learning Center bridges the gap between NASA scientists and students as young as five.

The center sponsors day, evening, weekend and summer-camp programs, and also coordinates special events such as an interactive video conference between students and NASA scientists during the *Mars Pathfinder* mission. But the most popular offering is a simulated space mission in which visitors take part in a space flight so realistic that they often forget they're really on earth in Wheeling.

Inside the bright, modern **Erma Ora Byrd Center for Educational Technologies**, the mission begins with a pre-flight orientation. Each person is assigned to a team—the communication team, medical team, probe team or one of several others, including a mission control team that monitors the flight. Flight members wear special vests and enter the space station by way of a revolving airlock door. Inside, the crew is in constant communication with mission control by audio, video and computer links. The teams work together, each performing specific scientific tasks, to bring their flight to a successful conclusion.

The Challenger Center is oriented toward group visits, which must be prearranged. Missions can be arranged for school groups, youth groups, clubs, corporate groups and the general public. They generally last between two and four hours, but some hour-long mini-missions are scheduled.

Mini-missions and student missions cost $10.00 to $15.00 per person, depending upon the length of the flight. For more information about corporate rates, or to schedule a mission, call (304)243-4325 or write Challenger Learning Center, Wheeling Jesuit University, 316 Washington Avenue, Wheeling, WV 26003-9908. You can find out more about the Classroom of the Future by visiting their web site (www.cotf.edu).

Directions: From I-70, take Exit 2B in Wheeling. Go north on Washington Avenue for about half a block. Wheeling Jesuit University is on the left, and the Challenger Learning Center is the first building on the left.

Oglebay Resort and Conference Center

Governed by the Wheeling Park Commission, **Oglebay Resort and**

Conference Center is likely the largest tourist attraction in West Virginia, drawing well over three million visitors from all 50 states and many other countries. Oglebay is for lovers of nature and animals, gardens and golf, history and shopping.

The park complex evolved from the 750-acre Waddington Farm, the elegant summer estate of industrialist Colonel Earl Oglebay, who bequeathed it to Wheeling in 1926 for "as long as the people shall operate it for purposes of public recreation and educations." It is the only major self-sustaining public park system in America.

Oglebay's 1,650 acres comprise what must be one of the most meticulously groomed public parks anywhere, a zoo, mansion, three golf courses, garden center, greenhouse, nature center, outdoor amphitheater, 217-room lodge, 50 cottages and seven specialty shops. Visitors can also enjoy tennis, swimming, fishing and boating. The park is home to several annual festivals, including one of the most extravagant holiday light shows in the country.

It's impossible to fully explore Oglebay in a single day, but you can make a good start. The best way to get the lay of the land is to pick up the park's handsome, helpful map and walking guide, "The Walks of Oglebay," at Wilson Lodge.

Mansion Museum

The centerpiece of Colonel Oglebay's large farm, this 1846 neoclassical mansion perched on a hill where summer breezes wafted through enormous rooms. It gave him a magnificent outlook from which to enjoy his gardens and orchards, including trial plots where he experimented with pioneering agricultural techniques.

Now a museum, the mansion has eight period rooms furnished with antiques, Oriental carpets, family portraits, glass and china collections. A Victorian parlor represents the 1860s. The Federal-style bedroom reflects the early 1800s. The replicated frontier kitchen with spartan furniture, its table set with pewter utensils, contrasts with the sharply elegant Hepplewhite dining room (1790-1810) with its glittering crystal and china. In the Waddington Room is a priceless silver service, which took two years to craft, with decorations depicting scenes of homes and places of worship.

A new wing, added through the generosity of the late Oglebay grandson Courtney Burton, provides a gallery for changing exhibits. Outside the mansion, a series of excellent interpretive displays details Colonel Oglebay's life and times.

The mansion museum is open 10:00 a.m. to 5:00 p.m. Monday through Saturday and noon to 5:00 p.m. Sunday during spring and fall seasons. There are extended hours during the winter holidays, and the museum is open weekends only, or by appointment, from January 5 through March 26. Closed during summer and on major holidays. Admission is $4.25 for adults and $2.00 for students (13-18). Children 12 and under are free with an adult.

Waddington Gardens and Oglebay Shops

Oglebay's **Waddington Gardens** are beautiful to behold in several seasons. The formal gardens, a re-creation of the ones that existed at the turn of the century, burst to life in spring with tulips, daffodils and flowering trees. Summer brings a bright parade of annual flowers, and from October through early November the gardens glow with the tawny beauty of chrysanthemums. Soft landscape lighting, stately pergolas and water displays add to the experience.

Within the gardens are several of Oglebay's shops. The **Garden Center Gift Shop** is filled with flower-arranging accessories as well as gifts made of natural materials, and the **Palm Room** offers seasonal plants, herbs and hanging baskets. **Christmas in the Gardens** is a year-round shop full of holiday items, including the unique and hard-to-find.

Nearby is **Carriage House Glass**, designed after an historic structure that was destroyed by fire half a century ago. The gem of Oglebay's specialty shops, it features the area's largest selection of West Virginia decorative glass plus exclusive items produced while you watch. One level of the building houses Oglebay's **Glass Museum**, which includes an audio tour on the history of glass-making in the area. Here you can see one-of-a-kind masterpieces like the Sweeney punch bowl, reportedly the largest piece of cut glass ever made, capable of holding 21 gallons of punch! Admission to the museum is $2.00 for adults, $1.00 for students aged 13–17, and free for children 12 and under with an adult. Entrance to the retail level is free. For more information call (304)243-4000.

You can pick up your very own Oglebay logo sweatshirt at the **Resort Shop**, located in Oglebay's **Wilson Lodge**, or visit the **Speidel Pro Shop** in the **Hamm Club House** at the Speidel championship golf course.

When the weather is warm, you can rent a boat, pack a picnic and feed the ducks on Schenk Lake, or watch the lakeside goings-on from a table in the Ihlenfeld Dining Room in Wilson Lodge. On summer nights, the many-windowed dining room is a good place from which to view the **Cascading Waters** on Schenk Lake, or you can walk the path around the lake to get other perspectives on the

Llamas are among the animals children can pet at the Good Zoo at Oglebay. COURTESY GOOD ZOO

free, multi-colored light show playing against the country's tallest free-flowing fountain, where water and light mingle in an undulating "dance" to a medley of computer-programmed musical selections. Half-hour shows begin at 6:30, 8:00 and 9:00 p.m.

Good Zoo

The zoo was a gift from the Good family in memory of their son Philip, and although the activities are designed specifically with children in mind, it's a wonderful place for adult animal lovers as well. Open since 1977, the 65-acre natural habitat for North American animals and endangered species is the only accredited zoo in West Virginia. An ocelot, red pandas, tamarins and red wolves are residents as part of the Species Survival Plan.

You can take a paved, easy walk (less than a mile) around and past the animal exhibits or, if the weather's uncooperative, ride the C.P Huntington train ($1.25) for a mile-and-a-half tour. Youngsters love the petting zoo, where goats and llamas wait for gentle touches from little hands. Children of all ages will enjoy the desert display with roadrunners and burrowing owls, the 3000-gallon fish tank and an exhibit of playful otters. There's a hands-on **Discovery Lab**, a miniature village capped by an O-gauge model train display and changing programs at the **Benedum Science Theater and Planetarium**. Special events like summer camp activities, laser shows and spooky Halloween rides are scheduled throughout the year. No food may be brought into the zoo.

The Good Zoo is open year-round, seven days a week. Summer weekdays 10:00 a.m. to 6:00 p.m., winter weekdays 11:00 a.m. to 5:00 p.m. Weekends, 10:00 a.m. to 7:00 p.m. Admission is $4.50 for adults and $3.50 for children aged 2-17. Group rates available. Rental strollers are available for very young children. For more information, call (304)243-4030.

Festival of Lights

From early November through February, Oglebay is a multi-colored riot of lights as part of the city-wide Festival of Lights. More than half a million lights encircle and glitter from 300 acres of trees, lake, roads and pathways. Those lights shine in the eyes of more than a million visitors every year. Huge scaffolds support holiday-theme outlines that wink, blink and twinkle—some, like the animated Jack-in-the-box, even jump up and wave to admirers.

Directions: About a ten-minute drive from downtown Wheeling. From I-70, take the Oglebay exit and follow Route 88 north for about 2 1/2 miles. Follow the signs. For information or reservations call (800)624-6988 or (304)243-4000 or write Oglebay, Wheeling, WV 26003.

Tip: Weekend traffic is heavy during winter holidays. If you hate crowds, opt for a weekday visit at this time of year.

Stifel Fine Arts Center

Located four miles from the park but part of the Oglebay Institute, the **Stifel Fine Arts Center** sponsors changing art exhibits as well as instruction in arts, crafts, music and dance. The 30-room mansion, named Edemar in honor of the Stifel children (EDward, EMily and MARy), was a gift from the civic-minded William E. Stifel family. Johann Stifel, a skilled fabric dyer, began his business in a log cabin in 1837 and built it into one of the largest producers of calico in the United States. The calico works operated in Wheeling until 1957.

Note the stained-glass window at the top of the grand staircase, which depicts the family's ancestral Bavarian castle, and the walnut paneling in the huge downstairs living and dining rooms. The library holds a permanent exhibit on the calico business, as well as portraits of the original owners. Studios, offices and a gallery space upstairs have replaced former bedrooms. Outside, enjoy the gardens and wide, gracious lawn.

Stifel Fine Arts Center is open 9:00 a.m. to 5:00 p.m. Monday through Saturday and 12:30 to 5:00 p.m. Sunday. Suggested donation is $1.00, and guided tours of the mansion are available for $3.00. For information about upcoming exhibits call (304)242-7700.

Directions: 1330 National Road, one mile from I-70. Take Exit 2B.

Victorian Wheeling Landmark Tours

Nineteenth-century Wheeling was a transportation hub, the Gateway to the West. As the last "civilized" stop for adventurers heading westward or south on the Ohio River, it was considered a "little New York"—a melting pot of ethnic diversity, industry and cultural activity. Thanks to all the travelers, Wheeling merchants prospered and built mansions near their factories along the river. And thanks to the talents of newly arrived, skilled immigrants, those homes were unsurpassed in craftsmanship and originality.

Most of the materials were made in Wheeling—the stained glass, brick, stone, tile, wood, chandeliers and even the nails. Built in an era when the homes of the affluent were considered works of art, each house was a one-of-a-kind tribute to its owner's fine taste and fabulous wealth. Because the houses were built in long, narrow lots along the river, their exteriors were understated, but inside they were bejeweled and embellished with no expense spared. Tiffany glass, bird's-eye maple and mahogany trim, marble mantels, ornamentally tiled fireplaces, filigrees of cast iron, lacy wooden screens

An innovative building for its day (1859), the Wheeling Customs House, now Independence Hall, was the scene of many political debates that led to statehood for the "Child of the Storm."

MICHAEL KELLER, WV DIVISION OF CULTURE & HISTORY

and elaborate inlaid floors were not uncommon. Between the years of 1837 and 1905 more than 600 houses were built here representing all stages of Victorian architecture.

Fortunately, some have survived intact and others are being

restored. Today, a few Victorian homes in the North Wheeling Historic District are among the city's most popular attractions. You'll feel that you've stepped back a century when you meet your docent—who wears a period costume including bonnet and parasol—for a stroll though Victorian Wheeling. Guides are well-informed about the history and highlights of each home on the tour, which begins at the **Eckhart House**, 810 Main Street.

You'll tour the **Hazlett-Fields** Richardson Romanesque-style house at 823 Main Street and its sister house next-door. Built for Jesse and John List by their father, they are masterpieces of fine woodwork, art glass and hand-wrought iron. The tour proceeds to the French Renaissance-style **Christian Hess House** at 811 Main Street, built in 1876; the 1885 **Holiday-Schaefer House** at 2307 Chapline Street, with its fabulous mixture of fretwork and woods, including maple, oak and beech; and the **L.S. Good House**, the first in Wheeling to acquire indoor plumbing, with its ingeniously built-in furniture, 22 Beaux Arts stained-glass windows, baronial mantels and mirrors.

Tours last about two hours and cost $12.00 per person. Buy tickets at the Eckhart House Gift Shop at 810 Main Street. To protect the wooden floors in the mansions, high heels are not allowed on this tour. Group rates are available for 20 or more. Tours begin at 10:00 a.m. and 1:00 p.m. Thursday through Sunday, from May through December. You can also indulge in an elegant high tea if you call at least four days in advance. For more information, call (304)233-1600 or (800)SEE-1870 or write Victorian Wheeling Landmark Foundation, PO Box 666, Wheeling, WV 26003.

Directions: From I-70 westbound, enter the right lane east of the Wheeling Tunnel. After the tunnel, exit in the right lane and turn right. You'll find 810 in the first block on your right. Watch for the Eckhart House sign. From I-70 eastbound, cross the Ohio River and pass through the Wheeling Tunnel, then take the Oglebay exit (2A) and immediately re-enter I-70 west, going back through the tunnel; then follow directions for I-70 west.

West Virginia Independence Hall

West Virginia was the only state to be created as a result of the Civil War. President Lincoln issued the proclamation approving the new state in April 1863, and West Virginia officially joined the Union on June 20, 1863.

Completed shortly before the Civil War as a customs collection house for Wheeling, a port of delivery since 1831, **West Virginia**

Independence Hall also provided postal services and served as the district court for the Western District of Virginia. It was soon to be the setting for far more unordinary events.

Step into the restored third-floor courtroom, and you can almost hear the oratory ringing. If it seems to you that the formal, dignified room has a lingering aura of important historic events, you're not mistaken. This room held the heated political discussions and constitutional conventions that led to statehood for West Virginia in 1863. Wheeling was the capital of the Restored Government of Virginia, which the Union recognized during the Civil War, and it was here, between 1861 and 1863, that the debates over taxation, boundaries, representation and emancipation were conducted in sessions of the Legislature and Constitutional Conventions. Some second-floor rooms were assigned as offices for the governor, lieutenant governor, auditor, treasurer and other state officials.

The new government moved to other quarters and eventually to Charleston, and this building passed into private hands. In 1964, the state purchased the structure and began to renovate it to its original appearance. Maintained by the Division of Culture and History, West Virginia Independence Hall offers special exhibits and programs focused on the state's history.

The three-story, hand-cut sandstone building is worth attention not only for its history, but for its architectural and engineering significance. Architect Ammi B. Young chose a balanced and stately Italianate Renaissance Revival design. Wrought iron "I" beams and box girders, along with cast iron columns, created an internal skeletal structure that was the precursor of the modern-day skyscraper's. The innovative building incorporated gas lighting and a convection current system for air circulation—and flushing toilets, the first in Wheeling.

Begin your visit on the lower level with the award-winning 20-minute film *For Liberty and Union,* which dramatizes the struggle for statehood during the Civil War. Be sure to look at the exhibit photos of Wheeling during its Victorian prime. Then explore the upper floors' changing exhibits and restored period rooms that interpret the beginnings of the Mountain State. In the courtroom, notice the original *trompe l'oeil* fresco, oak columns, iron shutters and mahogany benches and desks. Throughout the building, you'll marvel at massive 13-foot wooden doors and 20-foot ceilings. If you want, you can listen to an audio tour of the building and its history as you stroll through.

Mrs. Busbey Tours, a dramatic way of introducing history to groups of any age, appeal especially to young visitors. A living-history tour guide portrays Elizabeth Busbey, a colorful 19th-century character who was mother to a large family and wife to the proprietor of a carriage/wagon company once housed next to the hall. Beginning with a monologue scripted from Wheeling newspapers during 1862-63, she leads guests into a lively, interactive narrative of Wheeling daily life during the war.

Admission to West Virginia Independence Hall is $3.00 for adults and $2.00 for students. Tours with Mrs. Busbey require a minimum of ten persons at a cost of $3.00 per person; call (304)238-1300 to make reservations. The hall is open 10:00 a.m. to 4:00 p.m. seven days a week, except for Sundays in January and February and all state holidays. For more information call (304)238-1300 or write West Virginia Independence Hall, 1528 Market Street, Wheeling, WV 26003.

Directions: On the corner of 16th and Market streets. From I-70, take Exit 1A south on Main Street to 16th. Parking is available in back.

Tip: Combining this tour, which takes about an hour, with the two-hour **Victorian Wheeling Landmark Tour** will recreate the era from the 1850s through the turn of the century.

Wheeling Artisan Center

From the handcrafted door pulls by local artist Jeff Forster to the massive skylight that floods three open, airy floors with sunlight, the new Wheeling Artisan Center reflects a commitment to craftsmanship. It houses West Virginia's largest brew pub, a stunning collection of West Virginia crafts and a charming general store museum, along with gallery, festival and conference spaces.

First-time visitors should ascend the wide staircase to the second floor, where you'll walk into an engaging interactive exhibit about Wheeling's industrial history. The **"Wheeling Wheel of Industry"** is a self-guided tour: you take a "time card" and punch in at various stations, where historical characters including Mary Potter, Johann Stifel and Elizabeth Hess Beck represent Wheeling industries including tobacco, textiles and brewing.

After the self-guided tour you'll be a lot wiser about Wheeling, but don't miss the **Emporium** crafts shop or the delightful **Wymer's General Store Museum**, where you'll see, among hundreds of other curious objects, a collection of salesman's samples including miniature sewing machines, wringer washers, stoves and fiddles. (There is a $3.00 admission fee for the General Store Museum only.)

Then come back downstairs for steak, seafood, gourmet salads or a sampler of **Nail City Brewing Company's** six beers, brewed on-site in huge, gleaming vats.

The Wheeling Artisan Center is open 11:00 a.m. to 7:00 p.m. Monday through Thursday, 11:00 a.m. to 9:00 p.m. Friday and Saturday, and noon to 5:00 p.m. Sunday, with extended holiday hours. Call (304)232-1810 or write Wheeling Artisan Center, 1400 Main Street, Wheeling, WV 26003. For more information about the brewery or catering, call (304)233-5330.

Directions: From I-70, take Exit 1A and follow Main Street to 14th Street.

Wheeling Suspension Bridge

Before you leave Wheeling, take time to drive or walk across a National Historic Landmark. The **Wheeling Suspension Bridge**, also designated a National Civil Engineering Landmark, was completed in 1849. This was literally the gateway to the west for travelers on The National Road. It will take you to **Wheeling Island**, which itself includes one of several historic districts in the city.

This was originally a toll bridge; it cost $0.10 for a man and horse, $1.25 for a four-horse mail coach, and $0.02 per head for hogs and sheep. Now it's a free ride, and at night the towers, deck and cables are decoratively lit.

Directions: From I-70, take Exit 1A and go south a few blocks to 10th and Main Street. Turn right to go over the bridge.

Tip: If you're feeling lucky, stay on the island and look for treasure at **Wheeling Downs**. The racetrack and gaming center features live greyhound racing six days a week, off-track betting and video slot machines. Open seven days a week. For more information, call (800)445-9475 or (304) 232-5050, visit their web site (www.wheelingdowns.com) or write Wheeling Downs, 1 South Stone Street, Wheeling, WV 26003.

Directions: From I-70, take Exit 0 (Wheeling Island) and follow signs to Wheeling Downs.

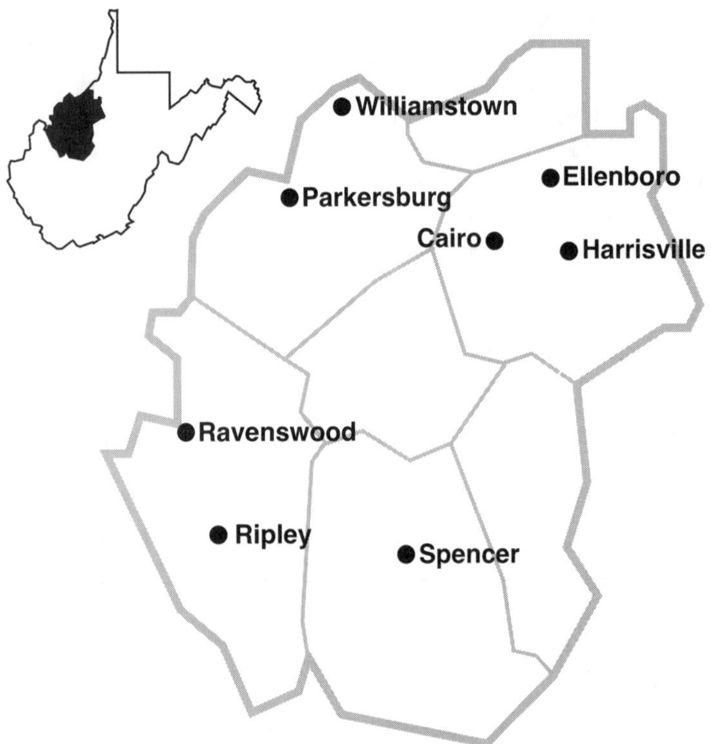

CAIRO
- R.C. Marshall Hardware Company
- North Bend State Park and Rail Trail

ELLENBORO
- Glass Factories

HARRISVILLE
- Berdine's Variety Store

PARKERSBURG
- Blennerhassett Island Historical State Park
  - The Blennerhassetts
  - Blennerhassett Island
  - Blennerhassett Mansion
  - Blennerhassett Museum
- Blennerhassett Hotel
- Cook House
- The Cultural Center of Fine Arts
- Henry Cooper Log House Museum
- Little Kanawha Crafthouse
- Ohio River Islands Natl Wildlife Refuge
- Oil and Gas Museum
- Smoot Theatre
- Sumner School Museum
- Trans Allegheny Books

RAVENSWOOD/RIPLEY
- Washington's Western Lands Museum
- Cedar Lakes Conference Center

SPENCER
- Charles Fork Lake

WILLIAMSTOWN
- Fenton Art Glass Factory & Museum
- Henderson Hall

Mid-Ohio Valley

According to archeologists, the green and fertile Mid-Ohio Valley has harbored humankind for over 11,000 years. Today's visitors can enjoy not only the landscape and climate that attracted all those prehistoric generations, but the rich tapestry of the region's more recent history. There are oil-boom stories of fortunes found and lost, a mansion filled with remembrances of antebellum plantation life and a moving tribute to early African-American educators. There's a five-and-dime from Victorian days and a turn-of-the-century hardware store where your great-grandfather would have felt at home. There's a vaudeville theater where the glamour and gaiety of the Roaring Twenties lives on. To top it all, you can visit the island retreat where one of America's most romantic and tragic love stories was lived out.

Much of the Mid-Ohio Valley's social life is centered in Parkersburg, a civic-minded city that is justifiably proud of its museums, restorations and diverse cultural life. Here as in every part of West Virginia, nature is always nearby: in a wetland wildlife refuge that now includes nearly a score of Ohio River islands, on a rail trail that spans the region, in a warm and welcoming state park.

Explore and discover. Tucked away among the hills and hollows throughout the region, you'll find pleasant parks, historic treasures and fine handcrafts. Watch herons in a protected habitat. Enjoy a splendid meal in a luxurious hotel where oil barons supped a century ago. Circle a pretty lake on a mountain bike. Learn how skilled glassblowers create sparkling crystal vases and goblets by watching them as they work. Let past and present blend into the perfect vacation in the green and gracious Mid-Ohio Valley.

For more information on visiting the Mid-Ohio Valley contact:

Jackson County Chamber of Commerce, PO Box 265, Ravenswood, WV 26164. Call (304)273-5367.

Ripley Area Chamber of Commerce, PO Box 282, Ripley, WV 25271.

Roane County Chamber of Commerce, PO Box 1, Spencer, WV

A game of checkers and a sip of sarsaparilla round out a visit to old-timey R.C. Marshall Hardware Company

COURTESY R.C. MARSHALL HARDWARE COMPANY.

acres, one side of the park bordered by the horseshoe-shaped "north bend" of the North Fork of Hughes River. As an overnight lodging, it features plenty of comfortable choices: a modern 29-room lodge overlooking the river valley, eight fully-equipped deluxe cottages and 78 campsites, each with its own grill and picnic table. The lodge, with its glass-enclosed restaurant, craft-filled gift shop and enormous sitting room—where the huge fireplace is always full of crackling logs in cold weather—is surely one of the most welcoming places in West Virginia.

North Bend's year-round recreation program includes activities for the whole family. Day visitors can play tennis, volleyball or miniature golf and use the large swimming pool at a nominal cost; picnicking, hiking and fishing (with proper licenses) are free. The park's **Extra Mile Trail** is a paved, accessible hiking trail with interpretive nature signage in print and in braille. Other trails take walkers through peaceful forest areas, along the riverbank and to interesting rock formations. In addition, the park sponsors quite a few special events, including a **Winter Wonder Weekend**, **Outdoor Adventure Weekend**, **Spring Nature Tour** and a **Mountain Bike Weekend** [see calendar of events].

The state park is also one of the major trail access points for the **North Bend Rail Trail**, stretching 72 miles from Parkersburg to Wolf Summit. It was created from an abandoned rail corridor originally constructed by the Baltimore and Ohio Railroad between 1853 and 1857. Traveling east and west, through ten tunnels and across 37 bridges, the trail passes through scenic and natural areas, farmland and a number of small communities whose history is very much bound to the railroad. Points of interest include a former stage coach inn, marble and glass factories, outlet stores, arts and crafts stores, sites of train robberies and tunnels with legends of ghosts.

The North Bend Rail Trail is an excellent way for hikers, bikers and horseback riders to explore the Mid-Ohio Valley and parts of Mountaineer Country. If you're not up to the whole 72 miles, go as far as you please. And if 72 miles isn't enough for you, keep in mind that this trail is just part of the 5,500-mile coast-to-coast **American Discovery Trail**.

The lodge and cabins at North Bend State Park are open year-round. Campgrounds are open from mid-April through November. Park hours are dawn to 10:00 p.m., but the office in the lodge is open 24 hours a day. For more information about the park or the North Bend Rail Trail, call (304)643-2931 or (800)CALL-WVA. You may also visit their web site (wvweb.com/www/NORTH_BEND.html) or write North Bend State Park, Route 1, Box 221, Cairo, WV 26337.

Directions: From Parkersburg take Route 50 east to Route 31, about 20 miles. Follow to Cairo and then follow signs to park.

Ellenboro

Glass Factories

Tiny **Ellenboro** is a fun place for glass lovers. Three small factories operate here, all within shouting distance of one another and each with its own specialties.

Chris A. Smith is the owner and chief designer at **C.A.S. Art Glass**, a company that devotes itself almost exclusively to handmade Christmas ornaments. Widely varied in color and shape, these artworks elicit smiles and expressions of pleasure when visitors walk in the small showroom—and the swirling or mosaic-like patterns really are too pretty to reserve for holidays. The company also carries large, decorative glass balls. The showroom/gift shop is generally open 10:00 a.m. to 4:00 p.m. Monday, Wednesday and Friday, and you may catch Chris or a helper there at other times as well.

Known for its colorful marbles and small hand-blown items like bells, vases and wine glasses, **Mid-Atlantic of West Virginia, Inc.** is a good place to watch skilled craftsmen blow glass the way it has been done for centuries. Although there is no tour guide to lead you step-by-step through the process, visitors are welcome to stand inside the door of the glass plant—a steamy place in summer, to be sure!—and watch as the glass is heated to a red-hot, molten state and manipulated by artisans who work together in a rhythm that seems choreographed. The company's marble and gem plant is not open to visitors, but marbles and other items are sold at the outlet shop directly behind the marble-making building. Mid-Atlantic is open 9:30 a.m. to noon and 12:30 to 5:00 p.m. Monday through Friday, except for major holidays; the outlet store is also open 9:00 a.m. to 2:00 p.m. Saturdays. If you want to make sure you'll see glass-blowers in action, it's best to call (304)869-3351 or write Mid-Atlantic of West Virginia, Inc., PO Box 279, Ellenboro, WV 26346. (Tour groups must call ahead.)

One specialty at **West Virginia Glass Specialties, Inc.** is the decoration and assembly of the company's own Victorian lamp design. The lamp pieces are glazed and fired in a variety of colors—amber, green, red, blue, purple, pink and a pearly, iridescent shade—then decorated with decals or hand-cutting. Assembled and wired, the 15-inch-tall lamps are favorite items at the gift shop. Although you will not see glass-blowing at this factory, you are welcome to watch the skilled cutter if she is in. West Virginia Glass Specialties does custom monogramming with advance notice. The gift shop is open 8:00 a.m. to 4:00 p.m. Monday through Friday and 9:00 a.m. to

4:00 p.m. Saturday. Call (304)869-3374 or write West Virginia Glass Specialties, PO Box 248, Ellenboro, WV 26346.

Directions: From Parkersburg, take Route 50 east about 30 miles to the Ellenboro exit. Go north (left). West Virginia Glass Specialties is on the right immediately after you go under the North Bend Rail Trail bridge. Continue a short distance to the fork in the road, and you'll see C.A.S. Art Glass directly ahead. At the fork, bear right and drive about three-fourths mile on Old Route 50 to Mid-Atlantic of West Virginia.

Harrisville

Berdine's Variety Store

Ninety years ago, two orphaned brothers named Kit Carson Berdine and Lafayette Marcus Hunt (the younger having taken the surname of his foster family) chose bustling Harrisville as the location for their new five-and-dime store. K.C. and Lafayette are gone, and nobody would argue that Harrisville is anything but a pleasant, small, quiet town—but **Berdine's Variety Store** is as busy as ever, catering to locals and visitors from every state and several foreign countries.

A look in the window will tell you why. Where else would a window display include Teddy bears, bird feeders, glassware, clocks, kitchenware, seeds, Rosebud Salve, thread and a nose flute? Step inside. If you're over 50, you'll be transported to the days of fifteen-cent movies and penny candy, when the local five-and-dime was the Victorian equivalent of today's department store. If you're under 12, you'll be able to choose all the penny candy you can eat from an antique glass-fronted confection counter—and still have some of your allowance left for a lightning bug lantern, a sling shot or a bag of marbles. And if you're somewhere in between, you're sure to find a few treasures—from glassware to books to antique porcelain dolls—you can't live without. Berdine's staggering stock ranges from the frivolously fun to the solidly functional. If you can't find something, ask. "We probably have it somewhere, if we can find it," says proprietor Dean Six.

Berdine's interior is half the fun. Its pressed tin ceiling is in excellent condition. Original oak shelves and counters line the walls. An old ceiling fan spins lazily. Vintage light fixtures cast a warm glow on original oak floors. Sections of the store are devoted to history, Christmas trimmings, housewares and collectibles. The proprietor's special interest is glass (he has written several books on the subject), and he has assembled a wonderful collection of antique and fine reproduction glassware, along with many made-in-West-Virginia handcrafts.

The store is open 9:00 a.m. to 5:00 p.m. every day except Sunday. For more information call (304)643-2217 or write Berdine's Variety Store, 106 Court Street, Harrisville, WV 26362.

Directions: From Route 50 take Route 16 south to Harrisville. As you pass through the downtown area turn right onto Court Street (NAPA store on corner). Berdine's is at #106.

Tip: Combine a visit to Berdine's with an outing to North Bend State Park a few miles away [see entry].

Parkersburg

If it seems that most tourist attractions in the Mid-Ohio Valley center around the city of **Parkersburg**, there's a good reason: it's an endlessly fascinating town to explore. Even without knowing about its rich history, a first-time visitor can sense that Parkersburg residents take pride in their town, as evidenced by the number of museums, historical sites and cultural facilities. Despite a century and a half of commercial development, the city at the junction of the Ohio and Little Kanawha rivers remains an undeniably pretty place. Given the placid setting, it's hard to imagine the enormous tolls flooding took on Parkersburg and its citizens until the late 1940s, when a huge floodwall was constructed.

Home to Native Americans for thousands of years, the area was first visited by European explorers in the mid-1600s. By 1800 it was a log-cabin town and in 1810 it was named. When oil was discovered, the town's economy exploded and continued to thrive, after the disruption of the Civil War, well into the 1900s. Oil and gas fortunes built some of the Victorian mansions on the town's walking tour.

Begin your visit at the **Parkersburg/Wood County Convention and Visitors Bureau** at 350 Seventh Street. Open 8:30 a.m. to 4:30 p.m. Monday through Friday, this friendly visitors center is well-stocked with brochures, up-to-date information, suggestions for driving tours and a 36-site Historical Walking Tour map. Call (800)752-4982 or (304)428-1130 or visit their web site (wvweb.com/parkersburg). Many of the walking-tour sites, like the Victorian homes in the **Julia-Ann Historic District**, are not open to the public, but some are, among them the elegantly Romanesque

St. Francis Xavier Church at 532 Market Street, built in 1869, with its pure-ringing bell-tower chimes, hand-carved altar and its own self-guided tour, available at the back of the church. The church is open to the public 9:00 a.m. to 5:00 p.m. Call (304)422-3142 for more information.

While you are in the Parkersburg area, and especially if you have children with you, consider a visit to **Blackwater Farms Zoological Park**, just off Route 14 on State Creek Road at Mineral Wells. The 12-acre park has the largest collection of exotic animals in the state on display in a natural setting, presided over by a zookeeper who treats the animals like adored children. Call (304)489-2370 for more information. You can have a delicious meal—and enjoy a magnificent view of the Ohio River—at the **Point of View Restaurant**, off Route 68 just west of town. It's open for lunch and dinner every day except Sunday. Call (304)863-3366. Woodworkers will want to spend some time at **Woodcraft Supply**, the Parkersburg outlet of the nationally-known catalog and retail store. From I-77, take the Emerson Avenue exit and follow Route 2 south to Rosemar Road. The store is on your left at the intersection. The toll-free number is (800)644-3106. And, for fast-paced fun, watch NASCAR racing at the **West Virginia Motor Speedway** at the Mineral Wells exit off I-77. Call (304)489-1889 for race schedules and more information.

Directions: The Convention and Visitors Bureau is at 350 Seventh Street. From I-77, follow Route 50 west (Seventh Street) into the city.

Blennerhassett Island Historical State Park

The Blennerhassetts

Riches, romance, political intrigue, adventure and tragedy—these are the ingredients of the **Harman and Margaret Blennerhassett** story. Wood County's most famous residents were born in England to closely-related families—too closely related. When the tall, musically talented, highly educated Harman, at 30, married his 23-year-old niece Margaret, the incestuous union disturbed his family. After he joined a secret society plotting a revolution to free Ireland from English rule, he and Margaret were forced to flee to America.

Their 1796 Atlantic crossing was turbulent and difficult, but the couple finally arrived in New York, bringing along servants, family heirlooms, scientific instruments, books, china, linens and everything else required to set up house in the grand manner they had enjoyed in the Old Country. From New York they headed to Philadelphia and then across the Pennsylvania mountains to Pittsburgh. But Harman was eager to put even more distance between himself and his enemies, so he and his wife pressed even deeper into the Ohio frontier to Marietta at the mouth of the Muskingum.

The Blennerhassetts soon found the ideal location for their estate, buying part of a 500-acre island in the Ohio River, 14 miles below Marietta. They proceeded to construct the largest and most opulent home in the Ohio Valley. The 7,000-square-foot mansion took more than two years to complete and borrowed its architectural configuration from the Palladian style, including semi-circular porticoes and flanking wings. What the wealthy young couple hadn't brought with them, they bought, spending lavishly on furniture, carpets and works of art. They established formal grounds with exotic trees and plants, hothouses and flower gardens on a magnificent scale—this during an age when most Ohio Valley residents lived in log cabins with dirt floors!

Here, for a few short years, the Blennerhassetts lived a charmed life, acknowledged as the most glamorous and cultivated citizens of the Ohio Valley. Harman pursued his scientific interests in his study wing and was also an important entrepreneur in the region, operating a store on the island and owning shares in others. Margaret wrote poetry (she was to become West Virginia's first published poet), rode on horseback around her island and gave lessons in cookery for local ladies. And they hosted parties, such gatherings as the Mid-Ohio Valley had never seen: formal balls, teas and salons for visitors from near and abroad. Locally, their island was nicknamed "Paradise." To complete the picture of Eden on earth, they were blessed with four children.

But their idyll was doomed to end tragically. In 1805 came the first sign of trouble—in the person of Aaron Burr, the former U.S. senator and vice president who recently had killed Alexander Hamilton in a duel. The bitter and desperate Burr persuaded Harman Blennerhassett, ever the reckless adventurer, to bankroll a scheme that would ruin them all—a daring plan to set up a separate country in the Southwest by seizing Spanish territory. When the plot was discovered, Harman was once again forced to flee, escaping downriver under cover of darkness. Within days, Margaret herself fled, with her children. She was never to see her beloved island again.

Harman was arrested, indicted and released. The family was reunited, albeit in much poorer circumstances. They made their way down the Mississippi and tried to run a cotton plantation, but their efforts met with failure. Meanwhile, their beautiful mansion, only 11 years old, was accidentally set on fire and burned to the ground in 1811.

From then on, all of the Blennerhassetts' endeavors seemed cursed. Unable to secure a position in Canada, Harman and Margaret went to England, where he spent the rest of his life in declining health. When he died in 1831, a poverty-stricken Margaret returned to America to visit her two sons and seek financial help. The elder, an alcoholic and a wastrel, had disappeared. The younger, a failed artist, died in poverty, as did Margaret herself in 1842. She left behind no fortune and no mansion, only a romantic legend unparalleled in American history.

The story has a spooky epilogue: Margaret's ghost often has been seen on the island through the years. One camper reported smelling a woman's perfume and seeing in the fog a tall, stately lady who resembled Margaret Blennerhassett. After the ghost refused his offer of coffee, it faded eerily into the fog. In the morning he found books removed from his knapsack and stacked in neat piles. Perhaps Margaret's ghost returns to her infant daughter, who is buried on the island, or to look at the new mansion that has risen from the ruins of the one she knew.

Blennerhassett Island

With a history like the Blennerhassetts', no visit to Parkersburg is complete without a trip to **Blennerhassett Island**. It is accessible only by means of an old-fashioned sternwheeler that runs May through October from the small park at "the point" near the Parkersburg floodwall. (The floodwall is worth a look in its own right.) The 20-minute ride is a pleasant, breezy excursion across a wide bend in the Ohio.

The fifth-largest island in the Ohio River shimmers mirage-like in the distance as the boat approaches. Nearly four miles long, with eight miles of shoreline, it is as fertile as it looks—naturalists have identified 112 different species of birds here, and deer and other small mammals are abundant. Near the water you may see freshwater mussels, an important part of the river's ecosystem as both food source and water filter.

Native Americans prized these mussels, eating them and using the shells for ornaments and weapons. Archeologists have unearthed weapons, tools, jewelry and other artifacts showing that Indians lived on this island for some 15,000 years before Europeans discovered it. The famous Delaware Indian Nemacolin called it home during the 1760s. Early European explorers and traders passed through during the 1700s, some staying to farm the river-enriched bottomland. When the Blennerhassetts arrived, years of bloody war between Indians and settlers had recently ended, opening the island for permanent settlement. After the Blennerhassetts left, the place was used for farming and as a private park for public gatherings. George Rogers Clark, King Charles X of France, Johnny Appleseed, Henry Clay and Walt Whitman all visited here.

In 1972, the island was placed on the National Register of Historic Places and the state authorized the Blennerhassett Island Historical Park Commission to preserve its heritage in a park. Archeologists discovered the foundations of the Blennerhassett's mansion in 1973, and the reconstruction of the splendid house began in 1984. Over the next decade and a half, the island was transformed from a neglected, overgrown tangle of weeds to a manicured park and estate. The work continues: a new archeological dig is currently underway, under the auspices of the West Virginia University Archeological Field School, aimed at locating and eventually reconstructing the Blennerhassetts' gardens as they once were, with serpentine paths, fountains and a fish pond.

You can explore the island on foot, by bicycle or by horse-drawn wagon. Birders should find the wetland at the western side of the island an excellent place for spotting a variety of waterfowl and other birds. Other spots worth noticing are the black walnut grove near the mansion and the "Great Tulip Poplar," an ancient tree measuring eight feet in diameter. It stood 125 feet high until it was unfortunately damaged by high winds in 1986 and 1994; leaves still sprout from its shortened trunk.

Blennerhassett Mansion

The mansion, reconstructed between 1984 and 1991, follows the Italian Palladian style admired and used by both George Washington and Thomas Jefferson for their own homes: a two-story central section connected to flanking wings by covered porticoes. Massive brick chimneys seem to anchor the mansion to the ground. But Harman Blennerhassett, for all his derring-do, was afraid of earthquakes; for this reason he chose to build his mansion of native hardwoods instead of brick, painting it white so that passengers in riverboats would see it gleaming against the island greenery. Like so many other choices in his life, it was a tragic decision: a candle in the wine cellar set some hemp afire and the conflagration spread.

You'll hear this story and others from costumed docents who lead visitors through the mansion. Most day-to-day activities took place in the central building, which held two parlors, two drawing rooms, a library, dining room, entrance hall, winter kitchen and four bedrooms. The brightly painted walls glow with light from large windows—the originals were some of the first glass-paned windows in this part of the country. Along with other antiques, including paintings and oriental rugs, are a few luckily-retrieved items, such as exquisite Italian alabaster vases, that once belonged to the Blennerhassetts. From the walnut-paneled drawing room to the upstairs ballroom with its marbled wallpaper, the mansion revives the aura of high-spirited elegance that graced the same space two hundred years ago.

In the south wing, originally the Blennerhassetts' summer kitchen, is one of the best-equipped 18th-century kitchens to be found. Although the huge hearth was tended by slaves, Margaret was an accomplished cook and prepared many of the meals herself. Some implements of 18th-century cookery are unrecognizable nowadays; fortunately, the docents can identify the long-handled coffee roaster and sugar cutter. You'll also see casks, pewter tableware and other utensils, some original to the house. Outside is an herb garden.

The north wing, site of the wine cellar where the fateful fire started, was Harman Blennerhassett's study and served as his scientific sanctuary. Here he kept his accounts and conducted chemical experiments. Take note of the handsome bookpress and original table, and be sure to press the button on the "magic message machine" for further details of each room.

Allow at least three hours to explore Blennerhassett Island. Near the mansion, you'll find craftspeople demonstrating during the season, a gift shop and a snack bar. The island is the site of several annual events, including a recreation of frontier life complete with muzzle-loaders and mountain men in May, a West Virginia Day festival in June and an October candlelight evening. If you happen to be in Parkersburg during early December, call the park for details on special holiday events.

Sternwheeler rides leave on the hour from Parkersburg and return from the island on the half hour. Hours are 10:00 a.m. to 5:30 p.m. Tuesday through Sunday, May through August. From September through October, boats operate from 10:00 a.m. to 4:30 p.m. Thursday through Saturday and noon to 4:30 p.m. on Sunday. Except for special holiday events, the island is closed from early November through April. The round-trip ride to the island is $6.00 for adults and $5.00 for children (ages 3 to 12). Mansion tours are $3.00 for adults and $2.00 for children, and wagon rides are $3.50. For more information call (304)420-4800 or (800)CALL-WVA or write Blennerhassett Island Historical State Park, 137 Juliana Street, Parkersburg, WV 26101.

This view of the east front of Blennerhassett Mansion shows the Italian Palladian style with semi-circular porticoes chosen by George Washington for Mount Vernon. BRIAN B. SCHROEDER

Directions: Board the sternwheeler at Point Park, at the foot of Second Street in Parkersburg. You can buy tickets at a booth beside the floodwall.

Blennerhassett Museum

You can begin or end your tour of the island at **Blennerhassett Museum**, on the mainland near the sternwheeler boarding point. Three floors of exhibits document 11,000 years of human occupation of the island, from Indian petrogylphs, arrowheads, pipes, pottery, weapons and ornaments to fine Blennerhassett furniture, china and glass. One glass case holds the huge bones of a mastodon. On the bottom level of this spacious building, a 12-minute video will acquaint you with the Blennerhassetts and their up-and-down fortunes. There are also a railroad exhibit and other interesting pieces unrelated to the Blennerhassetts, including 19th-century clothing and furniture, Civil War memorabilia, a Victorian wreath of human hair, a display on Parkersburg's "golden era," antique farming equipment and more.

Admission to the museum and its gift shop, which are open year-round, is $1.00 for adults and $0.50 for children. From April through August, hours are 9:30 a.m. to 6:00 p.m. Tuesday through Sunday. In September and October, hours are 9:30 a.m. to 5:00 p.m. on the same days, and November hours are similar, except that the museum opens 1½ hours later. From December through March, the museum is open Saturdays from 11:00 a.m. to 5:00 p.m. and Sundays from 1:00 to 5:00 p.m. During all seasons, you may visit at other times by appointment. Call (304)420-4800 or (800)CALL-WVA.

Directions: The museum is at the corner of Second and Juliana streets.

Blennerhassett Hotel

Built in 1889, the beautiful **Blennerhassett Hotel** dominates the corner of Fourth and Market streets and exudes the aura of another time, when horse-drawn carriages navigated streets lit by gaslights and the city was alive with the atmosphere only big money can create. It was a rough-and-ready time as well: back then, steel shutters protected the hotel lobby mirror from street shootings. Nowadays, the elegant foyer is a welcoming place, but the historic hotel's rich crown moldings, authentic English doors, brass and leaded chandeliers and antiques still bespeak fabulous wealth. Banker Colonel William Chancellor built the hotel to accommodate travelers brought here by the booming oil industry. The hotel was a showplace and an immediate success. Businessmen closed deals at the bar, ladies gossiped over tea and vaudeville stars rehearsed their acts in their rooms. In its time, the 50-room hotel was considered the state's finest.

Its aura of glamour undiminished, the Blennerhassett—now expanded and renovated to accommodate guests in 104 rooms—is still a wonderful place for an overnight stay. Now on the National Register of Historic Places, it was reopened in 1986. Although not original, the hotel's many antique chandeliers, sconces, mirrors and furniture revive its opulent early days. Some of the furnishings, like the clock in the entry lobby, are over 100 years old, and other details, such as the English prints on the guest floors and exterior lights made to resemble gaslights, impart a warm historical glow.

Off the main lobby, **Harman's Restaurant** serves gourmet meals suitable for hearty 19th-century appetites. A hostess greets diners from a 95-year-old ship clerk desk from England. The hotel's **American Harvest Cafe** features wholesome lunchtime fare. Spacious guest rooms, especially the ones in the restored older section of the hotel, are furnished with reproductions of Chippendale furniture and fabric. **The Peddlar Gift Shop** on the main floor offers fine regional arts and crafts.

For locals and visitors alike, the Blennerhassett is a favorite resting and meeting place, a welcome retreat in which Parkersburg's past still echoes. For reservations and more information, call (304)422-3131 or (800)262-2536 or write Blennerhassett Hotel, Fourth and Market streets, Parkersburg, WV 26101.

Directions: At the corner of Fourth and Market, the chateau-like building is hard to miss.

Tip: Ask about special weekend getaway packages, which can make a stay at this grand old hotel an affordable luxury.

Cook House

Driving a car, you might miss the **Cook House**—the quaint, cozy farmhouse at 1301 Murdoch Avenue is tucked between modern buildings and would be easy to overlook. If possible, see it as part of the walking tour or park your car at the adjacent shopping mall. One of the oldest existing buildings in Wood County, this beautifully preserved home dates back to about 1825. Under the care of the Junior League, the little gem is a living classroom for fourth-graders who come here to learn how a frontier family lived in the early half of the 19th century.

The Cook family, Quakers from New England, built the house with a great economy of construction and no frills. You won't see fancy moldings or interior decorations, but the house has an understated elegance: look for the unusual one-story wings on either side of the two-story core, the handsome Flemish bonding in the bricks and the balanced nine-over-six windows accented by an arched fanlight in the gable.

Tillinghast Cook came to the Mid-Ohio area with his family in 1795, when he was five years old. His father bought and left to him large, strategic tracts of land around Parkersburg, which was merely a settlement of log cabins at the confluence of the Ohio and Kanawha rivers at the time. Like other early settlers, Tillinghast was a man of many trades: farmer, merchant, surveyor, politician, land speculator. He built this home after marrying Betsey Russell in 1820, likely using slave labor to fire bricks on the site and cut hardwood timber from the virgin forest nearby. Here the Cooks lived together for 50 years, rearing seven of eight children. Meanwhile, Parkersburg grew up around them, changing from a mere crossroads to one of the richest cities in the new state of West Virginia.

Bright and welcoming inside, the house is furnished with some items that belonged to the Cooks and others authentic to their times. Above the fireplace (which was used for storing woolens during summer months!) a portrait of Tillinghast surveys the comings and goings of visitors. Visitors marvel over the fine needlework on a young girl's sampler and learn how to properly trim the wick of a candle. Perhaps most interesting to children is the collection of handmade toys—corn cob dolls, carved animals, puzzles and "Sunday toys" (the only toys allowed on the day of worship) like Jacob's Ladder.

Cook descendants lived in and cared for this house until the 1950s, when it was deeded to the Junior League. A family photo album documents every generation. During the Christmas season, docents in period costume show off the open house in full holiday finery of greens and candles. At other times, make arrangements for a tour at least a week ahead of time by calling (304)422-6961. Admission is $1.00 for adults, no charge for children under six. All fees are returned to the community through League service projects.

Directions: Follow Route 50 west. Stay in center lane when Route 50 becomes one-way (8th Street). The road curves right into Murdoch Avenue. Go about one-half mile; the house is on the left at 13th Street.

The Cultural Center of Fine Arts

Established in 1938, the Parkersburg Art Center is one of the oldest visual arts organizations in the state. Now the center has a beautiful new home—and a new name. **The Cultural Center of Fine Arts** has recently moved to a large Federalist-style building at 725 Market Street, increasing its floor space tenfold and placing it front and center among Parkersburg's many cultural offerings.

From its inception, the center has brought its community nationally recognized favorites like Winslow Homer as well as exhibits by local artists. The shows involve a wide variety of interests, including such imaginative themes as a "Touch and Feel" exhibit designed to enable blind persons to "see" celebrities by feeling their life masks, life-sized dinosaurs, wood engravings from children's classics, a photographic documentary of the Sioux, a competitive American Realism show, children's art, portraits and landscapes. Once a year the center sponsors an exhibit of regional artists who live and work within 75 miles of Parkersburg.

The new facility, at one of the busiest intersections in town, has space for much more: a permanent gallery for local artists, ongoing activities for children, an expanded gift shop featuring the works of local talent and a lending library of art books and videos. The center is handicapped-accessible from basement to attic, and very easy to include on a walking tour of Parkersburg because of its central location. It is open from 10:00 a.m. to 4:00 p.m. Tuesday through Friday, 1:00 to 4:00 p.m. Saturday and Sunday, closed Monday. Docent-led tours are available on request, and group and evening tours are available by appointment. Admission is $1.00 for adults and $0.50 for children. Call (304)485-3859 for more information, or write The Cultural Center of Fine Arts, 725 Market Street, Parkersburg, WV 26101.

Directions: Located at 725 Market Street.

Henry Cooper Log Cabin Museum

If you are in Parkersburg on a Sunday afternoon, take time to browse through the **Henry Cooper Log Cabin Museum**. In 1910, it was relocated, log by log, to the City Park in Parkersburg from its original site nine miles away. If the kids don't feel like seeing another "old place," they can feed the ducks in the park or play in the playground—but most children will find this cozy 1804 log home, with all its nooks and crannies, fascinating to explore. Under the auspices of the Centennial Chapter of the Daughters of American Pioneers, it is maintained as the museum "where time is stored in Parkersburg."

Larger than most dwellings of its time, the two-story cabin is chock-full of 19th-century Americana: photos (including Henry and his wife), Civil War and World War I uniforms, stuffed birds, rope beds, quilts, spinning wheels, vintage clothing, cradles, farm tools, a table original to the house, period hats and an astounding collection of some 45,000 buttons. Ask to see the red-and-blue eagle-patterned coverlet.

The museum is open Sunday afternoons from 1:30 to 4:30 p.m., Memorial Day to Labor Day. Call (304)422-7122 or 442-7841 to arrange group tours. Admission is $1.00 for adults, $0.50 for children 6-16, and no charge for children under six. For more information write: Curator, Daughters of American Pioneers, 3310 Kim Street, Parkersburg, WV 26104.

Directions: From Route 50 heading into Parkersburg, turn right on Park Avenue at Wendy's. Go two blocks to City Park.

Little Kanawha Crafthouse

If you arrive early to board the ferry for Blennerhassett Island, spend some time in the **Little Kanawha Crafthouse**. Tucked into the floodwall, it's a cute shop with a homespun feel and crafts from over 800 artisans, most representing the Mid-Ohio region. You'll find quilts, wooden furniture and toys, baskets, ironware, stained glass, painting, coal figurines, dolls, ceramics and a year-round Christmas craft selection. The shop's hours are 10:00 a.m. to 6:00 p.m. Monday through Saturday and noon to 6:00 p.m. on Sunday, May through August. Call (304)485-3149 or write Little Kanawha Crafthouse, 113 Ann Street, Parkersburg, WV 26101.

Directions: Between First and Second streets on Ann Street at the floodwall.

Ohio River Islands National Wildlife Refuge

West Virginia's first national wildlife refuge was dedicated in May 1992, after a decade of efforts by naturalists and supporters. Managed by the U.S. Fish and Wildlife Service, the **Ohio River Islands National Wildlife Refuge** currently comprises 21 islands (17 of them in West Virginia) with additional acquisitions in progress. The refuge includes 1,103 acres on land and 1,435 underwater.

Naturalists have long valued the Ohio River Islands and their back channels for the high quality of wildlife ecosystems used by migratory and resident waterfowl, shorebirds, songbirds, warm-water fish and rare freshwater mussels. Recent wildlife inventories have identified nearly 200 species of birds, including 17 raptors and 109 songbirds. Two of the largest great blue heron rookeries in the state are located on Grape and Fish Creek islands. Bald eagles and peregrine falcons visit here regularly, and mammals also proliferate—beaver, rabbit, mink, muskrat, opossum, raccoon, woodchuck and whitetail deer. Some of the over 50 species of fish breeding in these waters are drum, channel catfish, bluegill, largemouth bass and spotted bass. The refuge is home to over 40 species of freshwater mussels, including the endangered fanshell and pink mucket pearly mussel. The refuge's primary goal is to preserve, restore and enhance the diversity and abundance of these populations, and refuge staff are working hard to restore the bottomland hardwood forest habitat needed by wildlife native to the Ohio River's floodplain.

These islands played an important historical role in the region, supplying and harboring Native Americans, early European settlers and surveyors (including George Washington) and pioneers traveling west. Strategic Civil War battles were fought nearby. In this century, the islands witnessed the growth of commerce and served primarily agricultural, navigational and industrial purposes. Now, as refuge islands, they will ensure a wildlife legacy for present and future generations.

All refuge islands are open daily to the public from sunrise to sunset. Uses that are wildlife-dependent such as fishing, hunting (on some islands), bird-watching and wildlife photography are encouraged. Bridges to two of the islands, Middle and Wheeling, offer access to visitors without boats.

Before visiting the islands, you should request a refuge brochure to obtain current regulations. For more information, call (304)422-0752 or write Ohio River Islands National Wildlife Refuge, PO Box 1811, Parkersburg, WV 26102.

Oil and Gas Museum

Even if you think you have no interest in the topic, don't leave Parkersburg without seeing this museum. In fact, it would be a good place to visit first, because its contents document the history and character of Parkersburg so well that you'll take with you a much deeper appreciation of the city. The museum aims to preserve the heritage of the individuals in West Virginia and southeastern Ohio who created the oil and gas industry in the U.S.—and it succeeds admirably in illuminating the lives and times of some "rugged, resourceful, inventive, persistent and dynamic individuals."

Housed in the spacious, historic Smith Hardware store near Point Park, the **Oil and Gas Museum** also owns the adjacent land on which is parked a 1905 steam engine too big to fit into the building, as well as several other large pieces of drilling equipment.

Inside, exhibits illustrate that the Parkersburg area was the first

With the coming of the automotive age, many West Virginia communities became boom towns almost overnight. Once, the landscape was dotted with thousands of wooden oil derricks like this one.

Drawing by William D. Goebel

producer of oil and gas in the nation, starting with the major boom in oil in 1859. Early artifacts and equipment, along with models, letters, business documents and a video presentation trace the story of oil from its earliest use through the Civil War era, when Parkersburg's oil barons were a driving force in the creation of West Virginia. The first congressman, senator and governor of the state were oil men, all in positions to encourage the rapid growth of the industry and of Parkersburg. A huge collection of photos, lithographs, clothing and other memorabilia captures the colorful personalities who made Parkersburg, in its prime, one of the most dynamic cities in the country. Even before then, Indians and early settlers knew about the medicinal and industrial uses of oil. The slimy substance was so abundant and close to the surface that it oozed into the rivers. George Washington owned land aptly called Burning Springs, from which rich deposits were later extracted. An excellent book, *Where It All Began*, documents the area's history and is available for sale at the museum.

One of the most informative items in the museum is a wall-sized geological map showing the vast extent of oil exploration in the state—tens of thousands of wells since 1860. The museum's collection of Civil War artifacts is also outstanding.

The museum is open 10:00 a.m. to 6:00 p.m. Saturdays, noon to 6:00 p.m. Sundays and weekdays and evenings by appointment. Admission is $2.00 for adults and $1.00 for children. For more information call (304)485-5446 or 428-8015 or write Oil and Gas Museum, Box 1685, Parkersburg, WV 26102.

Directions: The museum is #24 on the Parkersburg walking tour, one block from Point Park at 119 Third Street.

Smoot Theatre

In 1989, Felice Jorgeson waved her magic wand and transformed a crumbling, shabby, demolition-bound movie house into an architectural gem. No, it didn't happen quite that way—the enthusiastic former high school teacher will tell you that the seemingly miraculous restoration of Parkersburg's **Smoot Theatre** took three long years and depended upon countless generous donors, hours and hours of volunteer manpower, gallons of paint and plenty of elbow grease.

Built in 1926 at a cost of $250,000 by the Smoot Amusement Company, the glittery new theater attracted famous vaudeville acts to booming Parkersburg. The Smoot's stage hosted saxophone-playing Siamese twins, dancing midgets, prancing elephants and saw-wielding magicians as well as more conventional entertainment like Guy Lombardo's band and beauty pageants. At its prime, the theater was packed for five shows a day, seven days a week.

Then the days of vaudeville ended. With the coming of the silent screen and later the "talkies," many of the nation's theaters, including the Smoot, were dismantled, mutilated and reshaped to accommodate movie screens, popcorn machines, projection rooms and streetside ticket booths. The Smoot Theatre served for over 50 years as a movie house, but finally fell to competition from mall theaters. Plans were made for its destruction to make way for a parking lot.

And then...enter Felice. With a growing group of local supporters, the indomitable fairy godmother spearheaded the effort to raise enough money to buy the building and open its doors for a historical big-band concert in May 1989.

These days, after many more hours of labor and even a generous donation from a local lottery winner to help replace the original 1928 pipe organ, the Smoot is transformed. Volunteer Tom Pliatt, who worked at the Smoot as a 10-year-old usher during its glory days, recollected the original paint colors—soft tones of beige, mauve, jade and blue—with help from old photos and documents. With the water-stained ceiling repaired and painted, the walls repapered, new carpets installed, wooden doors and brass fixtures replaced and polished, seats reupholstered, and chandeliers shined and relit, the curtain now rises on live performances.

If you visit, ask Felice to show you a superb slide show of the theater's history and some of the ads for early vaudeville shows and movies. You'll love the 1932 newspaper photo that shows nurses standing beside an ambulance in front of the marquee advertising *Frankenstein*. The ad promised that the theater would provide nursing, smelling salts and transportation to the hospital for overwhelmed audience members. You'll see the original lights and dimmers onstage, the pine-and-maple floors specially made to accentuate tap dancers' rhythms, the trap door and loft. You'll hear how a 1937 flood covered the stage, during a performance, with three feet of water. You'll see the old projection rooms and dressing rooms.

Felice will also tell you about the summer vaudeville camp she runs for young people, and will happily arrange a tailor-made tour to suit the interests of almost any group. A specialty is the dessert tour, with sumptuous pastries served to guests seated at tables onstage.

But a tour isn't a performance, and you really should try to catch a performance: the offerings include jazz, ragtime, opera, bluegrass, rock, children's theater, comedy and dance. All the hard work and fund-raising pay off when the stained-glass chandeliers dim, the music begins and the curtain goes up.

You must make advance reservations for tours either through the Parkersburg/Wood County Convention and Visitors Bureau at (800)752-4982 or (304)428-1130 or directly with the theater at (304)422-PLAY. Admission depends upon the type of tour. Full dessert tour with slide show is about $10.00; regular tour is $3.00.

Write the Smoot Theatre, PO Box 866, Parkersburg, WV 26102.

Directions: Five blocks east of the floodwall, at 231 Fifth Street, the theater is #31 on the Historical Walking Tour.

Sumner School Museum

In 1863, before West Virginia was a state, seven African-American businessmen in Parkersburg started a school in the basement of a local church. Now part of the **Avery Street Historic District** of Parkersburg, **Sumner School** was the first free school for blacks south of Mason-Dixon Line. It operated until 1954, when the landmark *Brown vs. the Board of Education* decision mandated integration of schools throughout the country.

Classrooms built in 1889 were destroyed, but a large brick gymnasium, built around 1926, remained. It has now been restored as a museum dedicated to preserving the African-American history of the Parkersburg area. It is operated by the Sumnerites, Inc., a nonprofit organization of former students who originally got together to collect school memorabilia such as trophies, class yearbooks and pictures.

The old gym is divided into four rooms—Family and Neighbors, Teachers, Community and School—and the hallway is a "memory lane" in honor of deceased classmates. The Sumnerites have collected over 1,500 photographs documenting the lives of Parkersburg's African-American community, as well as a number of artifacts. Be sure to look at Anna McClung Selby's beaten biscuit machine. Mrs. Selby was the town's acknowledged expert at making the afternoon tea delicacy; her machine, which she purchased in 1916, made her popular with Parkersburg's upper crust.

Guided tours are by appointment. Call (304)485-1152, or write Sumner School Museum, 1016 Avery Street, Parkersburg, WV 26101.

Directions: 1016 Avery Street, between 10th and 11th streets one block east of Market Street.

Trans Allegheny Books

If you love books *and* a bargain, you might just get lost for the whole day at **Trans Allegheny Books**. This book lover's paradise occupies the former Parkersburg Carnegie Public Library, built in 1906 and now on the National Register of Historic Places.

Reflecting the turn-of-the-century elegance of other Carnegie endowments, the stately brick neoclassic structure still has its original glass insets in the floor, providing light and a sense of space between levels. A winding spiral staircase leads three floors up to a

The Andrew Carnegie Public Library in Parkersburg now houses Trans Allegheny Books and their large selection of used, rare and new books. Courtesy Trans Allegheny Books

West Virginia history and genealogy section. The Carnegie coat of arms glows in stained glass behind the staircase.

Renovation and restoration costs topped $300,000 before the store opened its doors in 1985. It was popular from the outset and remains so. An excellent source of books about West Virginia and by West Virginia authors, Trans Allegheny also specializes in searching for rare and out-of-print books. The store owner's passion for historical volumes led to a personal collection of over 8,000 books. They honor requests from all over the country.

Spread over four floors, the inventory ranges from new West Virginia and regional titles to children's literature, magazines, postcards, sheet music, modern first editions, foreign language volumes and an extensive religion section. Over 200,000 used hardcover and paperback volumes, many from auctions and estate sales, cover every category under the sun.

Snoop to your heart's content, smell the old leather and read inscriptions inside book covers. Don't be surprised to find a signed copy by a favorite author, or a heartwarming inscription to the recipient of a gift book—and, while you're there, remember what great gifts books make, especially hard-to-find volumes. Buy an old copy of *Life Magazine* to commemorate someone's birth week, or a volume of 1920s nursery rhymes for a new baby. If you can't find what you're seeking, ask Trans Allegheny staffers for help—most of them are book lovers, too.

You can trade in your own books at Trans Allegheny. (Paperbacks are traded two for one.) Much as you might wish to get locked in this library overnight, hours are 10:00 a.m. to 6:00 p.m. Monday through Saturday, noon to 4:00 p.m. Sunday. E-mail the store (TABooks@TransAbooks.com) or call (304)422-4499.

Directions: 725 Green Street, #36 on the Parkersburg walking tour. As you enter Parkersburg on Route 50, turn right onto Green Street.

Ravenswood/Ripley

Washington's Western Lands Museum

If you are driving south from Parkersburg (or north from Charleston) on I-77, you'll find a pleasant, scenic picnic location beside the Ohio River in **Ravenswood** at the town's riverfront park. If it's a Sunday, top off your picnic with a visit to **Washington's Western Lands Museum** in the park. Maintained by the Jackson County Historical Society, the museum has a bit of everything, including old clothing, arrowheads, antique children's toys, paintings by a local folk artist, a country store exhibit and—occupying much of one two-story room—a large, horse-drawn hearse from the 1800's.

Also in the park, the restored 1875 **Sayre Log House** is filled with 19th-century furnishings, including the dough box, cupboard and sewing machine that belonged to the original family.

The museum and log house are free, but donations are welcome. There is no admission to the park except during the **Ohio River Festival** in August [see calendar of events]. For more information write Jackson County Historical Society, PO Box 22, Ripley, WV 25271. For information about arrangements to open the museum for special events, call the Jackson County Public Library: (304)372-5343.

Directions: From I-77, take the Ravenswood/Silverton exit and go west on Route 2 (four-lane) for three miles. Turn right at the second Ravenswood exit and go slightly more than a mile to the park entrance.

Tip: Just north of the Ravenswood/Silverton exit on I-77, look to the east side of interstate and you will see the **Rankin Octagonal**

Barn, the only survivor of two octagonal barns known to have been built in West Virginia. Built around the turn of the century, probably in the 1890s, the unique structure is on the National Register of Historic Places.

Cedar Lakes Conference Center

Established in 1949 as the state FFA-FHA Camp, **Cedar Lakes Conference Center** has become a hub of cultural, craft and recreational activity in Jackson County. Any warm day brings out hundreds of people to jog, walk, picnic, bike or hike on the 450-acre grounds. Paddleboats, canoes, miniature golf, swimming, fishing, basketball, volleyball and tennis are also available to the public. **The Heritage House**, a log cabin built in about 1850, was placed at Cedar Lakes complex in 1968, and the historic **Staats Mill Covered Bridge** [see appendix for a complete list of covered bridges] was moved here in 1983—two nostalgic additions to the picturesque grounds.

Throughout the year a variety of organizations use the complex as a meeting place, and craft workshops and Elderhostel classes are conducted on a regular schedule. Lodging choices include Holt Lodge, cabins and dormitories. The center's dining hall is open to the public. Cedar Lakes is the home of the gigantic **Mountain State Art & Craft Fair**, the granddaddy of West Virginia heritage fairs with over 200 juried exhibitors, held each year over the 4th of July weekend [see calendar of events].

The complex is open to the public during daylight hours. Admission to the park is free; there is a nominal charge for boat rentals, swimming and game courts. For more information call (304)372-7860 or write Cedar Lakes Conference Center, HC 88, Box 21, Ripley, WV 25271.

Directions: From I-77, take Exit 132 (the Fairplain exit, just south of Ripley). Turn right off exit ramp and, almost immediately, right again onto Cedar Lakes Drive (at the Burger King restaurant). Go 3½ miles to the entrance.

Spencer

Charles Fork Lake

Tucked away in the foothills in the southern part of the Mid-Ohio Valley region is a super day trip for mountain bikers of all ages and skill levels. **Charles Fork Lake** has about 20 miles of trails on 2,000 acres of land surrounding a pretty municipal lake. The excellent trails, built by mountain bikers for mountain bikers, are well-marked and color-coded. For variety and beautiful scenery, take the five-mile **Lakeview Trail**, an intermediate ride through deep coves, meadows and hardwood groves. If you're willing to make the climb back up, check out the old cemetery at the bottom of the very steep, half-mile **Tombstone Pass**. Other trails include **Charlie's Challenge**, **Trevor's Trail** and the **Jungle Pass**.

Charles Fork Lake is the location of the **ALLSPORT Tour de Lake Mountain Bike Festival** [see calendar of events] each summer, one of West Virginia's largest mountain biking events.

Hiking, fishing and primitive camping are also available. For more information, call (304)927-1780 or write Roane County Chamber of Commerce, PO Box 1, Spencer, WV 25276.

Directions: Charles Fork Lake is about two miles south of Spencer on Route 36. From Route 36, signs will direct you to the lake. From I-77, take Route 33 east to Spencer, then Route 36 south. From I-79, take the Amma exit. Drive north on Route 36 toward Spencer and watch for signs.

Williamstown

Fenton Art Glass Factory and Museum

If you have time and interest for only one glass factory tour, make it this one. A thriving business for over 90 years, **Fenton Glass** has outlasted many other glass companies in the Ohio Valley—a tribute to the company's marriage of old-fashioned glassmaking techniques, modern technology and business acumen. With a staff of over 500, Fenton runs a very efficient enterprise, including their comprehensive factory tour.

Two Fenton brothers started the company in 1907 with a combined capital investment of $284, wisely building their Williamstown plant near a cheap source of natural gas. Two more siblings soon joined them, establishing the dynasty that is now in its fourth generation. Fenton has consistently produced high-quality handmade glassware, using innovative techniques for such classic favorites as Carnival Glass, hobnail, milk glass, Cranberry and Burmese.

The showroom may dazzle you—lamps, vases, goblets, eggs, pitchers, dishes, figurines, paperweights in a multitude of colors, shapes, glazes and textures—but save your shopping spree for after the tour when you can better appreciate and evaluate the selection.

Begin with the free movie and museum upstairs, a fascinating introduction to the glass industry, particularly in this area. The 24-minute film takes you step-by-step through the glassmaking process at the Fenton factory, and the museum showcases irreplaceable pieces from early Fenton years as well as from other famous, now defunct, glass companies. Some, like the translucent amethyst "Goddess of Harvest," are truly breathtaking. You'll learn that Burmese glass is valuable for its contents (gold and uranium), that milk glass contains fluoride and that the iridescence of Carnival glass comes from a spray of metallic salts. The beauty of these amethyst, orange, jade, sapphire and ruby jewels is all the more impressive when you remember that humans made them with just sand, soda and few selected minerals.

You'll get acquainted with that miraculous process downstairs on the 40-minute factory tour. As you move through the different production areas, you'll see for yourself that no two handmade vases are exactly alike, and understand why each piece is individually signed by the artist. The tour varies slightly from hour to hour, depending upon what's in production. It takes years of training and experience to excel at any of the techniques that go into a piece of Fenton glass--and at each stage the worker must perform quickly and confidently. As you follow your guide through the factory, don't hesitate to ask questions.

After the tour, with a new body of knowledge and a deeper appreciation of the art, you're prepared to admire and purchase the products in the gift shop. (Seconds are discounted.) And you'll never again look at the fluted edges of a Cranberry vase, the painted hydrangeas on an opalescent lamp or the delicate etching on a beer stein with out remembering the talented Fenton artisans who created them.

Museum, movie and tours are free. Tours begin about every 45 minutes from 8:30 a.m. to 2:30 p.m. Monday through Friday. There is a limited tour at 4:15 p.m. When tours are not available (on weekends, major holidays and during the factory's two-week vacation in July), you may still visit the museum and watch the movie. The tour schedule is subject to change. Call for exact dates and to make arrangements for groups of 20 or more: (304)375-7772. Gift shop and factory outlet are open 8:00 a.m. to 5:00 p.m. Monday through Saturday and 12:15 to 5:00 p.m. Sunday. Evening hours are extended Monday through Friday from April to December. Children under two are not permitted on the factory tour, but they may watch the movie and visit the museum and gift shop. For more information call (304)375-7772 or write Fenton Art Glass Company, 420 Caroline

Three pieces from the historic "Topaz Opalescent" collection at Fenton Art Glass in Williamstown.

Avenue, Williamstown, WV 26187.

Directions: Williamstown is about ten miles north of Parkersburg on Route 14 and just across the river from Marietta, Ohio (accessible by I-77, Exit 185). After entering Williamstown, follow the signs to Fenton Glass, turning right on Henderson Avenue.

Henderson Hall

One of the most important historical sites in the Mid-Ohio Valley, **Henderson Hall** stands like a mighty monument to symmetry surrounded by 65 acres of what was once a 2,000-acre plantation overlooking the Ohio River. It rose to its three-story height in the decade preceding the Civil War when the Italianate Villa style of architecture was at the peak of its popularity.

Unlike most other great houses, it has never suffered a period of abandonment and is preserved in pristine condition. Better yet, according to the present owner, his ancestors apparently saved every scrap—including shopping lists, business accounts, bills, wedding dresses, candy boxes, children's shoes, Christmas decorations, the original land grant signed by Patrick Henry, diaries naming and describing the slaves who worked the land and letters from everyone they knew, including Robert E. Lee. The collection of memorabilia makes for a vivid picture of plantation life during the mid-1800s.

Portraits and photographs of previous generations hang in almost every room—strong, determined faces full of plans and dreams. These likenesses add meaning for a visitor touring the house. You are visiting a family, not the shell of a home, and sharing their lives—from household trivia to secrets, scandals, weddings and wakes.

Outside, notice the fine window and molding details, the entrance porch flanked by sandstone columns and the belvedere crowning the central roof. Inside, you'll tour a spacious entrance hall with a 35-foot curving cherry staircase; a parlor, wrapped in wallpaper carried on horseback from Cincinnati in 1870, with an 1875 rosewood piano that has never been moved from its position; a dining room chock-full of heirloom silver, china and linens; a front room that doubles as a library of priceless volumes; a boys' room with a diamond-etched message from 1893 in the window glass; Rosalie's room, in which almost everything—curtains, canopy and bedspread—was hand-crafted by its talented occupant; and the kitchen where meals for generations of Hendersons were prepared.

Henderson Hall is open to the public May through October. Guided tours are conducted anytime between 1:00 and 4:00 p.m.

Sunday. Monday through Friday there is a single tour beginning promptly at 2:00 p.m. Closed Saturday. Group tours at other times by appointment only. Admission is $4.00 for adults and $2.00 for children. Call (304)375-2129 or write Henderson Farms, Route 2, Box 103, Williamstown, WV 26187.

Directions: From Parkersburg take Route 14 north towards Williamstown. Approximately 4 1/2 miles beyond the Vienna line you will see a sign for River Road indicating a sharp, reverse left turn for Henderson Hall.

Tip: On the way to Williamstown is world-renowned **Holl's Chocolates** in Vienna. If you are a chocolate-lover, you owe it to yourself to try their handmade confections. One taste, and you'll probably want to send someone a box; Holl's will be happy to ship it anywhere. Call (304)295-6576. You'll find the store at 2001 Grand Central Avenue (Route 14) just north of Parkersburg in Vienna.

BELLE
- Samuel Shrewsbury House

CEREDO
- Pilgrim Glass Corporation
- Z.D. Ramsdell House

CHARLESTON
- Capitol Complex
  - Capitol Building
  - Cultural Center
  - Governor's Mansion
- Capitol Market
- Craik-Patton House
- Kanawha State Forest
- *P.A. Denny* Sternwheeler
- Sunrise Museum
- Town Center
- Watt Powell Baseball Park

CROSS LANES
- Tri-State Greyhound Park

DUNBAR
- Wine Cellars Park

HUNTINGTON
- Camden Park & The *Jewel City* Sternwheeler
- Heritage Village
- Huntington Museum of Art
- Huntington Area Parks
- Huntington Railroad Museum and New River Train Excursions
- Mountain State Balloon Company
- Mountain State Mystery Train
- Museum of Radio and Technology

HURRICANE/SCOTT DEPOT
- Hamon Glass Company
- Museum in the Community

LESAGE
- Jenkins Plantation Museum and Green Bottom Wildlife Management Area

LOGAN
- Chief Logan State Park

MALDEN
- Midland Trail
- African Zion Baptist Church
- Cabin Creek Quilts

MATEWAN

MILTON
- Blenko Glass Company

POINT PLEASANT
- Point Pleasant Battle Monument State Park
- Krodel Park
- West Virginia State Farm Museum

SOUTH CHARLESTON
- South Charleston Mound

WILLIAMSON
- The Coal House

Metro Valley

The southwestern region of the state holds, as its name suggests, West Virginia's largest cities, including Huntington and the state capital, Charleston. Here you'll find the sophistication of the urban—air service, good food and a busy arts and entertainment scene—winningly blended with a relaxed pace and old-fashioned hospitality. The gold dome of the State Capitol Complex is a gleaming beacon no visitor should overlook: including a visit to the state's Cultural Center and Governor's Mansion, it makes a good one-day trip in itself. Charleston's Sunrise Museum is an adventure for those with aesthetic or scientific inclinations, and the city's own sternwheeler presents the capital from the pleasing perspective of the Kanawha River.

Fifty miles west on I-64, Huntington's Museum of Art is a bright jewel in West Virginia's arts scene, and the university town's many beautiful parks show off the Ohio River Valley. You can view the Metro Valley from above—in a hot air balloon—or ride the rails through autumn foliage from the city that railroad magnate Collis P. Huntington built.

Throughout the region are other worthy attractions: the mysterious South Charleston Mound, evidence of the area's early Adena culture; world-renowned Pilgrim Glass artists at work on one-of-a-kind creations; a unique wetland habitat surrounding an antebellum mansion; a tranquil riverside park that was the site of the first battle of the American Revolution; a family-pleasing museum dedicated to the history of farming.

Dance to a lively fiddle tune at the Vandalia Gathering in Charleston. Visit the grave of "Devil Anse" Hatfield near Logan. Ride an old-time roller coaster at Huntington's Camden Park. Stand in the small church where Booker T. Washington taught Sunday school. From baseball to bluegrass, from quilts to coal mining lore, from greyhound racing to homegrown tomatoes, you'll find a bountiful harvest of day-trip options in the Metro Valley.

For more information on visiting the Metro Valley contact:

Cabell-Huntington Convention and Visitors Bureau, PO Box 347, #2 Civic Center Plaza, Huntington, WV 25708. Call (304)525-7333 or (800)635-6329, or visit their web site (www.wvvisit.org).

Charleston Convention and Visitors Bureau, 200 Civic Center Drive, Charleston, WV 25301. Call (304)344-5075 or (800)733-5469, or visit their web site (www.charlestonwv.com).

Hurricane Convention and Visitors Bureau, PO Box 186, Hurricane, WV 25526. Call (304)562-5896 or visit their web site (wvweb.com/www/CVB/HURRICANE/HURRICANE.html).

Main Street Point Pleasant, 305 Main Street, Point Pleasant, WV 25550. Call (304)675-3844.

Putnam County Visitors Bureau, 1 Valley Park Drive, Hurricane, WV 25526. Call (304)562-0518.

South Charleston Convention and Visitors Bureau, PO Box 8595, South Charleston, WV 25303. Call (304)746-5552 or (800)238-9488 or visit their web site (wvweb.com/www/so_charleston_cvb).

Belle

Samuel Shrewsbury House

Driving past the town of **Belle** on Route 60, you will see a huge chemical complex; if you take the time to go into Belle, however, you will discover a historical treasure beside it. The oldest house in Belle and the oldest of its kind in the Kanawha Valley, the **Samuel Shrewsbury House** was built in about 1800. It is also called the Old Stone House.

Samuel Shrewsbury and his brother John, Belle's first settlers in 1798, were both active in the early salt business. John built a house for his own family on the site now occupied by the DuPont chemical plant.

The handsome home, which served for several years as a stagecoach inn and has been continuously occupied since it was built, is made of hand-cut sandstone. Its hand-hewn interior walls, cupboards and woodwork were all cut from a surrounding walnut grove. Purchased in 1980 and restored by the Belle Historical Restoration Society, it now houses the Society's office.

Furnished with period antiques, it also contains photos and exhibits of local history. Also of interest: a time capsule dedicated in 1897 that will be opened in 2045 and a book of Belle history. You must schedule an appointment to see the house. Admission is $3.00 for adults and $2.00 for children. Call (304)949-2380 or -2398.

Belle's first settlers built a stone house that still stands. The Samuel Shrewsbury House, built about 1800, is one of the oldest structures in the Kanawha Valley. COURTESY BELLE HISTORICAL RESTORATION SOCIETY

Directions: From Charleston, take Route 60 east to the Belle exit, about 10 miles. Exit, turn left and proceed to Stubb Drive. Turn right on Stubb Drive, and you'll see the house on the left.

Ceredo

Pilgrim Glass Corporation

When you visit the showrooms at **Pilgrim Glass Corporation**, you will understand why the company's products are famous throughout the world. The company is especially known for two difficult-to-make forms of glass, Cranberry and Cameo, and you will see many stunning examples of each.

Cranberry Glass is, as its name implies, a rich, ripe color, the hardest of all glass colors to produce. It requires the fusion of solid gold with lead crystal—and its price reflects the gold content.

Cameo Glass is expensive for a different reason. It is created by encasing one layer of glass within another, adding layers one at a time. After the glass cools, an artist delicately carves into it. Pilgrim artists have successfully carved through as many as 12 layers of glass in one piece!

Pilgrim's many-layered, multi-colored glass is decorated with unique designs, each pattern used only once and destroyed in the carving of a single layer. Any Cameo glass bought here is signed by the artist, documented in the Pilgrim Registry and accompanied by a notarized certificate of authenticity. Collectors all over the world treasure Pilgrim's cameo creations for the vitality of their designs as well as the skill with which they are made.

The company was purchased by current owner Alfred Knobler in 1949. Knobler, already a glass lover, had been the main buyer of the glass produced by Walter Bailey and his small glass factory in Huntington before deciding to acquire the company itself. He built a new facility at the site of today's plant in 1956. The colored glass made in the early years was primarily ruby, tangerine, amethyst, smoke, amber, sapphire, green and crystal. Three Italian artisans, now all retired from Pilgrim, contributed greatly to its early success. In 1953, brothers Alessandro and Roberto Moretti, both trained at famed Murano Glass Center in Italy, joined the company. Roberto's skill was so great that he produced commissions for Chagall, Picasso, Cocteau and Paul Jenkins. A brother-in-law, Mario Sandon, joined the company in 1957 and was well known for his tiny, handmade glass animals.

In the 1980s, a New England graphic designer, Kelsey Murphy, discovered that a sandblasting technique she was using for signs was very effective for sanding designs on glass. She joined forces with Andy Rainey, who designed equipment that could accelerate production, in a company they called Glass Expectations. Machinist Robert Bomkamp joined them a year later and further improved their machinery. When they showed their portfolio of sand-carved glass to the Pilgrim Glass Corporation, a new partnership was born. Pilgrim contracted with Glass Expectations in 1985 for 100 each of 12 various-sized vessels and solid-glass eggs. Sales exceeded anyone's expectations—orders flooded in for 30,000 eggs alone.

Murphy and Bomkamp quickly met the demand and came up with further mechanical refinements. Included in their first successful group of Cameo pieces was the Liberty Vase, made for Lee Iacocca in 1986. The next year, Murphy and Bomkamp combined forces with Pilgrim Glass Corporation. After years of development, including a trying first year when breakage ran at 95 percent, their art glass division is producing editions of up to 250 pieces of Cameo ware. In 1996, Kelsey Murphy presented President Bill Clinton with a sculptural cameo glass eagle, valued at $45,000, for the White House art gallery.

You can watch all kinds of glass being made from Pilgrim's observation deck. It's open 9:00 a.m. to 5:00 p.m. Monday through Thursday. Call (304)453-3553 if you plan to come with a large group. Finished pieces are displayed and for sale in the handsome gift shop/gallery, open 9:00 a.m. to 5:00 p.m. Monday through Saturday and 1:00 to 5:00 p.m. Sunday.

Directions: Take Exit 1 from I-64 and follow the signs toward Tri-State Airport (Airport Road). The factory is on the left, at the intersection with Walker Branch Road. (If you reach Tri-State Airport, you've gone a little too far.)

Z.D. Ramsdell House

On the flatlands of the Ohio River floodplain a few miles west of Huntington is the small town of Ceredo. This rich land was named, appropriately, for the Greek goddess of grain, Ceres, and was founded in 1857 by abolitionist Eli Thayer, a proponent of steam power as a replacement for the labor of slaves in developing industry.

One of Thayer's supporters, a bootmaker named Z.D. Ramsdell, built the first brick house in Ceredo in 1858. Now on the National Register of Historic Places, it has been preserved by the Ceredo Historic Landmark Commission.

Interior restoration and furnishings are in keeping with its Civil War-era construction. Against a backdrop of random plank floors, cut nails and horse-hair plaster, display cases in the museum room contain Civil War artifacts, many of them recovered from the attic. Ramsdell's post-war service as a postal service special agent is reflected in a display of old post office delivery boxes.

The **Ramsdell House** is open for tours by appointment and for special occasions such as living history portrayals, craft demonstrations and craft sales. Luncheons and candlelight dinners are available for groups of 25 to 43. Call (304)453-2482 to arrange a tour, or write Ceredo Historic Landmark Commission, PO Box 544, Ceredo, WV 25507.

Directions: From I-64, take the Kenova/Ceredo exit and go toward Ceredo. Turn onto Route 60 East. After the third traffic light turn left on B Street. The house is located at 1108 B Street.

Charleston

Do all roads lead to West Virginia's capital? Well, not quite all, but three interstate highways (I-77, I-79 and I-64) do converge in downtown **Charleston**. Visitors also arrive by rail at the downtown Amtrak depot, disembarking at a restored 1905 Beaux Arts-style building originally constructed for the Chesapeake and Ohio Railroad. Others fly in to Yeager Airport, just minutes and a couple of miles from the Capitol Complex [see entry] with its shining gold dome.

Charleston has been called the "most northern of the southern cities and the most southern of the northern cities," and its personality is indeed a study in contrasts: expect the cosmopolitan confidence of a healthy economy mixed with a relaxed, come-as-you-are friendliness.

It's a fine town for taking a walk. Stroll along Kanawha Boulevard, beside the broad and beautiful Kanawha River, on five miles of walkways that offer golden displays when thousands of daffodils bloom in spring. Or hike the historic Carriage Trail—a 15-minute walk up a forested hillside leads from the South Side Bridge to Sunrise Museum [see entry] and rewards you along the way with wildflowers, ivy-covered stone walls and a mysterious monument marking the graves of two Civil War spies. If you want to feast on a smorgasbord of architectural styles while you wander, explore the **East End Historical District**, bounded by Bradford Street, Quarrier Street, East Avenue and Kanawha Boulevard. And when you're ready to pause, a good place is the downtown **Village District**, where you can browse bookstores and sip cappuccino at a cafe table while you admire the architecture of some of Charleston's oldest buildings, expertly restored to their 19th-century splendor. A favorite landmark is the 1891 turreted **Scott Building** at 227 Capitol Street. Nearby, at 820 Virginia Street, another notable building is the 1915 **Masonic Temple**, a veritable wedding cake of a structure bedecked with dozens of intricate Gothic pinnacles and arches. Just around the corner, where Capitol Street meets Kanawha Boulevard, the **Union Building** towers over the Kanawha River and **Haddad Riverfront Park**, hub of many activities during the annual **Sternwheel Regatta** [see calendar of events], a ten-day citywide celebration in late summer. For information about walking tours of downtown, the East End or the Edgewood area of Charleston, call the Convention and Visitors Bureau at (304)344-5075 or (800)733-5469 or visit their office at 200 Civic Center Drive.

Capitol Complex

Capitol Building

At 293 feet, the gold-leafed dome of West Virginia's main **capitol building** stands five feet higher than the U.S. Capitol dome in Washington, DC, and gracefully commands almost any view of Charleston's East End. Keystone of the pleasant, tree-shaded Capitol Complex, its east and west wings enclose a large, circular fountain on the north side, while the south entrance overlooks the Kanawha River. Designed by Cass Gilbert, who also designed the U.S. Treasury, Supreme Court and Chamber of Commerce buildings in the nation's capital, the Renaissance-style building was begun in 1924 and completed eight years later, two years before the architect's death, at a cost of about $10 million.

The huge marble and stone structure is the state's sixth capitol building. In fact, between 1863 and 1885, West Virginia's seat of government moved not only from building to building, but also from Wheeling to Charleston along the Ohio and Kanawha rivers so many times that it came to be known as the "floating capital." Wheeling served as the capital from 1863, when West Virginians elected Arthur I. Boreman as their first governor, until 1870, when legislators changed the location to Charleston. Five years later, they reversed their decision and moved back to Wheeling. Finally, in 1877, the choice of a permanent capital was turned over to West Virginia voters, who chose Charleston over two other proposed locations, Clarksburg and Martinsburg. By proclamation of the governor, the official move took place eight years later, in 1885.

The capitol building that served West Virginia beginning in 1885 was destroyed January 3, 1921 in a spectacular fire greatly aggravated by the explosion of cases of ammunition stored in the attic. Charleston historian Harry M. Brawley, then a boy, witnessed the fire and remembered: "By the time the explosions ceased and the crowds were under control, a single silvery stream of water reached the top of the roof. By then the fire was a raging inferno and fighting it was futile." The building burned for three days, and was a total loss. Heavy safes were removed from the smoldering remains and doused with water, but when they were opened their contents burst into flames.

For the next few years, the state's business was conducted from the so-called "Pasteboard Capitol," a large temporary structure erected on the governor's side lawn after the 1921 blaze. It, too, was destroyed by fire, in 1927. By then, government offices had

The brilliant gold dome of the main Capitol Building dominates Charleston's skyline. STEPHEN J. SHALUTA, JR.

already begun moving into the completed west wing of Cass Gilbert's magnificent complex, although the domed central building would not be completed for another five years.

Begin your tour of the capitol at the information desk on the lower level of the rotunda. Look up, and you'll see the building's dazzling focal point—a 4,000-pound, eight-foot-wide chandelier, hanging 54 feet from the top of the capitol dome, made of 10,080 pieces of hand-cut Czechoslovakian crystal and lit by 96 bulbs. Every four years, the chandelier is carefully lowered, and each piece of crystal is cleaned in preparation for the governor's inauguration.

Look in any other direction, and you'll see great walls of marble. Six types of marble (Imperial Danby, Italian Travertine, Tennessee, white Vermont, black Belgian and pink Georgian) are used throughout the building. The sounds of voices and footsteps reverberate in the huge rotunda, and the proportions are massive: porticoes at the north and south entrances are supported by limestone pillars weighing 86 tons each, and the sliding brass and copper doors (decorated with oak, elm, hickory, beech and maple leaves, all native hardwoods) weigh well over a ton. Walk along hallways to the east and west to see a gallery of portraits of West Virginia's governors.

If the legislature is in session, you can watch the proceedings. Visitor galleries are available on a first-come, first-served basis in both the Senate meeting room and the House of Delegates chamber. (The former is located on the west end of the capitol, the latter on the east.) Notice that the ceiling of the Senate chamber is domed, whereas the House chamber is flat; and the carved eagle in the Senate chamber spreads its wings, while the one in the House has its wings closed. Senators sit at hand-carved walnut desks, complete with telephones connected to their offices. Both chambers feature chandeliers with more Czechoslovakian crystal, and each holds a hand-carved replica of the Great Seal of West Virginia bearing the state motto, "Montani Semper Liberi"—Mountaineers Are Always Free.

Before leaving the building, do take a look into the governor's office, with its enormous, sky-blue Oriental rug. If you have time, stroll around the grounds to enjoy several fountains, as well as the newly completed, contemplative **Veterans Memorial.** You'll also see statues depicting Stonewall Jackson, Booker T. Washington, a Union Mountaineer and a somber, introspective Abraham Lincoln, *Lincoln Walks at Midnight,* inspired by the Vachel Lindsay poem of the same name.

Capitol hours are 7:00 a.m. to 7:00 p.m. Monday through Friday. Guided tours are available from 9:00 a.m. to 3:00 p.m. On Saturdays, the building is open from 9:00 a.m. to 7:00 p.m., with guided tours on the hour between 1:00 and 4:00 p.m. On Sundays, the building is open from noon to 7 p.m., but there are no guided tours.

Directions: From I-64-/77 take Exit 99, Greenbrier Street, and follow it south toward the Kanawha River. The Capitol Complex will be on your left. Phone: (304)558-3809. You may also call (800)CALL-WVA or (800)225-3982 and ask for the guide's desk in the rotunda.

Cultural Center

From the west wing of the capitol building, a walkway passes between several glossy-leaved magnolia trees to the entrance of the **Cultural Center**. This sleek, contemporary building is West Virginia's showcase for artistic, cultural and historical heritage, and a visitor of any age could happily spend an afternoon here.

The Cultural Center is home to both the state's Division of Culture and History and the West Virginia Library Commission. Within the purview of the Division of Culture and History are the Commission on the Arts, the Historic Preservation Office, the West Virginia State Museum, the State Archives and Library, and the state's folklife quarterly, *Goldenseal*. The Library Commission, which maintains more than 250,000 volumes for public use, administers the library reading room and microfilm library, a film and video library regarded as one of the country's finest, a video studio, and the Blind and Physically Handicapped Division.

Doorways on either side of a glass wall admit visitors to the Great Hall, the Cultural Center's welcoming entrance. This grand space, with marble floors, towering marble walls and a splendid chandelier, is a favorite place for receptions, festivals, exhibits and performances of jazz, dance, youth art, poetry and many other aspects of West Virginia culture. During the summer months, guests enjoy a display of colorful, award-winning quilts from a statewide quilt competition. Over Memorial Day weekend, thousands of visitors crowd in to enjoy traditional dancing and music at the **Vandalia Gathering**, a festival that celebrates West Virginia's folklife and spills into all areas of the Capitol Complex. Beginning the day after Thanksgiving, a month-long holiday celebration entices thousands of visitors, especially children, to the Cultural Center. Christmas tales and Hanukkah stories headline storytelling sessions, and every Saturday in December the center celebrates with crafts, music, food and children's activities. **Joyful Night**, the annual tree-lighting ceremony and musical walk through the Capitol and Governor's Mansion, ends in the Great Hall with a reception among holiday decorations.

Music lovers gather at the Cultural Center many Sundays throughout the year for **Mountain Stage**, the live weekly music radio show produced by West Virginia Public Radio for Public Radio International. Fans from across the U.S. and several foreign countries tune in this eclectic mix of popular, folk and world music—but it's much more fun to be in the live audience. Call (800)RADIO-87 for details about upcoming shows. (Tickets are sold at the door or in advance through TicketMaster: (304)342-5757.)

The **State Museum** includes exhibit areas on all three floors of the Cultural Center's public space. A good place to begin is on the lower level of the building, where permanent exhibits trace West Virginia's history from Indian migration to the early 20th century. Here you can look inside a typical settler's cabin or a quaint country store, inspect two genuine dressed fleas (one wears trousers, the other a skirt) or see George Washington's telescope. In the museum's lobby and balcony galleries, changing exhibits show work by the state's finest artists and craftspeople. A popular exhibit is the biennial **West Virginia Juried Exhibition**, for which the competition is keen, the cash prizes hefty and the opening night one of the most extravagant art events in town.

The restful courtyard views from the **State Archives Library** would be reason enough to sit for a while, but it is also an excellent research resource. State and public records and documents, private manuscript and photograph collections, video, film and microfilm collections and a genealogy research center make this the best beginning point for any scholarly or genealogical research in West Virginia.

The Cultural Center and State Museum are open 9:00 a.m. to 5:00 p.m. weekdays and 1:00 to 5:00 p.m. weekends. Hours for the Archives Library are the same, except that it is closed on Sundays. Call (304)558-0220 for information on all Cultural Center activities, or write: Communications, West Virginia Division of Culture and History, The Cultural Center, 1900 Kanawha Boulevard East, Charleston, WV 25305.

Directions: Take Exit 99 (Greenbrier Street) from I-64/77. The Capitol Complex is visible from the exit. Turn left into the complex at the light for metered parking.

Governor's Mansion

Part of the Capitol Complex, the 30-room **Governor's Mansion** is only a few steps west of the Capitol building. This handsome Georgian-style mansion was designed by prolific Charleston architect Walter F. Martens, who designed 89 churches in West Virginia alone. With its two-story portico supported by four white Corinthian columns, the red Harvard brick mansion proudly faces the Kanawha River.

The first eight governors of West Virginia didn't have such a splendid residence provided by citizens. It wasn't until 1893 that the Legislature agreed to purchase a residence for the chief executive. The first Governor's Mansion was a frame house on Capitol Street, across from the old capitol. Governor William A. MacCorkle was the first West Virginia governor to occupy it. After the capitol burned in 1921, the Legislature appropriated $100,000 for a permanent executive mansion to be built next to the new capitol. The first governor to occupy it, albeit briefly, was Ephraim Morgan, whose term expired a week after he moved in.

When you enter the mansion, you'll face two wide Georgian staircases flanking the large entry room, the highlight of which is the dramatic checkerboard floor of black Belgium and white Tennessee marble. The carpets incorporate symbols found in the capitol building. Among them are the state bird, the cardinal, and the state flower, rhododendron. Take special note of the ballroom's chandeliers, once fixtures in Scott's Drug Store on Capitol Street, and the warm butternut paneling in the library.

Guided tours of the first floor state rooms are available by appointment only. The tour, which takes about 20 minutes, may be scheduled for Thursday or Friday. On Thursdays, tours are conducted between the hours of 9:30 and 11:30 a.m. and 1:30 to 3:30 p.m.; on Fridays, between 9:30 and 11:30 a.m. only. Call (304)558-3809 to schedule a tour.

Directions: Leave the capitol building by the west door. The mansion is to your left.

Tip: Before leaving the complex, stroll past **Holly Grove**, just to the west of the Governor's Mansion. Also known as the Daniel Ruffner House, Holly Grove was built by Ruffner in 1815 on what was then a plantation east of Charleston, and served for a time as an inn. Well-known overnight guests included John James Audubon, Daniel Boone, Henry Clay, Samuel Houston and Andrew Jackson. The building is now headquarters for the West Virginia Commission on Aging.

Capitol Market

Where Capitol Street meets Smith Street in downtown Charleston, a bright new indoor/outdoor market, incorporating the city's former farmers market, has taken over three acres once occupied by a rail freight station built in 1905. A meeting place as well as a fresh food marketplace, the cheerful red-and-green renovation is complemented by matching cafe tables and inviting Adirondack rocking chairs. The year-round indoor market has just about everything an adventurous cook could want: in addition to fresh produce, the 16,000-square-foot space houses a coffee bar, fish market, wine shop, butcher shop, cheese shop, bakeries, West Virginia-made specialties and more. It's open 9:00 a.m. to 6:00 p.m. Monday through Saturday, and noon to 5:00 p.m. Sunday, with plenty of free parking. Call (304)344-1905 for more information.

Directions: 800 Smith Street, at the north end of Capitol Street. Take Exit 100 off I-77/64.

Craik-Patton House

This outwardly modest house about two miles east of Charleston, which you could easily overlook if you didn't know better, is one of Charleston's historical treasures. Here are preserved the lives and times of two prominent West Virginia families. Fully restored by the National Society of Colonial Dames of America for the 1976 Bicentennial and listed on the National Register of Historic Places, the Greek Revival-style building contains countless pieces of interest, many original to the home and used by the Craiks and the Pattons.

Originally called Elm Grove, the two-story house built in 1834 by James Craik was one of the first to be built with lumber from early sawmills. It first stood near what is now the downtown intersection of Virginia and Dunbar streets, and has twice been moved. Craik had inherited the land from his grandfather, Dr. James Craik, personal physician and close friend of George Washington. He and his family occupied it until 1846. In 1858, it was purchased by George Smith Patton, who later organized and led the Kanawha Riflemen in the Confederate Army. He was wounded in action at the Battle of Winchester and died in 1864.

Most rooms are furnished as they would have been when the Craiks raised seven of their 11 children here during the 1830s and early 1840s, but one room, the Patton Room, looks as it must have in 1865. Visitors who appreciate period architecture will be pleased by the numerous cut-outs in walls throughout the house that reveal different types of construction. With original floors, doors and hardware in place and every room full of antiques, this house will delight lovers of history.

Admission is $3.00 for adults and $2.00 for children and seniors.

Beautifully restored, the 1834 Craik-Patton House is furnished with many pieces that belonged to its early owners. RICK LEE

Hours are 1:00 p.m. to 4:00 p.m. Thursday through Sunday, April through October. Docents in period clothing lead tours of the house. Please write Craik-Patton, Inc., PO Box 175, Charleston, WV 25321 or call in advance to arrange group tours: (304)925-5341.

Directions: Two miles east of the Capitol Complex on Kanawha Boulevard (Route 60), adjacent to Daniel Boone Park.

Tip: While you are there, stroll outdoors and enjoy the herb and boxwood gardens at the Craik-Patton House. And, to see what homes were like before the introduction of sawmills, visit the **Ruffner Log House** on the same property. One of the earliest known structures in the area, the log house may date back to 1820. **Daniel Boone Park**, adjoining the Craik-Patton property, is a pleasant spot with a wheelchair-accessible deck overlooking the river. Unless it is out on the river, you will find the *P.A. Denny* [see entry] docked there.

Kanawha State Forest

One of the joys of being in Charleston is the ease with which you can leave the city behind. **Kanawha State Forest**, just seven miles to the south, is a 9,300-acre haven for picnickers, hikers, bikers, swimmers, horseback riders, campers, and—in season—those who want to hunt and fish in specified areas. The park maintains more than 25 miles of trails, ranging from seriously challenging climbs to the Salamander Trail, a wheelchair-accessible walkway. Plenty of playgrounds, picnic sites and shelters make it a favorite family place, and the park sponsors frequent weekend activities. Call (304)558-3500 or (800)CALL-WVA for more information, or write Kanawha State Forest, Route 2, Box 285, Charleston, WV 25314.

Directions: From I-64, take exit 58A and drive south on Route 119. Turn left onto Oakwood Road at the second stop light, and right onto Bridge Road. Follow Bridge Road to Connell Road. Turn right onto Connell Road. At the bottom of Connell Road, make a sharp left onto Kanawha Forest Drive and follow it to the forest entrance.

P.A. Denny *Sternwheeler*

Unlike some paddlewheel boats constructed as replicas of early transport ships that traveled America's rivers, the ***P.A. Denny*** is the real thing, and the waterway she travels is her own home. Built in 1930 by Charles Ward Engineering Works in Charleston and originally christened as the towboat *Scott*, she served the U.S. Army Corps of Engineers for many years. She was purchased in 1973 by Charleston riverman P.A. Denny, who rebuilt her from the hull up and renamed her in honor of a granddaughter. Following Mr. Denny's death in 1975, Charleston businessman Lawson W. Hamilton, Jr. bought the boat and renamed her again for his longtime friend. He continues to operate the grand old sternwheeler in memory of Mr. Denny.

She is a celebrated centerpiece of Charleston's ten-day **Sternwheel Regatta**, the annual river festival held just before Labor Day, but any warm day or starry evening is a good excuse for a cruise on the *P.A. Denny*. Watching Charleston from the top deck of the white, red-trimmed sternwheeler, with the wind in your hair and the big red paddlewheel churning, is a fine way to view the city. For year-round comfort, the boat's first level and most of the second are enclosed and heated. There is a cash bar on the first level.

With a comfy capacity of 150 passengers, the *P.A. Denny* is locally popular for catered charter cruises, luncheons, dinners, and celebrations of all kinds. For a complete price list, hours and schedules for public cruises or private charters, call (304)925-7899.

Directions: The *P.A. Denny* normally docks at **Daniel Boone Park** (beside the Craik-Patton House), east of the Capitol Complex on Route 60. Board there or at Haddad Riverfront Park in downtown Charleston.

Sunrise Museum

Across the Kanawha River from downtown Charleston, you can climb a pleasant, wooded trail to **Sunrise Museum** and discover a world where art meets science. The museum occupies two large stone mansions, one on either side of Myrtle Road. Built in 1905, the **Science Hall** is the former home of West Virginia's ninth governor, William A. MacCorkle, and was named after Sunrise, his family's Virginia plantation. The building that now houses the **Sunrise Art Museum**, Torquilstone, was the home of MacCorkle's son and was built in 1928.

In the Science Hall visitors can explore over 30 hands-on interactive science and arts exhibits that awaken new understandings about light and color, energy and magnetism, illusion and perception, art and architecture. Launch a hot air balloon, capture your shadow, explore laser holography or suspend a ball in mid-air with magnetism! An exhibit called **ScienceScape** lets very young scientists explore sound, shape and pattern. And be sure to step into **Stuffee's Kitchen**, where 9-foot-tall, soft-sculptured Stuffee actually unzips his skin to show the inner workings of the body. Kids and adults learn about stars, constellations, black holes and other astronomical wonders at the museum's planetarium, and **Science a la Carte**, an every-weekend series of interactive demonstrations, gets visitors involved in experiments. The museum brings in guest presenters for a new series of **Science Saturdays** each season, and **Funtastic Fridays** fill the summer months with special planetarium shows, art activities and more.

The history inside Sunrise is almost as interesting as the science. Be sure to take note of the huge fireplace in the Drawing Room. It contains stones that Governor MacCorkle collected from around the

The P.A. Denny *Sternwheeler is a familiar sight on the Kanawha River in her home port of Charleston.* DRAWING BY WILLIAM D. GOEBEL

world, many inscribed with their places of origin. Outside the Science Hall, try the amazing "whisper dishes" that make the faintest of whispers perfectly audible to a friend on the other side of the wide lawn, and stroll through the rose garden, where a bronze statue commemorates Christa McAuliffe, the beloved teacher who died in the *Challenger* space shuttle explosion.

Across the street at Sunrise Art Museum, you'll find locally-curated, traveling and multi-media exhibitions throughout the year, along with selections from the museum's permanent collection. Activities often include a popular artist-in-residence program: you can watch the artist at work and ask questions about their creations or creative process. **Art a la Carte**, an occasional program, engages visitors with interactive demonstrations and art lessons. Performance art enlivens Sunrise with the **Theater in the Galleries** program, which employs local actors in plays and skits that complement the museum's changing exhibits. And each year the museum hosts **Christmas at Sunrise**, featuring unusual holiday trees and wreaths created by local artist and designers, along with a delectable gingerbread village by area chefs. The program begins on the Friday after Thanksgiving with a day of family fun, **Holly Day**.

Admission is $3.50 for adults and $2.50 for students, teachers and seniors; there is no charge for museum members and children under three. Children under 16 should be accompanied by an adult in both buildings. Group tours can be easily arranged by calling the museum two weeks in advance at (304)344-8035. The museum is open 11:00 a.m. to 5:00 p.m. Wednesday through Saturday, noon to 5:00 p.m. Sunday. Holiday hours may differ. For more information, write: Sunrise Museum, 746 Myrtle Road, Charleston, WV 25314.

Directions: From I-64, take the Oakwood Road exit and turn left at the traffic light. Go to Route 60 and turn right (east). From Route 60, turn away from the river at the next traffic light, Thayer Street, and make an immediate left paralleling the river. Turn right onto Bridge Road and then right onto Myrtle Road. Proceed less than one-fourth mile to 746 Myrtle Road.

Town Center

Visitors to Charleston's historic districts don't need a car to get to the best and biggest shopping mall in the area. A short walk, or a fun 75-cent ride on one of Charleston's old-fashioned trolley buses (operating 9:30 a.m. to 5:30 p.m. weekdays and 10:30 a.m. to 5:00 p.m. Saturdays) will take you to one of the largest enclosed inner-city shopping malls in the United States. The vast, plant-filled structure holds more than 150 shops, four major department stores and a variety of restaurants, as well as a top-floor food court with a spectacular view of a waterfall that tumbles through the sunlit, three-story atrium. The mall occupies the full city block bounded by Court, Lee, Clendenin and Quarrier streets. Hours are 10:00 a.m. to 9:00 p.m Monday through Saturday and 12:30 to 6:00 p.m. Sunday, though doors open at 6:00 a.m. for morning walkers. Telephone (304)345-9525.

Watt Powell Baseball Park

Peanuts and popcorn and...baseball, of course! America's favorite pastime is alive and well at Charleston's **Watt Powell Baseball Park**. On many summer evenings, the cheers of loyal fans mingle with the sounds of trains passing near the 5,400-seat park. The city's resident team, the Charleston Alley Cats, is a single-A farm club for the Cincinnati Reds. These talented young players give the game their all and rarely disappoint the spectators. If you've never been to a minor league game, go see the Alley Cats and find out why this distinctively American form of family entertainment is more popular than ever. You might just see a future major-league star in the making. For a full season schedule, call (304)344-CATS or write: Charleston Alley Cats, PO Box 4669, Charleston, WV 25304.

Directions: From I-64/77, take the 35th Street Bridge exit. Watt Powell Park is straight ahead, at the intersection of 35th Street and MacCorkle Avenue.

Cross Lanes

Tri-State Greyhound Park

Seen close-up from the outdoor patio at the **Tri-State Greyhound Park**, the sleek greyhounds streak by at incredible speed. Whether you're betting on your favorite or just watching, this is the most exciting place from which to view the races in fair weather. The track has two other options for race-watchers: the casual environment of the enclosed grandstand section or the more formal atmosphere of the clubhouse, where each table is equipped with a TV that broadcasts replays of the live races as well as races from simulcast tracks.

Races are run year-round, rain or shine, at 7:30 p.m. Monday and Wednesday through Saturday and 1:30 p.m. on Saturdays, Sundays and some holidays. There's no charge for admission to the outdoor patio or grandstand, and a nominal per-person and per-table charge for the clubhouse. Call (304)776-1000 for more information and group rates.

The track also has 600 video lottery machines, including slot-style games, card games and keno. Hours are 11:00 a.m. to 12:30 a.m. Monday through Thursday, 1:00 p.m. to 12:30 a.m. Sunday, 11:00 a.m. 2:30 a.m Friday, and 11:00 a.m. to 2:00 a.m. Saturday. Youngsters under 18 are admitted with proper parental supervision, but are not allowed to wager, cash tickets or enter the video gaming area.

Directions: From Charleston take I-64 west to Exit 47 (Cross Lanes) and follow the signs one-half mile to the park. There is plenty of free parking.

Dunbar

Wine Cellars Park

If you are traveling west from Charleston to Huntington, you may want to take a relaxing break at a recreation area that is also on the National Register of Historic Places, **Wine Cellars Park** in **Dunbar**.

In the mid-1850s, Thomas Friend started a winery on a 448-acre tract of land once owned by George Washington. He planted hundreds of acres of "big blue" (probably Catawba) grapes, lining both sides of the hollow and extending to the next for half a mile or more. He also built three wine cellars to store and age the wine. According to newspaper accounts of the time, his business thrived. As happened to many commercial ventures of the day, unfortunately, the Civil War interrupted. The property passed through many hands—first at auction to settle Friend's bad debts—and the wine cellars were eventually abandoned.

Although unconfirmed by historians, Friend's winery may have served another purpose during his tenure. Popular legend has it that the cellars were part of the Underground Railroad. Purportedly, runaway slaves found their way to the vineyard, mixed with the other workers and then escaped by hiding in wine shipments destined for places where abolitionists could rescue and care for them.

The City of Dunbar bought 316 acres of the property, including the cellars, in 1974 and began an ambitious restoration. By 1982 they had not only refurbished the cellars, but added a caretaker's house, three covered picnic shelters (with fireplaces, tables and grills), restrooms, parking lots, a playground, nature paths and hiking trails, cross-country ski trails, camping areas, a game refuge and a seven-acre lake stocked with trout, bass, bluegill and catfish.

The park is open daily, dawn to dusk. (Night fishing is permitted, but you must make advance arrangements with the caretaker.) Hours for the recreation center are 11:00 a.m. to 8:00 p.m. Phone ahead for arrangements for handicapped access or to receive information on indoor basketball and the park's Olympic-sized pool: (304)766-0223.

Directions: Take the Dunbar exit from I-64. Go west on Route 25 and follow signs to the park.

Huntington

On the mid-section of the Ohio River at a point where West Virginia, Ohio and Kentucky meet is **Huntington**. Railroad magnate Collis P. Huntington built the city to serve as the western terminus for the Chesapeake and Ohio Railway—which he also built, owned and operated. The location was ideal: nearby timber tracts, coal fields, oil and natural gas deposits and an important river connection with Cincinnati. Huntington furthered his interests by pushing his rail line through the mountains to link it with the Union Pacific line, thereby establishing the long-dreamed-of Transcontinental Railroad. In 1884, Huntington did something no one had done before—he rode his own railroad car from the Atlantic Ocean to the Pacific over tracks he either owned or controlled.

Even today, the city's layout shows that it was planned around the development of rail travel. Tree-lined, 100-foot-wide avenues (large enough for four rail cars to pass abreast) run north and south while numbered streets run east and west.

The railways brought prosperity, dry goods, food, hardware, furniture, equipment and farm animals to Huntington. They also brought foreign entrepreneurs, farmers, caskets bearing the heroes of three wars and politicians. Presidents Teddy Roosevelt, Garfield and Eisenhower all stopped their campaign trains here.

Today, Huntington is a vibrant city blessed with beautiful parks, a busy riverfront, many fine Victorian homes and a respected art museum. It is also the home of **Marshall University**, the state's second-largest university, and the **Thundering Herd**, with football fans every bit as avid and loyal as their counterparts in Mountaineer Country. Call (304)525-7333 or (800)635-6329.

A self-guided walking tour of downtown historical buildings, *Streets of Style*, is available from **Huntington Main Street**. Call (304)529-0053 to get a copy, which includes a map and plenty of information about the structures. The walk begins at Tenth Street and Fourth Avenue.

Among its highlights: the ornate **Keith-Albee Theatre**, which opened in 1928 with the film *Good Morning Judge* starring Reginald Denny, and still brings regional crowds together for live theater and other presentations, including the Marshall Artists Series; the former **Hotel Frederick**, West Virginia's largest hotel when it opened in 1906 with 250 guest rooms, Turkish baths, hot vapor rooms and other amenities; **Reuschlein's Clock**, a four-faced cast-iron timepiece made by the famous clockmaker Seth Thomas around 1800 and still keeping time today; the **Old Post Office**, dating from about 1909; the former **Carnegie Library** (now the Huntington College of Business) and the **Central Huntington Garage**, one of the state's first indoor parking buildings when it opened in 1927.

Huntington's asymmetrical **East End Bridge** is definitely worth a look. The second concrete cable-stayed bridge erected in the country, it was the first to use high-strength concrete. Seen from the river, it rises overhead like a gigantic spider. If you can't see it from a boat, drive its one-mile length from Huntington's 31st Street to Ohio's Route 7 in Proctorville. But come right back to West Virginia!

Directions: You can pick up maps and brochures at the **Cabell-Huntington Convention and Visitors Bureau**. From I-64, take Exit 11 to Route 10, which becomes Hal Greer Boulevard. Follow it toward downtown. At 3rd Avenue, turn left. Go eight blocks to the intersection of 3rd Avenue and 8th Street. The visitors center is in the Civic Arena. Hours are 9:00 a.m. to 5:00 pm. Monday through Friday. You may also get information from the Information Center on I-64, located on the westbound side between Exits 6 and 11.

Tip: As you drive down Hal Greer Boulevard into Huntington, notice the new statue of **Carter G. Woodson** between 8th and 9th avenues. Known as the "Father of Black History," this remarkable American is credited with saving African-American history from oblivion. Founder of the Association for Negro Life and History, the *Negro History Bulletin* and Negro History Week, he authored many books, including the widely-used text *The Negro in Our History*. The Huntington native also served for a time as dean of West Virginia Collegiate Institute, now West Virginia State College.

Camden Park and the Jewel City *Sternwheeler*

Since 1902, West Virginia's only amusement park has thrilled and delighted children and adults. For an old-timey treat with a couple of new twists and loops, head for **Camden Park**, where the 28 rides include everything from the old-but-reliable Big Dipper roller coaster to the wild, looping Thunderbolt Express.

At Camden Park, the little ones aren't left out. If even the Big Dipper looks too scary, take them on the merry-go-round or into Kiddie Land. There's a roller skating rink, batting cages, an arcade full of blinking and buzzing games, miniature golf and a gift shop.

Bring your own picnic to the huge picnic area, buy hot dogs and cotton candy to eat while you stroll, or enjoy a meal in the air-conditioned cafeteria. On holidays and during special events, expect

The Big Dipper roller coaster is a favorite ride at Huntington's Camden Park, West Virginia's only amusement park. DAVID FATTALEH

fireworks and big-name entertainment in the amphitheater.

Also at the park is the state's third-largest Indian burial mound. Unexcavated, the conical, flat-topped mound is the largest in the Huntington area. It was built by the Adena between 1,000 B.C. and

A.D. 1. And, while you're at Camden Park, you can take a ride on the ***Jewel City Sternwheeler***. The excursion boat boards at the extreme western end of the park.

The fee to enter park gates is $1.00. After that, you can either pay one price ($12.50) to ride all day, or purchase individual ride tickets for $0.25. (Most rides require between three and eight tickets.) Camden Park is open Saturdays and Sundays in April and September, and seven days a week May through Labor Day. Hours are 10:00 a.m. to 10:00 p.m. (one hour later on Saturday). No alcoholic beverages are permitted. The *Jewel City Sternwheeler* operates whenever the park is open, unless it has been reserved for a private party. Hour-long boat rides begin at 1:00, 3:00, 5:00 and 7:00 p.m. and cost $4.00 for adults, $3.00 for children 12 and under. For more information call (304)429-4231.

Directions: From I-64, take Exit 6. Go west on Route 60 for three miles to the park entrance.

Heritage Village

This award-winning shopping and entertainment complex, in the former Baltimore and Ohio Station, is centrally located at 11th Street and Veterans Memorial Boulevard. The village owes its origin to the Cabell-Wayne Historical Society and the Collis P. Huntington Railroad Society. It's a good place to begin a tour of Huntington, especially if the city's railroad history captures your interest. And a good place to start here is the larger-than-life bronze likeness of Collis P. Huntington himself. Moved from its original home several blocks away and donated to the city by the Huntington family, it stands on a granite pedestal in the courtyard of **Heritage Village**. Its sculptor was Gutzon Borglum, of Mount Rushmore fame.

Heritage Village is home to an example of the kind of steam locomotive used during the city's railroad heyday. You can sit at the throttle of the old B&O 4559, a Mikado-class locomotive built in Ohio around 1911. You'll also see a Pullman Sleeper, which were often pulled by large engines with the rest of their load. Named for its inventor George Pullman, the sleeping car revolutionized rail travel. The one at Heritage Village was built for the Great Northern Railway's Oriental Limited in 1925 and named *Larpentuer*. It has 12 sleeping sections and a drawing room. Completely restored in 1988, it has been renamed—what else?—the *Collis P. Huntington*.

Browse through curio shops inside a boxcar, enjoy the attractive plaza and visit the old **Bank of Huntington**, the city's first, which was robbed by the Jesse James Gang on September 8, 1875.

According to local legend, the gang fled into Kentucky and beyond, never to be apprehended for the crime. The grillwork on the teller's cage is one of many interesting period pieces in the old brick bank.

For lunch or dinner, the **Station Restaurant** is a winning choice. The Victorian-style eatery, furnished with antiques, occupies the restored 1890s train depot and is a Huntington favorite. Be sure to look at the many photographs lining the stairway to the upper level. For more information call (304)696-5954 or write Heritage Village, PO Box 2985, Huntington, WV 25728.

Directions: From I-64 take Exit 8 (5th Street). Follow 5th Street to 8th Street and turn left. Turn right on Veterans Memorial Boulevard. Heritage Village is on the right.

Huntington Museum of Art

West Virginia's largest art museum could hold its own anywhere. Bright, pleasant and modern, the nationally acclaimed museum has outstanding permanent collections of 18th to 20th-century European and American paintings as well as Ohio River Valley historical glass, contemporary art glass, Georgian silver, Islamic prayer rugs, American furniture, Appalachian folk art and contemporary sculpture in addition to an ambitious schedule of changing shows. The museum provides studio classes, workshops, public lectures, a hands-on **Education Gallery**, a 10,000-volume art reference library, an auditorium for the performing arts and a very nice museum store.

The museum sits on a gentle hilltop surrounded by 50 acres of land with woodland nature trails, herb gardens, an outdoor amphitheater and a sculpture courtyard. The new **C. Fred Edwards Conservancy** is a lush, watery wonderland of subtropical palms and seasonal flowers in which to relax and contemplate your aesthetic experience. Spring and fall festivals add to the museum's other offerings.

Among other treasures in the permanent collection, be sure to see the 180-plus Near Eastern art objects donated by the Joseph and Omayma Touma family and the **Herman P. Dean Firearms Collection**, which traces the development of firearms from the 13th century, when gunpowder was invented, to the mid-19th century.

Docents will lead you through the museum, or you can explore on your own, with maps and brochures to help. The museum buildings are handicapped-accessible.

The museum does not charge admission, but suggests a donation of $2.00 for adults and $1.00 for children, students and seniors. Hours are 10:00 a.m. to 5:00 p.m. Tuesday through Saturday and noon to 5:00 p.m. Sunday. To find out about upcoming exhibitions or to arrange a tour for groups of ten or more, call (304)529-2701 or write **Huntington Museum of Art**, 2033 McCoy Road, Huntington, WV 25701.

Directions: From I-64, take Exit 8 and follow the signs. From downtown Huntington, take 8th Street away from the river and follow it to the museum.

Huntington Area Parks

Few cities can boast as many as many well-maintained and beautiful outdoor spaces as Huntington. Even if you have only a day to explore the town, plan to spend part of it in a park. Good maps and directions to city parks are available from the Greater Huntington Park and Recreation District, PO Box 2985, Huntington, WV 25728. Their phone is (304)696-5954. Depending upon your particular interest—tennis, soccer, basketball, walking, jogging, fishing, picnicking or just reading a book under a tree—you'll find a park to please you in Huntington.

Directly in front of Heritage Village at 10th Street and Veterans Memorial Boulevard is the **David Harris Riverfront Park**. Opened in 1984 on this wide stretch of the Ohio River, it's Huntington's newest park. Riverfront Park is a popular place where picnickers spread out on expansive lawns with plenty of tables and shelters, children squeal on the playgrounds, and powerboats whiz by on the water. At night, the 1,500-seat amphitheater, complete with a floating stage, holds concerts. Riverfront festivals take place here several times a year.

At the opposite side of Heritage Village (away from the river) is Huntington's most famous park, **Ritter Park**. With a new tennis center, a nationally recognized rose garden (over 1,500 plants and some 80 varieties of roses) and a playground recognized by *Child Magazine* as one of the "ten best playgrounds in America," the 100-acre park has something for outdoor lovers of all ages and interests. Its tree-shaded oval walking/jogging track is in use continuously. The children's play area, with its bigger-than-life columns, arches and triangles to climb on, is rarely without a few hide-and-seekers. The park also contains a pioneer cabin and a 1,200-seat amphitheater.

At the western edge of Ritter Park, look for a stone **Memorial Arch** placed in honor of "God and the men of Cabell County who served faithfully in the Great War." Then you can follow the extended jogging path through adjoining **Memorial, Kiwanis** and **Washington Avenue** parks, following Four Pole Creek along a swath of green that extends almost all the way through the city.

The Park District maintains several other parks and recreation areas, including **Altizer Park**, at the eastern end of Altizer Avenue, where you can find softball and soccer fields, large picnic shelters, a basketball court and a children's playground. **Westmoreland Park** is another neighborhood gathering place, this one on Vernon Street in Huntington's Westmoreland section. **Prindle Field** has both baseball and Little League fields. **Kiwanivista Park** is a popular roadside picnic stop between Barboursville and Milton on Route 60 outside of Huntington, and **April Dawn Park**, just two blocks north of Route 60 on Smith Street in downtown Milton, is a one-acre park with a picnic shelter and playground.

Huntington's largest park is **Rotary Park**, with a fine view of the city's east end from a tall observation tower. It features two ballfields, a basketball court, a playground, hiking trails, an 18-hole disc-golf course and a picnic shelter. Follow the signs off I-64 (Exit 15) to the park. At **St. Cloud Commons Park**, look for ballfields, basketball and tennis courts, a clubhouse and playground. The park is located at 1701 Jackson Avenue, off I-64 at Exit 16.

Wallace Park features a wilderness area, and adjoining **Camp Mad Anthony Wayne**, named for the frontier army general, has a newly renovated lodge and four rustic rental cabins, also recently refurbished. Also at this park is a tree nursery with 2,500 seedlings. These parks are eight miles west of the city on Spring Valley Drive off I-64 Exit 16. Be sure to make advance reservations if you want to stay here. Call (304)696-5954.

Finally, the westernmost point of West Virginia is also a park, **Virginia Point Park**. The Ohio and Big Sandy Rivers converge at this point where West Virginia, Kentucky and Ohio meet. You'll find campgrounds, a boat launch and a picnic shelter at this park, located at the end of Laurel Street in Kenova off I-64 Exit 1. Call (304)696-5954.

Huntington Railroad Museum and New River Train Excursions

All aboard, rail fans! Since 1959, the non-profit Collis B. Huntington Railroad Historical Society, Inc., a chapter of the National Railway Historical Society, has been preserving, promoting and inspiring railroad history in Huntington. At the **Huntington Railroad Museum**, the society maintains several impressive engines and cars resting on short tracks in the park and at its 8th Avenue work site near 11th Street. You are invited to climb aboard and inspect a large locomotive, formerly the Chesapeake and Ohio Railway Company's Mallet #1308, made in 1949 and one of only two of its class still in existence. Then walk inside the old C&O caboose for an up-close look at railroad life in days gone past. The fenced-in, outdoor museum also has a handcar you can ride if you're willing to provide the hand-cranked power.

The museum, established in 1962, charges no admission but gratefully accepts donations. Membership in the Collis P. Huntington Society is also encouraged; the only credential you need is a love of trains. Call the museum at (304)525-5884.

Directions: On the fringe of Ritter Park at 14th Street West and Memorial Boulevard.

Each year since 1966, on the most colorful fall foliage weekends, the Society has sponsored day-long trips through the scenic "Grand Canyon of the East," the New River Gorge. Usually on two weekends in October, engines and cars make their way through the entire length of the gorge, giving passengers a ride to remember for a lifetime.

Called the **World Famous New River Train Excursion**, the round trip begins in downtown Huntington early in the morning. The train picks up passengers in St. Albans and Montgomery and arrives about five hours later in Hinton, where the whole town is waiting, in a festival mood, for the train to pull in. Along the way, the train stops at Thurmond, where the National Park Service has restored the oldest station on the C&O main line, for a 45-minute tour of the town and depot. Passengers use a mile-by-mile guide to identify points of interest, including Gauley, where a restored New York Central depot houses town offices and a rail history exhibit, and Hawks Nest State Park [see entries].

You have a choice of Coach, Deluxe or Premium Service classes. Coach fares range from about $70.00 for children to about $100.00 for adults, including a continental breakfast and a boxed dinner at your seat. Premium Service, at about $180 (child or adult), allows you to watch the scenery roll by from a lounge car, day Pullman or other special car and includes a dinner prepared on the train and served in a special dining area. Premium Service passengers may request an upper level seat on the dome car, but these are assigned on a first-come, first-served basis, so ask early.

For the ultimate luxury in train travel, you can even rent your own rail car. The Society also sponsors other occasional excursions, including holiday trips. Call for more details about these options.

All cars have electric heat and air-conditioning. No alcoholic beverages are sold or permitted. The excursions run rain or shine.

Handicapped access is limited to coach service. For schedule information, or to make a reservation, call (304)453-1641 or write Collis P. Huntington Railroad Historical Society, 1429 Chestnut Street, 2nd Floor, Kenova, WV 25530.

Directions: Trains board at 7th Avenue and 9th Street in downtown Huntington.

Mountain State Balloon Company

Although it's not affiliated with the Park and Recreation District, there is an exhilarating trip that lifts off—literally—from Ritter Park. The **Mountain State Balloon Company** offers hot-air balloon rides from the park and other launch sites year-round.

It'll take you about an hour to get a bird's-eye view of Huntington, swoop down near the river and glide over the countryside before coming to rest in any one of three states. "Depending on which way the wind is blowing," says pilot Steve Bond, "you can leave West Virginia, fly through Kentucky and Ohio and land again in West Virginia." A chase truck follows to return passengers to the launch point. Flights are limited to two persons per balloon in addition to the pilot and generally last 60 to 90 minutes. The cost is $150.00 per person. You should call at least two weeks in advance to schedule a ride on either of the two balloons the company operates. A favorite time to fly is fall, when foliage colors are at their peak.

Mountain State Mystery Train

Get on board, get a new identity and get involved in solving a mystery that unfolds as you ride the train! The **Mountain State Mystery Train**, run by a commercial excursion company, combines rail travel with interactive mysteries suitable for the entire family. If interactive drama is a bit too much for you, travel the **Rails of Intrigue** to a "top secret" destination in West Virginia; you'll get clues with your boarding pass.

Or ask about other scenic tours—the **Sweetheart Express**, **Mother's Day Express**, **Santa Express** and **"Throw Momma on the Train"** mystery weekend shopping trip. The company also maintains the **Mountain State Rails to Rivers and Trails Train**, featuring one-way or round-trip scenic tours that showcase the New River Gorge National River and offer you the outdoor recreation of your choice upon arrival: guided skiing, rafting, hiking, biking, horseback-riding and other expeditions.

You'll ride diesel locomotives with modern passenger cars. There are five levels of service, and costs range from about $160.00 to about $400.00 per person. The company can also accommodate private parties and group charters up to 500 people. For complete timetables and reservations, call (800)CALL-WVA or (304)529-6412 or write Mountain State Mystery Train, PO Box 8254, Huntington, WV 25701.

Directions: Trains board in both Huntington and Charleston at the Amtrak passenger stations.

Museum of Radio and Technology

For another kind of excursion, take a trip through time and see how the medium of radio has changed since its birth in the 1920s—from the Atwater Kent breadboard radio to the sleek Art Deco consoles of the 1940s to a recreated 1950s studio—at the largest radio museum in the eastern United States.

In addition to a large collection of transistor radios from the 1950s and 1960s, you'll see early televisions and computers, walk through a re-created 1920s radio shop, and listen to some favorite programs from the 1940s. You can even try your hand at "tickling the crystal" on a real crystal set.

After you have looked at thousands of radio artifacts, stop at the museum's gift store, where you'll find lavishly illustrated collectors' books and tapes of old programs. The museum is open 10:00 a.m. to 4:00 p.m. Friday and Saturday and 1:00 to 4:00 p.m. Sunday, other times by appointment. Admission is free, but donations are welcome. Call (304)525-8890 or write **Museum of Radio and Technology**, 1640 Florence Avenue, Huntington, WV 25701.

Directions: From I-64, take Exit 6 and drive into Huntington on 17th Street. Turn right on Madison Avenue to 14th Street. Turn right on 14th Street and follow it south to Harvey Road. Turn right onto Harvey Road and follow it to Florence Avenue. Turn left onto Florence Avenue. The museum is on your right at 1640.

Hurricane/Scott Depot

Downtown Hurricane's "History Row" encompasses centuries of history in three exhibits: an ancient Indian petroglyph in sandstone, called **"The Maiden of the Rock"** (the maiden, hands on hips, looks distinctly aggravated, and has also been dubbed "The Water Monster's Daughter"); a mural dedicated to the town's volunteer fire department; and a cozy **Caboose Museum**, where you'll learn everything you ever wanted to know about cabooses and then some. Even though cabooses are no longer required on trains in West Virginia, some consider this the most important rail car. Find out why by calling (304)562-5896 to arrange a tour or write Downtown Hurricane Association, PO Box 186, Hurricane, WV 25526.

On Hurricane's Main Street is a high-quality cooperative gallery of fine arts and crafts, **Main Street Studio**, featuring paintings, prints, crafts, decorative boxes and birdhouses. Hours are 11:00 a.m. to 4:00 p.m. Thursday through Saturday, and other times by appointment. Stop by 2801 Main Street or call (304)562-5445.

Get refreshed at the **Root Cellar** at 2739 Main Street, where you'll find a large selection of herbs, soaps, skin-care products, teas, desserts and breads. Store hours are 10:00 a.m. to 5:00 p.m. Monday through Saturday, with evening hours to 8:00 p.m. on Thursday. Between 11:00 a.m. and 4:00 p.m. Tuesday through Saturday, stop in for lunch or high tea! Call (304)562-4139.

Directions: From I-64, take Exit 34 and follow the signs to downtown Hurricane.

Hamon Glass Studio

If you like to shop off the beaten path, look for a small glassmaking company, **Hamon Glass Studio**, in Scott Depot. Those who visit many glass factories soon learn that each, large or small, has its own specialties. [There are three others in this region. See also Blenko, Gibson and Pilgrim glassworks.] For Robert Hamon, a second-generation glassworker who began making glass at the age of ten, the specialties are paperweights, blown art glass and glass sculpture. The paperweights are truly works of art. Another colorful item is a "lollipop vase" with swirls of color just like an old-fashioned lollipop.

The gift shop is open 8:00 a.m. to 4:00 p.m. Monday through Friday. You may visit Saturday by advance appointment only. Tours of the studio are available by appointment as well. Call (304)757-9067.

Directions: From I-64, take Exit 39 (Route 34) toward Scott Depot. Go half a mile and turn left onto Teays Boulevard, then left again on Teays Valley Road. Proceed two miles to a right-hand turn on Scott Lane and then one mile to a right turn onto Hamon Drive. Finding the studio is almost as much fun as gazing at one of the dazzling paperweights!

This riverside facade shows off the balanced Georgian design of the 1835 house built by William Jenkins. ELLYN M. CAMERON

Museum in the Community

In 1983, teacher Bobbie Hill had an idea to show a group of high school students how a museum works: in a small donated space in a local shopping center, the students organized, advertised and mounted a real art exhibition. That idea grew into a new career for Hill and a new museum for Putnam County. Operating from its recently constructed, million-dollar-plus facility with two gallery spaces, classroom, pottery studio and sculpture garden, **Museum in the Community** still serves the residents of Putnam County. Its reputation as an innovative and exciting cultural, arts and education center attracts audiences from Charleston and Huntington as well.

The museum features ongoing exhibitions, special events, classes and workshops in all arts disciplines. Museum in the Community has become well known for its promotion of regional artists, children's art and hands-on interactive programs. It also sponsors a broad range of other programming, including Kidfest, Cultural Celebrations, Brown Bag Lunch Lecture Series, Summer Arts and Science Academies and Different Stages theater productions. Hours are 9:00 a.m. to 5:00 p.m. Tuesday, Wednesday and Friday, noon to 8:00 p.m. Thursday, 10:00 a.m. to 5:00 p.m. Saturday, and 1:00 to 5:00 p.m. Sunday. Call (304)562-0484 or write Museum in the Community, PO Box 251, Scott Depot, WV 25560.

Directions: Driving west on I-64, take the Winfield exit and turn south on Route 34. Go 3½ miles and turn right at the entrance to Valley Park on Valley Park Drive. If driving east on I-64, take the Hurricane exit and turn towards the town of Hurricane. Go to the light and turn left (north) on Route 34. Go about a mile and turn left on Valley Park Drive.

Tip: After you've had your aesthetic experience, take an exhilarating ride and make a splash on the Aqua Tube at Valley Park's popular **Waves of Fun** water park. Open 11:00 a.m. to 7:00 p.m. Monday through Saturday and noon to 7:00 p.m. Sunday, Memorial Day through Labor Day (except for early closing at 6:00 p.m. during August and September). Admission is $6.25, or $5.00 for seniors and children 5-11. Call (304)562-0518 for more information.

Lesage

Jenkins Plantation Museum and Green Bottom Wildlife Management Area

In 1826, a successful Tidewater shipping company owner named William Jenkins paid former Virginia governor William H. Cabell $15,000 for 4,400 acres of rich bottomland along the Ohio River. There he established a plantation and, in 1835, completed the house that still stands near the broad river. With access to both northern and southern river routes, the **Jenkins Plantation** greatly increased its owner's prosperity and influence. Slave labor built and sustained the vast "agricultural factory" that flourished just a stone's throw from the free state of Ohio.

Built of bricks handmade on the site, this late Georgian/McIntyre-style house reflected the Tidewater origins of the Jenkins family. If you visit, you may think at first that museum director Ellyn Cameron is leading you to the back of the house, but she will explain, "Back then, the river *was* the highway." There were at least two boat landings, one for shippers and one a "social landing" at the bottom of a long slope of grass. Indeed, the symmetrical plantation house atop a wide swath of lawn must have made an impressive sight for disembarking visitors.

William Jenkins and his wife had four children and 55 slaves (including a beloved governess named Mary, who raised two generations of Jenkins children). It is their youngest son, Albert Gallatin

Jenkins, with whom the house is most closely associated. Classically educated, daring and dashingly handsome, with a foot-long beard as symmetrical as his family home, Albert Jenkins inherited the house and a third of the land when his father died in 1858. He practiced law for a time and was elected to the U.S. Congress, a career that proved to be brief. When war threatened and Albert Jenkins had to choose between his loyalties to the Union and his state, he chose Virginia and, after her secession, the Confederacy.

He raised a unit, the 8th Virginia Cavalry, from among his neighbors. With Jenkins leading, the unit became famous for its bold raids into enemy territory (he was the first to lead Confederate forces into Ohio) and guerilla-like tactics. Jenkins, who eventually achieved the rank of General and survived Gettysburg, died at 33 as the result of a wound received at the battle of Cloyd's Mountain in 1864.

Museum director Ellyn Cameron's knowledge and enthusiasm make for a lively visit. There is a modest admission fee. Hours are 1:00 to 4:00 p.m. Wednesday through Sunday, year-round, except for major holidays. Write the Jenkins Plantation Museum, RR 1, Box 538, Lesage, WV 25537 or call in advance: (304)762-1059.

What was once the riverside approach to the Jenkins house is no longer a grassy slope, but one of the most unique wetland habitats in West Virginia. In fact, the museum is within the borders of the 1,100-acre **Green Bottom Wildlife Management Area**, a multiple-use area managed by the West Virginia Division of Natural Resources for hunting, trapping, fishing, hiking and wildlife observation. Rich in prehistory as well as Jenkins family history, the Green Bottom area was used by prehistoric Indians as long as 12,500 years ago. Eighteen recorded archeological sites are here, including the **Clover Archeological Site**, a National Historic Landmark.

Green Bottom is a favorite spot for some of the state's most avid birders, and its accessibility makes it ideal for beginners, too. Even amateur bird-watchers are likely to spot blue and green herons, hawks, wood ducks and other waterfowl. Listen for the eerie chortle of a rail while you admire the patchwork of buttonbush and willow emerging from a swamp marbled with brilliant green duckweed. Bowfin, bluegill and grass pickerel have been identified here, as well as the now-famous central mudminnow, a small fish whose only known habitat is the swamp at Green Bottom.

Directions: The Jenkins Plantation Museum and the headquarters for the Green Bottom Wildlife Management Area are located on Route 2, about 21 miles south of Point Pleasant and 16 miles north of Huntington.

Tip: One of the best observation points for birders is a bridge on

Route 2, about half a mile north of the Jenkins house, that overlooks a section of swampland. If you decide to get out here, watch carefully for traffic. You'll find the headquarters for the Wildlife Management Area just a few hundred yards south of the Jenkins House, accessible from Route 2. Stop to pick up a map. If you plan to explore, it's a good idea to wear waterproof boots. As in all state wildlife management areas, be aware of the hunting season calendar before you venture out, and wear bright colors if you must walk during hunting seasons. If you want to hunt or fish, make sure you have the proper licenses and know state regulations. For more information about Green Bottom Wildlife Management Area, write the Wildlife Resources Section, General Delivery, Lesage, WV 25537. Call (304)675-0871 or -0872.

Logan

The history of **Logan**, county and town, is inextricably woven with that of Native Americans. Both were named in honor of a Mingo Indian chief, Tahgahjute, who was called "Logan" after his teacher James Logan of Pennsylvania. (Logan's sister county of Mingo is named for Tahgahjute's tribe.) Established in 1836 as a city, Logan was first known as Lawnsville, but when it was incorporated in 1852, the town's name was changed to Aracoma in honor of legendary Princess Aracoma, daughter of Shawnee Chief Cornstalk. The name Logan didn't come along until 1907.

Logan is also famous as one site of the bitter Hatfield/McCoy feud that raged for years in the hills and mountains where West Virginia meets Kentucky. "Devil Anse" Hatfield, leader of the Hatfield clan, is buried in the **Hatfield Cemetery** in nearby Sarah Ann. A tall, life-sized marble statue of the patriarch—with a heavy beard, frock coat, vest, trousers tucked into knee-high boots, and a stern expression—marks the place. The cemetery is on the National Register of Historic Places.

Chief Logan State Park

This busy park, unlike other state parks in West Virginia, is located in a city. Come here any morning, and you will see Logan residents jogging and walking the path beside the road that leads into the park. Thanks in part to them, **Chief Logan State Park** is the most often visited park in the state system.

The pleasant park, on 3,303 acres, is a welcoming stop for day travelers. You can cool off in the swimming pool, get in a game of miniature golf, play tennis or explore one of eight hiking trails. A favorite trail in May is the **Guyandotte Beauty Trail**, named for an endangered wildflower species that blooms here. There are plenty of picnic and playground areas, including a therapeutic playground for children with disabilities. If you're hungry, enjoy a meal at the park's restaurant, where you can look out at a brand-new, life-sized statue of Chief Logan, created in white Cherokee marble by Vermont sculptor Seamus O'Mahoney. Be sure to stop and read the Native American's moving speech, called "Logan's Lament," as well as Thomas Jefferson's admiring words about him, on plaques at the statue's base.

For several weekends in July and August, an outdoor drama of love and war, ***The Aracoma Story***, unfolds in the park's amphitheater. The story of Chief Cornstalk's daughter and her ill-fated love for a British captive is set in the Appalachian hills in 1780. For information and reservations for this and other outdoor theater presentations, call (304)752-0253 or write The Aracoma Story, PO Box 2016, Logan, WV 25601.

In winter, the park glitters with an ever-growing, twinkling light display, **Christmas in the Park**.

Chief Logan has 25 campsites, 14 of them with electrical hookups. For more information, call (800)CALL-WVA or (304)792-7125, visit their web site (wvweb.com/www/CHIEF_LOGAN.html) or write Chief Logan State Park, Logan, WV 25601.

Directions: From Route 119, exit at Old Logan Road and travel south to the park entrance on the right. To find the Hatfield Cemetery, take Route 44 south from Logan 12 miles to the community of Sarah Ann. Park beside the small church and follow a well-marked path uphill to the cemetery.

Malden

Midland Trail

A few miles east of Charleston is the community of Malden, the western end of the historic **Midland Trail**, one of the oldest travel routes in the United States. If you travel through West Virginia by way of this 120-mile-long east-west route, you will proceed at a slower pace than on interstate highways, but you will be using the same route traveled by "Mad" Anne Bailey, Henry Clay, Daniel Webster, Booker T. Washington, Andrew Jackson, William McKinley, Rutherford B. Hayes and hundreds of thousands of hogs and sheep on their way to Eastern markets from Ohio and Kentucky (not all at the same time, of course). And you will be rewarded with dozens of historic small towns and sites, breathtaking views of the New River Gorge and plenty of quirky surprises.

Curving from White Sulphur Springs to Charleston, the Midland Trail was first cut by herds of buffalo, used by Indians and later expanded by pioneers. The trail was authorized by the Virginia Assembly as the State Road in 1790. By stagecoach (or "shakeguts," as coaches were known in the early 1800s) it took two long, dusty days to make the trip. By car today it is about a three-hour ride, but you'll want to take extra time to explore.

You can pick up a free, colorful map of the driving trail, packed with historical and geographical information as well as tips on good places to stop along the way, in Malden at Cabin Creek Quilts, an official Midland Trail visitors center, or by calling (800)822-US60.

African Zion Baptist Church

Originally known as Kanawha Salines, Malden was once a bustling salt-making center, larger than nearby Charleston. As a Shawnee captive, Mary Draper Ingles made salt at natural brine springs here in 1755. Fifty years later, Malden manufacturers were the largest salt producers in the world. The Salines thrived from the early part of the century until the Civil War, and great numbers of slaves came here, hired out by their masters to salt producers and shippers.

After the war, many freed slaves stayed in the Malden area. The **African Zion Baptist Church** was founded in 1863, first meeting in the home of Reverend Lewis Rice, its pastor and an early champion of education for his people. The small frame church that stands today was built in 1872. With symmetrical, gently arched windows and a graceful bell tower, it has retained its plain and simple lines through several restorations. It is listed on the National Register of Historic Places and is notable as one of the mother churches of black Baptists in West Virginia.

Undoubtedly, its most famous member was prominent educator Booker T. Washington. Born a slave, he came to Malden from Virginia with his mother, brother and sister after the Civil War. Washington's stepfather was already working in a salt-packing house when the family arrived, and his sons soon joined him. Booker T. Washington lived in Malden from the age of nine until he left for Hampton Institute at the age of 16. He returned in 1875 and continued his involvement with the community as a schoolmaster, church clerk and Sunday School leader. His first marriage took place in this church. Even after he left to head Tuskegee Institute in Alabama and went on to become a nationally-known speaker, he maintained close ties with friends and relatives in Malden.

A few hundred yards east of the church, on Malden Drive, you will find a small public park dedicated to Washington, as well as a monument inscribed with a poem honoring him by West Virginia's late poet laureate, Louise McNeill.

Cabin Creek Quilts

Malden's historic district comprises about a quarter-mile stretch along Malden Drive. An important landmark is **Hale House**, home-place of Mary Draper Ingles's great-grandson John Hale. The restored house is now the home of **Cabin Creek Quilts**, a cooperative founded in 1970 by six intrepid elderly ladies. That year James Thibeault, now the director of the cooperative, was a young VISTA (Volunteers In Service To America) worker from Massachusetts, working on a clean water project in the nearby hollow of Cabin Creek. He noticed that his neighbors, many of them miners' widows, made beautiful quilts and sometimes sold them to raise extra cash. When he asked elderly "Aunt Vick" Haggerty about one of her quilts, she quoted him a price of $10.

Haggerty's niece, Lena Hawkins, thought they were worth more. So did Thibeault, who left the water project to help the women market their handmade coverlets. "Lena got her aunt's and sister's quilts and some neighbors' quilts, packed them up into pasteboard suitcases, and sent me back to Boston," Thibeault remembers.

Things happened quickly. Jackie Onassis spotted the quilts in a Cape Cod shop, bought two and ordered two more, which Aunt Vick completed shortly before her death. The *Boston Globe* ran a story about the West Virginia quilters. Orders started pouring in. The cooperative moved from Lena Hawkins's living-room couch to a one-room coal-camp house; by 1972, it occupied the renovated second story of a general store. Membership grew steadily. The group weathered many hardships, including a 1975 fire that burned their building to the ground and destroyed the entire inventory.

In 1991 the quilters rescued the deteriorating 1838 Hale House in Malden and made it their new headquarters. Today it is completely refurbished and painted pink, and more than 300 quilters keep the shelves, cupboards and tables piled high.

The old mansion fairly bursts at the joints with patchwork quilts, wall hangings, potholders, placemats, aprons, hot mitts, baby toys,

Three presidents are among the many famous owners and admirers of Cabin Creek Quilts. STEPHEN J. SHALUTA, JR.

Christmas decorations, skirts, vests and coats. In one room are full-size quilts; in another, wall hangings. Baby quilts and clutch balls spill into the front hallway. The dining room is set for a holiday banquet, complete with a tree done up in patchwork ornaments. The kitchen is stocked with West Virginia-made food items as well as patchwork. Throughout the house are framed photographs and biographical sketches of quilters.

Anyone who loves beautiful handcrafts will enjoy Cabin Creek Quilts. Quilters will want to stay for hours. In addition to seeing the colorful, expertly-made quilts and other crafts, you can find quilting supplies and patterns.

Quilters should not hesitate to bring their families along; Malden has more than quilts. At Cabin Creek Quilts you can pick up a pleasant, self-guided walking tour of the town's historic district prepared by the Malden Historical Society. It includes several churches, one of the oldest Masonic lodges in the state and the ferry landing from which millions of bushels of salt were shipped.

Cabin Creek Quilts is open 10:00 a.m. to 5:00 p.m. Monday through Saturday and 1:00 to 4:00 p.m. on Sunday. For more information or to order a video catalog ($10, refundable with order), call (304)925-9499 or write Cabin Creek Quilts, 4208 Malden Drive, Malden, WV 25306.

Directions: From I-64, take Exit 96 (Route 60 East, toward Belle). Go one mile and take the Malden/Rand exit. Turn left after passing through the underpass and go three blocks. Cabin Creek Quilts is on the left.

Matewan

At the southwestern edge of West Virginia, deep in the heart of coal country, is a little town with a lot of history, the site of two memorable and violent events separated by almost forty years. Today, that history comes alive for visitors willing to drive the winding roads to **Matewan** in Mingo County, which in 1997 became the first National Historic Landmark in the coalfields.

During the 1880s, the famous feud between the Hatfields and the McCoys raged in this area. Nobody now alive knows for certain what precipitated the first violence, but on Election Day, August 7, 1882, three sons of Randolph McCoy stabbed and shot Ellison Hatfield, brother of "Devil Anse" Hatfield, in Pike County, Kentucky. Ellison was carried across the Tug Fork River and died shortly afterward in Matewan. Devil Anse retaliated by executing the three McCoys. The incidents made national headlines and created a violent image of Appalachia that lingers today, although the feud ended before 1890.

On May 19, 1920, Matewan was the scene of terrible violence again. During the years when the United Mine Workers of America attempted to organize coal miners, a confrontation between Matewan townspeople, miners and mine detectives ended in a bloody battle that came to be known as the Matewan Massacre. Afterwards, activist Sid Hatfield was a hero for miners—and a hated target of the coal bosses. He was acquitted of murder, but was gunned down on the McDowell County Courthouse steps in Welch [see entry] a year later, touching off unrest in the coalfields that eventually led to the miners' march on Blair Mountain in Logan County.

Although some folks in town still proudly trace their ancestry back to either the Hatfields or the McCoys, you'll find the atmosphere friendly when you visit Matewan. Stop at the **Matewan Development Center** in the McCoy Building (located centrally on Mate Street) to get a handsomely designed self-guided walking tour of the town. It's filled with historic photos, including portraits of Devil Anse and his kin. Stroll along awning-shaded Mate Street and have lunch or a glass of iced tea at the **Matewan Depot**, a restaurant decorated with historic railroad photographs from an exhibition originally assembled by the Huntington Museum of Art.

Probably the most compelling location on the tour is the **Old Matewan National Bank** building, which also housed the old post office next to the railroad tracks. Bullet holes are still visible in the brick wall facing the tracks, and you can push a button to hear an excellent 15-minute audio presentation about the 1920 massacre and the history of labor struggles in the region. The recording includes the voices of elderly Matewan residents who remember both the massacre and the subsequent trials and shootings.

For more information call (304)426-4239, visit their web site (www.matewan.com) or write Matewan Development Center, PO Box 368, Matewan, WV 25278.

Directions: From Charleston or Logan, follow Route 119 to Route 52 near the Kentucky border. Take Route 52 southeast for about 12 miles, past Williamson, then follow Route 49 southeast to Matewan.

Tip: A favorite place to stroll in Matewan is along the floodwall. The concrete wall has been decorated with scenes that illustrate the town's history.

Milton

For a small town, **Milton** has it all: two glassmaking factories, an historic covered bridge, a country, gospel and bluegrass music hall, a huge flea market, a luxury camping resort, access to a great hiking trail and one of West Virginia's happiest fall events, the **West Virginia Pumpkin Festival** [see calendar of events].

Close to the Milton exit off I-64 is the **Mountaineer Opry House**. Since 1971, weekend evenings here have been brightened by local and nationally known country, gospel and bluegrass stars—from Ricky Skaggs and Skeeter Davis to the Seldom Scene. The fun is the down-home type, with no alcohol, in the large cinder block building with theater-type seating—and the sound system is terrific.

The Opry House has a big concession stand and plenty of free parking. Admission is $8.00 for adults, $7.00 for seniors and $2.00 for children. It's open year-round for Saturday shows at 7:30 p.m. Specials shows take place on Friday or Sunday. Call (304)733-2721 for a schedule.

Directions: From I-64, take Exit 2-B and turn toward Milton. The Opry House is at the exit on your left.

In the mood for a bargain? Turn the opposite direction when you exit the interstate (toward Culloden) and follow Route 60 east to the giant **indoor/outdoor flea market**. Held Friday through Sunday during warm weather, the market is the tri-state area's largest. Call (304)529-4783 for more information.

Although smaller and without the history of its crosstown neighbor Blenko Glass, **Gibson Glass** appeals to shoppers. Among the highlights at this residential-area shop are handmade flower paperweights, cruets, vases, lamps, perfume bottles and a wonderful line of marbles. Like snowflakes, no two of Gibson's pieces are exactly alike. Look for bargains on seconds at Gibson, too.

There's an observation area where you can watch the glassmakers at work. Gift shop hours are 8:00 a.m. to 4:00 p.m. Monday through Saturday, and tours are available from 8:00 a.m. to 2:30 p.m. Monday through Friday. Call (304)743-5232 for more information or write Gibson Glass, Route 1, Box 8, Milton, WV 25541.

Directions: From I-64, take Exit 28 toward Milton. Turn right on Route 60 (west). At the light in the center of town, turn left. Go past Blenko Glass and, at the fork in the road, bear left. Pass Wetterau on the left and a church on the right. Turn right onto West Mud River Road, go under the railroad bridge and turn right. Turn right again at the second road and follow it to Gibson Glass.

If you still have the energy after your glass factory tour, how about a hike? Head to Camp Arrowhead for access to the peaceful, 32-mile-long **Kanawha Trace**, a foot trail that runs all the way from Barboursville, at the junction of the Mud and Guyandotte rivers, to Fraziers Bottom on the Kanawha River. Maintenance of this trail is a project of the Tri-State Council, Boy Scouts of America, and it is open year-round. Pack a picnic and bring along your camera. For serious hikers who want to cover the whole 32 miles, *A Guidebook* *to the Kanawha Trace* is available for $7.00 by calling (304)523-3408 or writing the Council at 733 7th Avenue, Huntington, WV 25701. Trail permits are required. Call (304)523-3408.

Directions: From Route 60 heading west, turn right on Blue Sulfur Road and follow to Camp Arrowhead.

If you'd like to stay nearby, you can combine the fun of camping with the luxury of resort living at **Fox Fire Resort**. This 72-acre camping resort offers a recreation banquet—everything from a 240-foot water slide to a hot air balloon ride, including volleyball, fishing, swimming, paddleboats, miniature golf, hayrides and, of course, singing around the campfire at night. For more information call (304)743-5622 or write Fox Fire Resort, Route 2, Box 655, Milton, WV 25541.

Directions: Located on Route 60 three miles west of Milton. If you're traveling east on I-64, take Exit 20A (Barboursville) and follow the signs. If you're headed west, take Exit 28 (Milton) to Route 60.

For more information about Milton, write the Milton Area Development Association, PO Box 123, Milton, WV 25541.

Blenko Glass Company

Milton's leading attraction is glass, and **Blenko Glass Company** is the headliner. Blenko's handblown glassware and blown stained glass, prized by designers of stained-glass windows, is famous throughout the world. Founded in 1922 by British glassmaker William Blenko, who persevered after earlier failures in the business, the company's explorations into handmade decorative glass paved the way for well-deserved success. The company is now into its fourth generation of Blenkos, including William H. Blenko, Jr., and Richard D. Blenko. It boasts major installations around the world, including those in St. Patrick's Cathedral in New York, the Washington Cathedral in the District of Columbia and Yale University. Blenko glass has been shown in museums and cultural exhibitions worldwide and won many awards. Its products are in gift shops everywhere.

A special observation deck at the factory provides an excellent, close-up view of glassmakers at their craft. Afterwards, visit the large, two-story visitors center next to the factory, where you can find multi-colored treasures (and some real bargains) at the factory outlet on the lower level, or see examples of different glassware produced through the years in the upstairs museum, which chronicles the history of the company and the Blenkos.

Factory tours are available 8:00 a.m. to noon and 12:30 to 3:15

p.m. Monday through Friday, except during the plant's two-week vacation (beginning about July 1) and the week between Christmas and New Year's Day as well as other major holidays. Visitors center hours are 8:00 a.m. to 4:00 p.m. Monday through Saturday and noon to 4:00 p.m. on Sunday. For more information call (304)743-9081 or write Blenko Glass Company, PO Box 67, Milton, WV 25541.

Directions: From I-64, take Exit 28 and go west on Route 60. A left at the light in the town center will lead you to the factory.

Tip: In Milton you can walk through history by crossing the **Mud River Covered Bridge** near Blenko. You'll find it on County Road 25 off Route 60. Built in 1876, the 112-foot-long bridge underwent extensive repairs in 1971 and is still open for foot traffic.

Point Pleasant

Point Pleasant Battle Monument State Park

Point Pleasant is first mentioned in George Washington's detailed 1770 diary of his journey to the place where the Kanawha and Ohio rivers flow together. Today, **Point Pleasant** would seem to be aptly named. It is hard to imagine that, over two centuries ago, on October 10, 1774, a bloody, day-long struggle occurred here—the first battle of the American Revolution. When Colonel Andrew Lewis's force of 1,100 Virginia militiamen finally defeated Shawnee Chief Cornstalk's party of equal number, it broke the power of the Indians in the Ohio Valley and prevented an Indian alliance with the British, one that might very well have altered the course of American history.

The story of the years preceding the Battle of Point Pleasant vividly illustrates the bitter struggle between European settlers hungry for land and Native Americans unwilling to give up their hunting grounds. When Lord Dunmore (John Murray) was appointed British governor of Virginia in 1771, he was charged with discouraging settlement of the land beyond the Alleghenies, partly to honor the Indians' right to their hunting grounds and partly to maintain a profitable fur trade with the tribes. But settlers continued to cross the mountains, and the Indians resisted. Their resistance turned violent after drunken settlers massacred the entire family of Mingo Chief Logan, whose relations with whites had been friendly. In his grief and wrath, the chief retaliated by leading many attacks on frontier settlements during the summer of 1774. More than 30 settlers were scalped or taken prisoner. The violence escalated from that time on, with both sides guilty of atrocities.

As a result, Lord Dunmore organized the border militia and appointed Andrew Lewis commander of the Virginia troops. After signing treaties with the Delaware and Six Nations of the Iroquois at Pittsburgh, Dunmore started down the Ohio River to battle the Shawnee, who had joined forces with Logan's Mingo tribe. Lewis's army, meanwhile, had marched from Fort Union (Lewisburg) and set up camp at Point Pleasant to await Dunmore's arrival from the north. But the Shawnee, led by Chief Cornstalk, struck before Dunmore could arrive.

This point, once known by the Wyandotte Indian name "Tu-Endie-Wei," meaning "point between two waters," was heavily wooded. Among the trees, men fought hand-to-hand. At times during the day Cornstalk's warriors seemed to hold the field; but at the end of the day the Virginians had won. More than 200 Indians and 50 white soldiers lay dead, among them Colonel Charles Lewis, the commanding officer's brother.

The centerpiece of the park is, of course, the battle monument. The 84-foot-high granite obelisk honors the militiamen who gave their lives during the battle, and a statue of a frontiersman stands at the base. Smaller memorial tablets in the park commemorate Chief Cornstalk and "Mad" Anne Bailey, who became a frontier fighter after her husband's death at Point Pleasant. An excellent rider and well-known scout, she saved Fort Lee in 1791 by riding 200 miles to get gunpowder. Another marker shows the place where French explorer Joseph Celoron de Blainville buried a leaden plate in 1749, claiming the land for France.

Also on the park grounds is the **Mansion House**, built in 1796 by Walter Newman. Originally a tavern, it is the oldest hewn log house in the Kanawha Valley. The Colonel Charles Lewis Chapter of the National Society of the Daughters of the American Revolution maintains a museum in this quite large, two-story house. You'll see many artifacts from the era, including an Indian flint-arrowhead collection and a piano that may have been the first square-leg piano carried over the Alleghenies. There is no admission charge, but donations are appreciated.

Point Pleasant Battle Monument State Park is open year-round. The museum is open May through October, from 10:00 a.m. to 4:30 p.m. Monday through Saturday and 1:00 to 4:30 p.m. Sunday. Restrooms are available, but no picnicking is allowed in this park. Phone (304)675-0869, visit their web site (wvweb.com/www/POINT_PLEASANT.html) or write Point Pleasant Battle Monument State Park, PO Box 486, Point Pleasant, WV 25550.

Directions: The park is at the southern end of Point Pleasant at 1 Main Street. From I-64 you may take either Route 35 or Route 62 to Point Pleasant (the two run on opposite sides of the Kanawha River). The park is one mile north of the junction of Routes 35 and 2, at the intersection of Routes 62 and 2.

Tip: The state park is also the beginning point for a self-guided walking tour of Point Pleasant's historic district prepared by Main Street Point Pleasant. Stop in their offices at 304 Main Street between 8:30 a.m. and 4:30 p.m. on Monday, Tuesday, Thursday or Friday to get a copy or call (304)675-3844. The tour takes you past the 1904 Lowe Hotel, a number of beautiful old homes and the site of the 1967 Silver Bridge collapse, which claimed the lives of 47 people.

Krodel Park

If you really want to have a picnic by the water in a Point Pleasant park, you'll find a very nice one just half a mile from the battle monument. **Krodel Park**, on the site where Daniel Boone once had a trading post, is a 44-acre city park, half of which is a lake stocked with trout, bass and bluegill. Admission to the park is free; for a nominal charge, you can swim, play miniature golf on the 18-hole course or rent a paddleboat. The park has a kitchen-equipped clubhouse and two picnic shelters for rent. Call the City of Point Pleasant at (304)675-2360 for more information.

Campers will enjoy this park, too. Sites are available from April 15 to November 1. Fees range from $5.00 for a tent without electrical hook-up to $16.00 for a camper site with full hook-up including air conditioning. Rentals are on a first-come, first-served basis. Call the park campground for more information: (304)675-1068.

Directions: One-half mile east of the Point Pleasant Battle Monument on Route 62.

West Virginia State Farm Museum

Threshing machines, cultivators, tractors, carriages, sleighs, looms, a potbellied stove, sewing machines, bottles, jars, tools—even a Maytag seed cleaner! Just about any sort of implement or artifact from 200 years of farm history in West Virginia can be found at the **West Virginia State Farm Museum**, and many have been restored to working order.

Six miles north of Point Pleasant, this is a must-see destination in the Metro Valley. Started in 1976, the complex comprises more than 30 period buildings spread over about 50 acres. The living farm museum is a tribute to West Virginia's farm life heritage and an attempt to preserve farm history in an era when the rapid advance of technology threatens the memory of older ways. The all-volunteer museum charges no admission fee and is supported entirely by donations, grants and income from several annual festivals.

On your guided tour through buildings, you'll see thousands of artifacts. Look for the large "cabinet" in the 19th-century log house that is actually a folding bed; the old wooden desks and potbellied stove in the 1870 one-room school house; the musket rack and pump organ inside the replica of a Lutheran church said to be the first of its kind west of the Alleghenies; and the authentic equipment and period medications in the doctor's office. There's also a country store with crafts and souvenirs for sale (including cornmeal and molasses made on the working farm), an old-time post office, a newspaper office with working presses and hand-set type, a blacksmith shop that compares favorably with the one at Williamsburg, an outstanding taxidermy collection (with a 1905 loon and a two-headed calf) and much more. New exhibits include a scale house, where farmers weighed crops, recently moved here from Minnehaha Springs, and a four-unit building that will replicate an old barber shop, post office, and veterinarian's office.

Children are particularly taken with **General**, reportedly the third largest horse ever to have lived. He's not living any longer, but he was mounted by the same company that mounted Trigger for Roy Rogers, and he's pretty impressive: 19½ hands high and 2,950 pounds. The registered Belgian gelding wore a 34-inch collar, the largest ever made.

The museum is open April 1 though November 15, from 9:00 a.m. to 5:00 p.m. Tuesday through Saturday and 1:00 to 5:00 p.m. Sunday. Throughout the year, the Farm Museum sponsors a number of festivals that include music, country cooking, gospel singing, a steam and gas engine show, quilt shows, horse pulls, auctions and craft demonstrations of all kinds. Call (304)675-5737 for a schedule of special events, or write West Virginia State Farm Museum, Route 1, Box 479, Point Pleasant, WV 25550.

Directions: From I-64, take Exit 45 and follow Route 62 north alongside the Kanawha River six miles to Point Pleasant. Signs on Route 62 lead you to the museum. Or take Route 35 north to Point Pleasant, then Route 62 north to the museum.

South Charleston

South Charleston Mound

Surrounded by a busy highway, large chemical plants, restaurants and shops, a mysterious mound rests in **South Charleston**. The grass-covered, 35-foot-high, 175-foot-wide mound is the second largest remaining Indian burial mound in the state. It was constructed as long as 2,000 years ago by the Adena, or Early Woodland people. Some scholars believe the Adena may have migrated from Mexico via the Mississippi and Ohio Rivers. Others think the culture came from Europe. Wherever their origin, the Adena left clear markers of their existence—burial mounds of varying sizes. An official report by the Bureau of Ethnology in 1890-91 cited 50 such mounds. Some have been destroyed. Others, like this one, have been carefully excavated.

From excavated artifacts, archeologists conclude that the Adena hunted and gathered food and also grew crops, particularly sunflowers, which they cultivated for the nutritious seeds. There is evidence to suggest that they practiced a custom of flattening and reshaping their infants' heads with cradle boards, and that they also practiced cremation. When the South Charleston mound was excavated in 1883-84 by Colonel P.W. Norris of the Smithsonian Institution, the many artifacts unearthed included 13 complete skeletons plus parts of another, a flint lance head, copper bracelets, arrowheads, tools and other items. One of the skeletons wore a copper headdress and was centered between two semi-circles formed by the other skeletons. Some of the artifacts found at the site are on loan to Sunrise Museum [see entry].

Directions: The mound fronts Oakes and Seventh avenues in South Charleston's Staunton Park. From I-64, take Exit 56 (Montrose Drive), and follow signs for Route 60. Go west on Route 60 for a few blocks. The mound is on the left.

Tip: A fun time to visit the Mound is during the annual **Mound Art and Craft Festival** in September [see calendar of events], when some 250 exhibitors set up displays around the landmark.

Williamson

The Coal House

In the courthouse square of **Williamson**, the county seat of Mingo County, stands a jet-black, fortress-like, rectangular building made entirely of coal—a tribute to the importance of coal in the region. The combination of the gleaming black surface and graceful arched entrance and windows makes for a surprising sight in downtown Williamson.

Now the home of the Tug Valley Chamber of Commerce, **The Coal House** was a pet project of O.W. Evans, manager of the Norfolk and Southern Railways Fuel Department in Williamson, and was built entirely with contributions and donated materials and labor. Designed by architect H.T. Hicks, it was completed in 1933 and is now on the National Register of Historic Places.

The coal blocks that form the building's exterior remain in amazingly good shape after more than 65 years, thanks in part to a biennial weather-proofing treatment. Don't be afraid to go inside: although it is made of combustible coal, the building poses no fire threat. It's open from 9:00 a.m. to 5:00 p.m. Monday through Friday. Call the Tug Valley Chamber of Commerce for more information: (304)235-5240.

Directions: In the courthouse square in downtown Williamson. From Huntington take I-64 to Route 52, and continue south to Williamson. From Charleston, take Route 119 (Robert C. Byrd Freeway) south to Williamson.

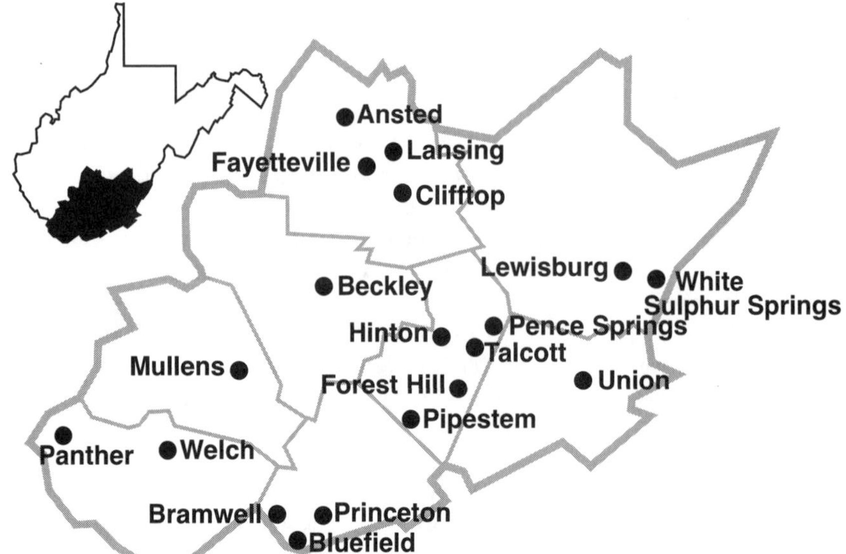

ANSTED
- African-Am. Heritage Family Tree Mus.
- Contentment
- Hawks Nest State Park

BECKLEY
- Grand View
- New River Park
- Tamarack
- Theatre West Virginia
- Wildwood House Museum

BLUEFIELD
- Bluefield Orioles
- Eastern Regional Coal Archives
- Science Center of West Virginia

BRAMWELL

CLIFFTOP
- Babcock State Park
- Camp Washington-Carver

COAL HERITAGE TRAIL

FAYETTEVILLE

FOREST HILL
- Wakerobin Gallery

GAULEY BRIDGE

HINTON
- Bluestone Dam and Bluestone Lake
- Historic District
- Three Rivers Avian Center

LANSING
- Canyon Rim Visitors Center

LEWISBURG
- Visitors Center and Walking Tours
- Lost World Caverns

MULLENS
- Twin Falls Resort State Park

PANTHER STATE FOREST
- Panther State Forest

PENCE SPRINGS
- Graham House
- Pence Springs Hotel

PIPESTEM
- Pipestem Resort State Park

PRINCETON

TALCOTT
- Big Bend Tunnel & John Henry Statue

UNION
- Walking Tour and Springs Trail

WELCH
- McDowell County Courthouse

WHITE SULPHUR SPRINGS
- The Greenbrier

New River/Greenbrier Valley

Historically, the riches of the New River/Greenbrier Valley region have always been its natural resources: coal, which made millionaires and blended a diversity of traditions into a distinctive Appalachian culture; mineral springs, the bubbling fountains around which antebellum high society gathered; powerful waterways that were natural transportation routes and forested hills teeming with wildlife.

Today these same rivers, forests, springs and mountains yield new treasures for travelers. Each year, whitewater rafters by the thousands run the ancient, awesome New River—53 miles of which is now a National River—while rock climbers scale the walls of the deep gorge. Hikers, bikers and horseback riders never run out of new paths to explore, with options ranging from gentle rail trails to truly rugged terrain. Anglers and hunters find plentiful fish and game in the region's wildlife management areas and state forests. History lovers walk, drive and ride on trails and rails traveled by Native Americans, pioneers, early spa visitors, Civil War soldiers and coal miners.

Steep your senses in fine arts, crafts, music and food at Tamarack, a bountiful gathering of West Virginia-made wares. Dig into coal mining history in Bluefield, Kaymoor or Beckley. Pamper yourself at a world-famous spa—or tour the top-secret hideaway beneath it. Play a round of golf on an 1884 course. Enrich your mind at dozens of museums. Retreat to one of the many beautiful state parks clustered in this region.

If you visit the New River/Greenbrier Valley region, bring a camera, a comfortable pair of shoes and a willingness to be surprised. And expect to take home some happy memories.

For more information on visiting the New River/Greenbrier Valley contact:

Bluestone Convention and Visitors Bureau, 500 Bland Street, Bluefield, WV 24701. Call (304)325-8438 or (800)221-3206.

Fayetteville Historic Visitors Bureau, 125 North Court Street, Fayetteville, WV 25840. Call (304)574-1500 or (888)574-1500 or visit their web site (www.visitwv.org).

Lewisburg Visitors Center, 105 Church Street, Lewisburg, WV 24901. Call (304)645-1000 or (800)833-2068 or visit their web site (wvweb.com/www/lewisburg).

New River Convention and Visitors Bureau, 310 Oyler Avenue, Oak Hill, WV 25901. Call (800)927-0263 or (304)465-5618 or visit their web site (wvweb.com/www/FAYETTE_CHAMBER/).

Southern West Virginia Convention and Visitors Bureau, PO Box 1799, Beckley, WV 25802. Call (800)VISIT-WV or (304)252-2244 or visit their web site (www.visitwv.org)).

Summers County Convention and Visitors Bureau, 206 Temple Street, Hinton, WV 25951. Call (304)466-5420 or visit their web site (www.visitwv.org).

White Sulphur Springs Convention and Visitors Bureau, 102 Main Street, White Sulphur Springs, WV 24986. Call (800)284-9440 or (304)536-9440.

Ansted

African-American Heritage Family Tree Museum

Just north of the Canyon Rim Visitors Center [see entry] on Route 60 is the town of **Ansted**. Here, in an original coal company house, a six-room museum is testimony to the small and large ways in which African-Americans have helped shape the history of West Virginia and the United States. It contains artifacts from the lives of both Booker T. Washington, who lived and taught school in Malden, West Virginia, and Carter G. Woodson, the founder of Negro History Week (later Black History Month), who once worked in a coal mine near Ansted. In addition, you'll see exhibits and objects documenting the work and domestic lives of area residents: coal mining and railroad memorabilia, an old sewing machine, a pair of high-topped boots with rows of tiny buttons.

The museum's centerpiece is a collection of photographs by William Harvey Jordan, born in 1886 in Black Hawk Hollow (Kanawha County), who operated a photography studio in Cleveland for many years. His Krona View camera and the bench he used for portrait subjects are exhibited along with more than 1,000 negatives and photographs documenting the life's work of this prolific photographer.

The museum is open from 2:00 to 7:00 p.m. Thursday, 11:00 a.m. to 4:00 p.m. Friday and Saturday, 1:00 to 4:00 p.m. Sunday, June 1

Many rafters consider West Virginia the whitewater capital of the East.
DAVID FATTALEH

to Labor Day. However, museum board president Genevieve Smallwood lives "just up the hill from the museum," and has been known to open it at other times of the year for interested visitors. Her number is (304)658-5889. Call her if you can't reach the museum at (304)658-5526, or write **African-American Heritage Family Tree Museum**, HC 67, Box 58, Ansted, WV 25812.

Directions: The museum is on Logtown Road at Jones Street. From Route 60, turn right on Rich Creek Road at the west end of Ansted (beside a bridge). Go less than one-half mile and bear left at Logtown Road (at the ballfield). Follow it to Jones Street.

Contentment

The three-building historic complex **Contentment**, under the auspices of the Fayette County Historical Society, contains a pre-Civil War home, a museum and a restored one-room country school.

The white frame house with a gray tin roof was built around 1830, a year before the founding of Fayette County, and purchased in 1872 by Colonel George W. Imboden when he came here as an early coal developer. During the Civil War, Imboden was the Confederate Commander of the 18th Virginia Cavalry Regiment; he was also Ansted's first mayor. His home, which his wife later named Contentment, still has the original walnut mantels in three rooms, and unusual alternating walnut and oak flooring. Period furnishings include a "fainting sofa," a handmade desk that once belonged to the family of West Virginia Governor Okey Patteson, a hand-cranked music box and children's toys.

The adjacent museum displays Civil War artifacts and other Fayette County memorabilia, including many pieces from the home of county leader Morris Harvey. Moonshine stills seized by revenuers, photographs of mining camps and Mrs. Imboden's wedding gown are among popular exhibits.

The restored schoolhouse on the grounds is one of only a few that remain of the nearly 1,000 once scattered over the West Virginia countryside. It is full of mementos from school days long past: a Burnside stove, benches and desks, copies of texts like *McGuffey's Reader*, handbells and photos. The names of dozens of former teachers are inscribed on the walls.

Admission is $2.00 for adults, $1.00 for children. Contentment is open 10:00 a.m. to 4:00 p.m. Monday through Saturday, June through August. Call (304)658-5695.

Directions: One mile east of Hawks Nest State Park on Route 60.

Tip: Thomas "Stonewall" Jackson's mother, Julia Neale Jackson, is buried in Westlake Cemetery, also in Ansted. Find Cemetery Street near the center of town and follow it for about half a block to the cemetery.

Hawks Nest State Park

One of the most photographed views in West Virginia, and for good reason, is the New River Gorge from the main overlook at **Hawks Nest State Park**. This 276-acre park is a favorite of West Virginians and tourists. The park has a 31-room lodge (many rooms have private balconies overlooking the same gorge view), a charming museum created by the Civilian Conservation Corps in the 1930s, a large gift shop with West Virginia crafts and glassware and a fun aerial tramway that travels from the lodge down to the marina at the bottom of the gorge.

At the tram office, you may also purchase tickets for the **New River Jetboat**. After the tram has taken you down to the river, the "Miss M Rocks" will take you upstream to the New River Gorge Bridge, towering 876 feet above. Bring your camera. The six-mile ride takes approximately half an hour, and the boat runs twice a day Tuesday through Sunday from Memorial Day through Labor Day, weekends only in September; then it's back to the summer schedule for the month of October. The cost is $15.00 for adults, $13.00 for seniors and $5.00 for children 5-16. The jetboat is run by a private concessionaire. Call (304)469-2525.

For more information about lodge rooms, the tramway or the museum, call (800)CALL-WVA or (304)658-5212, visit their web site (wvweb.com/www/HAWKS_NEST.html) or write Hawks Nest State Park, PO Box 857, Ansted, WV 25812.

Directions: Hawks Nest is on Route 60 one mile west of Ansted.

Beckley

New River Park

Families, history students and folks who are just plain curious will find much to engage them at **New River Park** in Beckley. Combine a visit to this learning park with a trip to Tamarack [see entry] for full, varied day.

If you have ever wondered what the inside of a real coal mine looks like, you can find out at the **Beckley Exhibition Coal Mine**, the only historically preserved coal mine in West Virginia. You'll see what it was like to work in a low-seam coal mine in the 1890s hand-loading era, then trace the industry's history up through modern, mechanized coal mining methods. The mine, once owned by a family named Phillips, was part of a 29-acre tract in the coalfields. Only about 11 acres were ever mined. In 1962, after careful safety preparations, 1,500 feet of the winding passageways were opened for public tours.

With a former coal miner as a guide, you'll begin your trip the way many miners started their workday—in a "man trip," the low rail car that transported work crews underground. As the clanking car takes you through the mine portal and into the underground city, you may be surprised to see that the walls of coal mines are not black, but "rock-dusted" white. You'll learn the reasons for that, and much more about mining techniques and tools, during the 45-minute tour. And when the guides turn out the lights, you'll gain a new appreciation of the phrase "pitch black."

The guides' stories are well worth the price of admission, and they'll give you a sense of the fierce love and loyalty West Virginia's coal miners have always felt for their difficult, dangerous profession.

Bring along a jacket. Even on the warmest day, the temperature inside a coal mine is a cool 58 degrees, and the fans that ventilate a mine pull a steady breeze through the tunnels.

When you purchase tickets for the exhibition mine, stop to explore the small coal museum in the same building. There is also a gift shop with coal-related mementos, West Virginia glass and pottery, homemade ice cream and some yummy fudge.

Tours are available from 10:00 a.m. to 5:30 p.m. April 1 to November 1. The gift shop is open from 10:00 a.m. to 6:00 p.m. Admission is $7.00 for adults, $6.25 for seniors and $4.00 for children aged 4–12. Group rates are available, and prices are subject to change. Call (304)256-1747 or write Exhibition Coal Mine, New River Park, Drawer AJ, Beckley, WV 25802.

Also at the park, adjacent to the Exhibition Coal Mine, take a walk through the **Coal Company House**. Just as the trip underground shows you how miners worked, the small, three-room house illustrates their home life. Coal companies often built camps near the mines they operated. The camps usually included a company-owned store, a school, churches and houses. Some coal camps had their own live-in doctors. The companies even issued currency, called "scrip," with which miners bought food and other supplies, often at inflated prices. Thus the company owners profited not only from the sale of coal but from the needs of workers and their families. Rent for a typical house, most of which were three to six rooms in size, ranged from $8.00 to $20.00 per month, a significant portion of a miner's income, and was sometimes deducted from their earnings before they were paid. The song lyric "I owe my soul to the company store" is telling: it was not unusual for miners to be in arrears.

The house you'll see, which has been restored by the City of Beckley, is a real coal company house that was moved here from the town of Sprague. Both house and camp were owned and used by the New River Coal Company between 1925 and the 1940s. Inside, it reflects those years and has been furnished with typical items used by coal mining families.

Nearby, the **Superintendent House** will give you an idea of how the mine superintendent lived. This "super's home," originally constructed in Skelton, dates from 1906. The restored three-story home resembles a small mansion from the English countryside, where its original owner was born. Among other rooms, you can tour the formal dining room, kitchen, super's office, master bedroom and nursery. Also in the mansion are a replicated company doctor's office, barbershop and company store post office.

A church and one-room **Miner's Shanty** complete the company town exhibits at the Exhibition Coal Mine. (Admission to the coal mine includes all of the company town exhibits.)

Next, walk a few yards through the park to the brightly decorated railroad boxcars that contain the **Youth Museum of Southern West Virginia**. This joyful place is an always-busy combination of permanent, changing and hands-on exhibits that will delight children and intrigue their elders as well. Ongoing attractions include a planetarium and the **Peace Totem**, an outdoor artwork. Inside the museum, book-loving children gravitate to the **Library Listening Loft**, an inviting, cozy reading and listening nook, its walls decorated with hand-carved West Virginia imagery including rhododendron blossoms and a black bear. Others head for **ScienceWorks**, a dozen or so hands-on physical science stations where kids and adults learn about levers, magnets, pulleys, simple electrical circuits and more. An example of the museum's changing exhibit schedule is a past exhibit called "Dinosaurs Alive," in which a life-like mechanical dinosaur roared and stomped its way through the museum.

Directly behind the museum's main gallery, you'll learn about frontier life at the **Mountain Homestead** exhibit. The one-acre complex includes an 1844 log house, barn, one-room school house, blacksmith shop, moonshine still, doll house and country store where kids can weigh and measure items just like old-time shopkeepers did. There are demonstrations of open-hearth cooking on the spider, a three-legged iron skillet popular during the late 1800s, and an example of a more modern kitchen from the 1930s.

The Youth Museum is open Memorial Day through Labor Day, from 10:00 a.m. to 6:00 p.m. Monday through Saturday and 1:00 to 5:00 p.m. Sunday, and 10:00 a.m. to 5:00 p.m. the rest of the year. For information on current events, permanent exhibits and corresponding admission fees, which are reasonable (a single $3.50 fee covers both the museum and the homestead), call the museum at (304)252-3730 or write Youth Museum of Southern West Virginia, New River Park, PO Box 1815, Beckley, WV 25802.

When you've learned about everything from mining to mountain living to magnets, move on to the rest of New River Park: an Olympic-sized pool with a water slide, tennis courts, horseshoes, basketball courts and a playground. Plan a picnic and, if you can't do it all in one day, ask about the park's campground. There are 17 full hook-up sites.

Directions: From I-77, Take Exit 44 (Harper Road). Go east on Harper Road/Route 3 about 1½ miles. Turn left on Ewart Avenue at the service station. Go one-fourth mile to the Exhibition Coal Mine or one mile to the Youth Museum entrance.

Tamarack

For drivers traveling I-77 near Beckley, it's well nigh impossible to miss the halo-shaped, multi-peaked roof line of **Tamarack**, the huge arts and crafts complex opened in 1996 by the West Virginia Parkways Authority. That's good, because it would be a shame to pass by this wonderful gathering of West Virginia handcrafts, fine art, live entertainment and good food.

Tamarack's unusual architecture echoes quilt patterns and mountains, and every detail—from the bronze door pulls to the stained glass window panels—incorporates the work of state artisans. Inside the complex, natural light floods the wide, tiled walkway between colorful displays of juried crafts, artworks, food products, recordings, clothing and souvenir items from all 55 West Virginia counties. The offerings range from small, affordable mementos to one-of-a-kind treasures.

Don't leave without sampling "A Taste of West Virginia." From savory sauteed greens to bread pudding topped with vanilla sauce, Tamarack's regional specialties, served up in a pleasant food court at moderate prices, are worth the visit. (Many local residents frequent Tamarack just for the food!) Not hungry at the moment? The gourmet shop is well-stocked with packaged goodies for your trip.

With five craft demonstration studios and a 200-seat theater featuring films and live performances (including a popular dinner theater series), there's always something happening at Tamarack. A fine arts gallery offers changing exhibits. Children gravitate to the outdoor playground and festival meadow, while others stroll the nature trail, inner courtyard, sculpture garden and herb gardens. The complex is also a tourist information center with a wealth of tips about attractions all over the state.

There is no admission charge and plenty of free parking. Hours are 8:00 a.m. to 8:00 p.m. April through December and 8:00 a.m. to 4:00 p.m. January through March. Tamarack is open every day except Christmas. For information about special events, call (304)256-6843 or 1-88-TAMARACK, or write Tamarack, One Tamarack Park, Beckley, WV 25801.

Directions: Tamarack is at Exit 45 on the West Virginia Turnpike (I-64/77).

Theatre West Virginia

At an elevation of 2,500 feet, **Grandview Park** offers a lovely view of the New River as it forms Horseshoe Bend. When evening comes, the 892-acre day-use park becomes the setting for another sort of scene. Two chapters of West Virginia's colorful history come alive each summer at Grandview Park's Cliffside Amphitheatre, just outside Beckley, thanks to the efforts of a repertory group called **Theatre West Virginia**.

The performances themselves have a venerable history: drama productions began here in 1961 when the West Virginia Historical Drama Association presented Kermit Hunter's epic of West Virginia's Civil War roots, *Honey in the Rock*. (The play's title refers to the Indian name for natural gas wells they found here.) In 1970, Billy Edd Wheeler's *Hatfields and McCoys*, the story of West Virginia's most famous feud, began its long run.

In addition to the two perennial favorites, Theatre West Virginia also features one musical each summer, such as *Fiddler on the Roof* or *The Wizard of Oz*. The performance season runs from early June to late August, with one play each night.

Grandview Park, now part of the New River Gorge National River, makes a fine destination even when the theater company is not in residence. On land once owned by Joseph Carper, the famous rifle maker, the park is especially popular when rhododendrons bloom in spring. There are picnic and playground areas, game courts, hiking/cross-country ski trails and a gift shop.

Theater tickets are $12.00 for adults and $6.00 for children under 12. Group rates are available. All performances begin at 8:30 p.m. at the Cliffside Amphitheatre. Call (304)256-6800 or (800)666-9142 for information on the revolving schedule.

Directions: From I-64, take Exit 129B and follow signs six miles to the park entrance.

Wildwood House Museum

General Alfred Beckley founded both the city of Beckley and Raleigh County. His house, built in 1836 and listed on the National Register of Historic Places, has been preserved as a museum. The white clapboard exterior, added in about 1850, conceals the original log structure, built for the Beckley family in 1836 by John Lilly, Sr.

Beckley inherited 170,038 acres of land in what was then the wilderness of western Virginia. Leaving behind a successful military career in Pittsburgh, Pennsylvania, he settled his family here and set out to develop the region. He drew up detailed plans—including streets, alleys, a courthouse, church, burial grounds, school, tavern and stores—for the founding, in 1838, of the town that bears the family name (in honor of the general's father). Beckley donated his own land for streets, half the building lots and the cemetery. Later, on condition that the town remain the county seat, he also donated two acres of land for the courthouse square.

Beckley returned to military life in 1849 when the General Assembly of Virginia commissioned him a Brigadier General of Militia. The following year, General Beckley put forth a bill proposing the formation of Raleigh County (named for Sir Walter Raleigh). His bill was approved by the Virginia General Assembly. After the Civil War, Beckley returned to his town and devoted himself to its future. He served as a lawyer, engineer, preacher, teacher, politician and peacemaker until his death on his birthday in 1888.

Wildwood, which he originally called Park Place, is preserved much as it was when he and his family occupied it. Note the old, wavy glass in the windows. A brick walkway that extends from the square front porch to a picket fence is made of bricks removed from Neville Street in downtown Beckley. Inside are a number of pieces of furniture that belonged to the Beckley family, who lived in the house until 1901.

Wildwood House Museum is open to the public on weekends from Memorial Day weekend through the end of October. Saturday hours are noon to 4:00 p.m. and Sunday hours are 2:00 to 4:00 p.m. Admission is $3.00 for adults and $2.00 for children.

Directions: Continue east on Route 3 from New River Park and turn left on F Street. Follow signs to the Laurel Terrace parking lot.

Bluefield

In the late 19th century, when the Norfolk and Western Railroad reached southern West Virginia, it connected huge tracts of coal-rich land with wide-ranging markets. Millionaires were made almost overnight, and busy towns suddenly sprouted where small farm communities had existed previously. Thousands of new laborers, including blacks from the South and European immigrants, settled in the rugged mountains and quickly growing towns of southern West Virginia. **Bluefield** was one of those towns. Once known as Higganbotham Summit, the area had been owned by two families descended from Revolutionary War veterans who built a fort there.

The coal industry in this area boomed from the 1890s into the 1920s, fed by a 900-square-mile coal bank near Pocahontas, Virginia. The coal found here became the standard by which all other bituminous coal was measured. So pure that it was called "smokeless," it was highly volatile and low in sulphur—and it fueled the industrial revolution around the world. Pocahontas coal was the choice of the U.S. Navy for its steam-powered battleships in both the Spanish-American War and World War I.

Bluefield, named for the color of the chicory flower, established itself as the corporate center of southern West Virginia's coalfields. Its huge trainyard served both business and pleasure travelers. Most of its venerable buildings—their construction supervised by a planning commission to assure compatible styles—were built during the successful coal mining years between 1900 and 1920. These buildings stand as a reminder of Bluefield's heritage, and may be seen on a self-guided walking tour prepared by the **Bluestone Convention and Visitors Bureau**.

Pick up a free copy of the tour guide at the Convention and Visitors Bureau on the second floor of the Old City Hall at 500 Bland Street. Now called the **Bluefield Area Arts and Science Center**, it is the tour's beginning point. The elegant Classical Revival-style building was designed by Wilbur Mills and is on the National Register of Historic Places. The Bluefield tour takes in nine historic buildings and can be easily covered in an hour, but you'll want to set aside some extra time to explore the Arts and Science Center, which includes an art gallery, a theater that produces six plays a year, a restaurant, and the fascinating Science Center of West Virginia [see entry].

The visitors bureau also offers guided coach tours of nearby attractions for groups of 16 or more. These weekend tours, which can include lunch and a choice of sites and activities, range from two to three hours. Some favorite tour stops are the Pocahontas Show Mine and Crab Orchard Museum in nearby Tazewell, Virginia and the Bluestone Gorge Canyon Rim Trail. The visitors bureau requires at least 48 hours notice to arrange coach tours, and the cost is about $15.00 per person. Lunch is extra.

As you leave the Arts and Science Center, be sure to look at the old **Ramsey School**, the oldest school in Bluefield, on your left. Perched on a hillside, it has seven entrances on seven different levels—a distinction that earned it a place in *Ripley's Believe It Or Not!*

For shoppers, the **Landmark Antique Mall** at 200 Federal Street in downtown Bluefield is a three-story gold mine of clocks, glassware, toys, stamps, coins, furniture, railroad memorabilia and much more. From April through September, it's open 9:00 a.m. to 5:00 p.m. Monday through Saturday and 1:00 to 5:00 p.m. Sunday. From October through March, hours are 9:00 a.m. to 4:00 p.m. Monday through Friday, 9:00 a.m. to 5:00 p.m. Saturday and 1:00 to 5:00 p.m. Sunday. Call (304)327-9686.

The visitors bureau is open Monday through Friday from 8:00 a.m. to 4:00 p.m. and Saturday by appointment. Call (304)325-8438 or (800)221-3206 for more information.

Directions: Downtown Bluefield is easily accessible off I-77 via Route 52. Follow the signs from the interstate to downtown along Routes 52 and 460. Route 52 becomes Bland Street, and the Arts and Science Center will be on your left.

Tip: While you are in the Bluefield area, be sure to drive up to the recently restored **East River Mountain Scenic Overlook**. From an elevation of 3,500 feet above sea level, you'll see the whole town of Bluefield sprawled beneath you and a truly breathtaking vista of mountain after mountain fading into the distance. Bring a picnic—you'll find pleasant shelters and hiking trails here in addition to two overlooks. From Route 460 in Bluefield, take Scenic Drive (Route 598) and follow it to the top of the mountain.

You'll also find two state parks near Bluefield. **Pinnacle Rock State Park**, on Route 52 just north of Bluefield, is a pleasant day-use park with picnic facilities and a two-mile hiking trail to the park's Jimmy Lewis Lake. **Camp Creek State Park** offers pretty waterfalls, hiking trails, camping areas, game courts, playgrounds and picnicking on 500 acres adjacent to the 5,000-acre **Camp Creek State Forest**. You'll find it by following signs from Exit 20 off I-77.

Bluefield Orioles

Bluefield is home to one of two minor league baseball teams in the area, the **Bluefield Orioles**. (The other is the Princeton Devil Rays.) The Orioles, affiliated with the big league Baltimore Orioles, play at lovely Bowen Field, recently featured as one of the nation's top ten minor league ballfields by *USA Weekend, National Geographic* and *Readers Digest* magazines. Built in 1939 and tucked into a narrow hollow of Bluefield's City Park, it was destroyed by fire in 1973. The reconstructed grandstand and recent renovations have made the diamond a showpiece—including new club houses, concession stand, lighted picnic pavilion, game courts and what "Doc" Gooden called "the best hot dog I've ever had at any ballpark." You can also expect beautiful sunsets and cool evenings at this park in "the air-conditioned city."

For more information on the park and a schedule of home games, call (504)326-1326.

Directions: From I-77, take Route 460 west to the Bluefield College exit. Fork left onto Stadium Drive at the light.

Tip: Don't worry when you arrive at the park and suddenly find yourself in Virginia. Bluefield is really twin cities, one in Virginia and one in West Virginia.

Eastern Regional Coal Archives

For travelers interested in coal mining history, a trip to the **Eastern Regional Coal Archives** is an absolute must. This excellent, comprehensive collection, located on the second floor of the Craft Library on Commerce Street, includes miners' tools, scrapbooks, company records, correspondence, diaries, newspapers, maps and blueprints, oral history tapes, films, 50,000 photographs and countless other materials and artifacts documenting the region's coal mining history. All of it is available for public viewing and use by scholars.

Don't imagine for a minute that a trip to this library will be dull. Dr. Stuart McGehee, the resident archivist, is an enthusiastic and helpful guide to the vast collection, and his passion for coal mining history is infectious.

The bulk of the material that lines the walls and fills the tabletops was initially assembled for a 1983 Pocahontas Coalfield Centennial Celebration. In the years since then, with support from the A.R. Mathews Foundation and the Craft Library, McGehee and his staff have continued to expand and refine the collection, and are always looking for materials that can help keep alive what McGehee feels is the "overlooked history" of the coalfields.

The collection is open to the public from 9:30 a.m. to 5:00 p.m. Monday through Friday. Those who want to conduct detailed research should call (304)325-3943 for an appointment.

Directions: Upstairs at the Craft Library at 600 Commerce Street in Bluefield.

Tip: Bluefield is the southern terminus of the Coal Heritage Trail [see entry], and a visit to the Eastern Regional Coal Archives would be a good way to acquaint yourself with mining history before driving the trail.

Science Center of West Virginia

In a 10,000-square-foot gallery on the third floor of the Arts and Science Center is one of the most exciting and fun interactive science museums in the state. If you cross the threshold of the **Science Center of West Virginia**, you can expect to spend at least an hour here—and you're guaranteed to have a good time, whatever your age.

Play Virtual Hoops, a basketball game without a basketball. Use the Video-microscope to examine coins, keys or a piece of your own

Most coal tipples, where coal was sorted by size, have been replaced by modern preparation plants. Coal mining history and artifacts are preserved at the Eastern Regional Coal Archives in Bluefield.

DRAWING BY WILLIAM D. GOEBEL

hair at 20 times actual size. Flap your arms and become a butterfly in the **Recollections** exhibit, which lets you watch yourself move through space and time in vivid color. Or visit the **Bone Zone**, a cozy living room where a human skeleton and its skeleton pets watch television. These are just a few of the exhibits at the Science Center, where every exhibit invites your active participation.

Exhibits and play areas designed for very young children occupy the original jail cells of this former city hall building. The Science Center also has a planetarium which groups can reserve for astronomy programs. On your way out, stop at the Science Center's second-floor gift shop.

The Science Center of West Virginia is open year-round. Summer hours (June through August) are 10:00 a.m. to 5:00 p.m. Monday through Saturday. From September through May, the hours are 9:00 a.m. to 3:00 p.m. Tuesday through Friday and 10:00 a.m. to 4:00 p.m. Saturday. Admission is $5.00. Children aged two and under are free. For more information call (304)325-8855.

Directions: The Science Center is located on the third floor of the Arts and Science Center at 500 Bland Street in Bluefield.

Bramwell

Bramwell, the way locals say it, rhymes with "camel." That's not the only unusual thing about this village cradled in a curve of the Bluestone River. More than half a century after its heyday, visitors are still amazed by the number of palatial mansions in the tiny town. In the early 1900s, investors made overnight fortunes from the rich Pocahontas coal seam. Estimates vary, but some say as many as 19 of the new millionaires chose Bramwell as home.

Most of the town's commercial section burned in a 1910 fire, and Bramwell was rebuilt under an ordinance requiring fireproof buildings; many notable buildings were constructed between 1910 and 1929, when Bramwell's fortunes came crashing down with the stock market. But the buildings survived, and the town was placed on the National Register of Historic Places in 1983.

Bramwell's **Town Hall**, built in 1888, is the first site on a self-guided walking/driving tour prepared by the Bramwell Millionaire Garden Club. The town's riverside location and quaint streets make for an exceptionally pleasant walk, and the tour features some of the town's oldest buildings, including the 1885 **McGuffin House**, along with some of its most lavish, such as the English Tudor **Thomas House** and the **Freeman House**. As you walk, you'll notice many beautiful old stone walls. Much of the stonework in Bramwell, including the stone church and bank building, was done by a family of Italian stonemasons, and the bluestone came from a quarry on the mountain above the Thomas House.

If the Town Hall is closed, you may also pick up tour guides at several bed-and-breakfast inns in Bramwell, including Perry House, Pack House and Three Oaks and Quilt, or at the Bluestone Convention and Visitors Bureau in nearby Bluefield. Twice a year, the Millionaire Garden Club sponsors guided tours of the mansions; for more information about the spring tour or candlelight Christmas tour, call the Town Hall at (304)248-7114, or call (304)248-7202 or -7252.

Directions: From I-77, take Exit 1 (Route 52) and travel 15 miles north to Bramwell. Follow signs to the historic district.

Clifftop

Babcock State Park

Route 60, the historic Midland Trail [see entry], offers many diversions for travelers, none more enticing than **Babcock State Park.** This 4,127-acre park features 51 campsites, 26 fully equipped cabins, a 19-acre lake, swimming pool, game courts, picnic areas, playgrounds and a fast-flowing trout stream in a ruggedly gorgeous canyon. Hikers love Babcock's 20 miles of trails, many of which have scenic outlooks; favorites include the **Island in the Sky Trail**, which looks down over the park's rustic, native sandstone headquarters, and the **Narrow Gauge Trail**, which follows an old railroad track. Guided horseback rides are offered at the park's stables during summer, and the park naturalist conducts regular wildflower walks and other presentations. One of the most-photographed attractions in the state park system, Babcock's **Glade Creek Grist Mill** was built in 1976 by combining parts from several abandoned mills around the state.

Babcock is a seasonal park, with most facilities open from mid-April through October 31 only. For more information about camping and cabin reservations, call (304)438-3003 or (800)CALL-WVA, or write Babcock State Park, HC 35, Box 150, Clifftop, WV 25831.

Directions: From Route 60, take Route 41 south to Clifftop. The campground is two miles south of Route 60, and the main park entrance is two miles further.

Camp Washington-Carver

From Babcock State Park you can hike a shady two-mile trail to nearby **Camp Washington-Carver**, stopping along the way to soak up the sun on flat rocks or wade in pretty Mann's Creek.

To fans of old-time music, Clifftop is familiar as the site (and the informal name) of one of the country's fastest growing music festivals and competitions. The early August **Appalachian String Band Music Festival** is one of a number of annual events at Camp Washington-Carver, the nation's first black 4-H camp. Built between 1939 and 1942 by the Civilian Conservation Corps, the camp is now a satellite location for the West Virginia Division of Culture and History. In addition to the string band festival, the camp is home to **Doo-Wop Saturday Night**, a popular oldies festival, **Mellow in the Mountains** (folk), **Clifftop Rocks** (classic rock and roll), **Mountain Knights and Crafts** (medieval festivities and crafts),

Haunted Hills (Halloween tricks and treats) and a regular schedule of dinner theater performances. Ticket prices range from $2.50 to $15.00, depending on the event.

The camp is dominated by the **Great Chestnut Lodge**, the largest chestnut log structure in the world, and is a fine place for fishing, hiking and picnicking during and between festivals. Others enjoy browsing in the old-fashioned **Country Store**.

Entertainment runs from July through October 31, but the grounds are open for day visitors year-round. For a schedule of events, call (304)438-3005 or write Camp Washington Carver, HC 35, Box 5, Clifftop, WV 25831.

Directions: From Route 60 take Route 41 to Clifftop.

Coal Heritage Trail

Ancient Greeks called it "the rock that burns." Coal powered the modernization of the United States, and beginning in the 1870s with the completion of the Chesapeake and Ohio and Norfolk and Western railroads, coal-rich southern West Virginia was transformed from rugged wilderness into a throbbing center of industry. Thousands of African-Americans from the deep South joined European immigrants and poured into the coal camps—privately owned towns, in fact—where mining companies housed their workers. During the early part of the 20th century, the region was bloodied by the Mine Wars, when federal troops were called in to suppress attempts to unionize coal miners.

Today, the coal industry in West Virginia is a highly mechanized business that produces more coal with fewer miners than ever before. Southern West Virginia is no longer the busy, growing place it was. Still, for the traveler who wants to learn more about a remarkable, sometimes violent chapter in American history, the Coal Heritage Trail is a fascinating route to explore.

The driving trail links Beckley and Bluefield via a string of towns in four counties—Raleigh, Wyoming, McDowell and Mercer—winding past company stores, miners' houses and massive railroad yards. Although you can pick it up at any point along the way, a good starting place is the Beckley Exhibition Coal Mine [see entry]. After exploring the mine, follow the trail southward. Stop and look at the huge company store at Itmann, the courthouse steps in Welch where organizer Sid Hatfield was shot to death, the intact mining town of Elkhorn and the "millionaires' town" of Bramwell. At trail's end in Bluefield, you'll see the "natural gravity" railroad yards that attract rail fans by the thousands; if your interest in coal history has been sparked, the Eastern Regional Coal Archives [see entry] is a good place to learn more.

For more information, contact the Coal Heritage Trail Association at the Eastern Regional Coal Archives, 600 Commerce Street, Bluefield, WV 24701, phone (304)325-3943; or Beckley Exhibition Coal Mine, New River Park, Beckley, WV 25802, phone (304)256-1747.

Fayetteville

Driving or walking down the main street, you might think **Fayetteville** is no more than a small, pleasant mountain town—except for the kayaks. Strapped to car-top carriers, propped in doorways, hanging from ceilings behind show windows, they serve notice that this little town is a major hub of outdoor recreation. Kayaking, whitewater rafting, mountain biking or rock climbing—choose your challenge, and you'll find some of the most challenging venues nearby. Adjacent to the New River Gorge National River and conveniently close to three state parks (Babcock, Carnifex Ferry and Hawks Nest), Fayetteville would be a good home base for any number of outdoor adventures. And the town is well worth exploring for its other charms.

Like many West Virginia towns, Fayetteville was the site of Civil War action—in September 1862, Confederate General W.W. Loring defeated the Union forces of General Joseph A.J. Lightburn here. Fayetteville is remembered by military historians as the first site of indirect firing, now in universal military use.

Stop at the **Fayetteville Historic Visitors Bureau** in the town hall at 125 North Court Street to pick up brochures about the area, including a map of the Fayetteville Historic District. Visitors center hours are 10:00 a.m. to 5:00 p.m. Call (304)574-1500 or (888)574-1500 or write Visitors Bureau, Historic Fayette Jail, Fayetteville, WV 25840. Or visit the **New River Convention and Visitors Bureau** in nearby Oak Hill. You'll find it on Route 19 at Oyler Avenue, across from the Holiday Inn. They're open 9:00 a.m. to 5:00 p.m. seven days a week. Call (800)927-0263 or (304)465-5618, visit their web site (wvweb.com/www/FAYETTE_CHAMBER/) or write New River Convention and Visitors Bureau, 310 Oyler Avenue, Oak Hill, WV 25901.

Across from the courthouse square you'll find the **Court Street Gallery**. The big display windows will give you a good view, but you'll want to go inside and look more closely at the collection of West Virginia pottery, jewelry, paintings, photography, sculpture, wood, stained glass and limited-edition prints. Summer gallery hours are 10:00 a.m. to 5:00 p.m. Monday through Thursday, 10:00 a.m. to 8:00 p.m. Friday and Saturday and 1:00 to 5:00 p.m. Sunday. Winter hours: 11:00 a.m. to 5:00 p.m. Tuesday through Saturday, Sunday and Monday by appointment. Call (304) 574-9010.

Perhaps because so many visitors are just in from activities guaranteed to work up a healthy appetite, Fayetteville has a remarkable number of good eateries. Among others, try the **Sedona Grille** at 106 East Maple Street for an excellent, generous meal in a Southwestern atmosphere. **Smokey's Charcoal Grill** at Class VI River Runners in nearby Lansing (Ames Heights Road just off Route 19) is another popular place for hungry adventurers during the season. Call (304)574-4905 for reservations, which are suggested. The **Breeze Hill Restaurant**, on Route 19 at Lansing Road, is a favorite place for seafood. Although casual dress is fine anywhere in Fayetteville, reservations are also suggested here: (304)574-0436.

At the **Cathedral Cafe and Bookstore**, scan the shelves for new and used books while you enjoy cappuccino or a meal in this converted church at 134 South Court Street. The pattern of the original stained glass windows is repeated on hand-painted tables and the coffee bar's tiled top, a creation of Julia Cassells, whose **Trillium Crafts**—a pleasing mix of art pottery, baskets, jewelry, marbled silk and more—overlooks the cafe from a balcony. Call (304)574-0202.

Check the marquee at the **Historic Fayette Theatre** across from the cafe. Small in size but ambitious in scope, the theater features an April-to-November season that includes children's mysteries and musical comedies, as well as some of the best old-time, folk and jazz musicians in the region. Call (304)574-4655 or write Historic Fayette Theater, PO Box 448, Fayetteville, WV 25840.

You can get hiking, backpacking, rock climbing, rafting or camping gear from several stores on Court Street. [see appendix for a list of whitewater rafting companies.] Within the historic district you'll find several shops with antiques and collectibles, as well as a good natural foods store.

Every October, Fayetteville floods with visitors on Bridge Day [see calendar of events]. A holiday in honor of a bridge? Once you've seen the **New River Gorge Bridge**, you'll understand. Towering above the gorge, it is an engineering marvel and a sight to behold—not to mention what you can behold *from* this perch. On Bridge Day, one side is closed to vehicular traffic and opened to hikers and a few brave souls who parachute the 876 feet to the New River. The holiday attracts as many as 100,000 and caps the region's whitewater season.

Forest Hill

Wakerobin Gallery

Lovers of Appalachian crafts and artworks will find them about ten miles south of Talcott at the **Wakerobin Gallery** in Forest Hill. Behind the old-timey storefront at the junction of Seminole Road and Route 12 is a tasteful array of fine hand-thrown pottery, paintings, weavings, dulcimers, stained glass, wooden toys, Shaker boxes, brooms, ironwork, afghans, rope hammocks and baskets from all over the Appalachian region.

Resident potter Marcia Springsteen has shown her work all over the U.S. and Canada. A potter for more than 20 years, she stresses function, texture and beauty in her work. The high-fired, lead-free vessels on display at Wakerobin Gallery are all the more impressive when you learn that she has been blind since birth.

Hours are 10:00 a.m. to 4:00 p.m. every day except Wednesday and Sunday. The phone is (304)466-2053.

Directions: Junction of Seminole Road and Route 12. For more information, write Wakerobin Gallery, HC 65, Box 112C, Forest Hill, WV 24935.

Gauley Bridge

Where the New and Gauley rivers meet to form the wide Kanawha River is the town of **Gauley Bridge**. Stop at the **Gauley Bridge Tourist Information and Craft Center** on Route 60 to get information about the area or the Midland Trail [see entry] or to find handcrafts created by 185 juried West Virginia crafters. Here also is the **Gauley Bridge Historical Society Museum**, filled with changing exhibits of art and artifacts of local and regional history. The museum is housed in a restored railroad yardhouse. A small restored post office building completes the complex.

Just across the river, take a look at the beautifully restored **Gauley Bridge Railroad Station**, placed on the National Register of Historic Places in 1980 and now used as the town hall. Built in 1893 by black railroad laborers, the station was the terminus for the Kanawha and Michigan Railroad and, in the early 1900s, a popular tourist destination for travelers from the North.

The Tourist Information Center is open March through December, seven days a week. Hours are 10:00 a.m. to 5:00 p.m. Monday through Saturday and noon to 5:00 p.m. Sunday. The museum is staffed by volunteers and is open weekends spring to fall, usually from 10:00 a.m. to 5:00 p.m., and other times by appointment. The museum charges no admission, but donations are accepted. Call (304)632-1284 or write Tourist Information Center, Box 490, Gauley Bridge, WV 25085.

Directions: Gauley Bridge is on Route 60 about 11 miles west of Ansted.

About a mile and a half east of Gauley Bridge on the Midland Trail, allow yourself a few minutes to view **Cathedral Falls**. This spectacular wayside waterfall is actually inside a stone room that was carved by the falling water. Walk inside, climbing carefully over the rocks and all the way to the base of the falls, and you can gaze up at an almost perfect circular opening in the ceiling. The small parking area has been recently repaved and lighted. In winter, the frozen falls make for a fantastical natural sculpture.

A mile west of Gauley Bridge on Route 60, at a picturesque setting beside the gently cascading Kanawha Falls, the historic **Glen Ferris Inn** is a lovely place for an elegant meal or an overnight stay. First opened in 1839 as Stockton's Inn, the Federal-style mansion with its large, stuccoed brick columns was a welcome sight for many a weary stagecoach passenger during the 19th century. It also housed both Confederate and Union soldiers during the Civil War and, in the first half of the 20th century, managers and workers in the developing chemical, manufacturing and hydroelectric generating industries. The inn continues to welcome visitors with gourmet cuisine and period furnishings. Guests love the carefully tended gardens almost as much as the view of the wide Kanawha River and falls. For rates and reservations call (304)632-1111 or write Glen Ferris Inn, PO Box 128, Glen Ferris, WV 25090.

Hinton

Bluestone Dam and Bluestone Lake

Just south of Hinton on Route 20, the huge **Bluestone Dam** holds back the waters of the New River and its nearby tributary, the Bluestone National Scenic River. Managed by the U.S. Army Corps of Engineers, the giant concrete facility is open for free guided tours from Memorial Day weekend through Labor Day weekend. Group tours are available year-round. The tour takes about an hour and is handicapped-accessible.

From the parking lot at the dam, you can see fishermen plying the dam's tailwaters, a popular and productive fishing spot.

Although it began in 1942, work on the Bluestone Dam was interrupted by World War II and continued in 1946. It was completed in 1952. The dam closes a 2,048-foot-wide gap between the mountainsides and rises 165 feet above the river bed, creating one of the state's largest lakes, the 2,040-acre **Bluestone Lake**.

The visitors center at Bluestone Dam is located on top of the dam near Route 20, and is open from 9:00 a.m. to 7:30 p.m. Wednesday through Sunday, Memorial Day through Labor Day. Guided tours are conducted at 1:30 p.m. Wednesday and Thursday and 2:00 p.m. Saturday and Sunday, and group tours are available anytime by appointment. The top of the dam is open daily, 9:00 a.m. to 7:30 p.m. during the same season, except for Monday and Tuesday, when it closes at 3:30 p.m. For more information and tour reservations, call (304)466-1234 or write Bluestone Lake, 701 Miller Avenue, Hinton, WV 25951. Call the same number for information on boating, fishing, water skiing and other lake recreation. Call (304)466-0156 for a recording of lake and stream information.

Bluestone Lake is sandwiched between large tracts of the 20,000-acre **Bluestone Wildlife Management Area**. Call (304)466-3398 for more information about hunting, fishing and hiking there. Or visit **Bluestone State Park**, on the west side of the lake where the Bluestone River meets the New River. This 2,155-acre park has 25 modern cabins, 87 campsites with full hook-ups, boat launch facilities, swimming, fishing, hiking trails, picnic areas, game courts and playgrounds. The park maintains year-round nature and recreation programs. Call (304)466-2805 or (800)CALL-WVA or write Bluestone State Park, HC 78, Box 3, Hinton, WV 25951.

Directions: The visitors center at Bluestone Dam is about five miles south of Hinton on Route 20.

Tip: While you are in the Hinton area, you may want to stop at the **Bluestone Museum** to see some fine examples of mounted fish, large and small game and reptiles. The museum also has a collection of local Indian artifacts. Built by a 20-year veteran of Alaskan big-game hunts and taxidermy, the small museum also has a gift shop with T-shirts, souvenirs and trophy mounts. You'll find the museum on Route 20/3 about a mile south of Hinton. Admission is $1.00, and the museum is open 10:00 a.m. to 6:00 p.m. daily, March through November. Phone (304)466-1454.

Historic District

The town of **Hinton** serves as a gateway to the many-splendored

New River Gorge National River, which was added to the national park system in 1978 to preserve 53 free-flowing miles of this ancient, majestic waterway from here to Fayetteville. In 1988 the **Gauley River National Recreation Area** and the **Bluestone National Scenic River** were added to the system, creating a large protected area filled with opportunities for whitewater rafting, boating, hunting, fishing, birding, hiking and camping.

If you are most interested in activities directly related to the New River Gorge National River, begin with a visit to the park system's **Hinton Visitors Center**, one of five visitors centers operated by the park system. Located on Route 20 in downtown Hinton and staffed by park rangers, the small center features a short slide show about the river and offers information on guided hikes, canoe trips, bus tours, evening programs, youth programs and more. It is open seasonally, and the phone is (304)466-0417. [See the entry on the Canyon Rim Visitors Center in Lansing for year-round operation.]

Much of the town of Hinton is a National Historic District, and the **Summers County Convention and Visitors Bureau** has prepared an informative self-guided walking tour for those who want to explore it. Stop by the visitors center at 206 Temple Street to pick up a copy or call (304)466-5420. Hours vary seasonally.

Like many other southern West Virginia towns, Hinton got its start with railroading and coal mining. In fact, the entire town was once owned by the Chesapeake and Ohio Railroad, which bought the property in 1871 and sold the first lot in 1874. A building boom ensued, and Hinton's historic district today reflects the eclectic styles of Victorian architecture. Churches in town include examples of American Gothic, Classical and Greek Revival styles. The residential architecture of the historic district includes fine examples of Classical Revival, High Victorian, American Four Square and even Second Empire. You'll see many large porches, various types of columns and plenty of gingerbread in Hinton.

Under the same roof as the Summers County Visitors Center is the **Hinton Railroad Museum**, where you'll find a wealth of railway history about this town that served for 75 years as a main terminal. Also in the museum is a unique treasure by folk artist Charlie Permelia, the **John Henry Woodcarvings** exhibit. This set of hand-carved figures, each 12 to 18 inches in height, makes use of some 80 different native hardwoods and records, in accurate detail, every job and tool that existed in an 1870 railroad. Full of emotion and detail, the carvings have been recognized as the work of a masterful self-taught artist. Admission to the railroad museum is $2.00 for adults and $1.00 for students. A not-for-profit **Crafter's Gallery** is also on the premises.

Hinton is home to West Virginia's first and only museum dedicated to the state's veterans. Located near the corner of 4th Avenue and Ballangee Street, the **Veterans Memorial Museum of Southern West Virginia** contains memorabilia of every major conflict from early frontier days to the Gulf War. Among other artifacts are General Douglas MacArthur's footlocker and a vintage jeep. Open noon to 4:00 p.m. Friday through Sunday, May through November, or by appointment. Admission is free but donations are appreciated. Call (304)466-3930.

Families with small children will enjoy the **City Sidetrack Park** and its 267-foot-long waterslide, located just off the path of the historical tour on Front Street. It's open Memorial Day through mid-August. Call (304)466-1600.

Directions: From I-64, take the Sandstone exit and follow Route 20 south to Hinton. From I-77, follow Route 20 north.

Tip: One of the best views in Hinton is from the riverside deck of the Dairy Queen restaurant! A giant sycamore tree beside the deck is home to many tree swallows that will entertain you with graceful aerobatics while you relax on the enclosed deck.

Three Rivers Avian Center

What happens to injured birds of prey, herons and other threatened birds? The lucky ones are taken to the **Three Rivers Avian Center** near Hinton, where Ron and Wendy Perrone and their staff devote themselves to the injured birds, nursing them back to health and releasing them in the area where they were found. Opened in 1990, the center has also become a clearinghouse for information about birds and their importance to West Virginia's ecosystem.

Operating from a 102-acre farm which they have converted to a wildlife sanctuary, Three Rivers Avian Center staff have organized a statewide hospice network of veterinarians and volunteers, established an internship program for college students, organized ongoing public education programs and built an impressive rehabilitation center.

Public tours of the center are conducted from 1:00 to 5:00 p.m. on the first Saturday of each month, May through October and there is a **Migration Celebration** [see calendar of events] in September. For more information, call (304)466-4683 or write Three Rivers Avian Center, HC 74, Box 279, Brooks, WV 25951.

Directions: From Hinton, take Route 20 north to Brooks Mountain Road, turn there and follow signs to the center.

Lansing

Canyon Rim Visitors Center

Between Hinton and Fayetteville, the awesome **New River Gorge National River** is the center of all attractions. Although the National Park Service maintains its headquarters in Glen Jean, day-trippers should start their visit at the **Canyon Rim Visitors Center** on Route 19 in Lansing, on the north side of the river near Fayetteville. With floor-to-ceiling windows, a terrace and a boardwalk, the large center offers perhaps the best views in the gorge. An 11-minute slide-show orientation is augmented by large exhibits detailing the gorge's geological and cultural history, and touch-screen information stations will tell you about the area's major industries and recreational opportunities. On weekends and holidays during summer, sightseers can take bus tours to the bottom of the gorge, and a number of trails are open for hikers year-round. The Canyon Rim Visitors Center is also the best place to find out about the many activities and interpretive programs conducted by park rangers—including guided hikes, evening storytelling, bird walks and star gazing.

You'll learn here that the New River is not at all new, but approximately 65 million years old! Geologists have confirmed that the river was once part of the ancient Teays River system that flowed through what is now the center of North America. Glacial activity during the ice age created other rivers, but this remnant of the original river—in place before the Appalachian Mountains took shape—still flows across the Appalachian Plateau in a northwesterly direction. Average depth of the gorge is 1,000 feet.

Its ancient history is fascinating, but no less interesting is the area's more recent history and folklore. The river's rapid descent, which makes it one of the best in the East for rafting, made it especially difficult for early settlers to navigate. Ferries were often the only means of crossing it. Not until the railroad arrived in 1873 did the inaccessible gorge become reachable. Its rich deposits of coal and acres of timber were great prizes, and communities sprang up almost overnight along the gorge. When the mines were played out and the forests exhausted, the towns were abandoned.

In 1978, the New River Gorge National River was established to preserve and protect 53 miles of the ancient river. The national park includes 70,000 acres of land along the river between the towns of Hinton and Fayetteville. A good way to appreciate the gorge's rich culture is to walk one of the many trails maintained by the National Park Service. Get maps and recommendations at the visitors cen-

Soaring 876 feet above the river, the New River Gorge Bridge is the world's longest single-arch steel span—1,700 feet long. LARRY BELCHER

ter or join one of the ranger-guided hikes. Trails range from one-fourth mile to more than six miles in length; the terrain varies from level to quite steep and rugged. Do be conscientious: stay on the trails, keep pets leashed and pack out anything you bring in.

The two-mile (one way) **Kaymoor Trail** takes you to the abandoned mine site of Kaymoor, with several remaining historic mine structures where thousands of miners lived and worked, beginning with the first shipment of coal in 1899 and ending with the mine's closure in 1962. You must look only and not enter the dangerous structures. The trail crosses a foot bridge over Wolf Creek and later follows the rim of the gorge, making for spectacular views from 400 to 500 feet above the river.

Another good hike is the **Thurmond-Minden Trail**. This easy trail, 3.2 miles in length one-way, and open to mountain bikers as well as hikers. It begins at trail heads either off Minden Road or off Route 25 near Thurmond. You'll follow the old railroad bed past McKinley Rock, a waterfall and views of both towns. While on this trail, pause at the view of the historic railroad town of Thurmond to reflect on its former life. Incorporated in 1903 with a peak population of 400 or more, Thurmond was the commercial and social center of the New River coal industry. The town and railroad were so integrally linked that Thurmond had no streets—the only such town in the country. Just the same, it produced as much as 20 percent of all C&O Railroad revenues by 1910 and supported two banks, two drugstores, two stores, a meat distributor, a movie theater, grocery stores and the lively Dun Glen Hotel where, according to legend, a 14-year-long poker game was played. The game might still be going had the hotel not burned. By the 1950s, with the end of the steam era of railroading, much of Thurmond had been abandoned, leaving behind colorful memories and one of the smallest incorporated towns in the state.

The **Thurmond Depot**, part of the **Thurmond Historic District**, has been restored to serve as a park visitors center, one of five maintained by the park service. To reach it by automobile, take Route 19 to the Glen Jean exit, north of Beckley, and follow the signs to Thurmond, seven miles down Route 25. (Be advised that Route 25 is narrow and winding, not suitable for recreational vehicles or trailers.) While there, stop in at **Thurmond Supply** for snacks, drinks, West Virginia crafts and foods, scenic and historic postcards, railroad pins, old-time toys, and outdoor gear and supplies. The store is open daily, 9:00 a.m. to dusk from April 1 to October 31 and 9:00 a.m. to 5:00 p.m. weekends during November and December, or by appointment. Call (304)469-2380.

Not surprisingly, outdoor activities dominate the scene along the New River Gorge. Whitewater rafting here is considered to be as good as it gets in the East—but it's not only for thrill-seekers. Mountain biking is also gaining in popularity; there are miles of trails along the 53-mile-long gorge. Rock climbers have a choice of 1,400 courses of climbing surface in the New River Gorge. On the third Saturday in October, **Bridge Day** attracts bands, jugglers, dancers, food vendors, parachuters, rappellers and as many as 100,000 visitors for a day-long festival that takes place on and around the **New River Gorge Bridge**. With a total roadbed length of 3,030 feet, the world's longest single-arch steel span perches 876 feet above the river (325 feet higher than the Washington Monument). Its construction was a ten-year project, completed in 1977, and it reduces to about a minute the gorge crossing that formerly took 40 minutes via winding mountain roads.

The Canyon Rim Visitors Center is open daily 9:00 a.m. to 5:00 p.m. during the winter and 9:00 a.m. to 8:00 p.m. Memorial Day though Labor Day. It is handicapped-accessible and has plenty of restrooms and parking. For more information on activities sponsored by the National Park Service, visit their web site (www.nps.gov/neri), e-mail the center (neri_interpretation@nps.gov), call Canyon Rim Visitors

Center at (304)574-2115 or park headquarters at (304)465-0508.

Directions: On Route 19 between Beckley and Summersville, two miles north of Fayetteville.

Lewisburg

Visitors Center and Walking Tour

Very few places in West Virginia are more amenable to a day or weekend trip than **Lewisburg**. Whether your interests run to history, scenery, outdoor recreation, antiques, arts or good food, Lewisburg will satisfy you and, almost certainly, bring you back again.

One of the oldest towns in the state, Lewisburg is named for Andrew Lewis, a surveyor who set up camp in 1751 near the spring behind today's courthouse. In 1774, Lewis (by then a general) assembled an army of frontier militia here and led them to Point Pleasant to defeat Chief Cornstalk in an epic battle [see entry on Point Pleasant Battle Monument]. The town was chartered in 1782 by the Virginia Assembly and prospered as a way-station on the James River and Kanawha Turnpike as well as a fertile farming area and a hub of education, government and law. (Among others, Patrick Henry practiced here.) In this region of many mineral springs, spa and resort hotels thrived during the 1800s.

The Civil War touched Lewisburg directly on May 23, 1862, when Union leader George Crook, who would later become famous for his defeat of the great Geronimo, led the well-trained 36th and 44th Ohio regiments in a stunning, early-morning victory over Confederate General Henry Heth. Nevertheless, Lewisburg remained strongly Southern in sympathy for most of the war. Many of the town's buildings were used as hospitals and barracks by both sides during the long conflict. In 1978, a 236-acre area of Lewisburg was designated a National Historic District, and many individual structures are on the National Register of Historic Places.

Begin your Lewisburg visit at the visitors center at 105 Church Street. Here you'll find every sort of resource a traveler could desire—an excellent self-guided walking tour, several suggestions for driving tours, guides to specialty shops and lodgings, historical and recreational information. The walking tour of Lewisburg—either the long version (72 sites), which will take you more than two hours, or an abbreviated, hour-long jaunt—is highly recommended, and begins with the building in which the visitors center is located, **Carnegie Hall**. Built in 1902 as a gift from Andrew

Instead of a main street, the Chesapeake and Ohio Railroad ran right through the middle of downtown Thurmond in 1910. Today, the New River Gorge town sees more whitewater rafts than rail cars.

Drawing by William D. Goebel

Carnegie to the Lewisburg Female Institute, the Greek Revival performance hall was acquired in the 1980s by a non-profit cultural and educational organization that now sponsors a diverse, year-round schedule of concerts, theater and dance performances, museum and art exhibits, school performances, studio classes, a children's summer arts program and a film series. The museum's Ivy Terrace is the setting for a popular summer series of picnic concerts featuring West Virginia artists. For a current schedule of events call (304)645-7917 or write Carnegie Hall, 105 Church Street, Lewisburg, WV 24901.

Just across the street, be sure to look at the **Old Stone Church**, one of the town's most beloved landmarks. The oldest church in continuous use west of the Alleghenies, it looks much as it did when it was built in 1796. The cemetery is full of old markers with interesting inscriptions. In another cemetery across the street lies Dick Pointer, the black slave whose heroic actions saved Fort Donnally during a 1778 Indian raid.

The John A. **North House** is remarkable not only because it was built in 1820 and run as the popular Star Tavern during the early 1800s; today, it is one of the liveliest and most captivating museums in West Virginia. Even children—perhaps especially children—can happily spend an hour or more here, exploring everything from a 1780 Conestoga wagon to the nation's first postal delivery buggy to the wooden saddle used to break Traveller, General Robert E. Lee's horse. Each room of North House tells a story; some are funny, some poignant. The museum sponsors a popular series of children's educational programs, including "Tea and Manners," for which young guests dress up in hoop skirts and and string ties to take tea and play 19th-century games. Also on the premises are public archives and a very nice museum shop. Museum hours are 10:00 a.m. to 4:00 p.m. Monday through Saturday, year-round. Call (304)645-3398 for more information.

The **Greenbrier Public Library,** at 301 Courtney Drive, was built in 1834; inside, you can look at a section of old plaster where Civil War soldiers scratched their names. At the **Lewis Spring** (in Andrew Lewis Park, near the corner of Jefferson and Randolph Streets), water still flows in the spot where Andrew Lewis found it. It was here that he gathered his forces before marching to Point Pleasant. You'll pass the imposing **Greenbrier County Courthouse** at 200 North Court Street, built in 1837, and continue eventually to the **Confederate Cemetery** on McElhenny Road. On this quiet hilltop, 95 unknown Confederate soldiers rest in a common, cross-shaped grave. Originally buried in a trench beside the Old Stone Church, their remains were moved here after the war.

Among the walking-tour sites is one that may entice you back, either for an excellent meal or an overnight stay. Look for the old stage coach in front of the **General Lewis Inn** at 301 East Washington Street—and look inside for an astounding collection of antique tools, guns, utensils and musical instruments lining the walls of the inn's Memory Hall. The dining room/restaurant is in the east wing of the 1834 John Withrow House; the large hand-hewn beams were once part of the slave quarters. The main section of the inn, all of it furnished with antiques, is a 1929 addition. Outside, the gardens and lily pond beckon guests in warm weather. Call (304)645-2600 to reserve one of the inn's 26 guest rooms.

Lewisburg is a pleasant place for walking, but you can also ride in style: the **Lewisburg Carriage and Horse Service** offers hour-long narrated tours of the town from a comfortable, 100-year-old Amish buggy pulled by Belgian draft horses. Tours run May through October, Tuesday through Saturday, from 9:00 a.m. to 5:00 p.m. During November and December, the service continues by special arrangement. Cost is $12.00 for adults, $10.00 for seniors or groups of four or more and $6.00 for children aged 12 and under. Call

(304)645-6593 for more information.

All the history notwithstanding, some people come to Lewisburg just for the shops—antique shops; fine art, craft and photography galleries; gourmet food and kitchen boutiques—and the many restaurants, including some pretty outdoor cafes. From wholesome health foods to handsome wearables to good books, Lewisburg is a buyer's paradise. The visitors center offers a handy map to guide you to the various treasures.

In August, Lewisburg is host to the **State Fair of West Virginia**, a big annual event in a state that values its agricultural heritage. More than 250,000 visitors come for horse and livestock shows, goat-milking contests, sheep shearings, draft horse pulls, harness races, cookery competitions and demonstrations, carnival rides, circus presentations, fireworks and nightly performances by national stars. Send a self-addressed envelope to Program of Events, State Fair of West Virginia, Drawer 986, Lewisburg, WV 24901 or call (304)645-1090 for more information.

After a day of sightseeing, check out the offerings at the **Greenbrier Valley Theatre** at 113 East Washington Street. Broadway musicals, classical and modern drama and children's theater matinees are among the presentations Thursday through Sunday from mid-June to early August. Phone (304)645-3838 for ticket information and reservations.

The visitors center is open year-round, Monday though Saturday, from 9:00 a.m. to 5:00 p.m. Call (304)645-1000 or (800)833-2068, visit their web site (wvweb.com/www/lewisburg) or write Lewisburg Visitors Center, 105 Church Street, Lewisburg, WV 24901.

Directions: From I-64 take Route 210 south to Lewisburg. Turn right on Washington Street, then left on Church Street. The visitors center will be on your right.

Tip: Don't forget that Lewisburg is just a couple of miles from Caldwell, the southern terminus for the **Greenbrier River Trail** [see entry in Potomac Highlands section], the 75-mile rail trail that follows the beautiful Greenbrier River. Fishing and canoeing are also popular activities on the Greenbrier.

Lost World Caverns

If you take one of the self-guided driving tours recommended by the Lewisburg Visitors Center, pay special attention to the gently rolling landscape. This area is richly underlaid with caves and caverns, about 100 named and up to 1,500 unnamed. A commercial enterprise, **Lost World Caverns**, provides a fascinating introduction to the ancient geological formations.

These caverns were discovered in 1942 by Virginia Polytechnic Institute explorers who descended 120 feet through a grapevine-covered opening to the floor of the cave. Known then as Grapevine Cave, it was explored and mapped for almost 30 years before a more accessible horizontal entrance was opened into the largest part of the caverns. Renamed in 1970 and designated a National Historic Landmark in 1977, it was opened for public tours in 1981 with extensive underground improvements as well as another entrance, new walkways and a large reception center and gift shop. It is an exceptionally large series of caves, with many rooms rivaling caverns in the West.

Among many points of interest along the 35-minute guided tour, notice the hex blocks, which cover much of the cavern floor. These patterns were created some 300 million years ago when ancient oceans subsided and limestone, formed from the sediment, was exposed and dried. One room features an Ice Cream Wall, complete with natural shades of vanilla, chocolate and butterscotch. In another, the mammoth flowstone column that goes by the name of Goliath measures 40 feet high and 25 feet around. An especially good example of brilliantly white calcite, the Snowy Chandelier is one of the largest compound stalactites in the United States, weighing in at a hefty 30 tons. Another stalactite in this cave, the War Club, provided the perch for patient Bob Addis, who sat in a platform attached to it for 15 days, 23 hours and 22 minutes to earn a place in the *Guinness Book of World Records.*

The caverns are open for tours year-round except for the month of January. Hours are 9:00 a.m. to 7:00 p.m. Memorial Day to Labor Day, 9:00 a.m. to 5:00 p.m. Labor Day to Thanksgiving and 10:00 a.m. to 4:00 p.m. from February 1 to Memorial Day. There is a fee for tours. Bring a light jacket, comfortable shoes and a camera. Lost World Caverns also offers three-hour-long wild walks for able-bodied explorers who wish to venture away from the commercial walkways and lights. Extra fees and reservations are required for these, and explorers must be at least 14 years of age. For more information call (304)645-6677 or (800)CALL-WVA or write Lost World Caverns, Route 6, Box 308, Lewisburg, WV 24901.

Directions: From Lewisburg, go north on Route 219. After crossing I-64, turn left on Arbuckle Road and left again on Fairview Road. The entrance will be on your right.

Mullens

Twin Falls Resort State Park

On the map, **Twin Falls Resort State Park** looks a bit isolated—well away from interstate highways and not close to any large cities. That is precisely its appeal. Once you get there, you may not ever want to leave this 3,776-acre haven. And there's no need—the resort has practically everything a civilized soul could desire right on the premises.

Perched on a wooded ridge, the park's 20-room lodge and conference facility overlooks an 18-hole championship golf course designed by George Cobb, with a pro shop at the center. Inside the lodge, the park's nature center is the headquarters for a year-round recreation/nature program. The facility also features a gift shop, restaurant and conference rooms. From Memorial Day to Labor Day, an outdoor pool is open to the public, along with tennis and other game courts.

The nine hiking trails at Twin Falls range from climbs to scenic overlooks to wooded paths. One leads to the falls for which the park is named and a moss-covered abandoned mill. Another takes hikers to a recreated 1830s pioneer farm on **Bowers Ridge**, where resident farmers Luther and Lottie Cook give friendly living history lessons to visitors.

Twin Falls boasts 13 modern, fully-equipped cottages—popular at all times of the year but especially inviting in cool weather, and stocked with an endless supply of firewood for the beautiful, large fireplaces—and 50 campsites with a convenience store, laundry facilities and bathhouses with hot showers. A large picnic area is adjacent to the campground.

Lodge and cottages are open year-round, and the campground is open from Easter weekend to October 31. No pets allowed in lodge rooms or cottages. Reservations are recommended. For rates and reservations, call (304)294-4000 or (800)CALL-WVA or write Twin Falls Resort State Park, Route 97, Box 1023, Mullens, WV 25882.

Directions: From I-77 or or I-64, take Route 16 south for 4.2 miles to the junction with Route 54. Drive southwest on Route 54 for 14 miles, to Maben. Turn right on Route 97 and drive 5 1/2 miles. At the stop sign, turn left onto Bear Hole Road; the park entrance is less than a mile, and the lodge just over four miles.

Tip: If you do want to venture away from the resort, you might want to drive to nearby **Itmann**, an interesting point on the **Coal Heritage Trail** [see entry]. In this old coal company town stands a huge and architecturally fascinating company store once operated by the **Pocahontas Fuel Company** and now listed on the National Register of Historic Places.

Panther

Panther State Forest

Panther State Forest is tucked away in the steep, mountainous country where West Virginia, Virginia and Kentucky meet. Depending upon which story you believe, a young hunter here fought off a panther with either his bare hands or no more than his knife. He survived, and the creek and later the state forest were named to commemorate the big cat.

You're not likely to see a panther, but the 7,810-acre forest is quiet, remote and beautiful. One reason is its isolation from major cities or roads—it's about two hours south of Charleston and more than an hour west of Bluefield or Beckley. However, if you are exploring the Coal Heritage Trail [see entry] that winds its way through southern West Virginia from Beckley to Bluefield, it will not be far off your route.

Six campsites with electricity, water and and fireplaces are located beside the lovely, trout-stocked Panther Creek. For groups, a 60-person barracks with kitchen and dining area may be rented by the week or, in spring and fall, for a minimum of two nights. There's a mountain-ringed swimming pool, open from Memorial Day to Labor Day, and plenty of picnic and playground areas.

If you hike, you'll like Panther's miles of trails and unimproved roads. One trail leads to the **Buzzard's Roost Overlook**. Another, the steep but well-kept **Drift Branch Trail**, follows a small stream and makes a series of switchbacks to a high ridge. There you'll find a fire tower built by the Civilian Conservation Corps. Climb to the top for a panoramic view of ridge after ridge stretching into three states.

Forest hours are 6:00 a.m. to 10:00 p.m. daily, and the forest office is open from 8:00 a.m. to 4:00 p.m. Monday through Friday. Call (800)CALL-WVA or (304)938-2252 or write Panther State Forest, PO Box 287, Panther, WV 24872.

Directions: From Route 52, one mile north of Iaeger, turn at forest sign to Panther and follow the road 3½ miles to the forest entrance.

Pence Springs

Graham House

Colonel James Graham built this log cabin, which is actually about a mile south of Pence Springs in the town of Lowell, between 1770 and 1772. An unusually large and spacious structure for its time, it reflected his affluence. With the exception of a modern wing at the rear of the building, the **Graham House** today looks much as it did when it was constructed more than 200 years ago.

The Graham House served as both a home and a sheltering fortress against Indian attacks—not altogether successfully, for Colonel Graham's ten-year-old son and a family friend were killed in a 1777 Shawnee raid. Graham's seven-year-old daughter Elizabeth was taken captive in the same attack. For the next eight years Graham searched for her, and finally bought her release near Maysville, Kentucky, with blankets and trinkets. Local lore says Graham turned the shoes on his horses around to avoid being followed home, and some maintain that teenaged Elizabeth returned reluctantly, having fallen in love and married a Shawnee prince.

The house is furnished with rope beds, a spinning wheel, trunks, family pictures and other pieces indigenous to the early 1800s. Now on the National Register of Historic Places and maintained by the Graham House Preservation Society, it is open weekends Memorial Day through Labor Day. Hours are 11:00 a.m. to 5:00 p.m. Friday and Saturday and 1:00 to 5:00 p.m. Sunday. Admission is $2.00 for adults and $1.00 for children. The house is open by appointment for groups, and may also be reserved for meetings, reunions and receptions. Call (304)466-5502 or -3321 or write Graham House Preservation Society, PO Box 218, Pence Springs, WV 24962.

Directions: On Routes 3 and 12 between Hinton and Alderson.

Pence Springs Hotel

About a mile north of the Graham House, a red brick Georgian mansion rises on a hillside. This is **Pence Springs Hotel**. During its heyday in the 1920s, it was considered the most lavish resort in West Virginia. Hotel and village are both named for Andrew Pence, a Confederate veteran who built his first hotel here in 1872, having observed that animals seemed to like the nearby mineral spring.

The spring water made Pence rich. Despite its strong sulphur taste, Pence Springs bottled water won a silver medal at the 1904 St. Louis World's Fair. Soon it was flowing out of the valley by rail at the rate

Pence Springs Hotel has been a gambling casino, a girls' finishing school and even a prison. The historic resort is now restored as a National Register country inn. COURTESY PENCE SPRINGS HOTEL

of three cars a week, while hotel visitors held sprigs of mint to their noses and gulped eight or more glasses a day for their health. You can drink it, too; the spring still bubbles inside a restored gazebo, one of the county's oldest structures, behind the hotel.

When his wooden hotel burned in 1912, Pence rebuilt in a grand manner. In fact, the mansion was originally called the Grand Hotel. To ensure that fire would not destroy his new hotel, Pence installed an elaborate sprinkler system—along with telephones in each of 60 guest rooms, showers and central vacuuming. On each floor was a large suite for nannies, maids and chauffeurs. A staff of 100 catered to guests. The price of lodging was $6.00 a day, including three meals.

For the revellers and gamblers who filled the hotel's adjacent casino during Prohibition years, luxury included liquor. The hotel had two cellars, accessible by removing bricks behind the English boxwood hedges, where bootleggers delivered moonshine while revenuers, aware of the Pence family's influence, winked obligingly. The liquor flowed in while the water flowed out.

The Great Depression spelled doom for the Grand Hotel; it closed in the early 1930s. For a few years, the building was home to a girls' finishing school founded by Eleanor Roosevelt and, briefly, a dude ranch. In 1946, the state took over the property and turned it into a maximum security women's prison. It remained a prison for almost four decades.

Remnants of its prison years are still in evidence. Each guest room has a peephole with a swinging steel cover. (The covers have been moved from the outside to the inside of each door.) And hotel proprietor Ashby Berkley has preserved a small room on north wing of the third floor—the solitary confinement area—which he invites guests to explore. Here, where massive steel doors still clang ominously, one can enter four dim, narrow cells to read prisoners' graffiti or look out barred windows toward Keeney's Mountain.

When the prison closed in the 1980s, Berkley (who grew up in the area) moved to have the hotel declared a historic site. All of the buildings except the prison guard house are now on the National Register of Historic Places. In 1986, Pence Springs Hotel was revived as an inn.

The very idea of luxury has changed. Instead of telephones in each room, today's rooms are telephone-free. You won't find an alarm clock, either, unless you request one. Suites are small, clean and furnished with plenty of fresh towels. Pence Springs should be considered a peaceful retreat, not a posh resort.

The hotel's parlor/music room takes one back in time to the 1920's. Stuffed ottomans, Art Deco chairs and a grand piano wait invitingly. Red oak floors and woodwork frame a massive fireplace. Double French doors open onto a wide Southern porch overlooking a brick-tiled terrace and an expanse of lawn. In the foyer, a beautiful curved oak staircase is the focal point.

Pence Springs Hotel has a large, formal dining room and an airy, windowed breakfast room, the two separated by eight sets of French doors. Ceiling fans turn overhead, ruffling the leaves of plants that hang from the pipes of Andrew Pence's sprinkler system. The hotel's menu reflects the tastes of early English settlers, with entrees like Old Virginia Chicken Peanut Pie and Fruit-Stuffed Duckling. Prices for a six-course meal range from $26 to $38. Sunday brunch is also served, from 11:00 a.m. to 3:00 p.m.

Rates for rooms begin at $60.00, including a full breakfast. The hotel is open April through December 31. and reservations are a must. Call (304)445-2606 or (800)826-1829 or write Pence Springs Hotel, PO Box 90, Pence Springs, WV 24962.

Directions: On Routes 3 and 12 between Hinton and Alderson.

Tip: If your visit falls on a Sunday, be sure to stop at the outdoor flea market beside the hotel, one of the largest in the state.

Pipestem

Pipestem Resort State Park

Sitting pretty on the rim of the Bluestone River Gorge in the New River area, **Pipestem Resort State Park** is unrivaled among state parks anywhere. Its 4,000 acres of scenic plateau and gorge provide ample pleasures for day-trippers as well as overnighters. Most visitors come for active recreation, many year after year, and they find it in abundance: two golf courses, two swimming pools (one indoor and heated), lighted tennis and basketball courts, paddle boats, horseback riding and bicycle rentals. Fishermen and boaters gravitate to Long Branch Lake and nearby **Bluestone River and Lake** [see entry]. In winter, Pipestem's hiking trails and hills attract cross-country skiers and sledders.

The resort's name was taken from the native Pipestem bush, which provided the hollow, woody stems nine different Indian tribes used to make pipes. Taking a tip from Native American handcrafters, the gift shop at Pipestem is a particularly attractive place, offering quality West Virginia handcrafts. The arts at this resort include the performing ones—an outdoor amphitheater is the setting for weekend musicals, concerts and plays. Park personnel also maintain a busy schedule of nature programs and activities.

The many lodging choices at Pipestem reflect its popularity. **McKeever Lodge**, with 113 luxurious rooms, rests on the rim of the gorge with a commanding view. Or take the aerial tramway, an enjoyable and scenic ride whether or not you're an overnight guest, down to the 30-room **Mountain Creek Lodge** and its gourmet restaurant, tucked into the base of the gorge near the river. The park also has 25 deluxe cabins that come with decks, televisions, fireplaces, fully equipped kitchens and baths, and 82 campsites with hot showers and laundry facilities.

Families with youngsters love Pipestem's **Honey Bear Lodge Child Care Center**. Children aged 2–12 are welcome for the day or an hour to a full program of exercise, crafts, drama and games designed to develop learning skills as well as entertain.

All recreational activities, including golf and tram rides, can be enjoyed by day-trippers at nominal rates. Rooms for two in the main lodge are under $70.00. Mountain Creek Lodge, open from May 1 to October 31, offers rooms for under $60.00. The park is open for day use from 6:00 a.m. to 10:00 p.m., and the front desk at the lodge is open 24 hours a day. For reservations or more information call (304)466-1800 or (800)CALL-WVA, visit their web site (wvweb.com/www/PIPESTEM.html) or write Pipestem Resort State Park, Box 150, Pipestem, WV 25979.

Directions: Pipestem is 14 miles north of Princeton and 12 miles south of Hinton on Route 20.

Princeton

Almost 25 years before the Civil War, Mercer County and the town of **Princeton** were founded and named to honor the Revolutionary War hero General Hugh Mercer, mortally wounded in battle at Princeton, New Jersey. An ideal home base for a number of one-day trips, Princeton is within half an hour of Bluefield, WinterPlace Ski Resort, Bluestone Lake and Pipestem Resort State Park. And you couldn't ask for a more peaceful place to call home, if only temporarily.

If you like books and antiques, make time for a visit to the **Olde Towne Shoppe**. You're sure to find a few collectibles you can't live without—especially if your interests include Depression glass, quilts, antique jewelry, old magazines, sheet music, signs, prints or reproductions. On the third floor is a shop specializing in musical items, including stringed instrument repairs and restorations. Summer hours (April 1 through Labor Day) are 10:00 a.m. to 5:00 p.m. Monday through Friday. From Labor Day to March 31, hours are 10:00 a.m. to 5:00 p.m. Monday through Friday. The shop is located at 929 Mercer Street in downtown Princeton. Call (304)425-3677. Also on Mercer Street is **Artifacts**, an unusual gallery/museum specializing in miniature paintings. Mostly watercolors, the works range from postage-stamp size to five by seven inches. They also feature World War I and II pieces, clothes and postcards. It's open by appointment only. Call (304)425-2697.

Like nearby Bluefield, Princeton is home to a Class A minor league baseball team, this one associated with the Tampa Bay Devil Rays. The **Princeton Devil Rays** play at Hunnicutt Field in Princeton—each year competing for the Mercer Cup, awarded to the winner of the regular season series between Princeton and their cross-county rivals, the Bluefield Orioles. Call (304)487-2000 for a season schedule.

For a nostalgic look back in time, visit the **Wiley Cabin and Museum**. From I-77, take Route 460 (Exit 9) west to the first stop light and turn right. Go to Oakvale Road and turn right again, where you'll find the Depression-era cabin built mostly by friends and neighbors of John Robert Wiley and his wife Lena. Donated to the Mercer County Historical Society and fully restored, it is the headquarters for the Society's museum. Three exhibit rooms and a gift shop are open Thursday from 10:00 a.m. to 2:00 p.m. or by appointment. Call (304)425-2697 or (304)384-9661 for more information.

If you want to camp near Princeton, take Exit 14 and follow the signs two miles west to **Grandfather Hollow Wilderness Campground**. Be prepared for quite a lot more, however, than an overnight stay. In addition to rental tents and luxurious cabins, there's a petting zoo, guided photo sessions through the world's most concentrated black bear habitat, horseback riding, hay rides, hiking, overnight trail rides and a 150-acre large animal habitat with bear, buffalo and wild boar in addition to deer and other native animals. Fishing in Grandfather Hollow's well-stocked ponds is sure to yield a catfish or trout for supper. Call (304)384-9736 for more information.

If you're in the mood to have someone else serve you breakfast, consider the historic 1906 **Hale House Bed & Breakfast** at 209 Hale Avenue. "Soothing" is the key word here: from the heathery wallpaper colors to a friendly family cat to the small fountains that bubble outside bedroom windows, everything about Hale House is calculated to help you rest easy (including the custom-made brass bed so high it comes equipped with a step-stool). If you ask, affable proprietors Norman and Diana Perry will even take you on their favorite brisk walk around the hilly neighborhood before you relax for a peaceful evening on the wrap-around porch, complete with fireflies and fragrant blessings from their lovely garden. Call (304)487-6783 or (888)843-4253 for rates and reservations.

Well worth a stop, at Exit 9 on I-77, is the **West Virginia Tourist Information Center**, where you'll find plenty of maps and brochures, friendly help and a quite stunning collection of West Virginia crafts displayed in a lovely gallery with a loft full of more handmade goodies. Outside, stop to look at the new Vietnam Veterans Memorial.

Talcott

Big Bend Tunnel and John Henry Statue

On Route 3 between Hinton and Pence Springs, you will come to a sharp curve on top of the mountain overlooking Talcott. As you peer down from the mountaintop, you can see the railroad tracks disappear into the hillside beneath your feet. The rails go through the mountain in **Big Bend Tunnel**. More than a mile of red shale was broken away by hand to make the original tunnel for the Chesapeake and Ohio Railroad in the early 1870s. (The original, no longer in use, is flanked by a sister tunnel that was completed 50 years afterwards.) Reportedly, one of every five workers was crushed to death by falling rock.

Was one of them the famous steel-drivin' man, John Henry? According to Louis Chappell, author of the 1933 *John Henry: A Folklore Study,* who in 1925 interviewed surviving workers in Talcott, a tall, 200-pound black man named John Henry did work for the C&O during the building of the tunnel. He was thought to have been a freed slave from the South, and Chappell's sources agreed that he was good-natured and loved a joke, and could sing and pick a banjo as well as anyone. Many of the workers also remembered that the man called John Henry did compete with a steam drill. But sources disagreed about the manner of his death. Although song and legend would have it that he died from exertion after the contest, it is probable that John Henry died the way so many others did in the tunnel—beneath a rock fall. Historian Lester N. Lively reports that in 1932 a hammer said to have been Henry's was found in a dirt fill in a tunnel shaft.

At the scenic overlook you'll find a historical plaque and a monumental statue honoring the big man, erected by the Hilldale Talcott Raritan Club 100 years after the completion of the tunnel. Bare-chested and holding his hammer as if to strike the next blow, this John Henry looks proud, strong and ready to whip that steam drill once again.

Directions: On Route 3 between Hinton and Pence Springs.

Union

Walking Tour and Springs Trail

There's not a traffic light, movie theater or mall in all of Monroe County, and folks in Monroe are proud of it. Just the same, the county seat of **Union** is still very much the "sprightly village" that 1830's visitor Samuel Kercheval described in *A History of the Valley of Virginia.* Your first stop should be the **Monroe County Historical Society Museum and Tourist Information Center**, where you'll find, in addition to a number of historical displays, a free, well-written self-guided walking tour of 46 historic buildings and the Green Hill Cemetery, resting place of soldiers from both the Revolutionary and Civil Wars. Adjacent to the museum, stop to look at the beautifully reconstructed **Clark-Wiseman House**, an 1810 log house discovered quite recently beneath the exterior of

The Talcott Ruritan Club erected this life-size statue of the Steel-Driving Man in 1972 to mark the John Henry centennial.

MICAHEL KELLER, COURTESY GOLDENSEAL

another building in town. Its high ceilings and many embellishments suggest that it was upscale housing for its time.

A building of particular note on the tour is the **Ames Methodist Church** at the corner of North and Pump streets, an elegantly simple board-and-batten church currently under restoration as a public performing arts space. It is named for Bishop Edward R. Ames. The 1857 structure has a balcony originally intended for slaves. In 1890 it became a black Methodist church, and on occasion was visited by Bishop Matthew Clair, a Union native who was the first black bishop of the Methodist Church.

A refreshing stop in Union is the **Moxie Cafe** on Main Street. In the cheery, book-and-greenery-filled interior beneath the embossed tin ceilings of the old 1905 Monroe Department Store, Chef Reed VanDenBerghe's eclectic, organically-grown menu is a real treat. The cafe serves continental breakfast and lunch Tuesday through Saturday and dinner on Friday and Saturday. Call (304)772-3068.

Union is the suggested starting point for a very interesting driving tour also prepared by the Historical Society. **The Springs Trail** is a self-guided tour that follows the footsteps (or rather, the stagecoach wheels) of 19th-century visitors to some of the many mineral springs in the area. The circular tour takes in eight springs and other sites of historical interest in the Greenbrier Valley, covering much of Monroe County and portions of Summers, Greenbrier and Virginia's Alleghany County. Along the way you'll see grand antebellum stone structures at Salt Sulphur Springs, Jeffersonian architecture on a monumental scale at Sweet Springs, a ghostly Classical pavilion standing in a wide pasture at the site of Blue Sulphur Springs and the very-much-alive Greenbrier Resort [see entry] at White Sulphur Springs. Also on the tour: a covered bridge, a perfectly preserved Art Deco clothing store in the town of Alderson and the working **Old Mill** at Greenville, a living museum where crafters demonstrate alongside exhibits on steam and gas engines. The mill is open weekends only, May until cold weather, 10:00 a.m. to 5:00 p.m. Friday and Saturday, noon to 5:00 p.m. Sunday. Call (304)832-6775 for more information.

Also on the Springs Trail is **Rehoboth Church**, about two miles east of Union on Route 3. The pioneer log church was built in 1786 and is the oldest Methodist church west of the Alleghenies. One of ten designated Methodist shrines in the country, it is on the National Register of Historic Places. Beside the church, stop at the small museum with no admission charge. Open April 15 to October 15, from 9:00 a.m. to 5:00 p.m. Tuesday through Saturday and 1:00 to 5:00 p.m. Sunday. Call the (304)772-3387.

A few miles north of Union, you can visit a gristmill operated since the 1790s and take home a bag of freshly-ground flour. **Reeds Mill**, like the Old Mill in Greenville, is on the National Register of Historic Places. Drive north from Union to the sign for Second Creek Bridge (just before the Greenbrier County line), then go about a mile east to the mill. Open 9:00 a.m. to 3:00 p.m. Saturdays or by appointment. Phone (304)772-5665.

Directions: Union is about 20 miles south of Lewisburg on Route 219.

Welch

McDowell County Courthouse

If you are traveling the Coal Heritage Trail [see entry] between Beckley and Bluefield, you will want to stop and stroll around the town of **Welch**. Snuggled into a narrow valley between nearly vertical mountains, its architecture tells much about its former days as a thriving industrial center. In 1992, the town's old commercial district was listed on the National Register of Historic Places. Stop at the Welch Municipal Building at 88 Howard Street for maps and information about tours.

The **McDowell County Courthouse**, included in the National Historic District, is notable for its architecture and its history. You'll find it right in the center of town—a massive rock-faced structure with a pyramid-roofed, three-story clock tower that emanates a sense of permanence, stability and authority. Built in 1893-94 to the specifications of 25-year-old Frank Pierce Milburn, who would go on to become an architect of importance in the southeastern United States, the courthouse is the most significant example of Romanesque Revival architecture in the extreme southern coalfields of West Virginia.

The booming coal economy that made such a building possible also laid the seeds for a most spectacular incident on these courthouse steps. What people remember most about the McDowell County Courthouse happened here on August 21, 1921, when union organizer Sid Hatfield and a companion, Edd Chambers, were gunned down by coal company agents as they climbed the courthouse steps.

A few years ago, during a remodeling of the building, McDowell County officials discovered original records from the subsequent trial of three coal company agents. County officials can show you a photocopy of the the actual indictment against those who "feloniously, wilfully, maliciously, deliberately and unlawfully did slay, kill and murder one Edd Chambers," along with a handwritten jury verdict finding the defendants not guilty.

For more information, call (304)436-3113 or write City of Welch, Welch Municipal Building, 88 Howard Street, Welch, WV 24801.

Directions: Welch is at the junction of Route 16 and Route 52. The courthouse is at the corner of Court and Wyoming streets.

White Sulphur Springs

Many attractions in and around **White Sulphur Springs** are mentioned elsewhere in this guide, including Greenbrier State Forest and the Greenbrier River Trail [see entry], a beautiful rail trail paralleling the Greenbrier River from nearby Caldwell to Cass. Hiking, fishing, hunting, swimming, picnicking, boating and camping are available at nearby **Blue Bend** and **Lake Sherwood** recreation areas. For more information about either, call the U.S. Department of Agriculture's White Sulphur Ranger District at (304)536-2144 or write them at 410 East Main Street, White Sulphur Springs, WV 24986.

The village of White Sulphur Springs is a small, pleasant place where craft and antique shoppers can easily spend an hour or two. Golfers will enjoy the nearby **Valley View Golf Course** (call (304)536-1600 for a tee time) or a round of golf the way it was played over a century ago, with hickory clubs and replica gutta-percha balls, at **1884 Oakhurst Links**, site of the first organized golf club in America. Call (304)536-1884 for reservations. After a day of sightseeing, come to the junction of Routes 60 and 92 for a relaxing meal at **Blake's Restaurant**, where Chef Blake serves up uncommonly good cookery in a casual atmosphere. Call (304)536-1221 for reservations.

The Greenbrier

In the 1830s, when cholera struck port cities, wealthy plantation owners in the East and South fled inland, seeking pure mountain air and the reportedly curative mineral waters from dozens of natural springs in the Greenbrier Valley. The journeys were social as well as therapeutic—spring-goers often visited six places or more during "the season." None was more beloved than The Old White—**The Greenbrier** at White Sulphur Springs. The resort still caters to presidents and princes, as well as thousands of other guests. Located on 6,500 mountainous acres, its vast manicured grounds and immense white, columned buildings bespeak privilege and grandeur.

At the entryway, where thousands of tulips bloom each spring in the center of an oval driveway, porters in white gloves greet travelers stepping out of limousines. In all, the resort offers nearly 700 guest rooms in addition to 30 cottages and 73 guest houses, three championship golf courses, 20 tennis courts, horseback riding, jogging and parcourse trails, trout-stocked streams, trap and skeet shooting fields, a falconry academy, indoor and outdoor pools fit for movie sets, extravagant afternoon teas with chamber music, luxurious spa facilities, a gallery of some 20 fine shops and world-renowned cuisine. Even with all the rooms filled, guests are outnumbered by a staff of 1,600, many of them second- and third-generation Greenbrier employees. The Greenbrier is a city unto itself—a splendid, serene place where every imaginable comfort is close at hand. Among many awards, the resort has consistently won five stars from Mobil and the AAA Five-Diamond award, and is rated one of the top three golf resorts by *Conde Nast Traveler.*

The opulence of The Greenbrier today belies its humble beginnings. Early visitors traveled long distances on treacherous roads, often sleeping in tents or wagons along the way, to bathe in and drink the sulphurous waters. In 1750, Nicholas and Kate Carpenter and their daughter Frances built a log home here on Howard's Creek. Kate's husband was killed in an Indian raid and she later married Michael Bowyer. When they died, Bowyer's daughter Mary and her husband, James Calwell, inherited the property and built a small tavern near the spring, the first building of a planned resort. In the early 1830s annual visitors began to add rows of bungalows and cottages, including the one now known as **President's Cottage**, where many presidents (beginning with Martin Van Buren) have stayed.

The symbol of the resort, its famous spring house, was built during the early 1830s and graced at the peak with a statue of Hygeia, the Greek goddess of health. Southern aristocrats gathered here to drink the water three times a day—and to stroll, chat and flirt. Indeed, White Sulphur Springs was renowned for something besides water: marriage-making. In his lively history, *The Springs of Virginia,* Perceval Renier calls the springs "the common ground where a widely scattered aristocracy foregathered to choose its mates. The business of healing and the business of pairing went on furiously, side by side.... You took the waters or you took a mate or you took both, and with both it was the same: there was no knowing what the effect would be." The business of pairing was ritualized to the extreme by one Colonel William Pope, who posted a list of 1,700 eligible gentlemen—the Billing, Wooing and Cooing Society—on a long roll of pink paper in the ballroom.

The Greenbrier's long history of plush resort life has coexisted with military uses. From 1861 to 1865, both North and South alternately occupied the resort, each using it as a hospital. Eighty years later, the hotel served as an internment center for German and Japanese diplomats for some six months and then as a government hospital for the remainder of World War II. During the Cold War, the reopened resort concealed an almost incredible military operation: between 1958 and 1962, the government constructed a top-secret, underground **Government Relocation Facility**, code-named "Project Greek Island," designed to accommodate both the U.S. Senate and House of Representatives in the event of nuclear war. For over 30 years, the massive bunker was maintained in a state of constant readiness by a small cadre of government employees posing as television repairmen. A 25-ton door guarded the West Tunnel entrance to the complex, which held decontamination areas, a huge power plant, state-of-the-art communication facilities, a clinic, a cafeteria and dormitory lodgings for up to 1,100 people. The bunker was "exposed" in 1992 by the *Washington Post,* and the last government official left in 1995. Today, resort guests and the public can tour the facility. Public tours are conducted Wednesday and Sunday at 1:30 p.m., beginning at the Greenbrier Bunker Tour Office on Tressel Street directly behind the White Sulphur Springs Civic Center on Main Street. Tours are $25.00 for adults and $10.00 for ages 10 to 18. From January through March, the adult tour price is lowered to $15.00. Children under ten may not join tours. Call (304)536-3595 for more information about bunker tours.

For reservations and information about The Greenbrier call (800)624-6070 or (304)536-1110 or write The Greenbrier, 300 West Main Street, White Sulphur Springs, WV 24986.

Directions: Located just off I-64 at White Sulphur Springs.

Calendar of Events

JANUARY

Early:

Davis, *Women's Pro Ski Tour Race Weekend,* (800)843-1751, (800)633-6682 or (304)866-4801

Lewisburg, *Shanghai Parade,* (800)833-2086 or (304)645-1000

Mid:

Cairo, *Winter Wonder Weekend at North Bend State Park,* (800)CALL-WVA or (304)643-2931

Moorefield, *Robert Burns Birthday Celebration,* (304)538-7173 or (800)298-2466

Late:

Berkeley Springs, *Spa Feast at the Winter Festival of the Waters,* (800)447-8797 or (304)258-9147

FEBRUARY

Early:

Helvetia, *Fasnacht,* (304)924-6435

Mid:

Williamstown, *Fenton Annual Gift Shop Sale,* (304)375-7772

Late:

Charleston, *West Virginia Black Sacred Music Festival,* (304) 342-3183

Berkeley Springs, *Toast to the Tap International Water Tasting and Competition,* (800)447-8797 or (304)258-9147

Morgantown, *Monongalia Arts Center Antique Show & Sale,* (304)599-4437

MARCH

Early:

Flat Top, *WV Shovel Race Championships,* (800)607-SNOW or (304)787-3221

South Charleston, *Native American Pow-wow,* (304)746-5552

Mid:

Ireland, *Irish Spring Festival,* (304)452-8962 or (304)269-7328

Mullens, *Go Hike Weekend,* (800)CALL-WVA or (304)294-4000

Pickens, *West Virginia Maple Syrup Festival*, (304)924-5096
Pipestem, *Appalachian Weekend*, (800)CALL-WVA or (304)466-1800

Late:

Beckley, *Irish Heritage Festival*, (304)256-1776

APRIL

Early:

Cairo, *Outdoor Adventure Weekend at North Bend State Park*, (800)CALL-WVA or (304)643-2931

Richwood, *Feast of the Ramson*, (304)846-6790

Wheeling, *Annual Antique Show and Sale*, (800)624-6988 or (304)242-7272

Mid:

Berkeley Springs, *Uniquely West Virginia Celebration of Wine and Food*, (800)447-8797 or (304)258-9147

Cairo, *Spring Nature Tour at North Bend State Park*, (800)CALL-WVA or (304)643-2931

Elkins, *Augusta Spring Dulcimer Week*, (304)637-1209

Late:

Clay, *Clay County High School Ramp Dinner*, (304)587-4274 or -4226
Elkins, *International Ramp Cook-off*, (800)422-3304 or (304)636-2717
Eastern Panhandle, *House and Garden Tour*, (800)848-8687, (800)498-2386, (304)264-8801, (304)535-2627
Helvetia, *Annual Ramp Supper*, (304)924-5455
Huntington, *Dogwood Arts & Crafts Festival*, (304)696-5990
Petersburg, *Spring Mountain Festival*, (304)257-2722

MAY

Early:

Bramwell, *Spring Tour of Homes*, (304)248-7252 or (304)248-7114
Davis, *Wildflower Pilgrimage*, (800)CALL-WVA or (304)558-2764
Mullens, *Pioneer Classic Golf Tournament*, (800)CALL-WVA or (304)294-4000
Parkersburg, *Rendezvous on the Island*, (800)CALL-WVA or (304)420-4800

Mid:

Grafton, *Mother's Day Observance*, (304)265-5549
Martinsburg, *Belle Boyd's Birthday Celebration*, (304)267-4713
Snowshoe, *Greenbrier River Trail Bike Trek*, (304)342-6600

Late:

Bluefield, *TeleScripps Mountain Festival*, (304)327-7184
Buckhannon, *West Virginia Strawberry Festival*, (304)472-9036
Charleston, *Vandalia Gathering*, (304)558-0220

Fairmont, *Three Rivers Festival and Regatta*, (304)363-2625
Martinsburg, *West Virginia Wine and Arts Festival*, (800)498-2386
Philippi, *Blue and Gray Reunion Civil War Re-enactment*, (304)457-4265
Webster Springs, *Webster County Woodchopping Festival*, (304)847-7666 or -2454
Wheeling, *National Pike Festival*, (304)233-7709
White Sulphur Springs, *West Virginia Dandelion Festival*, (800)284-9440 or (304)536-4007

JUNE

Early:
Belington, *West Virginia Timber and Wood Products Show*, (304)624-0682 or (304)372-1955
Bridgeport/Clarksburg, *Chili in the Hills Cook-Off*, (304)842-2795 or -5966
Cairo, *North Bend Rail Trail Festival*, (800)CALL-WVA or (304)643-2931
Canaan Valley/Davis, *24 Hours of Canaan Mountain Bike Race*, (304)259-5533
Charleston, *Rhododendron Outdoor Art & Craft Festival*, (304)744-4323
Hampshire County (countywide), *Confederate Memorial Weekend*, (304)856-2623
Harpers Ferry, *Mountain Heritage Arts & Crafts Festival*, (800)624-0577, (304)725-2055, or www.uconnect.com/mha&cf
Richwood, *Past 80 Party*, (304)846-6790
Union, *Farmer's Day*, (304)772-3003
Mid:
Glenville, *West Virginia State Folk Festival*, (304)462-8427
Lewisburg, *Lions Club Antique Show and Sale*, (800)833-2068 or (304)645-1000
Moundsville, *Fostoria Glass Society Convention, Show and Sale*, (304)843-1410
Morgantown, *Mountaineer Country Glass Festival*, (304)599-3550
Ronceverte, *Ronceverte River Festival*, (304)647-7554
Saint Marys, *West Virginia Bass Festival*, (304)684-2364
Salem, *Fort New Salem Heritage Arts Weekend*, (304)782-5245
Shepherdstown, *Upper Potomac June Dulcimer Fest*, (304)263-2531
Stonewall Jackson Lake State Park, *Sport and Water Show*, (304)269-7328
Wheeling, *Mountaineer Ribfest/Farm Days*, (800)624-6988

Late:

Bramwell, *Millionaires' Homecoming,* (304)248-7402
Fayetteville, *New River Gorge Triathlon,* (800)927-0264 or (304)465-5617
Grantsville, *Appalachian Classic Mountain Bike Race,* (304)655-7506
Parkersburg, *West Virginia Day Celebration,* (800)CALL-WVA or (304)420-4800
Princeton, *Summerfest,* (304)487-1502
Summersville, *"Music in the Mountains" Bluegrass Festival,* (304)872-3145
Wheeling, *West Virginia Day Celebration,* (304)238-1300
Wheeling, *Annual African-American Jubilee,* (304)233-4640

JULY

Early:

Davis, *July 4th Celebration Concert with the Wheeling Symphony,* (304)866-4710
Fayetteville, *New River Heritage Festival,* (304)574-0101
Ripley, *Mountain State Art and Craft Fair,* (304)372-7860 or (304)372-FAIR

Mid:

Belington, *Battle of Laurel Hill Re-enactment,* (304)624-0682
Fayetteville, *New River Funsplash Concert,* (800)879-7483 or (304)574-3834
Marlinton, *Pioneer Days in Pocahontas County,* (800)336-7009
Mineral Wells, *West Virginia Interstate Fair and Exposition,* (304)489-1301
Richwood, *Scenic Mountain Triathlon,* (304)846-6790
Salem, *Heritage Arts Weekend at Fort New Salem,* (304)782-5245
Shepherdstown, *Contemporary American Theater Festival,* (800)999-CATF or (304)876-3473
Snowshoe, *Fire on the Mountain Chili Cook-off,* (304)572-1000
Summersville, *"Singing in the Mountains" Gospel Sing,* (304)872-3145
Talcott, *John Henry Festival,* (304)466-5502 or -5420
Wheeling, *Jamboree in the Hills,* (800)624-5456 or (304)234-0050

Late:

Burlington, *"McNeill's Rangers" Outdoor Musical Drama,* (304)788-1105
Clifftop, *Doo-Wop Saturday Night,* (304)558-0220
Hinton, *West Virginia State Water Festival,* (304)466-5420
Moorefield, *West Virginia Poultry Festival,* (304)538-7173
Spencer, *Tour de Lake Mountain Bike Festival,* (304)927-4338

Wheeling, *American Heritage Glass and Craft Festival,* (800)624-6988 or (304)243-4010
Wheeling, *Upper Ohio Valley Italian Festival,* (304)233-1090

AUGUST

Early:
Charleston, *Multi-Fest,* (304)342-4600
Clifftop, *Appalachian String Band Music Festival,* (304)558-0220
Logan, *"The Aracoma Story",* (304)752-0253
Moorefield, *Battle of Moorefield Commemorative Weekend,* (800)298-2466 or (304)538-7173
New Creek, *Civil War Encampment,* (304)788-5129
New Martinsville, *Wetzel County Town and Country Days,* (304)386-4444 or (304)455-2418
Ravenswood, *Ohio River Festival,* (304)273-2293
Richwood, *Cherry River Festival,* (304)846-6790
Salem, *Heritage Workshops at Fort New Salem,* (304)782-5245
Mid:
Beckley, Charleston, Huntington, *WV State Fair Train,* (304)529-6412
Clifftop, *Clifftop Rocks,* (304)558-0220
Elkins, *Augusta Festival,* (304)637-1209
Lewisburg, *State Fair of West Virginia,* (304)645-1090
Parkersburg, *Homecoming Festival,* (304)422-3588
Snowshoe, *Snowshoe Mountain Bike Challenge,* (304)572-1000
White Sulphur Springs, *Battle of Dry Creek Civil War Re-enactment,* (304)536-4373 or (304)469-6994
Late:
Beckley, *Appalachian Arts and Crafts Festival,* (800)718-1474 or (304)252-7328
Charleston, *Sternwheel Regatta,* (304)348-6419
Clarksburg, *West Virginia Italian Heritage Festival,* (304)622-7314
Jane Lew, *Firemen's Arts and Crafts Festival*, (304)842-4095
Snowshoe, *West Virginia Symphony Weekend,* (304)572-1000
Weirton, *Greek Bazaar,* (304)797-9884 or -1725
Weston, *Stonewall Jackson Heritage Arts & Crafts Jubilee,* (800)296-1863 or (304)269-1863

SEPTEMBER

Early:
Huntington, *Chilifest,* (304)529-4857
Romney, *Hampshire Heritage Days,* (304)822-5013
South Charleston, *The Mound Art & Craft Festival,* (304)766-6369

Summersville, *Nicholas County Potato Festival,* (304)872-3722
Summersville, *Civil War Weekend,* (304)872-0825

Mid:

Brooks, *Migration Celebration at Three Rivers Avian Center,* (304)466-4683
Cairo, *Wild Foods Weekend at North Bend State Park,* (304)558-3370
Clifftop, *Mellow in the Mountains,* (304)558-0220
Gandeeville, *FOOTMAD Fall Festival of Music and Dance,* (304)768-9249
Mineral Wells, *West Virginia Honey Festival,* (800)752-4982 or (304)428-1130
Morgantown, *West Virginia Wine & Jazz Festival,* (800)458-7373
Shepherdstown, *Upper Potomac Dulcimer Fest,* (304)263-2531
Sistersville, *West Virginia Oil and Gas Festival,* (304)652-2939

Late:

Ansted, *Country Roads Festival,* (800)CALL-WVA or (304)658-5212
Arnoldsburg, *West Virginia Molasses Festival,* (304)655-8374
Clarksburg, *Black Heritage Festival,* (304)623-2335
Davis, *Leaf Peepers Festival,* (800)782-2775 or (304)259-5315
Elkins, *Mountain State Forest Festival,* (304)636-1824
Franklin, *Treasure Mountain Days,* (304)249-5422
French Creek, *National Hunting and Fishing Days,* (304)924-6211
Harpers Ferry, *Mountain Heritage Arts & Crafts Festival,* (800)624-0577, (304)725-2055 or www.uconnect.com/mha&cf
Keyser, *Fall Festival,* (304)788-1590
Kingwood, *Preston County Buckwheat Festival,* (304)329-0576 or -0021
Marlinton, *Autumn Harvest Festival and Roadkill Cook-off,* (800)336-7009 or (304)799-4636
Mineral Wells, *Harvest Moon Festival,* (304)422-7121
Moorefield, *Hardy County Heritage and Harvest Festival,* (304)538-6560
Morgantown, *Mason-Dixon Festival,* (304)599-1104
Parkersburg, *Civil War Weekend at Blennerhassett Island,* (800)CALL-WVA or (304)420-4800
Pipestem, *Fall Hawk Migration,* (800)CALL-WVA or (304)466-1800
Summersville, *Gauley River Festival,* (304)688-5569
Summersville, *Grape Stomping Wine Festival,* (304)872-7332
Union, *Autumn Harvest Festival,* (304)772-3003
Waverly, *Volcano Days,* (304)679-3611
Weston, *Oktoberfest-West Virginia,* (304)269-2608
Winfield, *Mary Ingles Trail Festival,* (304)562-0518

OCTOBER

Early:

Burlington, *Old-Fashioned Apple Harvest Festival,* (304)289-3511

Burnsville, *Battle of Bulltown Reenactment,* (304)853-2338

Canaan Valley State Park, *Wild Walks Weekend,* (800)CALL-WVA or (304)866-4121

Huntington, *Country Peddler Show,* (304)479-5005

Milton, *West Virginia Pumpkin Festival,* (304)743-9222 or (304)696-5954

Morgantown, *Mountaineer Balloon Festival,* (304)296-8356

Point Pleasant, *Battle Days,* (304)675-2170

Salem, *Apple Butter Festival,* (304)782-3565 or (304)624-6411

Salem, *Harvest Festival at Fort New Salem,* (304)782-5245

Wheeling, *Oglebayfest,* (800)624-6988 or (304)243-4010

Mid:

Berkeley Springs, *Apple Butter Harvest,* (304)258-3738

Elkins, *Augusta Old-Time Week and Fiddlers Reunion,* (304)637-1209

Fairmont, *Fall Festival at Pricketts Fort,* (304)363-3030

Fayetteville, *Bridge Day,* (800)879-7483 or (304)574-3834

Hinton, *Railroad Days,* (304)466-5420

Huntington, Charleston, Montgomery, Hinton, *New River Train Excursions,* (304)453-1641

Lewisburg, *Taste Of Our Town Festival,* (304)645-7917

Martinsburg, *Mountain State Apple Harvest Festival,* (304)263-2500

Mullens, *Lumberjackin' Bluegrassin' Jamboree,* (800)CALL-WVA or (304)294-4000

Harpers Ferry, *Election Day 1860,* (304)535-6748

Spencer, *West Virginia Black Walnut Festival,* (304)927-1780

Wardensville, *Fall Festival,* (304)874-3017

Weston, *Voices of the Mountains Storytelling Festival,* (304)269-7328

Late:

Hinton, *Hinton Railroad Days,* (304)453-1641 or (304)466-5420

NOVEMBER

Early:

Cairo, *Mountain Bike Weekend at North Bend State Park,* (800)CALL-WVA or (304)643-2931

Guyandotte, *Civil War Days,* (304)525-5720

Morgantown, *Mountaineer Heritage Festival,* (800)458-7373

Pipestem, *10K Pumpkin Run and 5K Walk,* (800)CALL-WVA or

(304)466-1800
Weirton, *Arts and Crafts Festival,* (304)748-3581
Wheeling, *City Festival of Lights,* (800)828-3097 or (304)233-2575
Wheeling, *Winter Festival of Lights,* (800)624-6988 or (304)243-4010
White Sulphur Springs, *Arts and Crafts Fair,* (304)536-4072

Mid:

Kearneysville, *Over the Mountain Studio Tour,* (304)725-0567 or -4553

Late:

Buckhannon, *Christmas Craft Show,* (304)472-4218 or -4115
Moorefield, *Art Show,* (800)298-2466 or (304)538-7173
Charleston, *Capital City Art and Craft Show,* (304)949-3205

DECEMBER

Early:

Ansted, *Lights Along the Midland Trail,* (800)CALL-WVA or (304)658-5212
Beckley, *Christmas at the Homestead,* (304)252-3730
Fairmont, *Christmas at Pricketts Fort,* (304)363-3030
Harpers Ferry, *Old Tyme Christmas,* (304)725-8019, (304)535-2511
Hinton, *Tour of Historic Homes,* (304)466-4490
Logan, *Christmas in the Park,* (304)792-7125
Lowell, *Olde Fashioned Christmas Dinner,* (304)466-5502
Parkersburg, *Christmas on the Island,* (800)CALL-WVA or (304)420-4800
Salem, *The Spirit of Christmas in the Mountains,* (304)782-5245
Shepherdstown, *Christmas in Shepherdstown,* (304)876-4553 or -9388
Martinsburg, *Belle Boyd Christmas,* (304)267-4713

Mid:

Bramwell, *Christmas Tour of Homes,* (304)248-7252
Pipestem, *Christmas Bird Count,* (304)466-1800

Late:

Beckley, *Peace Vigil,* (304)252-3730
Pipestem, *Christmas Bird Count,* (800)CALL-WVA or (304)466-1800

Biking

To say that West Virginia is becoming well known for bicycling is an understatement. Readers of *Mountain Bike* have ranked the Mountain State as one of the world's four favorite destinations for off-road biking. Bike shops and outfitters are sprouting up the way oil derricks did in turn-of-the-century Sistersville. New trails are being developed daily, and biking events are proliferating all over the state.

Much of what makes biking in West Virginia so attractive, of course, has been here all along: varied terrain, winding backcountry roads, scenic highways and an extensive network of rail trails. From rock-strewn high-country trails like The Plunge and Yabba Dabba at Snowshoe to the tunnel-rich North Bend Rail Trail, from the nearly vertical Black Bear Trail in Kanawha State Forest to the nearly level Greenbrier River Trail, from the 1,000-foot-high ridge overlooking the New River Gorge to the varied maze of trails surrounding Charles Fork Lake, there is a great bike ride in West Virginia for everyone—whether that someone is a thrill-seeking technical expert or a youngster who has just figured out how to make a two-wheeler stay up. Many state parks and forests have trails that are accessible and ideal for bikers.

A free annual guide, *Bicycle West Virginia Adventure Guide,* outlines the state's many opportunities for backroad touring, rugged mountain biking, rail trail biking and bike racing. To get a copy of the current guide, call (800)CALL-WVA. To access the magazine online, visit the web site (www.bicyclewv.com). Before you hit the trails, you may also want to check the West Virginia Web for biking information (wvweb.com/www/bikewv) or call (800)CALL-WVA to request a free copy of the West Virginia Trails Map.

Other helpful organizations are:

Blennerhassett Bicycle Club, PO Box 2262, Parkersburg, WV 26102

Greenbrier River Trail Association, General Delivery, Slatyfork, WV 26209

Greenbrier Valley Bike Club, Route 4, Box 77J, Frankfurt, WV 24938

Harrison County Bike Association, 515 S. Linden Avenue, Clarksburg, WV 26301, (304)624-9298

North Bend Rail-to-Trail Foundation, PO Box 206, Cairo, WV 26337

West Virginia Mountain Bike Association, PO Box 189, Davis, WV 26260. email: wvmba@aol.com

Mountain State Road Association, 18 Dayton Road, Philippi, WV 26416

Shepherdstown Trail Committee, PO Box 727, Shepherdstown, WV 25443

Tri-State Wheelers Bicycle Club, 590 Mahan Lane, Follansbee, WV 26307, (304)527-1154

West Virginia Rails-to-Trails Council, PO Box 8889, South Charleston, WV 25303, Web site: www.cwru.edu/lit/homes/rxr3/WVRTC/wvrtc.html

Note: *Shifting Gears: A Bicycling Guide to West Virginia* and *Bicycling Through Civil War History,* both written by history buff and cyclist Kurt Detwiler, are available at bookstores or from EPM, Box 490, McLean, VA 22101. Call (800)289-2339 or (703)442-7810.

Covered Bridges

An essential part of early transportation in West Virginia, covered bridges are now scenic reminders of the past—and any one of West Virginia's historic covered bridges will make for a lovely photograph.

Beginning in the mid-1800s, covered bridges were integral links in West Virginia's turnpike system. Generally they were patterned after German, Swiss and Austrian designs. Bridges were covered to protect the all-wood, hand-hewn supporting truss systems. A well-built covered bridge was a source of pride to the craftsman who designed it and, understandably, these bridges were often strategic prizes in Civil War battles.

Seven different truss types were used for West Virginia bridges. Although many were built over gentle creeks, some spanned wide, powerful rivers. Truss types were often named after their designers. In West Virginia, you can see examples of Long, Howe, Warren, Kingpost, Queenpost, Multiple Kingpost and Multiple Kingpost with Burr Arch trusses. All are based on the same idea: creating a support that is strengthened by joining together small triangles of timber. Some, like the fortuitously named Long type (named for designer Stephen Long), which supports the 285-foot-long Philippi Bridge, were adjusted to meet certain needs—in this case, length. Built by master builder Lemuel Chenoweth and his brother Eli in 1852, the Philippi Bridge is the oldest and longest in the state.

When railroads arrived in West Virginia during the 1870s, covered bridges were relegated to an eventual demise. Railroad bridges could be made quickly and relatively cheaply from prefabricated sections of iron. They required much less maintenance, didn't need to be covered and were not subject to the threat of fire. Nevertheless, as late as 1947, some 90 covered bridges were still in use in West Virginia. Today only 17 remain. Like the state's other historic attractions, covered bridges are now considered a precious resource.

Use the following list to find a covered bridge near your intended day trip. Most are located in Mountaineer Country and the New River/Greenbrier Valley regions and are short, ranging from 30 to 40 feet to about 100 feet in length. The smallest is the Laurel Creek Covered Bridge outside of Lillyville, measuring just 24 feet and 5 inches.

You may drive across most, but not all, of West Virginia's covered bridges. Some are open to pedestrians only, and a few are on private property.

Potomac Highlands

Locust Creek Covered Bridge: From Hillsboro, take Secondary Route 31 south approximately 6.3 miles. The only remaining covered bridge in Pocahontas County and the Potomac Highlands, the Locust Creek Bridge has a Warren Double Intersection truss, now rare in North America. Slightly under 113 feet in length, it was built during the 1870s and is in good condition.

Mountain Lakes

Walkersville Covered Bridge: On Route 119 one mile south of Walkersville. Lewis County's only remaining covered bridge, it was built in 1903. Just over 39 feet in length, it is in good condition and in use.

Mountaineer Country

Fish Creek Covered Bridge : Travel east on Route 250 from Hundred. Turn right on Secondary Route 13. Built in 1881, the bridge is 36 feet in length and is the only remaining covered bridge in Wetzel County. In use, its condition is fair.

Dents Run Covered Bridge: Take Route 19 south from Westover and turn right on Secondary Route 43 at historical marker. Go approximately .7 mile and turn left on Secondary Route 43/3. Proceed .3 mile to the bridge. Built in 1889, it is the only remaining covered bridge in Monongalia County. Forty feet long, the bridge is in good condition and in use.

Barrackville Covered Bridge: On Secondary Route 21 at the junction of Secondary Route 250/32 at Barrackville. A link in the Fairmont and Wheeling Turnpike, it was built in 1853 and is the second-oldest remaining covered bridge in the state. It is almost 146 feet long. In use, its condition is fair.

Center Point Covered Bridge: From Route 50, go 12 miles north on Route 23 to Center Point. The only remaining covered bridge in Doddridge County, it was built in 1888. Just over 42 feet in length, it is in use and in good condition.

Fletcher Covered Bridge: From Route 50, turn right (north) on Secondary Route 5 and proceed to Secondary Route 5/29. Go north .6 mile to the bridge. One of two covered bridges in Harrison County, it is slightly longer than 54 feet and has not been significantly altered since it was built in 1891. In use and in good condition.

Simpson Creek Covered Bridge: From I-77, take Exit 121 and follow Secondary Route 24 north approximately .2 mile. This is the other remaining covered bridge in Harrison County. Built in 1881, it originally stood one-half mile from its present site and was relocated here after being washed out in 1889. Just over 75 feet in length, it is in use and in good condition.

Philippi Covered Bridge: On Route 250 in Philippi. Built in 1852 by Lemuel and Eli Chenoweth, it is West Virginia's longest and oldest covered bridge [see entry] and one of two in Barbour County. Its condition is good, and it is used regularly.

Carrollton Covered Bridge: From Philippi, take Route 119 south to Secondary Route 36. Turn left and go .8 mile to Carrollton. The second-longest and third-oldest of West Virginia's covered bridges, it is 140 feet and nine inches in length. Built in 1856, it served traffic on the Middle Fork Turnpike. It is in good condition and in use.

Mid-Ohio Valley

Sarvis Fork Covered Bridge: From Sandyville, go north on Secondary Route 21 and turn right on Secondary Route 21/15. Originally built in 1889 over a branch of Big Mill Creek west of Ripley, it was dismantled in 1924 and rebuilt at its present location on the left fork of Sandy Creek. It is one of two covered bridges in Jackson County. Just over 101 feet in length, it is in fair condition and in use.

Staats Mill Covered Bridge: From I-77, take the Fairplain exit and follow signs to Cedar Lakes Conference Center just south of Ripley. Originally constructed over the Tug Fork of Mill Creek in 1887, this pretty bridge was moved to the Cedar Lakes complex in 1982 and restored. It is 97 feet long and in excellent condition.

Metro Valley

Milton (Mud River) Covered Bridge: At the junction of Route 60 and Secondary Route 25 in Milton. This is the only covered bridge in Cabell County and the only example of a Howe truss in the state. Just over 14 feet in length, it is in use and in fair condition.

Hokes Mill Covered Bridge: From Lewisburg, take Route 219 South through Ronceverte, to Secondary Route 48. Turn right and go approximately 3.6 miles to Secondary Route 62. Go south on Secondary Route 62 to Hokes Mill. This bridge was built over a two-year period from 1897 to 1899. It is in fair condition and in use.

Herns Mill Covered Bridge: From Lewisburg, go west approximately 2.6 miles on Route 60. Turn left on Secondary Route 60/11, then left again on Secondary Route 40. Built in 1884, this bridge and Hokes Mill Bridge are the only remaining covered bridges in Greenbrier County. It is in use and in good condition.

Indian Creek Covered Bridge: On Route 219 six miles south of Union, opposite St. John's Church. Among the most photographed of West Virginia's covered bridges and one of two remaining in Monroe County, Indian Creek Bridge is slightly over 49 feet in length and was built in 1903. Open for pedestrian traffic only, its condition is fair.

Laurel Creek Covered Bridge: From Route 219 just south of Salt Sulphur Springs, take Secondary Route 219/7 left to Lillydale. Turn right (north) on Secondary Route 219/11 and follow it through Lillydale to the bridge. This, the smallest covered bridge in West Virginia, is just over 24 feet in length. It was built in 1911. In use, its condition is fair.

Fishing and Hunting Guides

Many of the individual listings in this book recommend good fishing spots, and West Virginia's Division of Natural Resources can also be very helpful to anglers and hunters unfamiliar with the state [see appendix on wildlife management areas]. But, as outdoor lovers know, some of the best fishing and hunting locations are not necessarily easy to find. If you want expert advice on the most productive fishing holes and hunting grounds, or if you're looking for guidance on technique as well as location, you may want to consider hiring one of the guide services listed here.

Some of these are obviously whitewater rafting guides as well. [For a complete list of whitewater guides, consult the appendix on whitewater rafting.] One asterisk (*) denotes locations that offer both hunting and fishing guides. Two asterisks (**) denotes hunting only. Locations without asterisks offer fishing guides only.

Eastern Panhandle

Anglers Inn B&B, 846 Washington Street,Harpers Ferry, WV 25425 (304)535-1239

Potomac Highlands

Canyon Rim Outfitters, Route 32, Davis, WV 26260, (304)259-2236

Cheat Mountain Outfitting Guide Service*, Cheat Bridge, PO Box 217, Durbin, WV 26264

Eagle's Nest Outfitters, PO Box 731, Petersburg, WV 26847, (304)257-2393

Elk Mountain Outfitters, PO Box 8, Slatyfork, WV 26291, (304)572-3000

Elk River Trout Ranch, 14 Dry Branch Road, Monterville, WV 26282, (304)339-6455

Fastwater Flyfishing School, Route 3, Box 200, Harman, WV 26270, (304)227-4565

Hemlock Cove Fly Fishing School, HCR 79, Box 540, Davis, WV 26260, (304)866-6229

Riverside Outfitters, PO Box 61, Fisher, WV 26818, (304)538-6467

Smoke Hole Outfitters*, HC 59, Box 39, Seneca Rocks, WV 26884

Tory Mountain Outfitters, Front Street, Thomas, WV 26292, (304)463-4130

Mountain Lakes

Kincheloe Pheasant Hunting Preserve,** Route 2, Box 88A, Jane Lew, WV 24928, (304)884-7431

Mountaineer Country

Evergreen Fly Fishing Company, 768 Locust Avenue, Clarksburg, WV 26301, (304)623-3564

Metro Valley

Mullins Guide Service,** PO Box 572, Verdunville, WV 26378, (304)752-1020 or -4567

New River/Greenbrier Bass Unlimited*, Burdette Building, 308 Buchanan Street, Charleston, WV 25301, (800)649-0708 or (304)344-9832

New River/Greenbrier River

ACE (American Canadian Expeditions), PO Box 1168, Oak Hill, WV 25901, (800)223-2641 or (304)469-2651

Adventures, Inc., PO Box 39, Lansing, WV 25862, (800)879-7483 or (304)574-3834

Appalachian Back Country Expeditions*, PO Box 66, Sandstone, WV 25985, (888)642-3414 or (304)466-5546

Appalachian Outdoor Adventures*, PO Box 655, Fayetteville, WV 25840, (304)574-3559

Big Buck Hunting Camp*, Route 1, Box 31, Lookout, WV 25868, (304)965-0949 or (304)574-3820

Cantrell Ultimate Rafting, 504 Summers Street, Hinton, WV 25951, (800)470-7238 or (304)466-0595

Class VI River Runners, PO Box 78, Lansing, WV 25862, (800)252-7784 or (304)574-0704

Drift A Bit, Inc., PO Box 885, Fayetteville, WV 25840, (800)633-7238 or (304)574-3282

Fraley's Stables, Inc.*, Route 1, Box 880, Fayetteville, WV 25840, (304)457-2651

Go Fishin'*, Thurmond, WV 25936 , (304)469-9660 or (304)877-6649,

Gone Fishin' Fishing Guide, 1215 Main Street, Oak Hill, WV 25901, (888)470-3131

Greenbrier River Company, PO Box 265, Ronceverte, WV 24970, (800)775-2203 or (304)645-2760

High Mountain Outfitters*, Box 82, Loudermilk Rd., Clintonville, WV 24928

Horseshoe Creek Riding Stable, HC 81, Box 82C, Victor, WV 25938, (800)658-7433 or (304)658-3218

New River Scenic Whitewater Tours, Box 637, Hinton, WV 25951, (800)292-0880 or (304)466-2288

North American River Runners, PO Box 81, Hico, WV 25854, (800)950-2585 or (304)658-5277

Plateau Pheasant Reserve**, 112 Main Street, Oak Hill, WV 25901, (304)465-8882

Raft WV/Whitewater Info, Route 2, Box 459A, Fayetteville, WV 25840, (888)723-8982 or (304)574-1003

Riverchase Lodge, HC 74, Box 10, Meadow Creek, WV 25977 (304)466-1856

Songer Whitewater, PO Box 300, Fayetteville, WV 25840, (800)356-7238 or (304)658-9926

Twin River Outfitters*, PO Box 28, Daniels, WV 25832, (800)982-3467 or (304)763-5044

Whitewater Travel*, 109 Ankrom Street, Fayetteville, WV 25840 (800)723-8982 or (304)574-1298

Wildwater Expeditions Unlimited, PO Box 155, Lansing, WV 25862, (800)982-7238 or (304)658-4007

WV Lakes Fishing and Tours, 202 Haymarket Drive, Beckley, WV 25801, (304)255-2618 or (304)253-9656

Skiing

Although many of the destinations in this book are best enjoyed during warm weather, West Virginia does not close down when the snow flies! On the contrary: each year, more and more people discover that, in winter, West Virginia's mountains are transformed into spectacular slopes and tantalizing trails.

Because of its high-country location, which makes for longer winters and more snowfall, the Potomac Highlands claims much of West Virginia's downhill ski country. Southern West Virginia's WinterPlace, just south of Beckley, continues to expand its facilities, and is an especially friendly and popular place for beginners. In Mountaineer Country, Alpine Lake Resort also caters to novice skiers.

Downhill skiing can be expensive, but most resorts offer ski/lodging packages. Snowshoe Mountain Resort in Snowshoe, for instance, features weekday, weekend and holiday packages that can save you 15 to 50 percent on lodging, ski rental, lessons—even Thanksgiving dinner. One four-day holiday package ranges from about $300.00 to $450.00 for lodging (two to four people), with lift tickets discounted to about $100.00 per person, equipment rental to $31.00 and ski lessons as low as $9.00.

In winter, many of West Virginia's beautiful hiking trails become cross-country ski trails. You'll find nordic ski centers listed here in three regions of the state, but if you come to any part of West Virginia in winter, you'll find that a good snow brings out the cross-country skis, especially on state park trails. Some people much prefer the quiet of a snowy, wooded trail to the thrill of the plunge downhill—besides, cross-country skiing is excellent exercise and definitely less expensive.

The choice of ski/lodging/lesson packages can be mind-boggling. It's a good idea to contact resorts in advance and request their help in tailoring your ski vacation to suit your own needs and likes. Depending on the time of your trip, reservations should be made well in advance—sometimes months ahead.

To find out more about the thrill of West Virginia skiing, visit the Ski West Virginia web site (wvweb.com.www.wvsaa.html). For daily ski conditions, call (800)CALL-WVA or check with individual ski centers.

Downhill/Alpine

Potomac Highlands

Canaan Valley Resort State Park, HC 70, Box 330, Davis, WV 26260, (800)622-4121, wvweb.com/www/cvresort

Snowshoe/Silver Creek, PO Box 10, Snowshoe, WV 26209, (304)572-1000, wvweb.com/snowshoe

Timberline Four Seasons Resort, Canaan Valley, WV 26260, (800)SNOW-ING, wvweb.com/www/timberline

New River/Greenbrier Valley

WinterPlace Resort, PO Box 1, Flat Top, WV 25841, (800)607-SNOW, wvweb.com/www/winterplace.html

Cross-country/Nordic

Potomac Highlands

Blackwater Falls Ski Touring Center, Blackwater Falls State Park, Davis, WV 26260, (304)259-5117 or (800)CALL-WVA

Canaan Valley Resort State Park HC 70, Box 330, Davis, WV 26260, (800)622-4121, wvweb.com/www/cvresort

Elk River Touring Center, Highway 219, Slatyfork, WV 26291, (340)572-3771

Timberline Four Seasons Resort, Canaan Valley, WV 26260, (800)SNOWING, wvweb.com/www/timberline

White Grass Ski Touring Center, Canaan Valley, Davis, WV 26260, (800)866-4114

Mountaineer Country

Alpine Lake Resort Nordic Center, Route 2, Box 99-D2, Terra Alta, WV 26764, (800)752-7179

State Parks and Forests

West Virginia's mountains, forests and rivers are her greatest treasures, and the state's excellent system of public parks makes them available to everyone. Easy to get to and well managed, state parks are among the most popular destinations for West Virginians as well as visitors from other places.

Park facilities and recreational opportunities are widely varied, and each park has its own character and appeal. The parks fall generally into five categories: lodge and resort parks, cabin vacation parks, camping vacation parks, day use parks and natural/historical parks. Lodge and resort parks feature lodges, cottages, cabins and campsites ranging from rustic to luxurious, and prices for overnight stays are reasonable: a week in a cabin for two people averages less than $500.00 during the summer season, and rates are usually discounted during other seasons. Nightly and weekend rentals are available at some times of the year, and cabin sizes range from one to four bedrooms. Lodge rooms rent for about $60.00 to $70.00 per night for two persons. At several of the resort parks you will also find good restaurants, championship golf courses, tennis courts, horseback riding, swimming pools, skiing trails and fishing lakes as well as year-round nature programs, planned activities for children, craft shops and museums. Some parks offer dinner, dance and theater weekends, guided hikes and horseback rides, ski packages and romantic mid-winter getaways. Eight parks are currently categorized as lodge or resort parks: Blackwater Falls, Cacapon, Canaan Valley, Hawks Nest, North Bend, Pipestem, Twin Falls and Tygart Lake. (Plans are underway to add Stonewall Jackson Lake State Park to the list.)

At cabin and camping vacation parks, there is less emphasis on golf and tennis and more on nature—but the cabins are just as comfortable and well furnished, and some of these parks offer visitors nearly as many recreational opportunities as do the resort parks. Many have resident naturalists and offer wildflower and wildlife hikes, lectures and hands-on nature learning programs. Cabin vacation parks include Babcock, Bluestone, Holly River, Lost River and West Virginia's largest state park, Watoga. The state's camping parks are Audra, Beech Fork, Camp Creek, Cedar Creek, Chief Logan, Moncove Lake, Stonewall Jackson Lake and Tomlinson Run.

Day use parks—Little Beaver, Pinnacle Rock and Valley Falls—are wonderful places for picnics, family gatherings and hikes. And West Virginia's natural/historical parks are among its greatest gems. Explore awesome, ancient natural history at Beartown or living pioneer history at Pricketts Fort. Relive a legendary romance at Blennerhassett Island or ride the rails at Cass Scenic Railroad. These and the others—Berkeley Springs, Carnifex Ferry, Cathedral, Droop Mountain Battlefield, Fairfax Stone, Grave Creek Mound, Point Pleasant Battle Monument and Watters Smith Memorial—offer fascinating stories to accompany their natural beauty. Most of these popular parks are detailed in separate entries throughout this guide.

The following charts show locations and facilities of the various parks and forests. Use them to find the park that suits your interests and needs. Because they are so popular, it's necessary to make lodge and cabin reservations well in advance—in some cases, a year in advance. If you want more information about a specific park, remember that most state parks can be reached toll-free by calling (800)CALL-WVA and requesting the individual park.

West Virginia State Parks, Forests and Wildlife Management Areas Facilities Chart

		ACRES	Modern Cabins	Standard Cabins	Economy Cabins	Rustic Cabins	Lodge Rooms	Tent/Trailer Sites	Restaurant	Refreshments	Groceries	Golf Course	Swimming	Boat Rental	Boat Launch	Ramp	Fishing	Horseback Riding	Picnicking	Game Courts	Playgrounds	Hiking Trails	Natural Interest	Nature/Rec.	Program	Museum	Historical Interest
PARKS	Audra	355						65		X	N	N	S					X		X	X						
PARKS	Babcock	4,127		18	8			51	X	X	N	N	P	X		X	X	X	X	X	X	X	X			X	
PARKS	Beartown	110																X			X	X					
PARKS	Beech Fork	3,981						275		X	X	N		X	X	X		X	X	X	X	X	X			X	
PARKS	Berkeley Springs	4	N	N	N		N		N	N	N	N	P	N	N	N	N	N	N	N	N	X		X	X	X	
PARKS	Blackwater Falls	1,688	25				55	65	X	X	N	N	L	X		N	X	X	X	X	X	X	X			X	
PARKS	Blennerhassett Isl. Historical	500							N	X					X	X		X				X		X	X	N	
PARKS	Bluestone	2,155	25					87	N	X	N	N	P	X	X	X		X	X	X	X		X			X	
PARKS	Cacapon Resort	6,115	11	13	6		49		X	X	N	X	L	X		X	X	X	X	X	X	X	X	N	N	X	
PARKS	Camp Creek	500+						37								X		X	X	X	X						N
PARKS	Canaan Valley Resort	6,015	25				250	34	X	X	N	X	P			X	N	N	X	X	X	X	X			X	N
PARKS	Carnifex Ferry Battlefield	156						N	N	X		N			N	N		X	X	X	X	X		X	X		
PARKS	Cass Scenic Railroad	1,089		13				N	X	N	N							X		X	X			X	X	X	
PARKS	Cathedral	132							N	N								X		X	X	X					
PARKS	Cedar Creek	2,443						48		X	X		P	X		X		X	X	X	X		X			X	
PARKS	Chief Logan	3,303						25	X	X	N		P			X	X	X	X	X	X						
PARKS	Droop Mountain Battlefield	287																X		X	X			X	X		
PARKS	Fairfax Stone	4																							X		
PARKS	Greenbrier River Trail	950														X					X						
PARKS	Hawks Nest	276					31		X	X	N		P		X	N		X	X	X	X	X	X	X	X	X	
PARKS	Holly River	8,292		9				88	X	X	X		P			X		X	X	X	X		X		X	X	
PARKS	Little Beaver	562						30	N		N	N	L	X		X		X		X	X			X			
PARKS	Lost River	3,712	9	15				N	X	X	N		P				X	X	X	X	X	X	X	X	X	X	
PARKS	Moncove Lake	896						50					L	X		X		X	X	X	X						N
PARKS	North Bend	1,405	8				29	80	X	X	N	N	P			X		X	X	X	X		X			X	
PARKS	North Bend Rail Trail	61 mi.															X				X						
PARKS	Pinnacle Rock	364							N							X		X			X	X					
PARKS	Pipestem Resort	4,023	25				143	82	X	X	N	X	P	X	N	X	X	X	X	X	X	X	X			X	
PARKS	Pt. Pleasant Monument	4																						X	X		
PARKS	Prickett's Fort	188													X	X		X						X	X	X	
PARKS	Stonewall Jackson Lake	2000+						34		X	N			X	X	X		X			X					X	N
PARKS	Tomlinson Run	1,398						54		X	N		P	X		X		X	X	X	X		X			X	
PARKS	Twin Falls Resort	3,776	13				20	50	X	X	N	X	P					X	X	X	X	X	X	X	X	X	
PARKS	Tygart Lake	2,134	10				20	40	X	X	N	N	L	X	X	X		X	X	X	X		X			X	
PARKS	Valley Falls	1,145														X		X		X	X	X					
PARKS	Watoga	10,100	8	25				88	X	X	N	N	P	X		X	X	X	X	X	X		X			X	N
PARKS	Watters Smith Memorial	532								X			P					X	X	X	X			X	X	X	
FORESTS	Cabwaylingo	8,123		13				34	N	N	N	N	P			X		X		X	X					X	X
FORESTS	Calvin Price	9,482														X											X
FORESTS	Camp Creek	5,300+														X					X						X
FORESTS	Coopers Rock	12,713						25		X						X		X		X	X		X		X	X	X
FORESTS	Greenbrier	5,130		12				16	N	X	N	N	P	N		N	N	X		X	X		X		N	X	X
FORESTS	Kanawha	9,302						46		X	N		P				X	X		X	X						X
FORESTS	Kumbrabow	9,474				5		13								X		X		X	X						X
FORESTS	Panther	7,810						6		X			P			X		X		X	X						X
FORESTS	Seneca	11,684				7		10			N			X		X		X		X	X						X
WMA	Berwind Lake	18,093											X					X			X						
WMA	Bluestone	17,632						330				N	N	N		X	N	X	N	N	X						X
WMA	Laurel Lake	12,855						25					X	X		X		X	X	X	X						X
WMA	Plum Orchard Lake	2,953						43						X	X	X		X			X						X

N-Nearby P-Pool L-Lake S-Stream

* RAMPED OR GROUND FLOOR 4/96

ACCOMMODATIONS FOR DISABLED GUESTS

at West Virginia State Parks, Forests and Wildlife Management Areas

* REASONABLE ACCOMMODATION WITH ASSISTANCE/UPON REQUEST

	Picnic Shelter/sites	Campsites	Trail	Braille Trail	Campground Toilet or Showers	Lodge Rooms	Cabins	Public Rest Rooms	Chair Lift to Dining Area	Wheelchair Overlook	Softball	Basketball	Horseshoes	Dining Room	Hospitality Room	Recreation Room	Conference Room	Water Fountain	Group Camp Toilets & Showers	Elevator	Swimming Area	Fishing Pier	Playground	Marina/Boatdocks	Nature Center/Visitor Center	Skiing	Lift Access to Train	Amphitheater/Theater	Museum/Exhibit Area	Gift Shop	TTD
Audra State Park	2	4			X*			X*																							
Babcock State Park	1							2						X				X				X									
Beech Fork State Park	X	X			X			X								X		X													
Berwind Lake Wildlife Mgt. Area	X																					X									
Blackwater Falls State Park	X		X				1	1		X				X		X	X	X		X					X					X	
Blennerhassett Island Hist. State Park	X							X							X		X	X		X									X	X	
Bluestone State Park	X	4			X		4*									X	X	X				X			X						
Bluestone Wildlife Mgt. Area	X	2			2																										
Cacapon Resort State Park	X					2	1	1						X								X	X								
Camp Creek State Park	X	X	X		X			X																							
Canaan Valley Resort State Park		X				8	2	6						X	X*	X*	X*	X			X				X	X					
Carnifex Ferry State Park	X																														
Cass Scenic Railroad State Park							1	1						X*													X				
Cathedral State Park	X*							X*																							
Cedar Creek State Park		2			1											X		X			X	X								X	
Chief Logan State Park	X	X	X		X	X		X						X	X			X					X						X		
Coopers Rock State Forest		X		X	X			X		X												X									
Greenbrier State Forest	2						1*	1*													X										
Hawks Nest State Park	X					2		1		X				X	X	X	X	X		X										X	X
Holly River State Park								2						X*					X												
Kanawha State Forest	X*	X	X	X	X*			2																							
Kumbrabow State Forest	1						1*																								
Laurel Lake Wildlife Mgt. Area	1							2																							
Little Beaver State Park	4		1					2								X					X	X	X	X							
Lost River State Park	1							2													X										
Moncove Lake State Park	2				1			1														X									
North Bend State Park	1	X	X	X		2	1							X			X	X		X	X							X			X
Panther State Forest	X																		X		X*										
Pipestem Resort State Park	2	2				5	1	4	X					X*		X	1	2		X	X				X			X			
Pinnacle Rock State Park	X							X														X									
Plum Orchard Lake Wildlife Mgt. Area					X			X														X		X							
Prickett's Fort State Park	X							X										X				X			X			X	X		
Seneca State Forest	X	X*			X			X																							
Stonewall Jackson Lake State Park		X			X			X								X	X	X				X		X							
Tomlinson Run State Park	X				X			X				X																			
Twin Falls Resort State Park	2		X		X	9*	2*	X						X			2	1												X	
Tygart Lake State Park	X	2				2		2						X		X		X			*			*							
Valley Falls State Park	X							X										X													
Watoga State Park	X				X		1	2						X		X															

Whitewater Rafting

In the past 20 years, West Virginia's whitewater industry has grown into a big business and attracted a great deal of attention. With good reason: the state's mountainous terrain, natural beauty and almost 2,000 miles of streams and rivers add up to the best whitewater rafting in the East. Indeed, many return visitors first discover the state on a rafting trip.

If you haven't tried it, don't be intimidated by the pictures you've probably seen. Although some of West Virginia's rivers, in some seasons, can satisfy thrill-seekers, the joy of rafting in the Mountain State is its almost infinite variety. Rapids are classed by their difficulty, from class I, the most tranquil, to VI, the most technical and difficult. There are trips for those who prefer to float peacefully and watch the scenery go by at a leisurely pace; trips for those who want to run the most challenging and turbulent rapids; and plenty of in-between options.

Although the fun and thrill of whitewater rafting is not limited to these three, West Virginia's most famous whitewater flows on the New, Gauley and Cheat rivers. The New has many moods: the calm upper section, ideal for beginners and those who want to fish while they float; the middle, with class II and III rapids, great fun and good for skill-building; and the lower section, which passes through the deep gorge between high mountains and provides exciting class IV and V rapids along with some calm, deep pools perfect for swimming.

Rafting on the lower and middle Gauley during spring and summer can be a fun, fast-paced ride, depending on the amount of rainfall. On fall weekends, controlled releases from the Summersville Dam turn the upper Gauley, a steep and challenging run even at medium water levels, into what is probably North America's most exciting stretch of river—a trip that is not only the ultimate in watery thrills but physically demanding.

The Cheat River, the third of the "big three" in West Virginia, has one of the longer regularly rafted sections in the state. The rapids come fast and furious, though no individual section is quite as wild as the Gauley in fall. The Cheat, like the New, can be rafted year-round.

Other rivers to consider are the Tygart, with class I to V rapids; the Bluestone, Meadow and Big Sandy Creek, where seasons are short-lived and depend on spring rains; the North Branch of the Potomac, especially during springtime releases from Jennings Randolph Dam; the Shenandoah, which passes through Harpers Ferry National Historical Park; the generally tranquil, gorgeous Greenbrier; and the gentle South Branch of the Potomac.

Most outfitters operate during spring, summer and fall, and many offer a number of different trips or packages, depending upon the river, their experience and their facilities. In fact, the choices can be daunting. Your planning should take into account the ages of your party—although children as young as six are welcome on easier runs, some rapids are limited to those over 16—and your experience with whitewater. Don't be shy about comparing companies. A reputable outfitter will gladly tell you about their safety record, what sorts of runs they specialize in, their guides' experience, and how long they have been in business. Some companies add gourmet meals to the equation—a particularly welcome treat after a day of paddling.

Fishing/raft trips are a popular combination, especially for smallmouth bass and muskie; *Sports Afield* has rated the New River one of the top four fishing rivers in the United States, and the Gauley is also becoming well known for its great muskie fishing. Other specialty trips can combine rafting with bird-watching, environmental education, rock climbing, mountain biking or hiking. Some outfitters offer corporate team-building trips and kayak clinics.

Depending on the river, you are likely to have a choice about the kind of boat you use. The most common is a large, inflatable raft, 12 to 16 feet long, that accommodates four to ten people. Gaining in popularity is the ducky, a one- or two-person craft that is essentially a cross between a raft, a canoe and a kayak—more stable than a canoe or kayak and more maneuverable than a raft. Kayaks and canoes are versatile, but are easily tipped and not recommended for beginners; a couple of days of training and skill-building are usually required, but the practice pays off in fun and maneuverability. For raft/fishing trips, outfitters may use rafts fitted with special pedestal seats, or dories, flat-bottomed boats of fiberglass, wood or aluminum.

You can expect to pay about $75.00 to $100.00 for a one-day trip including food and transportation to the put-in point on a weekend day, and there are often discounts on weekdays. Two- and three-day camping packages range from about $175.00 to $330.00, depending upon many variables. West Virginia's rivers are filled to capacity on many summer and fall weekends, so it's a good idea to do your planning early and make reservations as far in advance as you can. When you make reservations, be sure to inform your outfitter about children's ages, as well any medical conditions and/or special dietary needs that may need to be accommodated.

Your outfitter should advise you about what to wear. Basics include a swim suit, T-shirt, shorts, old sneakers or river sandals that fasten securely, sun visor or ball cap, windbreaker, sunglasses and sunscreen. In spring and fall, you'll want to bring warm outerwear. Bear in mind that, whether you intend to or not, you *will* get wet.

Use the following list of licensed whitewater outfitters to find out more about scheduling a trip.

Eastern Panhandle

Blue Ridge Outfitters, PO Box 750, Harpers Ferry, WV 25425 (304)725-3444

Historical River Tours, RR 3, Box 1258, Harpers Ferry, WV 25425 (410)489-2837

Mountaineer Whitewater, PO Box 1060, Charles Town, WV 25414 (540)667-1149

River Riders, Inc. , Route 3, Box 1260, Harpers Ferry, WV 25425, (800)326-7238 or (304)535-2663

Metro Valley

Mountain State Mystery Train (train/outdoor adventures), PO Box 8254, Huntington, WV 25705, (304)529-6412

Mountaineer Country

Appalachian Wildwaters, Inc., PO Box 100, Rowlesburg, WV 26425, (800)624-8060 or (304)454-2475

Cheat River Outfitters, Box 196, Albright, WV 26519, (410)489-2837

New River/Greenbrier Valley

ACE Whitewater, PO Box 1168, Oak Hill, WV 25901 (800)SURF-WVA or (304)469-2651

Adventure Expedition, PO Box 269, Glen Jean, WV 25846(304)469-2955

Appalachian Whitewater, PO Box 510, Fayetteville, WV 25840(304)574-2413

Cantrell Ultimate Rafting, HC 76, Box 11, Hinton, WV 25951 (800)470-7238 or (304)466-0595

Class VI River Runners, PO Box 78, Lansing, WV 25862 (800)CLASS-VI or (304)574-0704

Drift A Bit, PO Box 885, Fayetteville, WV 25840(800)633-RAFT or (304)574-3282

Extreme Expeditions, PO Drawer 9, Lansing, WV 25862 (888)463-9873 or (304)574-2827

Greenbrier River Company, PO Box 265, Ronceverte, WV 24970 (800)775-2203 or (304)645-2760

Madd Jack's Trading Post and Camp, HC 81, Box 45A, Ramsey, WV 25938 (800)822-1386 or (304)658-5505

Mountain River Tours, Box 88, Sunday Road, Hico, WV 25854 (800)822-1FUN or (304)658-5266

Mountain State Outdoor Center Campground, PO Box 98, Lansing, WV 25862 (304)574-0947

New & Gauley River Adventures, Box 44, Lansing, WV 25862, (800)759-7238 or (304)574-3008

New River Rafting Company, PO Box 249, Glen Jean, WV 25846, (800)639-7238

New River Scenic Whitewater Tours, PO Box 637, Hinton, WV 25951,, (800)292-0880 or (304)466-2288

North American River Runners/West Virginia River Adventures, PO Box 81, Hico, WV 25854, (800)950-2585 or (304)658-5276

Outside Adventures, Box ABC, Bradley, WV 25818, (304)877-6427

Passages to Adventure, PO Box 71, Fayetteville, WV 25840 (800)634-3785 or (304)574-1037

Rivermen, PO Box 220, Lansing, WV 25862, (800)545-RAFT or (304)574-0515

Rivers, PO Box 30, Lansing, WV 25862, (800)879-7483 or (304)574-3834

Riverworks, PO Box 268, Glen Jean, WV 25846, (800)223-2641 or (304)255-6563

Songer Whitewater, PO Box 300, Fayetteville, WV 25840, (800)356-RAFT or (304)658-9926

USA Raft, Route 1, Box 430, Fayetteville, WV 25840, (800)346-RAFT or (304)574-3655

West Virginia River Adventures, PO Box 95, Hico, WV 25854, (800)950-2585 or (304)658-5241

West Virginia Whitewater, Box 30, Fayetteville, WV 25840, (800)989-7238 or (304)574-0871

Whitewater Information, Route 2, Box 459A, Fayetteville, WV 25840 (888)723-8982 or (304)574-1003

Wildwater Expeditions Unlimited, PO Box 155, Lansing, WV 25862 (800)WVA-RAFT or (304)658-4007

Potomac Highlands

Blackwater Outdoor Center, Box 325, Davis, WV 26260, (800)328-4798 or (304)478-4456

Eagle's Nest Outfitters, PO Box 731, Petersburg, WV 26847, (304)257-2393

Wildlife Management Areas

West Virginians have a long tradition of hunting, trapping and fishing—and some of the best places on earth in which to pursue their prey. The West Virginia Division of Natural Resources maintains 59 public areas throughout the state that are open year-round. These Wildlife Management Areas (WMAs) include areas owned by the

Division, national and state forests and lands leased by the Division from the U.S. Army Corps of Engineers and corporations. The WMAs are maintained with funds that come from the sale of hunting and fishing licenses and from taxes paid on hunting and fishing equipment.

Very few states can boast such a well-organized and successful program, and West Virginia's WMAs rival any in the country for beauty, diversity and abundant fish and game. Surprisingly, the relatively populated Metro Valley region—the area in which you might expect to find fewer hunting and fishing opportunities—has the largest number of WMAs.

These areas are for the use and enjoyment of all outdoor enthusiasts. The Division of Natural Resources asks all visitors to respect the lands and use them wisely. You should be aware that most are not developed; roads are unpaved and may require four-wheel-drive vehicles, and you should not expect to find comfort facilities, telephones, etc. For hiking or walking the dog, trails in state parks and national forests will probably serve you better. If you must walk through WMA lands, wear bright colors, preferably blaze orange, and know the hunting season calendar.

A typical WMA ranges in size from 2,000 to 12,000 acres. Burches Run Lake WMA south of Wheeling is only 54 acres, and both Sleepy Creek WMA near Berkeley Springs and East Lynn Lake WMA outside of Wayne occupy more than 22,000 acres. The terrain varies from heavily forested hillsides to open fields, from high ridges to wetlands. Game may include deer, bear, bobcat, wild turkey, raccoon, grouse, quail, crow, starling, pheasant, squirrel, rabbit, skunk, opossum, coyote, weasel and, by special permit, wild boar. Trapping for muskrat, beaver, fox and mink is permitted in some locations. West Virginia has strict, specific laws about firearms; be sure to check current regulations before planning a hunting trip. In some areas only bowhunting is permitted.

Bass, trout, muskie, walleye and catfish are a few favorites of West Virginia fishermen; the state maintains a regular trout stocking schedule on more than 125 streams and rivers. There are strict limits on the number of fish that may be taken, and some areas are designated as catch and release streams.

Some WMAs are equipped for tent and trailer camping, and a few have cabins. Others have only picnic tables, well water and pit toilets. Boat launches are available at some areas. Others place limits on motor horsepower.

Thirteen of the 46 WMAs—and some of the largest and most remote—are located in the state's three national forests (Monongahela, George Washington and Jefferson), all in the Potomac Highlands region. To hunt or fish in these areas, you will also need a national forest stamp, available at all license locations. Other WMAs are located within state forests. In state parks, you may fish, but no hunting is permitted.

Before you hunt or fish in West Virginia, you will need to secure the proper licenses and familiarize yourself with state laws and regulations. You should also check signs at each location for specific rules. Be sure to respect "No Trespassing" signs on contiguous private property. The Division of Natural Resources can provide you with a complete list of WMAs, hunting and fishing season schedules, stocking schedules and game maps, as well as camping and float trip information. Resident and nonresident licenses are available at about 800 locations throughout the state or in advance by mail. For more information call (304)558-2771, visit the state's hunting web site (wvweb.com/www/hunting) or fishing web site (wvweb.com/www/wvfishing.html), or write Division of Natural Resources, 1900 Kanawha Boulevard, East, Building 3, Room 812, Charleston, WV 25305, Attention: Hunting and Fishing License Section.

Wineries

Clean water, sunshine, rich soil and a climate conducive to many different varieties of grapes all combine to make West Virginia surprisingly good wine country. Small wineries are nestled in hollows and strung along ridgetops throughout the Mountain State, most of them offering scenic views to rival their award-winning wines.

Winemaking in West Virginia is not a new phenomenon. Five years before the Civil War, cellars in Dunbar were stocked with the fruits of the Friend Brothers Winery. Although the site is now a park instead of a winery, its name—Wine Cellars Park—commemorates the early West Virginia vineyard and the old cellars, which have been restored and are listed on the National Register of Historic Places.

Among the many different varieties of American wine grapes grown in the state are Concord, Niagara and Delaware. Proprietors of West Virginia vineyards also tend French hybrids such as Seyval, Blanc, Aurore, Foch and Vidal Blanc. In order to create unique blends, state winemakers rely on outside sources for about 25 percent of their fruit. From all these sources, Mountain State vintners create red, white and blush wines, both sweet and dry—along with some excellent berry and even honey wines.

For a mellow taste of West Virginia, visit one of the following wineries. Tours and tastings are available at most, and getting to them will be an enjoyable part of your day trip.

Eastern Panhandle

A.T. Gift Company Farm Winery
Route 3, Box 802, Harpers Ferry, WV 25425
(304)876-6680
Tours, tastings and sales. Call for hours.

Potomac Highlands

Robert F. Pliska and Company Winery
101 Piterra Place, Purgitsville, WV 26852
(304)289-3493
Tours, tastings and sales. Hours are 1:00 to 4:00 p.m. Tuesday through Saturday, mid-April to mid-September, or by appointment.

Potomac Highland Winery
Route 1, Box 247-A, Keyser, WV 26726
(304)788-3066
Tours, tastings and sales. Call for hours.

Schneider's Winery
PO Box 1950, Romney, WV 26757
(304)822-7434
Tours, tastings and sales. Hours are noon to 6:00 p.m. Wednesday through Saturday, 1:00 to 6:00 p.m. Sunday.

West-Whitehill Winery, Ltd.
HC 85, Box 153, Moorefield, WV 26836
(304)538-2605
Tours, tastings and sales. Open 1:00 to 5:00 p.m. Saturday and Sunday.

Mountain Lakes

Kirkwood Limited
Route 1, Box 24, Summersville, WV 26651
(304)872-2134
Tours, tastings and sales. Hours are 9:00 a.m. to 7:00 p.m. Monday through Saturday and 1:00 to 7:00 p.m. Sunday.

Little Hungary Farm Winery
Ferenc Androczi
Route 6, Box 323, Buckhannon, WV 26201
(304)472-6634
Tours, tastings and sales. Call for hours.

Mountaineer Country

Forks of Cheat Winery
Route 4, Box 224E

Morgantown, WV 26505
(304)598-2019 or (304)599-8660
Tours, tastings and sales. Hours are 10:00 a.m. to 5:00 p.m. Monday through Saturday and 1:00 to 5:00 p.m. Sunday, except for January through March, when the winery is closed on Sundays.

Metro Valley

Fisher Ridge Winery
1021 Quarrier Street, Suite 201, Charleston, WV 25301
(304)342-8702
Tours, tastings and sales. Call for hours.

New River/Greenbrier Valley

Laurel Creek Winery
Route 4, Box 280-B, Lewisburg, WV 24901
(304)645-5870
Tours, tastings and sales. Call for hours.

Index

Acknowledgments

Hundreds of people helped make this book. They graciously showed me around their museums, zoos, parks, shops, factories, railroads, trails and towns. They called me to make clarifications and additions. They wrote me letters and sent me clippings. To all who shared with me their little bit of West Virginia, thank you.

To Suzanne Lord and Jon Metzger, authors of the original *West Virginia One-Day Trip Book,* I am deeply grateful. Their scholarship, lively writing and goodwill made my own traveling and writing a pleasure. And to the staff and editors at EPM Publications, thank you so much.

Many thanks to the staff of the West Virginia Division of Tourism, every single one of you! (I'm sure I talked with every single one of you on the phone!) Cindy Harrington's support and encouragement are especially appreciated. Many others helped me with printed materials, maps, charts and more.

Thank you to the talented staff photographers at the West Virginia Division of Tourism and West Virginia Division of Culture and History, who generously allowed me to look through thousands of images and furnished most of the photographs in this book.

Thank you to artist William D. Goebel, whose beautiful pen-and-ink illustrations would appear in many more places throughout the book if I were not so wordy.

Thank you to the West Virginia Division of Natural Resources, U.S.D.A. Forest Service and National Park Service.

Too numerous to acknowledge individually are the many directors and volunteers at hundreds of large and small Convention & Visitors Bureaus, Chambers of Commerce, Main Street projects and historical societies. Thank you for your expertise and enthusiasm.

Thank you to the following friends, each of whom has contributed something important, from research assistance to lodging to moral support: Julie Adams, Elena Bailey, Ancella Bickley, Joan Browning, George Castelle, Grace Cavalieri, Amanda Cox, Scott Finn, Denise Giardina, Rebecca Kimmons, Cecelia Mason, Gail Michelson, Jeanne Mozier, Bruce Perrone, Ren Petersen, Neal Peterson, Arla Ralston, John Stone, Arline Thorn and Michael Titus.

Thanks especially to my family and to my friend and work associate Nancy Balow—for your loving support, willingness to listen, steady nerves and loyalty.

Richard S. Lee

About the Author

Colleen Anderson has been a West Virginian by choice since 1970, when she came to the state as a VISTA volunteer. Her stories, poems, essays, songs and articles—many inspired by the land and people of the Mountain State—have been honored by the PEN Syndication Fiction Project, broadcast on West Virginia Public Radio and published in *Redbook* and other periodicals. She owns Mother Wit Writing & Design, a creative studio in Charleston. Beginning in 1999, she will edit *West Virginia—It's You*, the state's tourism annual.